Violence and Pow

This book is a significant contribution to the study of Egyptology and ancient art history, delivering the results of cutting-edge research in an area of central importance. Its essential focus is violence in Ancient Egypt, which is a topic of increasing interest in current historical and cultural studies, and discusses a large corpus of images of great value, recognizing the need for a more theoretical approach to the study of Egyptian artistic expression, and emphasizing the critical importance of context in evaluating the function of representations. Throughout, the analysis shows a healthy awareness of the problem of evidence—or lack thereof. The book has a valuable cross-cultural dimension that makes it relevant not only to the Egyptological community, but also to art historians, ancient historians in general, and anthropologists. The result is a study that breaks much new ground and forces the reconsideration of entrenched views.

Dr Alan Lloyd, Swansea University, UK

Violence and Power in Ancient Egypt examines the use of Egyptian pictures of violence prior to the New Kingdom. Starting with the assertion that making and displaying such images served as a tactic of power, related to but separate from the actual practice of violence, the book explores the development and deployment of this imagery across different contexts. By comparatively utilizing violent images from a variety of other times and cultures, the book asks that we consider not only how Egyptian imagery was related to Egyptian violence, but also why people create pictures of violence and place them where they do, and how such images communicate what to whom. By cataloging and querying Egyptian imagery of violence from different periods and different contexts—royal tombs, divine temples, the landscape, portable objects, and private tombs—*Violence and Power* highlights the nuances of the relationship between aspects of royal ideology, art, and its audiences in the first half of pharaonic Egyptian history.

Laurel Bestock is an Associate Professor of Archaeology and Egyptology at Brown University (USA). She received her PhD in Egyptian Archaeology and Art from the Institute of Fine Arts, New York University (USA). She directs excavations in Egypt at the site of Abydos, where she investigates early kingship. In the Sudan, she co-directs excavations at the Egyptian fortress of Uronarti, seeking to understand lifestyles and cultural interactions in a colonial outpost from nearly 4,000 years ago. For her next project, she hopes to work on a book focused on food and culture at Uronarti, both in antiquity and in the context of a modern excavation team camping in tents along the Nile.

Routledge Studies in Egyptology

Available titles:

**Women, Gender, and Identity in Third Intermediate Period Egypt:
The Theban Case Study**
Jean Li

Ancient Egyptian Temple Ritual: Performance, Patterns, and Practice
Katherine Eaton

Science in the Study of Ancient Egypt
Sonia Zakrzewski, Andrew Shortland, Joanne Rowland

Histories of Egyptology: Interdisciplinary Measures
Edited by William Carruthers

www.routledge.com/Routledge-Studies-in-Egyptology/book-series/RSEGY

Violence and Power in Ancient Egypt

Image and Ideology before the New Kingdom

Laurel Bestock

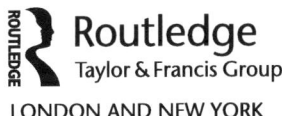
Routledge
Taylor & Francis Group

LONDON AND NEW YORK

First published 2018
by Routledge

2 Park Square, Milton Park, Abingdon, Oxfordshire OX14 4RN
52 Vanderbilt Avenue, New York, NY 10017

Routledge is an imprint of the Taylor & Francis Group, an informa business

First issued in paperback 2019

British Library Cataloguing-in-Publication Data
A catalogue record for this book is available from the British Library

Library of Congress Cataloging-in-Publication Data
Names: Bestock, Laurel, author.
Title: Violence and power in ancient Egypt: image and ideology before the New Kingdom/Laurel Bestock.
Other titles: Routledge studies in Egyptology.
Description: Abingdon, Oxon; New York, NY: Routledge, 2018. | Series: Routledge studies in Egyptology | Includes bibliographical references and index.
Identifiers: LCCN 2017015115| ISBN 9781138685055 (hardback: alk. paper) | ISBN 9781315543505 (ebook)
Subjects: LCSH: Art, Egyptian. | Art, Ancient—Egypt. | Violence in art. | Egypt—Antiquities.
Classification: LCC N5350.B39 2018 | DDC 709.32—dc23
LC record available at https://lccn.loc.gov/2017015115

ISBN: 978-1-138-68505-5 (hbk)
ISBN: 978-0-367-87854-2 (pbk)

Typeset in Times New Roman
by Swales & Willis Ltd, Exeter, Devon, UK

For Lutz

Contents

List of figures   ix
Acknowledgments   xvi
The chronology and contexts of scenes of violence from Egypt
through the Middle Kingdom   xviii

1 Picturing violence   1

The structure of this book 5
Themes 9

2 The origins of violent imagery   14

The earliest images of violence in Egypt 16
The evidence from early Egypt: Naqada I 18
The evidence from early Egypt: Naqada II 24
Order and chaos 33

**3 The violence inherent in the system: imagery and royal
ideology in the period of state formation**   40

Violence in Egyptian art in the period of state formation 41
Continuity and discontinuity 74

4 To live forever: the decoration of royal mortuary complexes   85

The Old Kingdom 90
The Middle Kingdom 127
Interpreting imagery of violence from royal tombs 143

5 Uniter of the two lands: images of violence in divine temples   154

Egyptian temples as a context for imagery 156

6 The preservation of order: images in the landscape 172

The Early Dynastic Period 175
The Old Kingdom 179
Reading rock carvings of smiting 193

7 Out and about: images of violence on portable objects 201

Images of triumph on portable objects 203
Images of captivity on portable objects 209
Movement and meaning 216

8 Who is who? Private monumental images of war 222

The Old Kingdom 225
The First Intermediate Period 232
The Middle Kingdom 235
Inscriptions and images in private tombs 252
Interpreting private images of war 255

9 Violence, power, ideology 264

Bibliography 269
Index 285

Figures

Note: dimensions are given in captions so as to allow the reader to gauge the size of any object while viewing it. Dimensions given are those published. Copyright information can be found in the Acknowledgments and in the endnotes associated with each image.

1.1	Belgian €2.5 coin issued to commemorate the 200th anniversary of the Battle of Waterloo	2
1.2	Line drawing of the reliefs showing Ramses II triumphant at the Battle of Qadesh, Ramesseum, Thebes	8
2.1	"Skirmish" scene, painting on rock face, near Deaf Adder Gorge, Arnhem Land, Northern Territory, Australia	14
2.2	White Cross-Lined Ware vase with possible captivity scene. Provenance unknown. Brussels, E. 3200	19
2.3	White Cross-Lined Ware vase with possible captivity scene. Provenance unknown. University College London, Petrie Museum	19
2.4	White Cross-Lined Ware vase with possible captivity scene. Abydos, Umm el-Qaab, tomb U-239 vessel 1. Cairo JdE 99072	20
2.5	White Cross-Lined Ware vase with possible captivity scene. Abydos, Umm el-Qaab, tomb U-415 vessel 1. Abydos SCA storeroom	20
2.6	White Cross-Lined Ware vase with possible captivity scene. Abydos, Umm el-Qaab, tomb U-415 vessel 2. Abydos SCA storeroom	21
2.7	Naqada II Decorated Ware pot with boat scene	25
2.8	Detail of the fragmentary Gebelein textile showing boats and a possible bound captive	26
2.9	Watercolor facsimile of Hierakonpolis Tomb 100, southwest wall, paint on mud plaster	28
2.10	Detail of the lower left corner of the southwest wall of Hierakonpolis Tomb 100; smiting	29

2.11   Detail of the lower part of the southwest wall of Hierakonpolis
       Tomb 100; possible combat   30
2.12   Detail of the upper left of the southwest wall of Hierakonpolis
       Tomb 100; royal ritual (?)   32
3.1   The Battlefield Palette   45
3.2   The Libyan Palette   47
3.3   The Bull Palette   50
3.4   Line drawing of the Oxford knife handle showing bound
       prisoners   51
3.5   Line drawing of the Metropolitan Museum knife handle
       26.241.1   51
3.6   The Gebel el-Arak knife   52
3.7   Detailed view of the two sides of the Gebel el-Arak knife
       handle   53
3.8   Line drawing of the relief image on the Scorpion Macehead   56
3.9   Three ivory cylinders, perhaps from a handle, from the
       Hierakonpolis Main Deposit   58
3.10   Ivory macehead from the Hierakonpolis Main Deposit   59
3.11   Three figurines from temple deposits at Tell el-Farkha,
       possibly showing captives   60
3.12   Figurines from Tell Ibrahim Awad, possibly showing
       captivity or submission   61
3.13   Line drawing of the rock carving at Gebel Sheikh Suleiman   63
3.14   Line drawing of the Narmer Palette   65
3.15   Maceheads from the Hierakonpolis Main Deposit   69
3.16   Line drawing of the relief scene on the Narmer Macehead   69
3.17   Line drawing of the ivory cylinder of Narmer from the
       Hierakonpolis Main Deposit with the king's *serekh* smiting   71
3.18   Line drawing of ivory tag of Narmer with the king's name
       smiting   72
4.1   *La Liberté guidant le peuple*, oil on canvas, Eugene Delacroix 85
4.2   Sahure pyramid complex plan   87
4.3   Relief of bound captive, detail. Giza, pyramid complex of
       Khafre   91
4.4   Relief fragment showing archers firing in unison, probably
       from the pyramid complex of Khafre at Giza, Fourth Dynasty   92
4.5   Line drawing of relief showing the Libyan Family Scene,
       pyramid temple of Sahure at Abusir, Fifth Dynasty   95
4.6   Line drawing of relief showing bound prisoners, causeway
       of the pyramid complex of Sahure at Abusir, Fifth Dynasty   97
4.7   Detail of row of prisoners from the scene of bound prisoners,
       causeway of the pyramid complex of Sahure at Abusir,
       Fifth Dynasty   98

4.8   Relief fragment showing an Asiatic beard from a trampling
      scene, causeway of the pyramid complex of Sahure at Abusir,
      Fifth Dynasty   99
4.9   Detail of relief with archers taking target practice, causeway
      of the pyramid complex of Sahure at Abusir, Fifth Dynasty   100
4.10 Line drawing of relief showing Sahure as griffin trampling, valley
      temple of the pyramid complex of Sahure at Abusir, Fifth Dynasty 101
4.11 Line drawings of relief fragments from smiting scenes,
      pyramid temple of Niuserra at Abusir, Fifth Dynasty   104
4.12 Line drawings of relief fragments from trampling scenes,
      causeway of the pyramid of Niuserra at Abusir, Fifth Dynasty   105
4.13 Line drawing of relief fragment showing an arm wearing a
      bracelet with a smiting scene, valley temple of Niuserra at
      Abusir, Fifth Dynasty   107
4.14 Line drawing of a relief fragment showing smiting, pyramid
      temple of Unis at Saqqara, Fifth Dynasty   108
4.15 Line drawing of a relief fragment showing a bound captive
      herded by a god, pyramid temple of Unis at Saqqara,
      Fifth Dynasty   108
4.16 Line drawing of a relief fragment showing bound prisoners,
      pyramid temple of Unis at Saqqara, Fifth Dynasty   109
4.17 Line drawing showing the reconstruction of a possible trampling
      scene from the causeway of Unis at Saqqara, Fifth Dynasty   110
4.18 Line drawing of a relief fragment showing battle against
      Asiatics from the causeway of Unis at Saqqara, Fifth Dynasty   111
4.19 Line drawing of a relief fragment showing battle against
      Asiatics from the causeway of Unis at Saqqara, Fifth Dynasty   112
4.20 Relief fragment with an axe-wielding Egyptian, from the
      causeway of Unis at Saqqara, Fifth Dynasty   113
4.21 Relief fragment with combat, from the causeway of Unis at
      Saqqara, Fifth Dynasty   114
4.22 Relief fragment with possible combat, from the causeway of
      Unis at Saqqara, Fifth Dynasty   115
4.23 Line drawing of partial relief showing the Libyan Family Scene,
      pyramid temple of Pepy I at Saqqara, Sixth Dynasty   116
4.24 Line drawing showing the reconstruction of a Libyan Family
      Scene from the pyramid temple of Pepy II at Saqqara,
      Sixth Dynasty   117
4.25 Line drawing showing the reconstruction of a smiting scene
      from the pyramid temple of Pepy II at Saqqara, Sixth Dynasty   118
4.26 Line drawing showing bound prisoners and the crown of
      Seshat from the pyramid temple of Pepy II at Saqqara,
      Sixth Dynasty   119

4.27 Relief with three prisoners from the pyramid temple of Pepy II
at Saqqara, Sixth Dynasty   120

4.28 Line drawing showing the reconstruction of two trampling
scenes from the causeway of Pepy II at Saqqara, Sixth Dynasty   121

4.29 Line drawing showing the reconstruction of two trampling
scenes from the causeway of Pepy II at Saqqara, Sixth Dynasty   122

4.30 Line drawing showing the reconstruction of the presentation
of prisoners from the causeway of Pepy II at Saqqara,
Sixth Dynasty   123

4.31 Line drawing showing the reconstruction of a smiting scene
from the valley temple of Pepy II at Saqqara, Sixth Dynasty   124

4.32 Sculptures of bound, bearded captives from the pyramid
complex of Pepy II at Saqqara, Sixth Dynasty.   125

4.33 Sculpture of a bound prisoner—an Egyptian?—from the pyramid
complex of Pepy II, Saqqara   126

4.34 Relief fragment with yellow-skinned, arrow-shot victims
tumbling next to a ladder, mortuary complex of Nebhepetra
Mentuhotep at Deir el-Bahri, Eleventh Dynasty.   129

4.35 Relief fragment with victims of combat, mortuary complex
of Nebhepetra Mentuhotep at Deir el-Bahri, Eleventh Dynasty   130

4.36 Relief fragment with an archer shooting, mortuary complex of
Nebhepetra Mentuhotep at Deir el-Bahri, Eleventh Dynasty   131

4.37 Relief fragment with archers firing in unison, mortuary complex
of Nebhepetra Mentuhotep at Deir el-Bahri, Eleventh Dynasty   132

4.38 Relief fragment of combat, mortuary complex of Nebhepetra
Mentuhotep at Deir el-Bahri, Eleventh Dynasty   133

4.39 Relief fragment of combat, mortuary complex of Nebhepetra
Mentuhotep at Deir el-Bahri, Eleventh Dynasty.   133

4.40 Relief fragment with mixed troops, mortuary complex of
Nebhepetra Mentuhotep at Deir el-Bahri, Eleventh Dynasty.   134

4.41 Relief fragment with combat and captivity, mortuary complex
of Nebhepetra Mentuhotep at Deir el-Bahri, Eleventh Dynasty.   135

4.42 Relief fragment with a dark-skinned archer firing his bow,
mortuary complex of Nebhepetra Mentuhotep at Deir el-Bahri,
Eleventh Dynasty   136

4.43 Relief fragment with a victim, mortuary complex of Nebhepetra
Mentuhotep at Deir el-Bahri, Eleventh Dynasty   136

4.44 Relief fragment with a woman and child being herded by an
archer, mortuary complex of Nebhepetra Mentuhotep at
Deir el-Bahri, Eleventh Dynasty.   137

4.45 Relief fragment from a smiting scene from the pyramid
complex of Senwosret I at Lisht, Twelfth Dynasty   140

4.46 Relief fragment with a foreigner throwing a spear from the
pyramid temple of Senwosret I at Lisht, Twelfth Dynasty 141
5.1 Line drawing of relief. Late Classic Maya Stela 11, Yaxchilan,
Chiapas Mexico 154
5.2 Line drawing of an architectural relief fragment from
Hierakonpolis, reign of Khasekhem, Second Dynasty 158
5.3 Limestone statue of Khasekhem from Hierakonpolis,
Second Dynasty 160
5.4 Line drawing of the front of the base of a limestone statue
of Khasekhem showing apparent combat casualties, from
Hierakonpolis, Second Dynasty 161
5.5 Line drawing showing Nebhepetra Montuhotep smiting an
Egyptian on a relief fragment from Gebelein, Eleventh
Dynasty 162
5.6 Line drawing showing Nebhepetra Montuhotep smiting a
Libyan on a relief fragment from Gebelein, Eleventh Dynasty 164
5.7 Line drawing showing Nebhepetra Montuhotep smiting an
abstract emblem from Denderah, Eleventh Dynasty 166
6.1 Relief of Hormizd II, Naqsh-e-Rustam, Iran 172
6.2 Naqsh-e-Rustam, Iran 173
6.3 Line drawing of a relief with the *serekh* of Djer smiting, Wadi
Ameyra, Sinai, First Dynasty 175
6.4 Line drawing of a relief of Den smiting, Wadi el-Humur, Sinai,
First Dynasty 177
6.5 Line drawing of a relief of Den smiting, Wadi el-Humur, Sinai,
First Dynasty 177
6.6 Line drawing of a relief of a king in the Red Crown smiting,
Wadi el-Humur, Sinai, First Dynasty 178
6.7 Line drawing of a relief of Netjerikhet (Djoser) smiting,
Wadi Maghara, Sinai, Third Dynasty 180
6.8 Line drawing of a relief of Sekhemkhet smiting, Wadi Maghara,
Sinai, Third Dynasty 181
6.9 A relief of Sekhemkhet smiting, Wadi Maghara, Sinai,
Third Dynasty 183
6.10 Line drawing of the second relief of Sekhemkhet smiting,
Wadi Maghara, Sinai, Third Dynasty 183
6.11 Fragment of relief of Sanakht smiting, Wadi Maghara, Sinai,
Third Dynasty 184
6.12 Line drawing of a relief of Snefru smiting, Wadi Maghara, Sinai,
Fourth Dynasty 186
6.13 Line drawing of a relief of Snefru smiting, Wadi Maghara,
Sinai, Fourth Dynasty 187

6.14 Double-panel relief with Khufu smiting, Wadi Maghara,
Sinai, Fourth Dynasty   188

6.15 Line drawing of relief showing Khufu smiting, Wadi Maghara,
Sinai, Fourth Dynasty   188

6.16 Line drawing of relief showing Sahure smiting, Wadi Maghara,
Sinai, Fifth Dynasty   189

6.17 Line drawing of relief showing Niuserra smiting, Wadi Maghara,
Sinai, Fifth Dynasty   190

6.18 Line drawing of relief showing Djedkare Izezi smiting,
Wadi Maghara, Sinai, Fifth Dynasty   191

6.19 Line drawing of relief showing Pepy I smiting, Wadi Maghara,
Sinai, Sixth Dynasty.   192

7.1 Ivory armlet from Benin showing warriors   201

7.2 Line drawing of an ivory tag with a smiting *serekh* from the
tomb of Aha at Abydos, First Dynasty   204

7.3 Ivory tag showing Den smiting, from his tomb at Abydos,
First Dynasty   205

7.4 Top: gold and inlay pectoral with symmetrical images of
Senwosret III smiting. Bottom: gold and inlay pectoral with
symmetrical images of Amenemhat III smiting. Both from
the tomb of Mereret at Dahshur, Twelfth Dynasty   208

7.5 Ivory rod, possibly for gaming, with a relief carving of a
bound prisoner. From the tomb of Qa'a at Abydos, First Dynasty   210

7.6 Clay execration figurine with schematically rendered bound arms,
Saqqara, Twelfth Dynasty.   212

7.7 Line drawings and photograph of mud stamp sealings from
Nubian fortresses showing captives and captors, Twelfth Dynasty   214

8.1 The Alexander Mosaic from the House of the Faun, Pompeii   222

8.2 Line drawing of an attack on a settlement from the tomb of
Khaemhesy at Saqqara, Fifth Dynasty   226

8.3 Line drawing of an attack on a fortified place from the tomb of
Inti at Deshasha, Fifth Dynasty   228

8.4 Painting from the tomb of Setka at Aswan showing dark-skinned
bowmen in combat, late Old Kingdom (?).   231

8.5 Line drawing of a fragmentary scene from the tomb of Iti-ibi at
Asyut, First Intermediate Period   233

8.6 Line drawing of fragmentary figures from the tomb of Ankhtifi
at Moalla, First Intermediate Period   234

8.7 Watercolor facsimile of the attack on a fortified place, tomb of
Intef at Thebes, Eleventh Dynasty   236

8.8 Line drawing of three boats with soldiers brandishing weapons,
tomb of Intef at Thebes, Eleventh Dynasty   240

8.9	Line drawing of Beni Hasan Tomb 15, belonging to Baqt, east wall of the main chamber, showing a complex battle scene, early Middle Kingdom	243
8.10	Line drawing of Beni Hasan Tomb 17, belonging to Khety, east wall of the main chamber, showing a complex battle scene, early Middle Kingdom	245
8.11	Detail of the fortress and its defenders from the east wall of the tomb of Khety at Beni Hasan, early Middle Kingdom	245
8.12	Line drawing of scenes from the damaged east wall of Beni Hasan Tomb 14, belonging to Khnumhotep I, early Middle Kingdom	246
8.13	Line drawing of Beni Hasan Tomb 2, belonging to Amenemhat, north half of the east wall of the main chamber, showing a complex battle scene, early Middle Kingdom	248
8.14	Detail of the attack on the fortress shown in Amenemhat's tomb, Beni Hasan, early Middle Kingdom	249
8.15	Line drawing of Beni Hasan Tomb 2, belonging to Amenemhat, south half of the east wall of the main chamber, showing a complex battle scene, early Middle Kingdom	250
8.16	Detail of the combat in the tomb of Amenemhat, Beni Hasan, early Middle Kingdom	251

Acknowledgments

I am grateful for the intellectual and personal support of many people during the process of writing this book. Foremost among them is Luiza Silva, whose help editing the manuscript, tracking down sources, gaining image permissions, and generally being a model of both organization and critical thinking has been essential. I quite literally could not have finished the book without her. I am fortunate in my students, and others also served as research assistants at critical periods: thank you Kathryn Howley, Simon Hochberg, and especially Jessica Tomkins, who first imposed order on my chaos. Three reviewers of the book proposal gave comments that shaped the project, and I would particularly like to thank Alan Lloyd, who not only gave very constructive criticism but also signed his review. Adela Oppenheim generously gathered and then discussed with me unpublished relief fragments from Middle Kingdom pyramid complexes, for which I am thankful. The larger group of my colleagues and students at Brown has been so long supportive and is so numerous that I will not name you all, but thank you—and particularly to the participants in the seminar on violence in Egyptian art in the Spring of 2015, during which many of the ideas in this book were tested. I would be remiss not to mention, too, the two different classes of Egyptian Warfare that I have taught at Brown University— you guys did marvelous reconstructions of the Battle of Qadesh, and teaching you helped me realize how much I wanted to write this book. The Howard Foundation generously supported a sabbatical semester during the beginning stages of research for this project, and further support from the Joukowsky Institute for Archaeology and the Ancient World and the Department of Egyptology and Assyriology at Brown University has also been helpful. Finally, some friends and family have been so consistently supportive that I wish to mention them particularly. David Sherry, Ralph Bestock, Donna Bestock, Simon Sullivan, and especially my daughters, Rose and Norah, thank you.

It was clear to me from the first that this book could not work without thorough illustrations, and the process of getting them has not been easy. Ben Tyler and Ann Caldwell at the Rockefeller Library at Brown University scanned images when files could not be obtained elsewhere; most of the drawings and photographs illustrated here from old excavations are thanks to their help, which was considerable. Jessica Porter's assistance with logistics of image acquisition was also critical. Endnotes for images that come from texts give their citations. A large number of figures were given by scholars and artists, and I would like to thank them and acknowledge the copyright for the following (figure numbers given after names): Paul Taçon: 2.1; Stan Hendrickx: 2.2; Royal Museums of Art and History: 2.2, 7.6; Barbara Adams: 2.3; Daniel Polz and the German Archaeological Institute Cairo: 2.4, 2.5, 2.6, 3.4, 3.18, 8.7, 8.8; Günter Dreyer and Christiana Köhler: 2.4, 2.5, 2.6, 3.5, 3.18; Metropolitan Museum of Art: 2.7, 4.4, 4.46; Museo Egizio di Torino and the photographer Pino Dell'Aquila: 2.8; British Museum: 3.1, 4.34, 4.35, 4.38, 4.39, 4.40, 4.41, 4.42, 4.44, 6.11, 7.1, 7.3; Ashmolean Museum: 3.1, 3.8, 3.16, 5.3; Jürgen Liepe: 3.2, 7.4; The Louvre Museum: 3.3, 3.6, 3.7; Krzysztof Ciałowicz: 3.11; Willem van Haarlem: 3.12; Barry J. Kemp: 3.14; Miroslav Bárta: 4.8, 4.9; Institut Français d'Archéologie Orientale: 4.14, 4.15, 4.16, 4.17, 4.18, 4.19, 4.23, 4.24, 4.25, 4.26, 4.27, 4.28, 4.29, 4.30, 4.31, 4.32, 4.33, 6.3, 8.6; Peabody Museum of Natural History: 4.36; Egypt Exploration Society: 4.37, 4.43, 6.7, 6.10, 6.12, 6.13, 6.14, 6.15, 6.16, 6.17, 6.18, 6.19, 7.2, 7.5, 8.9, 8.10, 8.12, 8.13, 8.15; Los Angeles County Museum of Art: 5.1; Elisa Fiore Marochetti: 5.5, 5.6; Pierre Tallet: 6.4, 6.5, 6.6; American School of Oriental Research: 6.8; Francis Lankester: 6.9; Josef Wegner: 7.7; Ann McFarlane: 8.2; Naguib Kanawati: 8.3; Deborah Vischak: 8.4; Jochem Kahl: 8.5; Brigitte Jaroš-Deckert: 8.7, 8.8; Linda Evans: 8.11, 8.14, 8.16.

Laurel Bestock

The chronology and contexts of scenes of violence from Egypt through the Middle Kingdom*

	Mortuary triumph	Mortuary battle	Divine temple	Landscape	Object
Naqada I (*c.*4000–3500 BCE)					
Naqada II (*c.*3500–3200)					
Naqada III (*c.*3200–3000)					
Early Dynastic Period (*c.*3000–2686)					
First Dynasty					
Narmer					x
Aha					x
Djer				x	
Djet					x
Den				x	x
Semerkhet				?	
Second Dynasty					
Khasekhem(wy)			x		x
Old Kingdom (*c.*2686–2160)					
Third Dynasty					
Djoser				x	
Sekhemkhet				x	
Sanakht				x	
Fourth Dynasty					
Snefru				x	
Khufu				x	
Khafre		x			
Fifth Dynasty					
Userkaf	?				
Sahure	x	x		x	

Niuserra	x		x	
Djedkare Izezi			x	
Unis	x	x		
Sixth Dynasty				
Pepy I	x		x	
Pepy II	x			
First Intermediate Period (*c.*2160–2055)				
Middle Kingdom (*c.*2055–1650)				
Eleventh Dynasty				
Nebhepetra Mentuhotep	?	x	x	
Twelfth Dynasty				
Senwosret I	x	x		
Senwosret III	x	x		x
Amenemhat III				x

* Only those kings from whose reigns we have images of violence are listed. The chart shows the contexts within which we find those images, excluding private tombs as those are often difficult to date precisely and the imagery is quite different. Question marks indicate uncertain readings or scant evidence. The purpose of this chart is to show relative chronology within Egypt and to track changes in use of violent imagery in the historic periods. Dates given are approximate and based on Shaw (2000); that the chronology of the earlier Naqada should be significantly shortened has been convincingly demonstrated by Dee et al. (2014).

1   Picturing violence

This is not a book about violence. A reader could be forgiven for thinking it so; a flip through its pages will give numerous images of soldiers firing arrows, of kings preparing to bash in the heads of opponents, of fortress walls being stormed. But this is a book about pictures of violence, and where and why Egyptians made them for the first half of pharaonic history. Many societies made or make images of or related to violence, and their use is often complex. An example from our own time, and another not much older, serve to demonstrate some of the ways in which such images can function, some of the reasons why it is important to distinguish pictures of violence from the practice of it, and thus some of the questions that will structure the examination of Egyptian pictures of violence that follows.

2015 was the 200th anniversary of the Battle of Waterloo. To commemorate the battle, Belgium, where Waterloo lies, decided to issue a coin with a schematic image of the battlefield on its reverse (Figure 1.1). The most prominent visual component of the scene is the lion-topped commemorative mound erected on the site; the dirt for the mound was excavated from what had been a key position during the battle. Represented schematically against this on the coin are the roads and troop positions of the battlefield from a contest in which a coalition composed primarily of British and Prussian troops decisively defeated Napoleon Bonaparte and put an end to French ambitions for European hegemony.

Belgium is part of the eurozone. Countries in the eurozone issue their own coins, which may be decorated with images of national significance, but the coins are legal tender throughout the zone and so become dispersed. While the importance of Waterloo for shaping European history is universally acknowledged, the emotional relationship to that battle is different in different places, and has itself changed over time. No better understanding of the changes in emotional impact of the battle can be achieved than by recalling the celebration of its 100th anniversary. There was no celebration. 1915 was not a good time for any of the parties involved to recall a battle in which combined English and German troops kept Europe from being overrun by a violently expansionist France. In 2015, conversely, the shaping of modern Europe could be celebrated, if not without some ambivalence.

The coin itself proved to be a point of more than ambivalence—it became a point of active anger. The first issue struck was a €2 coin. France, which is a

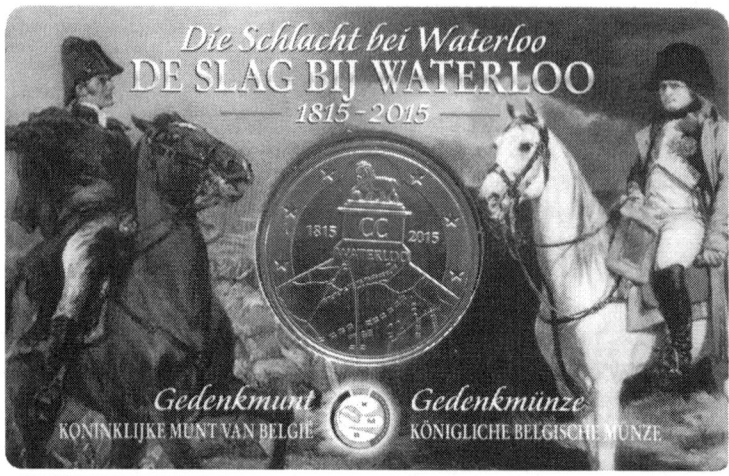

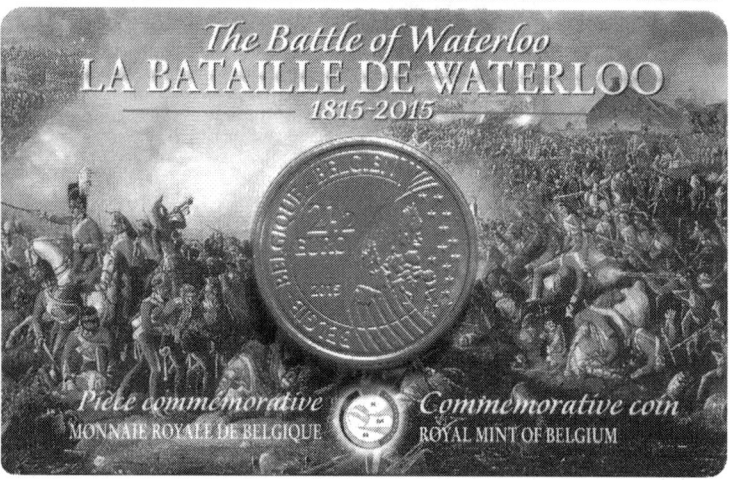

Figure 1.1 Belgian €2.5 coin issued to commemorate the 200th anniversary of the battle of Waterloo, in which a British and German coalition defeated the armies of Napoleon. The reverse of the coin shows the monument erected at the battlefield and the field itself, with dotted lines indicating the position of troops.

member of the eurozone and so a place where the coin would be legal tender, was insulted and required the withdrawal of the issue as a matter of national pride.[1] In the end, a commemorative €2.5 coin was issued. This, as an irregular denomination, is legal tender only within Belgium (which did not exist in 1815). Rather than a European piece of money that commemorated an event of international significance, the coin became national and almost entirely symbolic, as well as much more limited in distribution. It was packaged in a cardboard sleeve decorated with a reproduction of a painting of the battle and sold for more than its face value.

Several points raised by the Belgian coin picturing the Waterloo battlefield help us question the relationship between images and violence more generally. At its most basic, what constitutes an image of violence? No overt violence is shown on the coin itself, though the sleeve in which it was sold was more direct, but even the reference of the schematic image is to an extremely violent event. Without the historical knowledge of what Waterloo was, would we interpret this as an image of violence at all? When are we looking at pictures of violence, or pictures about violence, and how can we tell where the boundaries are when we lack specific knowledge?

Another issue raised by the coin is that of authors and audience. One point of concern in revoking the first issue was that viewing the coin would not be voluntary, but would rather be forced on the audience by its circulation. France itself has issued commemorative images of the 200th anniversary of Waterloo, so in this case it was a combination of the author and audience that was toxic: for Belgium to force the French to be confronted with an image that elicited memories of French defeat was more of a problem than the French-controlled commemoration of that defeat. This not only suggests that we need to pay attention to who makes and who sees images referring to violence, but also that we should be alert to restrictions placed on viewership. That states are directly concerned with the ideological import of circulating such images is also clear in this case.

In the case of the coin, it is not the image itself but rather, as already suggested, the relation of that image to a real and historically well-attested event that is effective. The image tells us nothing of the event. If it were not labeled, it is unlikely that any but a select audience of military history enthusiasts would recognize it. The image does not say anything about who won, or even who fought. It works only in a context where its audience has other means of understanding what happened at Waterloo and what that meant. As such, while the image relies on a relationship to an actual event, it does not show a picture of that event or directly communicate through visual means any information about it. How can this help us approach Egypt?

In part because we lack the same kinds of detailed historical records for Egypt that we have for Europe, we generally cannot know if we have an image that refers to violence unless it directly shows it. Nonetheless, many of the questions raised above are relevant to a study of the fairly large number of remaining pictures from Egypt that do directly show violence. The first question raised by the coin, that of "what is an image of violence?" is a good starting point. From Egypt, I have identified two basic types of images that I am confident speak about violence: triumph scenes that either show the king smiting an enemy with a weapon or, in the form of a fantastical beast, trampling him; and battle images, which show troops in combat. These categories are not necessarily intrinsic to the material, and we must recognize that there may have been additional visual references to violence that we now cannot see as such. Furthermore, even though the pictures that we can study as images of violence are overt in their imagery, can we really use them as the basis of an understanding of royal actions, weapons and battlefield organization, friends and foes, specific campaigns, and booty? Or are their references as oblique as the battlefield image on the €2.5 coin? The temptation to read Egyptian imagery of violence as a direct report on the practice of violence has been strong in scholarship, for the understandable reason that if these pictures do not answer questions about historical violence, we have very little evidence to answer them at all.[2]

An argument against giving in to this temptation of expecting violent imagery to communicate clearly and directly about war and the practice of violence can be advanced on two fronts. This whole book will offer a sustained discussion of specificity and what we might call reliability, and will show time and again that there are internal details of the images, either present or deliberately left out, that make reading them as 1:1 reports on actual events impossible. This does not make them entirely divorced from history, as we will repeatedly see, only unreliable guides. But beyond this, even if real events were pictured, though perhaps not with total accuracy, an attempt to understand them primarily as historical documents misses an essential point. The act of picturing violence is necessarily an act of recasting that violence, of making it tell a story that fits a bigger narrative, one that is ideologically driven rather than true to history—even if we were to assume something so simplistic as the existence of *a* history. The €2.5 coin—with its de-peopled imagery and surrounding political kerfuffle—demonstrates one way in which an image could be caught up in conflicting ways to remember and interpret a war, but a further example serves to demonstrate that issues of reinterpretation, context, audience, and reference to reality are present even with pictures that more realistically and directly present acts of violence.

In the 1880s, there was a craze in America (and elsewhere) for cycloramas showing various battles of the American Civil War. These enormous panoramic canvases were painted on the basis of photographs, displayed in cylindrical halls built for the purpose of making an audience feel immersed in the experience of the battlefield, and augmented by the presence of artifacts—even dummies of dead soldiers—carefully arranged before the canvas. They were the nineteenth-century precursor to IMAX. No "realer" art of war has ever existed. Yet, as Yoni Appelbaum has written,

> [Their] stunning rendition of a battle utterly divorced from context appealed to a nation as eager to remember the valor of those who fought as it was to forget the purpose of their fight. [Their] version of the conflict proved so alluring, in fact, that it changed the way America remembered the Civil War.[3]

Only 20 years after it had been fought, with Reconstruction a demonstrable disaster, many Americans wanted to remember a different war than had happened. They wanted it to have been a shared national traumatic birth in which the valor and bravery of both sides shone—not the moral opposition it was largely understood to be at the time. With an exodus of black Americans leaving the still-repressive south, the role of slavery in the war was actively erased. The memory of the war was simplified and cleansed and images of Pickett's Charge at Gettysburg could be refashioned into a moment—a single moment to represent a bloody four years!—of valor and courage that failed, but in failing birthed a new era for the prosperous emergence of America on the world stage. The most visually realistic imagery could be employed to tell a story different from the one understood by the protagonists at the time. Pickett hated that his name was attached to the charge, about which there had been serious disagreement among the Confederate generals.[4] Meade and Lee did not do battle to give rise to rampant industrialized capitalism. But the context and audience for the display of this image, much more even than what it particularly depicted, drove home the new message.

The coin and the cyclorama together illustrate the starting point behind this study: committing violence and making pictures of it are fundamentally different tactics of power, regardless of the "realism" of the image. Both can be used as means of control. They can be exercised at vastly different times, and by very different people, to widely different ends. Even when exercised by the same people at the same time, they function differently and produce different outcomes. Pictures, even realistic ones, are so prone to manipulation and are so context-dependent in their meaning that they must be approached in their own light rather than as direct evidence of the practice of violence. Pictures can show violence differently than it happened. Pictures can show violence that never happened. Violence that did happen is also certainly not always turned into a picture. As such, studying the images left to us from Egypt allows us to better understand one tactic of pharaonic power: that of imaging it. These images do not give us reliable insight into the practice of violence itself any more than the coin tells us about Waterloo or the cyclorama lets us understand Gettysburg. This is first surprising, then disappointing. But, once accepted, it frees us to consider the images and their power on their own.

The structure of this book

I have gathered and present here all extant images of violence from Egypt that I know of dating prior to the New Kingdom. One goal of this book is that it be a sourcebook for anyone else who wishes to address how and why Egyptians visualized violence, and this is the reason I have striven both to include as much evidence as I know to exist and to illustrate as much of it as I could. The inclusion of images themselves is critical to allowing the reader to accept or challenge my own observations of each piece and the interpretations I suggest. Dimensions given are those published. Every piece for which I could obtain permission to publish is illustrated, and all, including the few I was not able to illustrate, are described.

Because my goal is not to illuminate historical events but rather to examine how pictures of violence in Egypt communicated what to whom, I have chosen to organize this material primarily by context. It has become clear to me that the same image could work differently in different places—that the king smiting an Asiatic on the walls of his tomb does something else than the same picture on a rock face in the Sinai. Context and audience were deeply entwined and often heavily regulated in ancient Egypt. "Where," or perhaps more precisely "on what," was thus the guiding principle followed in organizing this book.

The material of pharaonic date is divided into contextual chapters, addressing the royal tomb; divine temples; the landscape; portable objects; and private tombs. The chapters are of wildly uneven length because these contexts are represented by vastly different amounts of material. The kings of the first half of Egyptian history spent much more time and effort on decorating their tombs with violence than anywhere else. The variety as well as the number of violent pictures from royal tombs is overwhelming even in its very fragmentary current state.

That a contextual organization makes sense can be seen from a simple chart, such as the chronological table in the front matter. Trends of scene type by context are very consistent and support the argument that the relationship between image and context was meaningful and controlled. For instance, battle scenes are known only from tombs, both royal and private. Smiting scenes are found in all contexts except private tombs. Smiting is the only scene type found in the landscape., etc.

While I thus thought the Dynastic material would be best organized contextually, the issue of the origin of violent imagery is not easy to treat in the same way. This is in part because the types of contexts on which we have violent imagery— the contexts arguably more than the images themselves—changed fundamentally both during the period of state formation in the late fourth millennium and between that period and the Old Kingdom. Consequently, the first two chapters of the book are organized chronologically and present the early occurrences of themes of violence and domination in Egyptian art. The most significant suggestion I have made on the basis of this material is that we cannot observe a coherent development of such imagery with a defined relation to nascent power structures prior to the very late Predynastic Period.[5] The reign of Narmer at the start of the First Dynasty is the reign from which we have the greatest variety and number of such pictures, and it is only with his reign and perhaps the generations immediately preceding it that we see the kinds of specificity and historicity combined with general statements that we expect from later violent images. I do not think this is an accident; I think both kingship itself and visual means of depicting and upholding its ideology underwent a very rapid growth and transformation, and that pictures of violence are a good illustration of how exceptional this period was. The pivot between a chronological and a contextual discussion is thus the reign of Narmer, whose imagery looks more like that which followed but whose contexts for using it were more like those of his predecessors. Still, there is no neat dividing line and the inclusion of First and Second Dynasty material in the contextual chapters has often been awkward, though I felt it to work better than attaching it to the chronological chapters.

Another point of structure is the opening of each chapter with a comparative image. I have tried to use these as I have used the coin and cyclorama here in the introduction: to raise questions about the ways in which violent pictures, or pictures of domination in some cases, could work. In no case have I attempted to write an interpretation of the comparative image itself, nor to be comprehensive in citing bibliography about it. In the end, some of these comparisons have proved more useful than others, but they all at some point made me stop and step back from assumptions I was making about how Egyptian images must have functioned.

Two major omissions, both intentional, must be explained: I have not dealt with texts in much detail, and I have not included New Kingdom or later material. The decision to leave out texts would be insupportable if this were a book about violence, rather than a book about pictures of violence. But texts can communicate differently, sometimes to different audiences and in different contexts than images, and my primary aim has been to ask how the imagery functions. When images and texts are together and I am confident they rely upon one another to communicate, I have usually noted the text. This primarily means image captions where those are present. In a handful of instances where texts about violence and images of violence are found in the same context but not directly together, I have brought in quotes from these texts. However, in these cases it has usually seemed to me that the texts and images are demonstrably different in intent, and this has supported rather than undermined the decision to consider imagery separately. For instance, in the most completely considered example, the private tomb of Amenemhat from Beni Hasan has both an autobiographical account of his participation in military campaigns and an image of troops attacking a fortified place (Chapter 8). They do not match; the picture is not an illustration of the text. The text can be read, to oversimplify a bit, as an indication of the close relationship between the king and his trusted official Amenemhat, and as a celebration of Amenemhat's personal qualities. The image is doing something else entirely, and not only does it not include the king, but it also does not even include Amenemhat. This type of mismatch itself helps us understand what both the texts and the images were intended to do; here my focus is on the images, but a similarly contextual examination of texts that speak of violence would complement this study.

The decision to consider only the first half of pharaonic history has three bases, one of overwhelming importance and the other two not negligible. The smaller reasons are simpler: later Egyptian imagery has been quite extensively studied, including from the perspective of power and ideology;[6] it also would have made the book much too long. But the most important reason is that I do not think it belongs in the same study. The material from the New Kingdom is much richer but it is also quite different, both in terms of content and in terms of context. This makes it on the one hand very tempting to use it to explain the earlier material, since it is much better understood, and on the other dangerous to do so. By way of an example we can look at the famous Qadesh reliefs of Ramses II (Figure 1.2),[7] which show the king triumphantly riding his chariot and firing his bow, personally snatching victory from the jaws of defeat as his army reels in chaos during a massive battle against the wily and well-organized Hittites.

Superficially, this image has a great deal in common with what will be examined in this study. Here we have a scene of violence from the royal mortuary temple, which shows the king acting in unique splendor and the chaos of a battlefield. But neither in context nor in content are the similarities as close as they appear. The outside of a pylon, where the Ramses image is located, is a more or less public space, visible to everyone. The inside of a mortuary temple, where reliefs of violence in the Old and Middle Kingdoms are located, had a

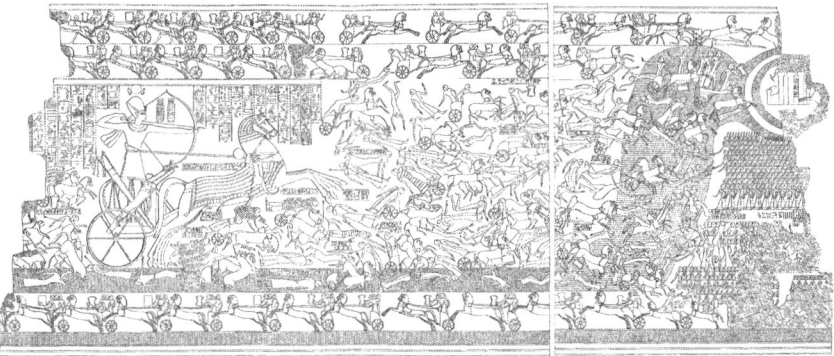

Figure 1.2 Ramses II of the New Kingdom rides his chariot and fires his bow in attacking the Hittites at Qadesh, Syria. From the second pylon of his mortuary temple at Thebes.

much more restricted audience. Qadesh scenes were also carved for Ramses in divine temples—a context that is so ill-represented prior to the New Kingdom that Chapter 5 of this book cannot come to any reasonable conclusions at all about how or even if images of violence regularly worked there. The Qadesh scene combines royal action and the battlefield; this is not known from earlier imagery, where icons of royal violence appear to have been separated from war itself and where battle was not utilized to demonstrate personal valor of the king or anyone else. For Qadesh, elements of landscape are present—a sense of place is given. This is never true in earlier imagery. This image tells a story: it does so itself, and it does so in combination with extensive texts. The image is not a perfect illustration of the story, but the two are very closely tied and are explicitly related to actual events—they say so, and we have other documentary evidence for the events. We may laugh about how "true" the picture is, how heroic Ramses really was or if he really won, but that it purports to represent a series of actual events is unquestionable.

Earlier images are much less obviously narrative and do not have this relationship to texts, as suggested above. In part because of this, they also have a much less direct interest in appearing historical. We will find specificity and historicity regularly as elements of earlier images, but no attempt—and I think even a deliberate avoidance—to claim that a picture is a report in the way Qadesh claims to be. The coin and the cyclorama were used to suggest that it would be a mistake to use any image as a straightforward report on an event, and indeed no scholarship of the scenes of Qadesh fails to make the point that this is not pure historical reporting. But if we cannot use scenes of Qadesh as a simple report on Qadesh, it is equally true that we cannot use them as a simple guide to understanding earlier images of violence in Egypt. Some visual elements of violent imagery were incredibly static over time, particularly the so-called smiting scene, in which the king prepares to bash an enemy on the head with a weapon. Because of contextual changes, however, we should not assume that even such an icon—which like Qadesh could appear on the pylons of New Kingdom temples—had a static function over the whole course of Egyptian history.

Themes

Several themes appear across different contexts with images of violence from Egypt. First and foremost is scene type; this is limited, and has already been noted above, with due caveats about our creation of categories. It was noted that explicitly violent imagery, in which a person or people are shown in the act of damaging other persons or people, can be grouped into two categories in this material: triumph (smiting, trampling) and battle. Triumph in our periods is exclusively the province of the king. Trampling is accomplished by the king in the form of a mythical animal. Smiting, in which he clubs one or more prostate prisoners with a mace, is performed usually by the king in human form but very occasionally, in early periods, by the king's name. Is this a moment of violence or a preparation for violence, given that the mace has not yet hit the head, and is that distinction meaningful? Battle scenes include both hand-to-hand combat and ranks of soldiers attacking in unison. Often, including in all completely preserved cases, the battle occurs outside the walls of a fortified place. There is, as noted above, no evidence that battle and triumph were closely linked scene types during this period, though they became so in the New Kingdom.

Given differences in their use and apparent meaning, and remembering the questions raised by the €2.5 coin, we must question if these categories or even the category "images of violence" are inherent to the material or our own. Even the boundaries of the category as thus defined are difficult to find. Aside from the explicit images, there are several cases of imagery showing bound captives who are not being actively damaged that I have included in this study; these could be used beside images of violence or independently. I have not attempted to gather such images comprehensively. Images of captivity are included here when I have felt that they can help us understand either the presence or the absence of explicit violence in specific contexts.

The theme of the relationship between depiction and event is one that is inherent to the topic, and while I used two more recent images above to show how problematic it would be to assume a one-to-one correspondence between the two, "reality" also cannot be avoided entirely. If I have tried to not be trapped by an expectation that real events are depicted realistically, I have not tried to avoid thinking about what might have actually taken place as well as how images might relate to that. Here it is important to recognize that images might influence future events as well as reflect past events. This is abundantly clear with figurines of bound captives used ritually to damn potential enemies, but might also be a factor with other types of imagery. When is an image intended to show, and perhaps recast, what has happened, and when is it intended to influence what will happen? In fact, the relationship of such images to time seems particularly critical to me. If I were to accord them a single overarching purpose, I would say that they take events, real, ritual, or imagined, past, present, or future, and cast them timelessly, so that they tie the practice of violence to a theory or an ideal.

Another constant theme already mentioned is that of audience. I argue that most of the contexts in which we find violent imagery before the New Kingdom were highly restricted, meaning that in most cases these pictures spoke to a selected audience. This is particularly true for triumph scenes, which would have been seen, I think, by a limited number of largely divine and perhaps priestly eyes. To such an audience, such images are reassuring rather than threatening; it is an audience that is supported rather than hurt by royal violence. The opposite may be true of the same image when deployed in the landscape; there it might have been seen by a broader audience, including people who were threatened by its promise. It is worth remembering, too, that images in ancient Egypt were often considered to have considerably more agency than we are used to according them. It may have mattered not only who could see an image, but also what the image itself could have seen and what it could have done in response to what it saw. Images as audiences themselves would likewise have played different roles in different contexts.

Related to the theme of audience is that of transmission of imagery. The smiting icon in particular is so entirely canonical from so early in pharaonic history that we can be certain it was known and seen even in periods from which we have no extant evidence. Those periods can be significantly long, such as the entire Second Dynasty. Someone in some context must have seen images of smiting that we do not have during these reigns, and made new ones. I have tried to show in Chapter 7 why I think portable objects are unlikely to have been the main carriers of such imagery, as I think they themselves were quite restricted in circulation, but I remain uncertain of what filled the gap. The one place where mode of transmission may be reasonably reconstructed is the landscape, where the images were available to be seen and could be copied directly from one another, but this is also in many ways the least typical context we have and it seems unlikely that it had a larger role in the process of transmission.

A final theme that comes up repeatedly is that of the visual representation of stereotypes of groups of people. It is a difficult topic to treat for several reasons. That there are visual ethnic stereotypes is so abundantly obvious, from all periods of Egyptian history, that it is easy to simply accept them as present, identify "peoples," and move on. But in the nitty-gritty it is much more complicated, in terms of which attributes are static and which change, which attributes belong to which peoples, and which peoples play what roles. Furthermore, that there was an element of ideology to identifying others is clear, and some of the mismatches between visual attributes, texts, and what we know of "foreigners" on the ground may result from a different rate of change between ideological markers and actual interactions between peoples.[8] Identifying "who" is thus not straightforward, particularly early on when visual stereotypes were in greater flux, and in fact I am not so confident that ambiguity was always meant to be absent; plurality and differentiation mattered more than accuracy. Even if the Egyptians did mean to designate static and bounded groups of people with these visual stereotypes, it is not so clear that they are meant to be representative of places, or that we should understand them territorially.[9]

Despite real misgivings about terminology and a recognition that the issue is more complex than I had originally thought, I have used the terms common in scholarship to refer to broad groups of people: Libyans, Asiatics, and Nubians. To avoid them seemed more complicated than to use them. All deserve more attention and qualification than I can give, and many issues will be raised within discussions of individual depictions, but a few observations here will help the reader navigate what follows. "Libyans" are by far the most consistent of the visual depictions but are also the hardest to identify with a people, polity, or place known from other sources for the period considered here—an interesting combination. "Asiatics" are a group within which there are subgroups that are sometimes specified in texts and perhaps in imagery as well. Notable here are the *Mentiu*, a group of Asiatics who are named in inscriptions in various contexts and are the only named group of people in the images in the landscape, which themselves are restricted to the Sinai. We may see here a very deliberate and pointed reference to a particular ethnicity instead of the "all" common in other contexts. "Nubians," who are also frequently differentiated into subgroups in texts, surprised me the most. I expected and did not find a static visual representation for people from the south, and I expected southerners to be common. This was not the case. I remain uncertain of how and when Egyptian imagery of violence includes Nubians, and which Nubians. They do not seem ever to be the victims of attack in battle in the periods under study here. A final critical note about the "who" of ethnicity is that Egyptians were given visual stereotypes, too, and that people with Egyptian stereotypical features could appear as victims in all types of scenes of violence, though they are less common than "foreigners." Whatever else these stereotypes are doing, they are not creating a binary world in which Egypt is the good and foreigners the evil. If there is a binary at all, it is that the Egyptian king is in power and everyone else is, at least potentially, violently subject to him.[10]

I have tried to keep ethnic stereotypes from taking over the book, and I have not at all tried to be comprehensive in tracing the rise of visual stereotypes or including all iterations of them; like captivity, they are here only if and when they contribute to our understanding of active scenes of violence.

In the end, scenes of violence may not be straightforward historical documents, but they are rich sources for helping us understand the ways in which their contexts functioned and the ways in which ideal kingship was conceived. The ideology expressed in this imagery seems to me quite simple. Theoretical Egyptian kingship required that the king be violently physically dominant over everyone. Events, whether ritual or not, were cast in line with this theory and displayed in contexts that helped to maintain this ideal of kingship. The king's right, even requirement, to be shown smashing heads was exclusive to him. Much less exceptional was the imagery of war, which—perhaps surprisingly—does not seem in these periods to have been closely tied to royal ideology at all. If triumph was exclusive and spectacular, warfare was rather ordinary and conflict an assumed part of life.[11] But if these strains of ideology and worldview are themselves simple and far from unexpected or previously unexamined, there is no simple and single answer to the question of how images of violence worked, and we should not expect one. They worked differently, and the same image could do different things, depending on where it was and who could see it.

Notes

1 Michaël Torfs, "Belgium withdraws 'Controversial' Waterloo Coin under French Pressure, but has a Plan B," *FlandersNews.be*, March 12, 2015, http://deredactie.be/cm/vrtnieuws.english/News/1.2267618.

2 Schulman, for example, has used imagery of violence to examine both supposed historic events and tactics of war: Alan R. Schulman, "Siege Warfare in Pharaonic Egypt," *Natural History Magazine* 73, no. 3 (1964): 12–21; Alan R. Schulman, "The Battle Scenes of the Middle Kingdom," *Journal of the Society for the Study of Egyptian Antiquities* 12, no. 4 (1982): 165–183. Spalinger deals extremely briefly with early periods from a quite traditional military–history perspective: Anthony J. Spalinger, *War in Ancient Egypt: The New Kingdom* (Malden, MA and Oxford: Blackwell, 2005); Anthony J. Spalinger, *Icons of Power: A Strategy of Reinterpretation* (Prague: Charles University in Prague, Faculty of Arts, 2011). Alberto Giannese, "Conflict-Related Representations in the 4th Millennium Egypt. A Study on Ideology of Violence" (Master's thesis, University College London, 2012), provides an examination of violent imagery from the Naqada I-III in hopes of analyzing the relationship between ideology and Egyptian state formation. Gregory has studied war in early Egypt, relying on material culture but also pictorial representations: Gilbert Gregory, *Weapons, Warriors and Warfare in Early Egypt* (Oxford: Archaeopress, 2004). Juan Carlos Moreno García, "War in Old Kingdom Egypt (2686–2125 BCE)," in *Studies on War in the Ancient Near East: Collected Essays on Military History*, Ed. Jordi Vidal (Münster: Ugarit-Verlag, 2010), discusses different aspects of Old Kingdom warfare. Shaw has dealt with the relationship between economy and war: Ian Shaw, "Battle in Ancient Egypt: The Triumph of Horus or the Cutting Edge of the Temple Economy?" in *Battle in Antiquity*, Ed. Alan B. Lloyd (London: Duckworth in association with the Classical Press of Wales, 1996); Ian Shaw, "Socio-Economic and Iconographic Contexts for Egyptian Military Technology: The Knowledge Economy and 'Technology Transfer' in Late Bronze Age Warfare," in *The Knowledge Economy and Technological Capabilities: Egypt, the Near East and the Mediterranean 2nd Millennium BC–1st Millennium AD Proceedings of a Conference Held at the Maison de La Chimie Paris, France 9–10 December 200*, Ed. M. Wissa (Barcelona: Aula Orientalis, 2010), 77–85. Popular treatments of war in ancient Egypt have tended to be broad in scope: Robert Partridge, *Fighting Pharaohs: Weapons and Warfare in Ancient Egypt* (Manchester: Peartree Publishing, 2002); Bridget McDermott, *Warfare in Ancient Egypt* (Stroud: Sutton Publishing, 2004).

3 Yoni Appelbaum, "The Great Illusion of Gettysburg," *The Atlantic*, February 5, 2012, www.theatlantic.com/national/archive/2012/02/the—great—illusion—of—gettysburg/238870/.

4 James Longstreet, for example, was against making the charge at all: "I do not want to make this charge. I do not see how it can succeed. I would not make it now but that Gen. Lee has ordered it and is expecting it," Edward P. Alexander, *Military Memoirs of a Confederate: A Critical Narrative* (New York: C. Scribner's Sons, 1907), 424. Pickett was left frantic with grief after the charge and the deaths of so many of his men. In a letter to his wife, he wrote:

Well, it is all over now. The battle is lost, and many of us are prisoners, many are dead, many wounded, bleeding and dying. Your Soldier lives and mourns and but for you, my darling, he would rather, a million times rather, be back there with his dead, to sleep for all time in an unknown grave.

Letter sent by Pickett to LaSalle Corbell Pickett on July 4, 1863: George E. Pickett, *Soldier of the South: General Pickett's War Letters to His Wife*, Ed. Arthur C. Inman (Boston, MA and New York: Houghton Mifflin Company, 1928), 59–62.

5 Most studies of early imagery of domination and violence have concluded rather the opposite. The development of my point of view with full references to those who would argue otherwise can be found in Chapter 2.

6 Most recently and in most depth, Spalinger, *Icons of Power: A Strategy of Reinterpretation*. Also G.A. Gaballa, *Narrative in Egyptian Art* (Mainz am Rhein: Philipp von Zabern, 1976).

7 James Henry Breasted, *The Battle of Kadesh: A Study in the Earliest Known Military Strategy* (Chicago, IL: The University of Chicago Press, 1903), pl. 3.

8 Dominique Valbelle, *Les neuf arcs: L'égyptien et les étrangers de la préhistoire à la conquête d'Alexandre* (Paris: Armand Colin, 1990), 46.

9 That foreign people rather than foreign places are the focus of Egyptian domination has also been suggested in analyses of the Pyramid Texts, inscribed in the interiors of late Old Kingdom pyramids. See a discussion in Eric Uphill, "The Nine Bows," *Jaarbericht van het Vooraziatische—Egyptisch Genootschap Ex Oriente Lux* 19 (1967): 394, where he cites Kurt Sethe, *Die altägyptischen Pyramidentexte, nach den Papierabdrücken und Photographien des Berliner Museums, neu Herausgegeben und Erläutert* (Hildesheim: Georg Olms Verlagsbuchhandlung, 1960), spell 202b.

10 The inclusion of Egyptians as enemies appears in texts, too. For instance, Uphill reminds us that the developed list of the Nine Bows, the traditional "others" who needed to be crushed by the king, included Upper and Lower Egypt. Eric Uphill, "The Nine Bows," 394–395.

11 Whether or not there even was a notion of "peace" in ancient Egypt is an interesting question that has received recent attention. Bickel notes that a state in which conflict existed was more or less assumed as the baseline normal; she also finds that in discussing peace in ancient Egypt it is important to recognize that worldview and actual political behavior were "intensely interwoven but did not always coincide," an observation quite in line with the discussion of violence here. Susanne Bickel, "Peace in the Ancient World: Concepts and Theories," in *Peace in the Ancient World: Concepts and Theories*, Ed. Kurt A. Raaflaub (Chichester and Malden, MA: John Wiley & Sons, 2016), 44.

2   The origins of violent imagery

In the Northern Territory of Australia, in a shelter on the Arnhem Land plateau deep above Deaf Adder Gorge, there lies a painted rock face that has been understood as showing a skirmish, with several figures wounded by spears (Figure 2.1). The image belongs to the "Dynamic Figures" tradition, which has been dated to approximately 10,000 BC;[1] this tradition is the earliest utilizing figural imagery in this region, and its violent images are the oldest pictures of humans inflicting harm on one another known anywhere in the world.[2] Images of fighting are rare in hunter-gatherer societies at all, and are not the most prevalent type of Dynamic

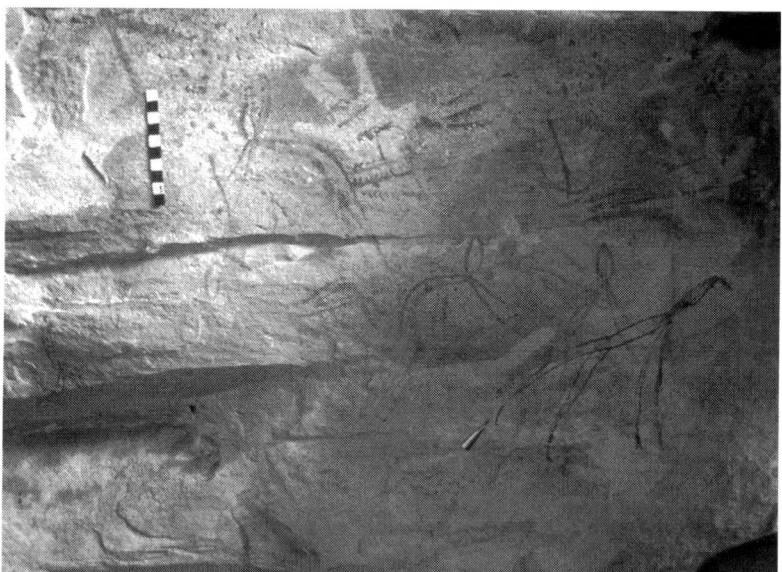

Figure 2.1 "Skirmish" scene, painting on rock face, near Deaf Adder Gorge, Arnhem Land, Northern Territory, Australia. Figures are shown ducking spears, lying on the ground, and reaching to help one another. No indication of spear throwers is evident in the image, but that it represents a moment of violence is suggested by the spears evidently still in flight.

Figures imagery in Arnhem Land, where male figures in ceremonial headdresses predominate, though domestic and hunting scenes are also not uncommon.[3]

Understanding the figures of this scene and their relation to each other is difficult. They appear to have been added in at least three phases. The clearest grouping is of six figures at the left rendered in the same pigment and style as one another.[4] Immediately to the right of the scale in the image above, faint and difficult to see, is a prone figure reaching up and a second figure bending down toward it. This leaning figure, who faces to the left, has three almost vertical lines coming out the back of its leg; these lines have many shorter lines coming out of them, making them look like feathers. In the middle of the scene a figure ducks; there are three more lines of the same fletched nature to the right, not in contact with anything else. Beneath these lines is another figure leaning forward, to the right, not as severely stooped as the middle figure. The darker and more easily seen figure at the right was a later addition, indicating continued changing of and interaction with the image over time.

The Deaf Adder Gorge image does not make much immediate sense to an uninitiated viewer. It appears relatively simple, with only a small number of figures and objects shown, but reading it and advancing possible interpretations, even understanding that it is an image of violence, require knowledge of a broader corpus of images, including some that date to later periods.[5] For example, would I have read the fletched-looking lines as spears if I had not been told by an expert to do so? On the leaning figure at the upper left, might I have read them instead as elements of clothing indicating the role of the figure, an iconographic device indicating power that is repeated elsewhere in the scene?

The type of spear shown here is present in other Dynamic Figures Period images, which include several cases of figures with similarly barbed shafts sticking out of different places in their bodies. There are also cases of opposed figures brandishing weapons, but this is the sole Dynamic Figures image of anything like mass combat, and groups of figures at all are quite rare in this tradition.[6] This scarcity is one reason it is difficult to determine what is meant by this scene, and again one reason comparison to later scenes seems helpful. In the later Stick Figure Period, violence is a much more prevalent aspect of imagery. At that time, the scope of violence in individual images is much greater, with the introduction of large battle scenes; new motifs including different weaponry are present; and the corpus of imagery as a whole shows much greater regional variation. The interpreters of the violent imagery of Arnhem Land rock art have correlated the changes in the corpuses of these periods to substantial shifts in social and economic structures and suggest that they are reflective of actual changes in who fought, how, and why.[7] From our perspective it is equally of interest that changing social and economic realities resulted in changing modes of representation, even within the same medium of expression. This rock art is no more a simple report on wars fought than is a Belgian €2.50 coin with an image of Waterloo a simple report on that battle.

Some questions about the development of early imagery of violence as well as reasonable approaches to it, which are suggested on the basis of the Arnhem

Land skirmish scene, are also applicable to Egyptian art. When do such images first occur? In what media and to what end? How do those images relate to contemporary images that are not violent? How can we tell that violence is pictured? What relation might such imagery have to actual violence or other aspects of social and economic structures? Who is shown? Why were such images made? And as has already been made clear, we must ask what level of knowledge is needed to read such images, and to what degree is it safe to build on knowledge of later images—knowledge we have, but that the creators of the images in question did not.

The earliest images of violence in Egypt

Imagery of physical domination in Egypt is known from the first major tradition of figured representation in the Nile valley: painted pottery from the Naqada I Period of the Upper Egyptian Predynastic. There is no clear relationship between the practice of violence in early Egypt and these depictions of domination. The first occurrence of such images is many thousand years after the first archaeologically attested evidence of violence on more than an interpersonal scale.[8] More critically, the first attested images are extremely limited and known only from one site and in a small handful of examples, while violence itself was probably much more widespread. They are also part of scenes that include postures and iconography that suggest they are ritualized in nature rather than reportorial; the degree to which these images intended to picture either violence or accurate reports is questionable. In the subsequent Naqada II Period images of violence are even more poorly attested, though richer in content. They, too, are impossible to divorce from their ceremonial settings. From the first, then, it seems important to examine such images not as simple indications of the presence or roles of violence in Egyptian society, but rather as deliberately deployed messages intended to function in specific contexts.

   Understanding the meaning of the messages in these earliest images of violence seems simpler than it is, particularly if one tries to consider such art within its own contexts, without reliance on later pharaonic traditions. Such an attempt should be made. The chief reason for caution in relating Predynastic images of violence to later periods is a lack of continuity, notable in chronological gaps, in changes of context for the display of such images, and in both modes and motifs of representation. A tendency in much recent scholarship has been to see ever-greater continuity between early Predynastic and pharaonic Egypt, particularly in terms of artistic motifs and their ideological meanings; an effect of this has been to see the ideas of Egyptian kingship, particularly about violence, as nascent in even the earliest periods.[9] Especially with the earliest material, this tracing of continuity has relied primarily on presumed concepts embedded within images rather than on visual similarities, but to me the risk seems great that we only see the concepts as continuous because we expect them to be. While a focus on continuity has been a welcome corrective to earlier ideas of pharaonic Egypt's rise as due to the invasion of a "Dynastic race,"[10] there is room for more consideration of dynamism and difference within the indigenous traditions of the Nile valley.

This chapter will deal selectively with some images of domination and violence from the Predynastic Period, in particular Naqada I-II, and the following chapter will focus on art of the Naqada III and the transition to the Early Dynastic Period. These chapters together will show that the relationship between power, violence, and iconography was flexible, though also uncommon, before the enshrinement of violence as an icon in the pharaonic smiting scene. This suggests that the development toward that scene was not linear, and that we should be quite cautious in assuming that the specifically pharaonic conceptions of violence and order communicated by that icon were already present in Predynastic power structures. Because the contexts we have in general from these early periods are not always directly comparable to later contexts—for instance, there is no standardized royal tomb, and royal involvement with divine temples is not clear—this material is organized roughly chronologically rather than contextually in the way of later chapters. However, as even relative dating is not always particularly precise, and as some categories of evidence are themselves fairly restricted chronologically, there are clusters by medium within the chronological framework. I also include a few pieces of unknown provenance.

The images treated in this chapter are found exclusively in relation to tombs and, with one exception, are found on objects in tombs rather than on the tombs themselves. It is not clear how much this mortuary prevalence is an accurate reflection of early use, since tombs in general are far and away the best-preserved type of context we have from Egypt. The mortuary context raises immediate questions about the audience for such images: who could have seen them? In the case of pots or textiles painted with images of violence, they might well have had a use in life before their interment. The case of a subterranean burial chamber with a painted wall cannot have been intended primarily for a living human viewership. Either its audience was the buried individual, and perhaps other beings in the afterlife, or its function relied most on knowledge among the living that it was there, not on them actually seeing it. Some of the early graves containing such images may have belonged to local rulers; all were unquestionably burial places for members of the emerging elite. But the relation between the people pictured in the imagery and the occupants of the tombs in which it has been found is never clear in these periods. We can never be certain if we are looking at a specific person or event, at the representation of cosmic processes, or at some combination of the two. The move from such ambiguous, perhaps general, images in the early Predynastic to exceptionally specific, labeled images in the Protodynastic and Early Dynastic is one of the most dramatic developments of Egyptian art. This is particularly the case as it accompanies in lock-step the development of what is often called the artistic canon of Egypt, that typical mode of representation that sees, among other things, Egyptians "walking like Egyptians." No such canon, no such specificity, can be demonstrated in the early art of Egypt. But those few images of violence we have from such periods do suggest that some of the general ideas and universal forces that would be important later were in play back then as well.

The evidence from early Egypt: Naqada I

Domination on White Cross-Lined Ware

Identifying the earliest Egyptian images of violence between people is not straightforward as the content and particularly meaning of some early representations are often unclear; a viewer without knowledge of later Egyptian art might not read these as violent at all. The first images usually discussed in this context come from pottery vessels dated to the Naqada IA-C Period (roughly 3800–3400 BC).[11] The pots in question belong to a tradition variously called White Cross-Line Ware or C-Ware; this pottery is characterized by its deep red surface decorated with white lines. Five vessels of this type have been interpreted as showing larger figures dominating smaller captives, and these have been accepted by many as scenes of triumph or victory, though captivity or domination might be less loaded terms.[12] The Naqada I itself was a period of increasing social stratification, read from tomb sizes and differential amounts of grave goods, but we are uncertain of its structures of power.

Naqada I material culture is limited geographically to a relatively small area in Upper Egypt. White Cross-Lined Ware, while one of the type-materials of the Naqada I, has been found in a limited number of graves. Its motifs include geometric designs, grazing animals, and hunting. There may be regional variations in the painting style and content of images.[13] Images appear on multiple different types of vessels, including both open and closed forms; they are known to us almost exclusively as grave goods, though a relatively large percentage of known examples of this type is unprovenanced. White Cross-Lined Ware is the first regularly decorated type of artifact in Egypt. As such, if we accept that some White Cross-Lined Ware vessels show domination, possibly as an aftermath of violence, this motif is present as soon as objects carry images at all.[14]

Three of the five White Cross-Lined Ware vessels with possible captivity scenes were excavated in the Predynastic cemetery at Umm el-Qaab, Abydos, two from the same grave; the other two are unprovenanced (Figures 2.2–2.6).[15] Given regional variations in the corpus, it may be reasonable to assume that these two were from Abydos. All five are tall, narrow jars with flaring rims, though the shape of their bodies varies. The representations are in all cases schematic, with figures heavily abbreviated and unrealistically depicted; arms in particular are not clear and in many cases seem to be absent.[16] Where the figures have obvious markers of sex, they are male, indicated by what appear to be penis sheaths. Four of the five scenes have clear visual means of distinguishing between the protagonists, and in all cases they employ at least two of the same methods of distinction: size and headgear. The headgear itself is not entirely consistent, but in three cases the larger figures wear what seem to be rather tall headdresses composed of multiple upright elements, perhaps feathers or branches. The heads of the smaller figures on all five vessels seem to have rather wavy long hair that goes back behind their heads, or else headdresses that give this impression. Two of the scenes further distinguish the larger figures by giving them some sort of tail, and this may be indicated on a third by the presence of dots going down the back legs of the two larger figures. On three of the vessels, one or more of the large figures raises his curving arms above his head; this is a pose that will become familiar on later Naqada II Decorated Ware pottery and on ceramic figurines, and that is generally recognized as ritual in nature though its precise meaning is debated.[17]

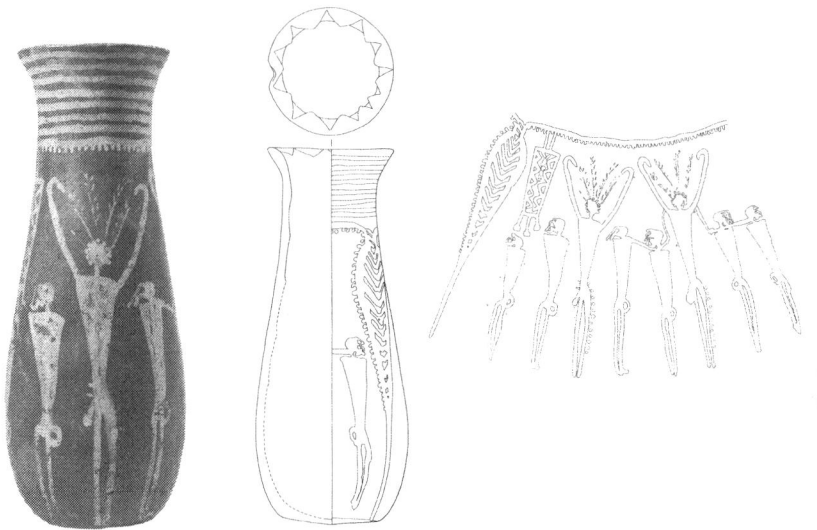

Figure 2.2 A vase of the White Cross-Lined Ware tradition with eight figures shown on its side. The larger two, with arms raised, have often been interpreted as dominating the smaller figures. Provenance unknown. Height: 28.6 cm. Width: 11.8 cm.

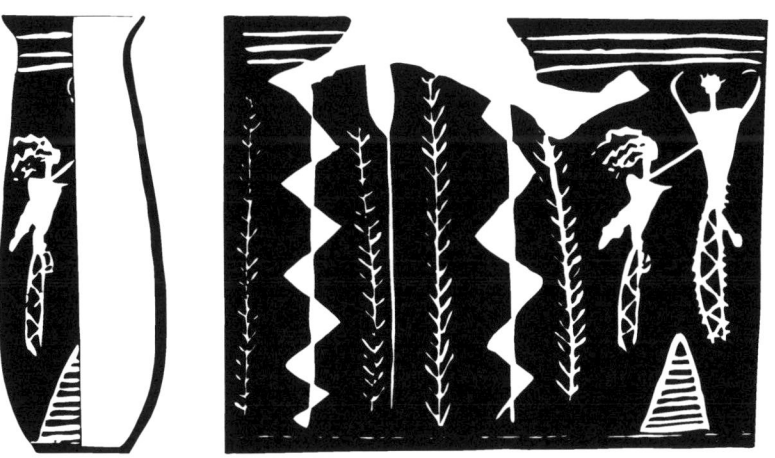

Figure 2.3 Another White Cross-Lined Ware vase interpreted as showing domination, with a raised-arm figure apparently connected by a line to a smaller person. Provenance unknown. Height: 31.5 cm.

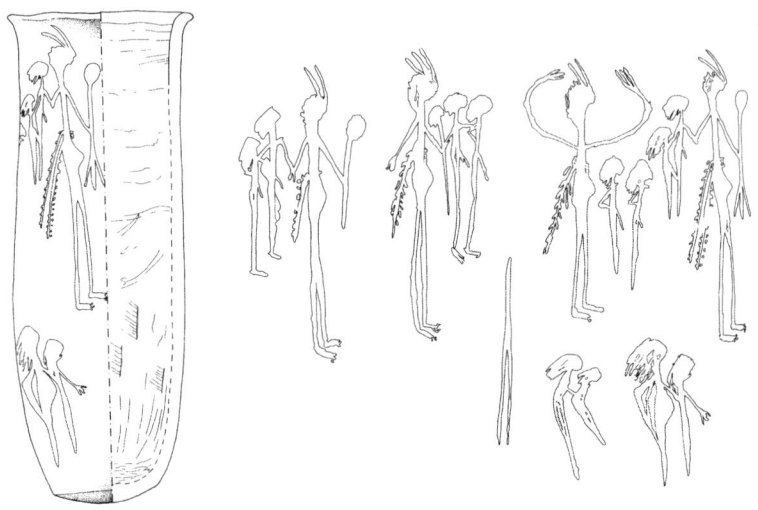

Figure 2.4 White Cross-Lined Ware vase with large and small figures, possibly in poses of domination. On the left of the rolled-out scene the large figure can be seen to clutch an object that has sometimes been called a mace. Abydos, Umm el-Qaab, tomb U-239 vessel 1. Height: 29.8 cm. Rim diameter: 11.5 cm.

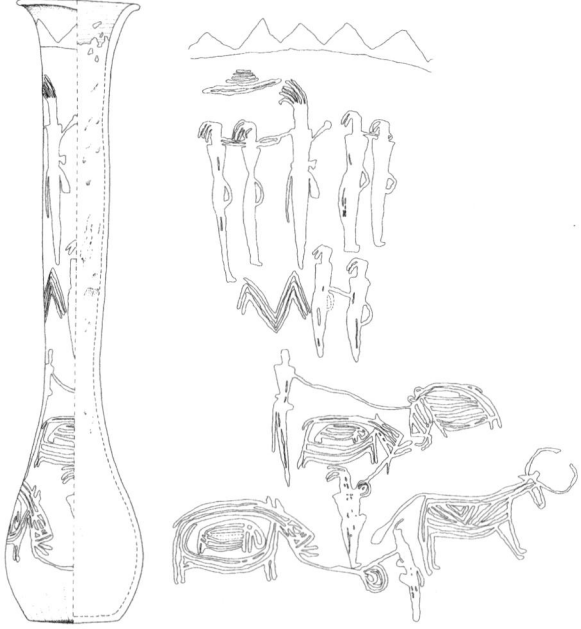

Figure 2.5 White Cross-Lined Ware bulbous vase with a possible domination scene as well as captive animals. Abydos, Umm el-Qaab, tomb U-415 vessel 1. Height: 50.6 cm.

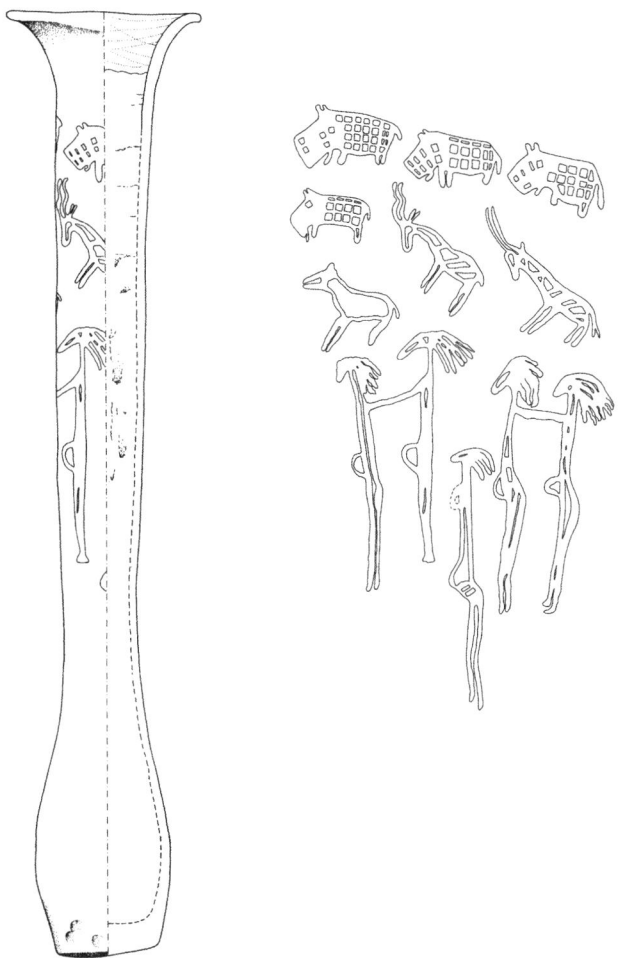

Figure 2.6 White Cross-Lined Ware bulbous vase with animals and figures akin to those in "domination" scenes shown above, but without the presence of a captor. Abydos, Umm el-Qaab, tomb U-415 vessel 2. Height: 46.6 cm.

Each one of these vessels has been said to show domination of the smaller figures by the larger (implied, in the case of Abydos U-415/2, since there are no larger figures). This has been asserted on the basis of the differences in size of the figures; the attachments between smaller figures, and sometimes between larger and smaller figures, which have been interpreted as binding ropes; and analogy to later scenes in which domination and binding are more unambiguously present.[18]

The number of people in these scenes ranges from 2 to 16 and some vessels also depict animals or vegetation and geometric motifs. The Brussels vessel (Figure 2.2) and Abydos U-239/1 (Figure 2.4) include both multiple large and small figures. It is not clear if these scenes show different episodes of a narrative with a single set of actors, who are then repeated in the image, or a single scene. If a general rule can be observed in such a small corpus, there seems to be a preference for grouping the smaller figures in twos. In several places small figures seem to be bound by the neck. On those vessels with clear dominant figures, at least some of the captives are always physically tied to their captors, either because he holds them with an outstretched arm or because the lines that can be interpreted as ropes that bind their necks lead back to the larger figures. In no case is the means of domination given particular visual emphasis, and no one stands in a posture that is either overtly threatening or abjectly cowed.

The bottom sections of two of the vessels include human figures who are not obviously part of the main scene. In Figure 2.5, the bottom and bulbous part of the vessel is covered with a scene of three people holding leashed and apparently pregnant hippopotami. An unleashed bovine is also present. One of these people is rendered with a tail, and one with the hairstyle of a captor; this and the fact that they hold animals captive suggests a conceptual relationship with the scene of human captivity above.[19] In Figure 2.4, four figures at the bottom bear quite a different relationship to what is over their heads. These figures, all small and one possibly held by another figure, have the hairstyle of the smaller figures. They are not obviously distinguished with regards to sex. Their relationship to the groups above them is not clear, but if they are part of the same scene at all they are there as observers rather than participants.[20]

In Figure 2.4, three of the four large figures hold long implements with bulbous heads that are sometimes interpreted as weapons among the scene of captivity. In one case this implement has a split tail, but in the other two it has only a straight handle. A similar object may be represented as coming from the shoulder of the large figure on U-415/1 (Figure 2.5). The bulbous-headed implement has often been interpreted as a mace, presumably both because of its shape and because it is held by figures who are thought to be dominating others.[21] The forked tail of the implement is not known from any definitive depiction of a mace and would seem to make the implement more like a standard or staff than a weapon. These implement-holding figures are each attached to two smaller figures.

How should we interpret the scenes of large and small people, physically connected, on Naqada I White Cross-Lined Ware? Many of the questions we might ask were raised already with regard to the Arnhem Land skirmish scene: questions about first appearances, about prevalence of the motif when it appears, about the relationship of motifs of violence to social and economic structures and changes in them. But all such questions, when put to Naqada Egypt, must come after the most basic one: do these White Cross-Lined Ware scenes even show violent domination of a person or people over others? Our ability to answer that question also shows parallels to the Arnhem Land case. Can we, and should we, try to filter out our knowledge of what would come? Would Egyptologists read this as violence if we did not know a broader corpus, did not know that canonical Egyptian art would use differences of size to indicate differences of importance? That the mace would be a fundamental image of royal control several hundred years later, that the very site where these pots were found was itself the place where the first kings to rule a unified Egypt would be buried?

I am cautiously willing to accept that these images on Naqada I White Cross-Lined Ware show domination of the larger figures over the smaller ones. I think the strongest argument in support of this comes from the images themselves, not on the basis of later, far from close, parallels.[22] The differential size and accoutrements do seem to me to make a clear and consistent distinction between the large and small figures.[23] I see no reason to think that we have here adults and children, meaning that the difference in size most likely relates to a difference in importance, not physical stature.[24] I acknowledge that this reading does depend on my own awareness of a hierarchy of size in later Egyptian art, but I think this is at least a fairly straightforward way of establishing meaning. Another feature of the images that goes some way toward convincing me is the lines linking figures. They seem to me in most cases most easily read as ropes, particularly where they seem to come from the necks of the smaller figures. I am less certain of this; it relies in part on the understanding that the smaller figures are not shown with arms. In some places this is clearly the case, such as the two leftmost figures shown in Figure 2.2, but in others where the connecting line is lower than the neck it is not so clear. It gives me pause that the larger figures do not hold the ropes—definitively not, as their arms are elsewhere. My daughters have not seen ropes at all, and their reading of the scene in Figure 2.3 as showing a small figure sticking a spear into a larger figure, who throws his arms up in response, gives me pause enough to include it here. I am unconvinced about the "mace," particularly because of the spikes on its bottom in one iteration.

If these are scenes of dominance, the coherent and consistent, if very small, body of evidence suggests a defined relationship between a general concept—physical control—and a type of image. The group is clearly a group. The provenanced examples all come from one site, and their images include repeated visual motifs that are not present on other contemporary pots. The general idea that important people are in physical control over subject people seems supported by the imagery, and the elevation of this to ideology can be argued on the basis of the consistent differences of clothing, hair, size, posture, and relationship between large and small figures. The corpus is too small to assert with any confidence that iconographic differences are meant to reflect ethnic differences, but they serve as identifiers of groups within the specific context of dominator/dominated.

The images themselves can be said to make a claim about dominance, but they do this generally. The only thing that might be said to link an individual to any one of these images is its context in his grave, not inherent in the image itself. As we will see repeatedly with pharaonic scenes, the link between the general and the specific can be critical to the functioning of the image. Here we have only the general. Finally, there is no evidence that an established underlying idea about power and captivity and its depiction in imagery was broadly shared in either space or time, since all provenanced examples come from Abydos with two from a single tomb. It has been argued that the motif must have been more often used on other media, now missing, allowing both its greater dissemination in the Naqada I and its communication across time.[25] But such an argument is only necessary if these scenes are seen as a direct linear precursor to the smiting scene, meaning a bridge that is not extant must once have existed. If they are a more general statement about physical domination as an aspect of power for important people at Abydos in the Naqada I Period, it remains an open question as to whether the deployment of this motif in art was a broader tactic for demonstrating and exerting that power.

In part because scenes on these vessels cannot, I think, be clearly connected to later images of smiting, I am not comfortable calling the captors here kings. The visual discrepancies between these images and pharaonic smiting scenes are far more notable than any similarities, and include everything from posture to iconography to the context of painting on a pot. Even the differences in modes of representing the human figure, so schematized here, are relevant: the developed pharaonic mode of representing humans is extremely consistent and it is accepted that this is because the mode as well as the content of the images played a role in conveying its meaning.[26] That mode is absent in Naqada I. Naqada I art was complete in and of itself; it was not a half-baked anticipation, imperfectly capable of achieving its own goals, of what was to come. Even though this is not a proto-smiting scene, there is in its own right a relationship between imagery and power here, deployed in a way and context that suggest it had a codified meaning. The further development of this relationship was far from linear.

The evidence from early Egypt: Naqada II

Like the Naqada I, the Naqada II Period is notable from our perspective chiefly for the near total lack of violent imagery. At a time when Upper Egyptian Naqada culture was growing more stratified and expanding territorially, there is very little evidence that making and displaying pictures of violence were deliberate tactics of asserting power. In terms of numbers, we have only one artifact and one decorated tomb to consider. What little Naqada II imagery of violence we have does show again the Naqada I motifs of domination and binding of figures; however, additional motifs are also present, and the connection to later imagery is clearer than any continuity with the Naqada I. The Naqada II imagery of violence (and in general) is considerably denser than that from Naqada I, but like the images considered above it continues to be general rather than inherently specific in its references.

A break with the past is evident in Naqada II art. White Cross-Lined Ware, the main extant vehicle for images of people from the Naqada I, was not produced after this period. The subsequent decorated ceramic tradition of the Naqada II does not seem to be a direct descendant of it in any way, from fabric, to form, to motifs of decoration; there is also a gap in time between the two. Violence is not shown in the figural scenes on the Decorated (D-Ware) vessels of the Naqada IIC-D Period (roughly 3500–3300 BC). The Decorated Ware images as a corpus are unambiguously related to ritual action and appear to display a consistent and developed worldview (Figure 2.7).[27] Decorated vessels are clearly elite artifacts that played a role in social display during a period when social stratification seems to have increased dramatically. Why is captivity not present on this pottery as it was, if in a very limited way, earlier? It seems far more likely that this argues for a relatively narrow use of imagery on pottery in this period, instead of for a diminished importance of violence in Naqada II society and power structures. This is suggested by the Naqada II tomb painting from Hierakonpolis (Figures 2.9–2.11), which is the main evidence of violent imagery in the period, but the real rarity of such imagery in the preserved record should still caution us against too complete and confident an understanding of the role of either violence or iconography at this time.

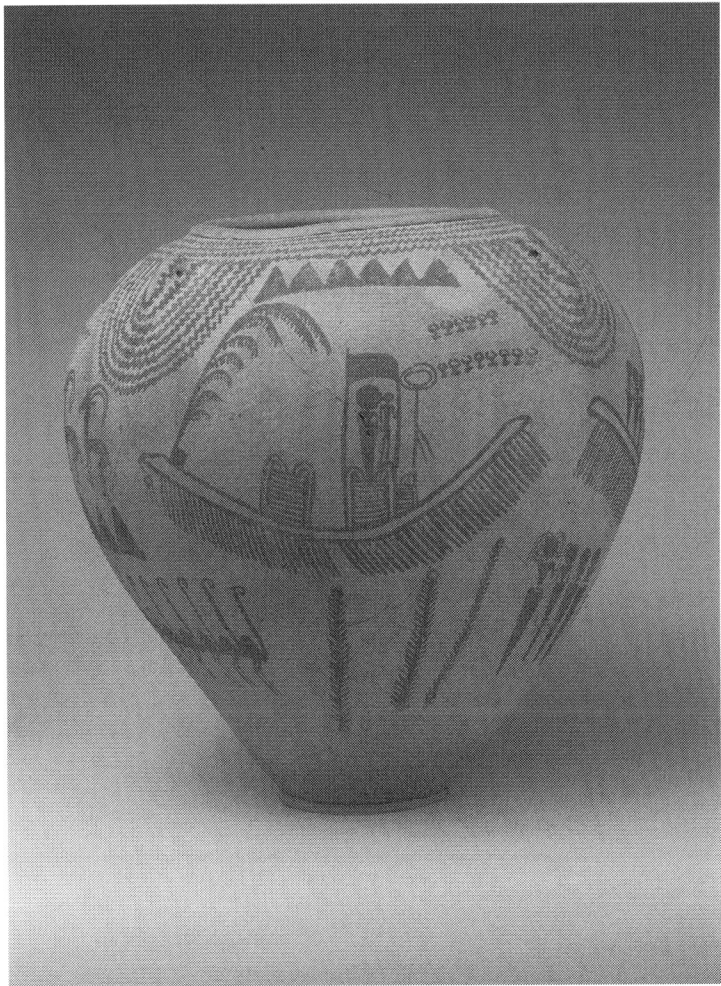

Figure 2.7 A Naqada II Decorated Ware pot. The decoration on this type of vessel includes several standardized elements, of which boats are particularly common. Its depictions are almost certainly ritualized in nature, but are not well understood. Violence is not a known motif on Decorated Ware.

The Gebelein textile

The first image to consider is known as the Gebelein textile. Fragments of a large piece of linen painted with figural scenes were excavated in a Naqada II grave at the Upper Egyptian site of Gebelein in 1930 (Figure 2.8).[28] Reconstruction of the whole piece is not possible but enough remains on the fragments to see some of its motifs, rendered schematically in brown and black, with a few bits of white. The majority of its decoration has no obvious relation to violence at all, and the sole part that has been so interpreted is as ambiguous and reliant on analogy to later material in this regard as was true of the White Cross-Lined Ware scenes.

Parts of at least four boats are present on the Gebelein textile. The largest, shown at the bottom of Figure 2.8, includes a figure manning a rudder at the rear and four preserved oarsmen; more oars show they are missing their fellows. Amidships are two structures: one on the right, toward the prow, with a steeply angled roof, and the other behind, with a rounded roof. Between them sits or kneels a figure whose arms seem to be behind his back. This figure is distinguished from the others in the boat only by his posture—in size and color they are all similar, and none has clear indication of clothing or other identifying marks. A round object hangs off the left pavilion, over the head of the figure.

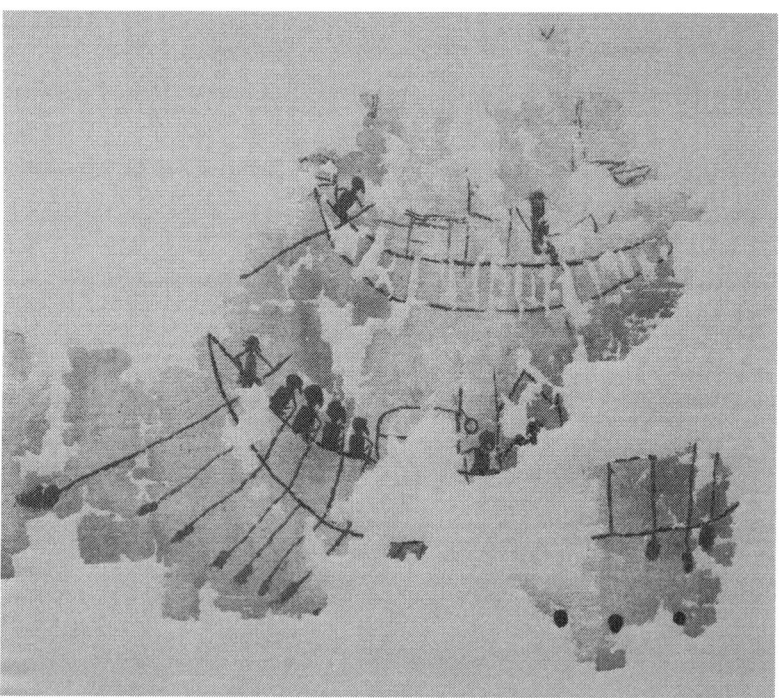

Figure 2.8 Detail of the fragmentary Gebelein textile. The boat at the bottom includes a figure between the two structures amidships that may represent a bound captive. Dimensions: maximum height 77.47 cm, maximum width 134.62 cm.

The figure between the pavilions on the boat of the Gebelein textile has often been interpreted as a bound captive. The posture does seem similar to later images of such prisoners, particularly the statues from royal pyramid complexes, and it has been suggested that the object behind him is a mace.[29] It is possible that this shows a bound prisoner being transported as part of some ritual, but this identification relies on comparison to later imagery. If we accept this as a scene of captivity, it contrasts with the Naqada I images especially in the relative lack of visual distinction between actors, but also in the possible use of a symbol rather than a figure in the dominating position (though Abydos U 239/2 also had only captives without a dominant figure present) and in that there is only one captive. While in both cases there are elements in addition to the presumed scene of domination, those elements themselves are very different: domination over animals in the earlier case, and boating activity, possibly ceremonial, here. It seems a bit of a stretch even to say we are looking at a scene descended from what was present in Naqada I; visually there is no point of comparison at all, and conceptually any relation seems too general to be meaningful.

Other aspects of the imagery on the Gebelein textile have been understood as representing ritual actions and have been specifically linked to later pharaonic rituals. This issue is relevant to a discussion of violent imagery because it becomes more likely that the scene of domination is linked to later ideas of violent kingship if other aspects of developed pharaonic ideology are also present in the image. As the Gebelein textile is so fragmentary, and as the issue is equally applicable in the better-preserved scene in Hierakonpolis Tomb 100, a discussion of explicitly royal ritual in Naqada II imagery will be addressed below. That the tomb and textile, as well as Decorated Ware, engage in a shared visual vocabulary that can inform us of some of the most important motifs across media is clear, for instance, in their use of boats. That the boats are differently represented (see the rowers, here, which are not clear in other contexts), as well as the presence of motifs that are present sometimes but not always, shows the manipulation of this visual vocabulary toward specific ends based at least in part on medium and/or context.

Hierakonpolis Tomb 100

It is with some relief that we turn to Hierakonpolis Tomb 100, which contains the first unambiguously violent imagery from Egypt (Figures 2.9–2.11).[30] Its precise meanings are still somewhat obscure, but there can no longer be any question that we are looking at physical domination of some people over others, at smiting and fighting. The tomb itself consists of a rectangular subterranean chamber with mudbrick walls. It measures approximately 4.5 by 2 m, with a depth of 1.5 m, and is subdivided by a low and short brick wall into two rooms; this wall does not touch the southwest long wall, leaving a passage between the rooms.[31] In form, this type of double-chambered tomb has probable contemporary parallels at both Hierakonpolis and Naqada,[32] but this is the only case of extant decoration. Two of the walls of Hierakonpolis Tomb 100 were decorated with representational scenes in paint on mud plaster. A complex scene or scenes including boats, humans, and

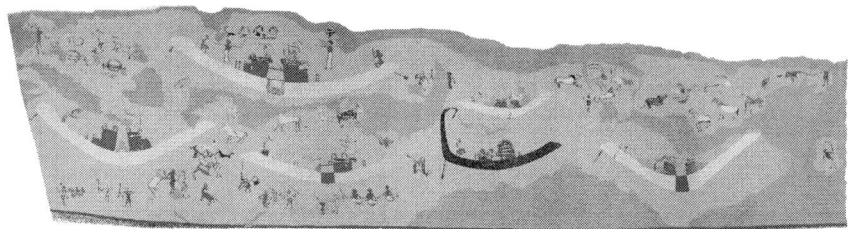

Figure 2.9 Hierakonpolis Tomb 100, southwest wall, paint on mud plaster. Scenes of domination and violence anchor the corners and are arranged along the bottom.

animals decorated the southwest wall, which runs the length of the tomb. Human figures, possibly in procession, were also painted on the end and the southeast side of the dividing wall; these may be part of a single composition.[33] The painting on the short wall was very badly preserved and no facsimile of it was ever published, so it is not possible to speak of its particular attributes or significance but only to note that more than one wall was decorated with humans.

The damaged but largely legible southwest wall was copied in the field and was removed and taken to the Egyptian Museum in Cairo. It has unfortunately suffered greatly in the years since its discovery, and so discussions of this painting are necessarily based almost entirely on the facsimile published by Quibell and Green.[34] The composition as a whole almost certainly includes different phases of painting, though there is disagreement about how much time separates these phases.[35] In its final form, the painting has three main types of components: boats, people, and animals. It is not clear to what degree all elements should be understood together, and no indication is given of landscape or setting aside from the boats themselves. It is not possible to say if the mural depicts things that are related in space or time. The painting as a whole could show a single moment, a narrative of connected moments, or unrelated episodes, and this ambiguity makes the image difficult not only to interpret but even to describe. This is also, of course, a point of commonality between the painting and the images on earlier White Cross-Lined Ware discussed above, as well as the non-violent ritual scenes on contemporary Decorated Ware.

The violence in this tomb painting takes place on the periphery, while boats occupy the central space of the scene(s). In the lower left corner a figure, shown in outline, faces right and raises a club-like weapon behind his head (Figure 2.10).[36] This weapon does not have a defined head and so cannot be identified with certainty as the type of mace known from later smiting scenes, but the posture is strikingly similar. This figure's front hand reaches out to grasp three much smaller figures, who appear to be kneeling captives (the main figure stands at 10.35 cm while the captives measure just 4.05 cm). They kneel not on the same level as their oppressor, but on what appears to be a groundline extending right from the region of the weapon-holder's kilt. They are sketchily rendered, but the two on the right appear

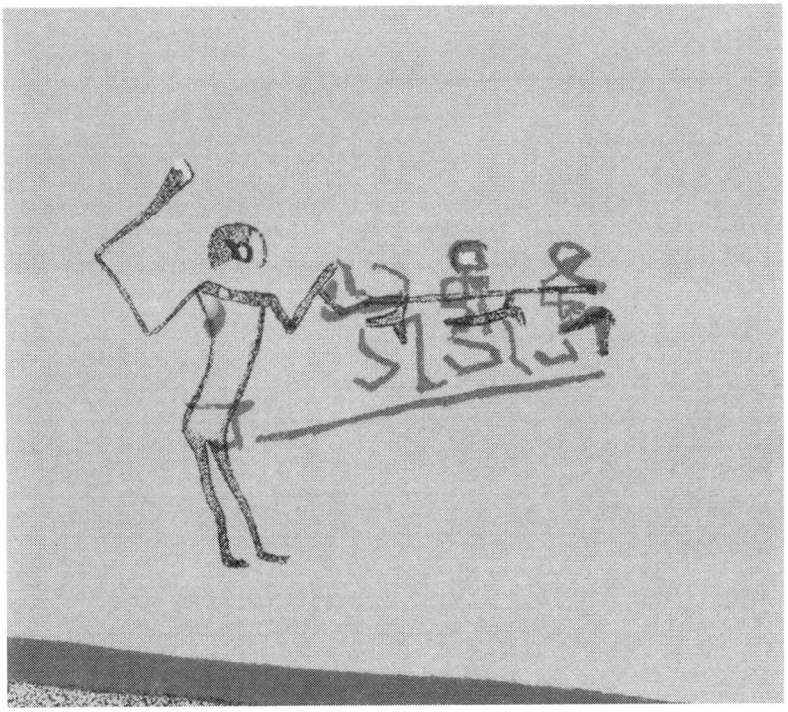

Figure 2.10 Detail of the lower left corner of the southwest wall of Hierakonpolis Tomb 100; a larger figure rendered in black paint prepares to hit with a weapon what appear to be three bound red captives.

to have one knee on the ground and one raised. The captive most immediately in the grasp of the smiter is in more disarray—it looks as though his head is pulled back and his arm raised to his face. While the weapon-wielder is shown in black with red details, his victims are shown in red with black details. Black lines may show binding of the captives together at the chest and also individually at the arms. Distinction between these figures is thus made in multiple ways: size, color, and posture. That these figures are thus distinguished and multiple makes them more like the Naqada I captives than the lone subject on the Gebelein textile. In this tomb, the relationship of the figures to one another and the violence of the pictured action are unambiguous. The posture of smiting is repeated in the lower right corner of the tomb wall, where a single figure is shown with a raised implement in his hand. He leans forward, his legs slightly apart. Damage in this section makes it impossible to say what he was preparing to hit.

Other clearly violent humans are beneath the white boat and to the left of the black boat. Here, two sets of opponents appear to be engaged in hand-to-hand combat (Figure 2.11).[37] Directly beneath the middle of the boat, a figure on the right raises a hand behind him with a long weapon. His outstretched front arm

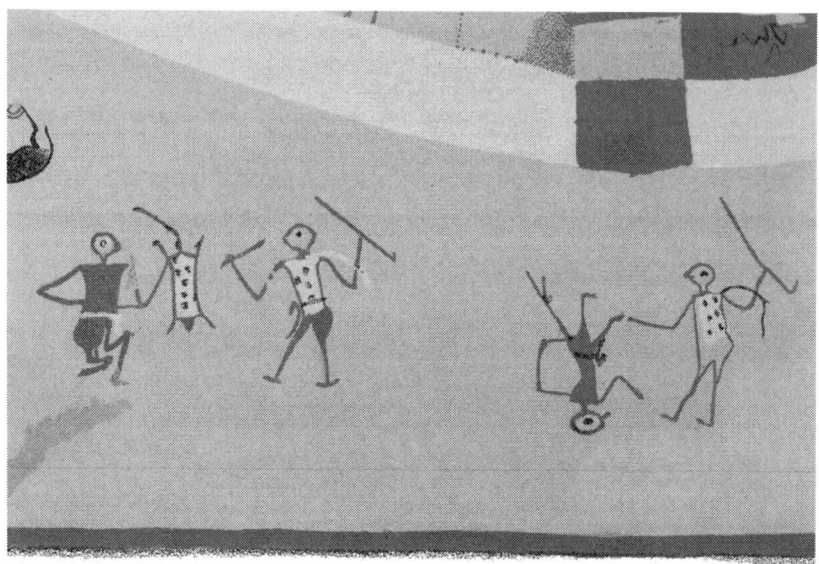

Figure 2.11 Detail of the lower part of the southwest wall of Hierakonpolis Tomb 100;
two groups of two men are shown in what may be combat.

puts him again in a posture related to the to-be-canonical smiting pose. Here,
however, his front hand stretches out to an opponent who is shown upside down
and at the same scale as his menacer. The upside-down figure, too, holds a long
implement that may be a weapon, but he seems to trail it behind him rather than
raise it in a threatening way. His front arm reaches forward, too, in a fashion reminiscent of warding off a blow. Left of these figures are two others, both upright in
this case, who may be in combat. The figure to the right holds long implements
in both of his upraised hands, one in front of his head and one behind. Facing him
is a figure who holds an object that may be a skin-covered shield, though it also
resembles an upside-down animal with a tail; he appears ready to parry a blow
from his opponent with this object. Both of these sets of combatants at the bottom
appear to be visually distinguished from one another by their clothing. In each
case, one has a white torso with black spots, likely representing animal skin, and
the other a red and presumably unclothed torso. No other figures in the painting as
a whole wear such skins, though the object held forth by the leftmost combatant
is similarly marked. It is certainly notable that these figures are all the same size.

A complete analysis of the painting of Hierakonpolis Tomb 100 is not possible or necessary here, but several points can be made about the relationship of
the violence shown to earlier and later imagery, as well as possible connections
this scene has to kingship. The figure holding a weapon and smiting multiple
bound captives may be related to the images we have already seen on Naqada
I White Cross-Line Ware, but the differences between the two are as obvious as

the similarities. Similarities include the size difference between captor and captive; the presence of multiple captives; the generally schematic rendering of the human figures; the apparent binding of the prisoners; and possibly the presence of a mace. Differences include a different pose for the captor, who is actively in the process of swinging his weapon, presumably to kill; a greatly reduced differentiation between captor and captives by means of attributes such as hair style (perhaps because the figures in Hierakonpolis Tomb 100 are so small); and the type of mace held by the captor, if it was a mace at all in the first instance.

The other images of violence from Hierakonpolis Tomb 100, which show hand-to-hand fighting between pairs of figures, have no known precedent. Combat is quite different from preparing to smite an already subdued enemy. In these cases the combat is depicted as taking place between individuals; however, visual distinctions between the opponents might suggest that they represent groups. Skin-covered torsos seem too specific to be just a pattern for the sake of visual separation, though a skin-covered shield held by a bare-torsoed fighter would seem to rather blur the distinction. In both of the cases of combat, the skin-wearing figure seems to have the best of the current situation, though in one case it is less resolved. This might seem a bit odd, given that only two skin-wearers are present in the composition as a whole and they are therefore rather more easily understood as enemies. The failure to differentiate fighters on the basis of size also certainly leads to confusion about which faction is the "good guy," and suggests a quite fundamental difference between the meaning of smiting and fighting scenes here. This can be seen in many ways as a parallel to the use of smiting and fighting scenes in later pyramid complexes (see Chapter 4).

Among the human figures in the painting as a whole, not only the violent ones, there is a notable lack of apparent focus: no prominent individual is singled out within the evident logic of the composition itself. Most of the human figures are of roughly the same scale. It is only in the lower-left smiting scene that a deliberate hierarchy of size appears to have been used, and here it only distinguishes the smiter from the smitees, who are very small. There is nothing about the position or details of this element that inherently suggest that the smiter is the most important person in the scene as a whole, and I do not think we would read him as such if we did not know that smiting is an exclusively royal prerogative in later iconography.

That another smiting figure may be shown in the opposite corner provides the only point of visual symmetry in the entire composition. Are these two depictions of the same individual, anchoring the scene at its corners? Are they related to figures smiting and perhaps holding leashed animals in the top two corners? I would suggest that perhaps these are related images of control over humans and animals that were quite deliberately placed at all four corners of the composition, all facing inwards toward the other representations. These icons of bashing and binding may have had a protective function that made them appropriate for corners.[38] The juxtaposition of domination over people with domination over animals may be seen as parallel to the Naqada I scene in Figure 2.5. I also suggest and would emphasize that the actions thus shown were more important than distinguishing the individual(s) who performed them. If the smiting image is not a royal image, what about the rest of the scene?

Two human figures in the painting, in addition to the smiters, have sometimes been thought to represent kings on the basis of their apparent participation in what is understood as royal ritual. Although these are not violent images, they are relevant to a discussion of general versus specific in early imagery and the relation of Predynastic to later royal iconography. In this way they help contextualize the arguments being developed about the role of violence in early imagery. The two figures thus interpreted are that in the pavilion on the boat on the upper left, and that to the right of the same boat who appears to be striding while holding a crook and perhaps a flail (Figure 2.12).[39] Interestingly, these two figures are not in relation to the one boat that is distinguished by color, which we might thus have wanted to read as the most significant of the boats. Similar to the corner figures, the distinction of these two figures is indicated not by scale, but rather by their poses, as well as by the pavilion and the implements held by the figures. All of these aspects have been taken as evidence that the scene represents a *heb-sed*, the festival of the royal jubilee that was central to Egyptian kingship from at least the First Dynasty.[40]

There are many problems with such a specific link to the imagery of a particular later royal festival. First, it is probably inaccurate to consider every royal ceremony illustrated even in early pharaonic material itself a *heb-sed*, given that we know other early royal ceremonies existed. Some aspects of *heb-sed* ritual and hence iconography appear to have been quite specific, but others, including a royal audience in a pavilion and race-running, may have been more generally ceremonial and therefore not necessarily references to that particular event.[41] Second, there is a roughly contemporary depiction of a similar pavillion in a similar position on a boat on a Decorated Ware vessel in the Metropolitan Museum.[42] In this case there are two figures in the pavilion, one clearly female; this is not part of later *heb-sed* iconography. Third, while a pavilion of this type and striding are both characteristic of the *heb-sed*, they are not combined in later cases. Fourth, there is no known relationship between the *heb-sed* and boats in later Egypt; rather, the *heb-sed* pavilion is invariably shown at the top of a staircase. Boats are the most prominent aspect of this scene. Finally, the figure that may run with a crook and

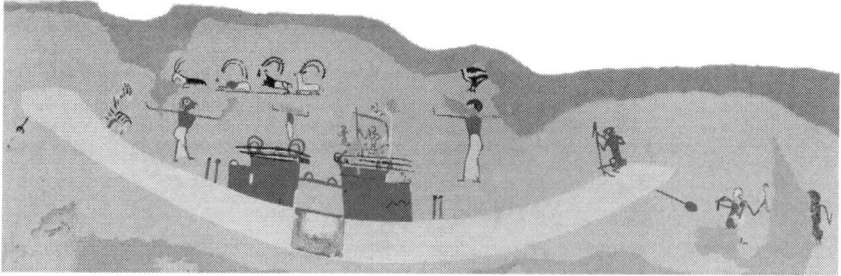

Figure 2.12 Detail of the upper left of the southwest wall of Hierakonpolis Tomb 100; possible royal ritual on a boat, with combat (?) to the right.

flail does not have boundary markers near him, while these are never omitted later. While it is not impossible that the *heb-sed* existed early but changed dramatically, so that its imagery was thus in a state of flux in this period, it would in that case be problematic to assume that the *heb-sed* meant the same thing in the Naqada II as it did in later periods when it was pictured differently. I think it is safer not to assume that we can put a later name to the activities pictured here.

If the specific link to the *heb-sed* is untenable, a more general connection to ritual does not seem improbable, and this is true of the violence depicted here, too. Even then, however, it is remarkable that these figures are not clearly visually distinguished by size or accoutrements, with the possible exception of the presumed crook and flail. As was the case with images from White Cross-Lined Ware, and indeed from the larger corpus of Decorated Ware, the painting of Hierakonpolis Tomb 100 is more notable for what appears to be a generalized depiction of ritual and worldview than one anchored to specific people. Specificity is there—this is a specific tomb, and clearly belonged to a person of extreme importance—but it is not a focus of the image itself. The several figures within the painting that might be considered kings could be called such only on the basis of comparison to later images, not on the basis of anything in this painting itself. In later depictions of smiting and royal ceremonies no such ambiguity is present.

A final point of note about the violence depicted in Hierakonpolis Tomb 100 is that the images do not seem to have been felt to be in any way threatening. They are there immediately beside the deceased. If they had the power to hurt him, they would not be there. Rather, they surround a scene of apparently ritual significance, enclose and perhaps protect it. That images of domination on White Cross-Lined Ware were not threatening can be inferred from their presence in tombs, too, but here we have something that might be much more: the deliberate placement of images of violence to keep other things outside. They were powerful, but were themselves under the control of the one who commissioned them. This highlights the degree to which such images spoke to an audience for whom the pictured violence was a good thing, was reassuring and right. This will be characteristic of most later Egyptian imagery of violence.

Order and chaos

The Naqada I and II Periods saw increasing social stratification within Egypt as well as a growing use of imagery. Violence is only a very minor part of that imagery. There is no reason to suggest that violence itself was not an important part of Naqada society and a tactic by which the increasingly separate elite enforced their dominance. In fact, weapons, including maceheads, are a common type of grave good in elite tombs throughout this time.[43] That violence occurs so rarely in the pictorial record might, of course, be due to an accident of preservation. But given the absence of violence in such important contexts as Naqada II Decorated Ware, which clearly was a vehicle for images of significance, I think it is more likely that there was not yet a developed or continuous relation between imagery and violence at this time. What images we do have that can be called violent much more often show physical domination and perhaps the threat of violence than overtly violent acts.

Because of both its rarity and its focus on domination, it is important to reconsider the assumption, widespread in Egyptology, that the seeds of pharaonic ideology are already indicated by imagery of violence in the Naqada I and II Periods. The rarity would argue against it, but the focus on domination might suggest otherwise, since physical domination over captives is such an important part of royal iconography and ideology later. In particular, it has usually been assumed that these very early scenes of domination are direct ancestors of later scenes of royal smiting, which themselves are interpreted as showing the king preserving order by controlling chaos. In historic Egypt, the maintenance of order—*ma'at*— over chaos—*isfet*—is arguably the single most important responsibility of the king, even the structuring principle of the whole cosmos. *Ma'at* can also be defined as right action, or "connective justice";[44] it ties together all of Egyptian society through a series of rights, obligations, and actions.[45] The pharaonic opposition between *ma'at* and *isfet* was present from relatively early in pharaonic Egypt, though it does seem to have undergone substantial elaboration and refinement.[46] The word *ma'at* is present as an element of royal names as early as the Second Dynasty, and the royal responsibility to set *ma'at* in the place of *isfet* is alluded to in the Pyramid Texts of the late Old Kingdom.[47] The question for us is whether or not this concept stretches back further, if this is what is shown in images of domination in Naqada I and II art.

This is in itself a two-part question. First: is the imposition of order represented in imagery of the Naqada I and II Periods? And second: if so, what is its relationship to *ma'at* and *isfet*? I think the answer to the first question is yes: images of controlling people and animals and images of rituals with boats, too, can be read as the imposition of order. They suggest that there is a proper way to do things, that structure is positive, that danger should be contained. They suggest that there are differences between people, and that physical domination can be part of enforcing the proper order between them. They also suggest that imagery is already involved in the process of procuring order.

It is, however, much more difficult to support an argument that such images are embryonic depictions of *ma'at*. *Ma'at* versus *isfet* is a complex principle, one we might call philosophical or theological, and is very explicitly Egyptian. But the idea of an opposition between order and chaos is rather laughably simple. It is also close to universal. If you say "order and chaos" in a room full of people who are not Egyptologists, you will not evoke stares of incomprehension. Some might think you are speaking of physics, some of university administration, some of online gaming, some of the relationship between your daughter's room and the rest of the house.[48] All hunting, all political systems aside from anarchy, nearly anything with any relation to system, in the end, can be read as the imposition of order. It is thus unreasonable to classify Naqada I and II images of the imposition of order as images of *ma'at*. They may be precursors, may be preconditions, but *ma'at* they are not. As such, they cannot be used to suggest that an ideology of kingship is already present in earliest Egypt. Here we have a general idea suggested by generalizing imagery.

The development of a close relationship between an ideology of kingship and violent imagery is in part a process of increasing specificity and codification in pictures. It belongs, in Egypt, to the Protodynastic Period, when smiting in particular becomes an iconic representation of kingship. The development of such an icon of violence does draw on earlier ideas of power and imagery and, as strongly suggested by Hierakonpolis Tomb 100, also has visual precedent. Egypt is not unique in seeing a quick boil of ideas, violence, and means of communicating at around the time of state formation. The rise of the Islamic State in the Middle East during the time I have worked on this book serves in many ways as a good parallel, and also reminds us that while our topic may be academic, violence and its depiction are not always so. They can be terrifying.

Notes

1 George Chaloupka and Northern Territory Museum of Arts and Sciences, *From Palaeoart to Casual Paintings: The Chronological Sequence of Arnhem Land Plateau Rock Art* (Darwin: Northern Territory Museum of Arts and Sciences, 1984).
2 Paul Taçon and Christopher Chippindale, "Australia's Ancient Warriors: Changing Depictions of Fighting in the Rock Art of Arnhem Land, N.T.," *Cambridge Archaeological Journal* 4, no. 2 (1994): 217, with bibliography.
3 Paul Taçon, personal communication.
4 Taçon and Chippendale, "Australia's Ancient Warriors," 220.
5 It was not recognized until the 1980s that some Dynamic Figure imagery included fighting. Taçon and Chippindale, "Australia's Ancient Warriors," 220, citing an unpublished report: Chaloupka, "G. Rock Art of the Arnhem Land Plateau: Paintings of the Dynamic Figure Style."
6 Taçon and Chippendale, "Australia's Ancient Warriors," 213, fig. 1, 219–220.
7 Taçon and Chippindale, "Australia's Ancient Warriors."
8 The first archaeological evidence of violence in the Nile valley comes from Gebel Sahaba, where a cemetery dated to approximately 12,000 years before present included numerous bodies with embedded projectile points. Fred Wendorf, "Site 117: A Nubian Final Paleolithic Graveyard near Jebel Sahaba, Sudan," in *The Prehistory of Nubia 2*, Ed. Fred Wendorf (Dallas, TX: Southern Methodist University Press, 1968).
9 This claim is made directly or by inference in much recent scholarship. For instance, Andelković has written,

> Ideological "patterns of continuity," archaeologically perceivable as early as Naqada I … that constitute the most distinctive hallmarks of nascent Egyptian civilization, are to a great extent defined by the concept of Divine Ruler, "presiding over everything," acting as an eternal promise to nullify chaos, enemies and death, that seems to be a key ideological issue in the rapid political transformation of Predynastic Egypt.
> Branislav Andelković, "The Molding Power of Ideology: Political Transformations of Predynastic Egypt," *Issues in Ethnology and Anthropology, n.s.* 9, no. 3 (2014): 713–722 [quote from p. 715].

Similarly, Kerry Muhlestein, *Violence in the Service of Order: The Religious Framework for Sanctioned Killing in Ancient Egypt* (Oxford: Archaeopress, 2011), 10, 85; Stan Hendrickx, "Iconography of the Predynastic and Early Dynastic Periods," in *Before the Pyramids*, Ed. Emily Teeter (Chicago, IL: The Oriental Institute of the University of Chicago, 2011), 76; Stan Hendrickx and Merel Eyckerman, "Continuity and Change in the Visual Representations of Predynastic Egypt," in *Recent Discoveries and Latest Researches in Egyptology: Proceedings of the First Neapolitan Congress of Egyptology. Naples, June 18th–20th 2008*, Ed. Francesco Raffaele et al. (Wiesbaden: Harrassowitz Verlag, 2010), 121–144. I would argue that neither continuity nor rapidity really describe the evidence well if we start in the Naqada I Period, and that the ideas, particularly about chaos and order, are present long before there is anyone we can understand as a divine ruler.

10 Petrie called it a "Dynastic race" from the East. W.M. Flinders Petrie, *The Making of Egypt* (London: Sheldon Press, 1939). For a brief discussion of the origins and long acceptance of this explanation for pharaonic culture, with bibliography, see Bruce Trigger et al., *Ancient Egypt: A Social History* (Cambridge: Cambridge University Press, 1983), 2–3.

11 Both the absolute and relative chronologies of Predynastic Egypt have been a matter of contention. The relative sequence as currently used was largely established by Kaiser, with modification by Hendrickx: Werner Kaiser, "Zur inneren Chronologie der Naqadakultur," *Archaeologia Geographica* 6 (1957): 69–77; Stan Hendrickx, "The Relative Chronology of the Naqada Culture: Problems and Possibilities," in *Aspects of Early Egypt*, Ed. Jeffrey Spencer (London: British Museum Press, 1996), 39–69. A large recent 14C study confirmed the overall integrity of the relative dating system of the Naqada Period, but also suggested that some divisions within periods were questionable, that the overall Upper Egyptian Predynastic and Protodynastic Periods were shorter than previously thought, and that allowance for regional variation is needed. The results are convincing. Michael Dee et al., "Radiocarbon Dating and the Naqada Relative Chronology," *Journal of Archaeological Science* 46 (2014): 319–323.

12 Stan Hendrickx and Merel Eyckerman, "Visual Representation and State Development in Egypt," *Archéo-Nil* 22 (2012): 25–27. The theme is also addressed in an earlier article by the same authors: Hendrickx and Eyckerman, "Continuity and Change in the Visual Representations of Predynastic Egypt," 122–126.

13 For instance, hunting scenes are known only from the site of Abydos, not the type-site of Naqada. Elizabeth Finkenstaedt, "The Location of Styles in Painting: White Cross-Lined Ware at Naqada," *Journal of the American Research Center in Egypt* 18 (1981): 7–10.

14 The relation of such images to earlier rock art, which is also ambiguous in its use of violent imagery and often quite difficult to date, is uncertain. The images on White Cross-Lined Ware are included in the study by Gwenola Graff, *Les peintures sur vases de Nagada I—Nagada II: nouvelle approche sémiologique de l'iconographie prédynastique* (Leuven: Leuven University Press, 2009).

15 Figure 2.2: Brussels E.3002. Line drawing by Stan Hendrickx, "Peaux d'animaux comme symboles prédynastiques. À propos de quelques représentations sur les vases White Cross-lined," *Chronique d'Égypte* 73 (1998): 203–230, 206–207, figs. 5–6; Original photograph in Alexander Scharff, "Some Prehistoric Vases in the British Museum and Remarks on Egyptian Prehistory," *The Journal of Egyptian Archaeology* 14, no. 4 (1928): 261–276, pl. 28; Figure 2.3: University College London, Petrie Museum 15339. © Barbara Adams, *Predynastic Egypt* (London: Shire Publications [part of Bloomsbury], 1988), 46, fig. 28d; Figure 2.4: Abydos U-239/1; Cairo JdE 99072. © German Archaeological Institute Cairo. Line drawing in Günter Dreyer et al., "Umm el-Qaab: Nachuntersuchungen im frühzeitlichen Königsfriedhof: 9./10. Vorbericht," *Mitteilungen des Deutschen Archäologischen Instituts, Abteilung Kairo* 54 (1998): 77–167, 113–114, figs. 12.1, 13; Figure 2.5: Abydos U-415/1; Abydos SCA storeroom. © German Archaeological Institute Cairo. Line drawing in Günter Dreyer et al., "Umm el-Qaab: Nachuntersuchungen im frühzeitlichen Königsfriedhof: 13./14./15. Vorbericht," *Mitteilungen des Deutschen Archäologischen Instituts, Abteilung Kairo* 59 (2003): 67–138, 81, fig. 5; Figure 2.6: Abydos U-415/2; Abydos SCA storeroom. © German Archaeological Institute Cairo. Line drawing in Dreyer et al., "13./14./15. Vorbericht," 83, fig. 6; Ulrich Hartung, "Hippopotamus Hunters and Bureaucrats: Elite Burials at Cemetery U," in *Recent*

Discoveries and Latest Researches in Egyptology: Proceedings of the First Neapolitan Congress of Egyptology. Naples, June 18th–20th 2008, Ed. Francesco Raffaele et al. (Wiesbaden: Harrassowitz Verlag, 2010), 118, fig. 4c.

16 Hendrickx and Eyckerman take the absence of arms as indicative of the subject status of the smaller figures in "Continuity and Change in the Visual Representations of Predynastic Egypt," 122. This may well be so, but there is a danger of bending all evidence to support the already accepted contention that these are victory scenes.

17 This pose is most frequently described as a ritual dance. Other interpretations include celebration of a victory and imitation of bull horns. For bibliography, see Hendrickx and Eyckerman, "Visual Representation and State Development in Egypt," 25–27. Additionally, James Allen, personal communication, suggests that it is a gesture of mourning, pouring dust on the head. It is not clear to me that the gesture should always be read as representing the same thing, as it occurs in scenes showing very different types of actions and probably actors.

18 The assumption that these are victory scenes is more often than not felt to need no explicit justification at all, for instance by Hartung, who says the scenes are "without a doubt the depiction of a chief who presents captured enemies": "Hippopotamus Hunters and Bureaucrats: Elite Burials at Cemetery U," 110. But the reasons for the assertion are clear in, among others, Hendrickx and Eyckerman, "Continuity and Change in the Visual Representations of Predynastic Egypt," 122.

19 Hendrickx and Eyckerman argue for an early and close connection between victory and hunting in part on the basis of these vessels: "Continuity and Change in the Visual Representations of Predynastic Egypt," 122–127, and I agree that the connection between the motif of human captivity and animal captivity is close not only on White Cross-Lined Ware but also in later Predynastic art. Bound hippopotami will become a pharaonic motif as well, but it is again not clear that there is a simple connection between this motif on White Cross-Lined Ware and the pharaonic image. Of note here is that the hippopotami on Abydos U-415/1 are apparently pregnant.

20 See Chapter 4, where women and children observers are often parts of smiting scenes in royal mortuary complexes.

21 Hendrickx and Eyckerman, "Visual Representation and State Development in Egypt," 25; Muhlestein, *Violence in the Service of Order*, 85; Toby Wilkinson, "What a King Is This: Narmer and the Concept of the Ruler," *The Journal of Egyptian Archaeology* 86 (2000): 23–32, 29. Archaeologically attested maces in Upper Egypt at this time come in a variety of shapes, including disc-shaped and round, but not yet the pear-shape that would become the standard ceremonial mace type. Alice Stevenson, "Material Culture of the Predynastic Period," in *Before the Pyramids*, Ed. Emily Teeter (Chicago, IL: The Oriental Institute of the University of Chicago, 2011), 70–71.

22 Purely anecdotally, the six students in a seminar I taught on Images and Ideology at Brown University in Spring 2015 were unanimously unwilling to assume that these were scenes of domination. They were all very familiar with the later material, but deeply uncomfortable reading backwards from it. My daughter Rose, then 8 years old, took one look at the line drawing of Abydos U-239/1 and proclaimed that "the big guys are holding the same thing Narmer does." See Figure 3.14.

23 The wearing of a tail is a well-known royal prerogative in pharaonic art, but on White Cross-Lined Ware appears only to signify status. Some but not all hunters wear tails on vessels with motifs not considered here, for instance. Diana Craig Patch, "From Land to Landscape," in *Dawn of Egyptian Art* (New York: Metropolitan Museum of Art, 2011), 37.

24 The two are not necessarily mutually exclusive. Abydos Tomb U-415 itself contained two skeletons, the topmost a very large adult male, the second, below the first body, a much smaller and younger male. Hartung cautiously suggested that this might be a subordinate buried with, even killed to be buried with, his superior: "Hippopotamus Hunters and Bureaucrats," 108. Sacrificial subsidiary burials are characteristic of the First Dynasty and this interpretation thus again rests in part on reading backwards from much later evidence.

25 Hendrickx and Eykerman, "Continuity and Change in the Visual Representations of Predynastic Egypt," 125; Hendrickx and Eyckerman, "Visual Representation and State Development in Egypt," 32–33.

26 Heinrich Schäfer, "Das Niederschlagen der Feinde: zur Gesichte eines ägyptischen Sinnbildes," *Weiner Zeitschrift für die Kunde des Morgenlandes* 54 (1957): 168–176; William Peck, "The Ordering of the Figure," in *A Companion to Ancient Egyptian Art*, Ed. Melinda Hartwig (Chichester, West Sussex: John Wiley & Sons, 2015), 360–374.

27 Metropolitan Museum of Art 20.2.10; www.metmuseum.org.

28 Courtesy of the Museo Egizio di Torino, S. 17138. Photographer: Pino Dell'Aquila. Giuseppe Galassi, "L'arte del più antico Egitto nel Museo di Torino: preistoria E protostoria mediterranea," *Rivista dell'Istituto Nazionale d'Archeologia e Storia dell'Arte*, Nuova Serie 4 (1955): 5–94, pl. 1, figs. 1–12 (main fragment discussed here: pl. 1); Ernesto Scamuzzi, *Museo Egizio di Torino* (Turin: Edizioni d'arte Fratelli Pozzo, 1964), pls. 1–5.

29 Krzysztof Ciałowicz, "Le plus ancien témoignage de la tradition du heb-sed?" *Folia orientalia* 33 (1997): 42.

30 This is the only known decorated tomb chamber from the Naqada II Period, or indeed Predynastic Egypt as a whole. Recent discovery of painted plaster fragments that appear to be from a somewhat earlier superstructure associated with a tomb at Hierakonpolis indicates that painting in funerary contexts may have been at least somewhat more common than existing evidence suggests, and that it may have been in places accessible to a living audience. These badly preserved fragments do not show anything that appears to be violent. Renée Friedman, "Excavating Egypt's Early Kings: Recent Discoveries in the Elite Cemetery at Hierakonpolis," in *Egypt at Its Origins 2: Proceedings of the International Conference "Origin of the State. Predynastic and Early Dynastic Egypt," Toulouse (France), 5th–8th September 2005*, Ed. Béatrix Midant-Reynes et al. (Leuven: Peeters Publishers, 2008), 1186–1187, fig. 15. The precise dating of Hierakonpolis Tomb 100 has been a matter of discussion. It is usually considered to date to the Naqada IIC, this date being consistent with all of the artifacts in the tomb. Some of the iconography of the painted wall also has very clear parallels to Decorated Ware of the Naqada IIC-D, but it has also been noted that some elements of the painting, including the shape of the black boat and the human figures, have better parallels in Naqada III art: Béatrix Midant-Reynes, *The Prehistory of Egypt: From the First Egyptians to the First Pharaohs* (Oxford, and Malden, MA: Wiley-Blackwell, 2000), 208; George Reisner, *The Development of the Egyptian Tomb down to the Accession of Cheops* (Cambridge and London: Harvard University Press and Oxford University Press, 1936), 362; Elise Baumgartel, *The Cultures of Prehistoric Egypt II* (London: Oxford University Press, 1960), 126. Most recently this has been attributed to a possible repainting and intended reuse of the tomb in the Naqada III: Dirk Huyge, "The Painted Tomb, Rock Art and the Recycling of Predynastic Egyptian Imagery,"*Archéo-Nil* 24 (2014): 93–102. This explanation is not entirely satisfying given that Naqada II pottery vessels appear to have been found next to the painted wall. This can be quite clearly seen in the center left of a photograph from the excavation published by Barry Kemp, "Photographs of the Decorated Tomb at Hierakonpolis," *Journal of Egyptian Archaeology* 59 (1973): 36–43, pl. 23, whereas it seems likely that they would have been moved had there been a need to access the wall at a time after the interment of the original occupant.

31 James Quibell and Frederick W. Green, *Hierakonpolis: Part II* (London: Bernard Quaritch, 1902), 20. The tomb was excavated in 1899 and has subsequently been lost.

32 Kemp, "Photographs of the Decorated Tomb at Hierakonpolis."

33 Quibell and Green, *Hierakonpolis: Part II*, 21; visible in Kemp, "Photographs of the Decorated Tomb at Hierakonpolis," pl. 23.

34 Quibell and Green, *Hierakonpolis: Part II*, pls. 75–79.

35 Quibell and Green, *Hierakonpolis: Part II*, 21; David Wengrow, *The Archaeology of Early Egypt: Social Transformations in North-East Africa, 10,000 to 2,650 BC* (Cambridge: Cambridge University Press, 2006), 115; Huyge, "The Painted Tomb, Rock Art and the Recycling of Predynastic Egyptian Imagery," 98; Patrick Gautier, "Analyse de L'espace Figuratif Par Dipôles: la Tombe Décorée No. 100 de Hiérakonpolis," *Archéo-Nil* 3 (1993): 35–47.

36 Quibell and Green, *Hierakonpolis: Part II*, pl. 76.

37 Quibell and Green, *Hierakonpolis: Part II*, pl. 76.

38 Wengrow, *The Archaeology of Early Egypt*, 195. The idea that corners might get special treatment, might need protection, is also suggested by roughly contemporary intentional deposits within ritual buildings at Hierakonpolis. Renée Friedman, "The Early Royal Cemetery at Hierakonpolis: An Overview," in *Recent Discoveries and Latest Researches in Egyptology: Proceedings of the First Neapolitan Congress of Egyptology. Naples, June 18th–20th 2008*, Ed. Francesco Raffaele et al. (Wiesbaden: Harrassowitz Verlag, 2010), 72.

39 Quibell and Green, *Hierakonpolis: Part II*, pl. 76.

40 Humphrey Case and Joan Crowfoot Payne, "Tomb 100: The Decorated Tomb at Hierakonpolis," *Journal of Egyptian Archaeology* 48 (1962): 5–18; Bruce Williams, Thomas J. Logan, and William J. Murnane, "The Metropolitan Museum Knife Handle and Aspects of Pharaonic Imagery before Narmer," *Journal of Near Eastern Studies* 46, no. 4 (1987): 271–272; Barry Kemp, *Ancient Egypt: Anatomy of a Civilization*, 2nd Revised ed. (London: Routledge, 2006).

41 Kathryn Howley, "A Re-Examination of Early 'Sed Festival' Representations" (paper presented at the annual meeting for the American Research Center in Egypt, Providence, Rhode Island, April 27, 2012).

42 Metropolitan Museum of Art 20.2.10; Diana Craig Patch, *Dawn of Egyptian Art* (New York: Metropolitan Museum of Art, 2011), 70.

43 Gregory Gilbert, *Weapons, Warriors and Warfare in Early Egypt* (Oxford: Archaeopress, 2004).

44 Jan Assmann, *The Mind of Egypt: History and Meaning in the Time of the Pharaohs*, trans. Andrew Jenkins (Cambridge, MA: Harvard University Press, 2003), 127.

45 The bibliography on *ma'at* is extensive. Important treatments include Wolfgang Helck, "Maat," in *Lexikon der Ägyptologie, Band III*, Ed. Wolfgang Helck and Eberhard Otto (Wiesbaden: Harrassowitz, 1981), columns 1110–1119; Erik Hornung, "Maat— Gerechtigkeit für alle? Zur altägyptischen Ethik," in *Wegkreuzungen/Crossroads/ La croisée des chemins*, Ed. Rudolf Ritsema (Frankfurt am Main: Eranos Foundation Ascona, 1989); and Jan Assmann, *Ma'at: Gerechtigkeit und Unsterblichkeit im alten Ägypten*, 2nd ed. (Munich: Beck, 2006).

46 For a historical survey of the usage of the word *ma'at* and what it meant, see Harry Smith, "Ma'et and Isfet," *Bulletin of the American Schools of Oriental Research* 5 (1994): 67–88.

47 Unis Recitation 160, in the translation of James P. Allen, *The Ancient Egyptian Pyramid Texts*, Writings from the Ancient World 23 (Atlanta and Leiden: Brill, 2005), 42.

48 A quick search on Googlescholar of the term "order versus chaos" yielded articles, on the first page alone, about reef fish, human resources, Bram Stoker's Dracula, physics, psychology, and electroencephalography among others. Order and chaos is so very broad a model that, in fact, I think we should be far more wary than we are of using it to interpret even pharaonic imagery. Perhaps we should confine our use of the word *ma'at* to times when it is in fact explicit in the ancient evidence, and move away from an expectation that everything in Egypt can be explained in terms of a binary opposition between order and chaos.

3 The violence inherent in the system

Imagery and royal ideology in the period of state formation

2014. Two men. The background is blank, an anonymous desert. Both men face the camera. The one in front kneels, hands bound behind his back. He wears orange. The man behind him stands, clothed entirely in black, even across his face. He reaches one hand to touch the shoulder of the man in front of him, and in the other hand he holds a knife.

This image has many iterations, both as still photographs and as videos, and has been widely disseminated via the Internet and to a lesser degree in print media. The description above captures its first moment, which is how it is usually shown when it is a still rather than a video. The two men clearly represent different things. Their differences are marked by clothing, by posture, by their relationship to one another, by that knife. As a still the image is static and calm, but any viewer of the image at the time it was made knew precisely what action inevitably followed: the beheading of the man in orange.

This contemporary iconic image of violence raises questions about ancient Egyptian images; the amount of continuity can be shocking. In fact, one of the most important reasons to discuss modern imagery is precisely to return the sense of shock—the visceral emotional reaction that is missing from our confrontation with ancient art—to an understanding of how such pictures work within their own cultural contexts. While the comparative examples utilized in the rest of this book are illustrated, I have chosen not to include an image of this example. For readers who pick up this book soon after its publication, inclusion will not be necessary. It is my profound hope that in the future this will no longer be a familiar image, that my omission here will be confusing, my reference of only historical interest.

This image is particularly relevant for an appreciation of early royal images of violence in Egypt, especially to the smiting scene and its connection to early royal ideology. The Islamic State is, at the time I write, an expansionist polity, a new political and social force on the scene in the Middle East, a group with some military power aspiring to become a state. This image serves to proclaim an aspect of the ideology of this polity. It both represents and affects the actual relations between worldviews and between the political actors who embody those worldviews. The icon is of course a simplistic expression of both theology and politics, but its very simplicity is one reason it is an effective *image*. Images of violence in early Egypt were always associated with power, but became iconic representations of kingship only at the time when the Egyptian state itself was assuming a new form, only when kingship and ideology and writing and art all coalesced into the recognizably pharaonic state that would be recognizably itself from 3000–300 BC.

The Islamic State beheading image derives its power from several interwoven factors, all of which are relevant to interpreting Egyptian imagery. In particular it is effective because it is both real and ritual, because it is repeated and easily recognizable but also individual each time—a new person dies. It is effective because it absolutely sets up an us/them using immediate visual clues to distinguish between the two, making individuals representative of larger entities or positions. The horror created in an audience outside the Islamic State provokes fear that is disproportionate to the actual threat and causes false comparisons with other movements that were also exceptionally violent but did not utilize images of violence in the same way;[1] the Islamic State is not more violent than other insurgencies, but seems so because it looks so. It is the image in combination with the violence, not just the violence or knowledge of the violence, which horrifies. The events filmed are real, but the power of the pictures is only partly related to that reality.

While the Islamic State beheading image is horrifying to an outsider, it has other audiences, sympathetic audiences. The same image speaks differently across this divide, and it is this that is acknowledged in controversy over dissemination of the images. Facebook, for instance, will allow users to post the video of the beheading of James Foley for condemnation or news, but will remove the same video when used to "glorify violence."[2] To audiences who are "them" from the standpoint of this image, it is horrifying and induces fear. To audiences who are "us" from the standpoint of the image, it is glorious and even reassuring, and therefore censored by those on the opposite side of the ideological divide.

The parallels between the Islamic State beheading images and the Egyptian smiting icon are the closest demonstrated by any of the comparative images utilized in this book. They include formal visual elements, an interplay between general and specific meanings, and widespread dissemination at a time of state formation. It is the latter that makes this image so apt for a chapter on violent imagery in Egypt during the transition from the Predynastic to the Dynastic. But, in fact, the relevance of the Islamic State image could be invoked throughout this book, for instance in Chapter 4 where images of smiting in royal tombs display many of the same variations seen in the beheading scenes, such as differences in the number and ethnicity of those being killed. Then, in Chapter 6, we will see the ancient Egyptian smiting scene utilized in the landscape for a different audience than in royal tombs, and there we will confront the fact that the same icon—by speaking in different contexts to a different part of the us/them divide—operates in a range of ways.

Violence in Egyptian art in the period of state formation

As we have seen, the earlier Predynastic Period was characterized by a notable paucity of violent imagery. What we have tends to focus on domination, and its relation to later pharaonic ideas of violent kingship is not clear. This is not the case in the Naqada III Period. In the time leading up to the political unification of Egypt as a territorial state ruled by a line of hereditary kings, the prevalence and variety of violent imagery veritably explodes. That imagery is also much more obviously connected to pharaonic imagery.

The terminology of chronology of this period can be confusing in Egyptological literature because we switch from defining eras on the basis of material culture changes—the Naqada sequence of Predynastic cultures—to using political designations related to dynasties. The political history of the period of state formation in Egypt used to be understood in quite simple terms as a war in which an Upper Egyptian state conquered a Lower Egyptian state and produced a unified Egypt. This idea of a single moment of unification seemed to be confirmed by the Narmer Palette, which was once thought to represent precisely the conquest of Lower Egypt by Narmer, king of Upper Egypt. This also seemed to make sense in terms of later Egyptian tradition, which credited a single semi-mythic king named Menes with the original unification of the Two Lands.[3]

We now understand the period of state formation to have been much more complex, and to have taken place over generations.[4] Egyptologists now identify a "Dynasty 0" before the start of the First Dynasty; this refers to a time in which kings wrote their names with *serekhs*—a heraldic device including, in its fully developed form, a representation of the falcon god Horus, with whom the king was identified, and a building (this device can be clearly seen, for instance, on ivory tags from kings' tombs of the First Dynasty, see Figures 7.2 and 7.3). The *serekh* was one of the most consistent markers of kingship over the course of Egyptian history, and even minimalists can be confident we are dealing with a form of pharaonic kingship once we see the *serekh*. What we cannot be so sure of, in part because the earliest *serekhs* are anonymous, is how many people in how many places might have made such claims to kingship in the generations preceding the named Dynasty 0 kings. To make things even more complicated, Naqada III material culture spans the gap and is still present into the First Dynasty proper.

The term Protodynastic will be used here to refer broadly to the period from early Naqada III through Dynasty 0; I have grouped images of this period by the types of artifacts on which they occur rather than attempting to order them according to a precise chronology, as such precision is difficult to establish with confidence. Such precision is possible once such images regularly include royal names. Narmer, a king who stands at the transition from Dynasties 0 to 1, has left us an unprecedented wealth of violent imagery incomparable either to what came before or to what came after, and will receive his own section.

While everything after the reign of Narmer is discussed in the contextual chapters, it will be seen that there is often a tension; for instance, two First Dynasty kings have ivory labels that look much more like Narmer's labels than like anything from the Old Kingdom. This reminds us that, though Narmer's reign was certainly a turning point, and as can be seen with images of violence, there is no hard and fast line in the sand that separates these periods.

Violent imagery is part of the development of kingship, and we can from this period speak of such depictions as being used as a consistent and coherent tactic of demonstrating a particular worldview and even ideology. Violent images in the Protodynastic were much more prevalent than previously and were used creatively, with the introduction of new motifs and—particularly important—the use of clear abstractions, with animals standing in for people and with impossible combinations depicted. In the Early Dynastic Period images of violence were both less common and more standardized; gone are the variety and creativity of the preceding period. A few particular elements survive—the binding of prisoners' arms at the elbow behind the back, the disarray of dead bodies that seem to be almost swimming in space—but only the smiting image becomes iconic. This process of standardization was accompanied by a great growth in specificity, particularly in references to people. The ability to include such specificity in images is due both to the introduction of writing—many images will have labels by the end of the Protodynastic Period—and to the increasing use of visual stereotypes. This itself is possible in part because the media of art in this period allowed for a great level of detail.

From the Protodynastic Period and perhaps into the reign of Narmer we see a continuation of images that appear to make general statements about power and violence, but such general images, without specific labels and iconographic distinctions, disappear by the Early Dynastic Period. This does not mean that references to generalizations about power and violence were absent, but rather that kings of Egypt were careful to link themselves, as specific incarnations of the god Horus, to general structures. Creation of violent imagery thus enabled kings of the nascent state to tie themselves, and perhaps their historical uses of violence, into a larger ideology of royal domination. This drew on earlier pictorial traditions but also greatly restricted what had been in use before.[5]

Protodynastic art in general, in the centuries immediately preceding the unification of Egypt, was much more prevalent, more complicated, and utilized more media, than that of earlier periods. It was, however, in most ways a clear development out of forms that had been present in the Naqada II. While Decorated Ware ceased to be made and was not replaced by a subsequent decorated pottery type, many other kinds of objects persisted. These include stone maceheads, ivory knife handles, small carved ivory objects, and mudstone grinding palettes. Earlier these tended to be plain or only slightly decorated, but by the Naqada III they had come to bear, in some cases, complex scenes.[6] Such relief-decorated objects are instantly recognizable and very characteristic of this period. None of them survived as major artifact categories into the Dynastic Period, though their imagery and the style in which it is rendered are the closest forerunners to canonical pharaonic art known from the Predynastic Period.

All of these types of instantly recognizable and highly decorated Protodynastic objects sometimes bore images of violence. This is most notable on the palettes and knife handles, which will be treated here first before turning to object categories that bear less evidence of such imagery. There are some additional types of image that are less diagnostic of the period but that also contain references to violence. These include faience figurines, a common artifact category of which a few examples seem to show captives, and rock carvings. That violent imagery is present on every type of decorated object from the Protodynastic Period in fact makes it difficult to determine how such imagery might have contributed to the specific functions of the objects it is found on. What we have is a general picture that objects carried meaningful pictures, but not that there was a close relationship between the meaning of the pictures and the use of the objects.[7]

In addition to an increase in the number and variety of violent motifs, the Protodynastic Period saw new contexts for the use of violent imagery. This is not only true for the types of objects that bore such imagery—on that front there is a complete shift, with no overlap whatsoever with earlier. But even the places where those objects were used undergoes a change; while much decorated Naqada III material still comes from elite graves, including some with our images of violence, a great deal of it has also been found in deposits associated with temples. These collections of objects were usually buried substantially later than the Protodynastic Period, and are generally understood as the cleaning up and ritual interment of objects that had served cultic purposes in the temple in earlier times.[8] The best-known such deposit, and the one that has yielded by far the greatest wealth of images of violence from this period, is the so-called Hierakonpolis Main Deposit.[9] While we have very little understanding of how early temples looked or worked, such a context for images of violence—for imagery at all—suggests that its audience was expanding in this period and that one of its purposes was to communicate to the divine.

Ceremonial relief palettes

The class of objects best known for its use of violent imagery in Predynastic Egypt is mudstone palettes. Palettes for grinding colored stone into powder, presumably to use as cosmetics, were in use as early as the Naqada I Period. In the late Naqada II and early Naqada III these palettes were not infrequently ceremonial objects with elaborate relief scenes.[10] The level of detail on these palettes is higher than on any other previous or contemporary image-bearing objects. Most of the palettes of known provenance come from graves; however, the highly decorated later palettes that are the best-known examples of the genre are almost all of unknown provenance. Violence as a whole is a very common motif on these palettes, but in many cases it takes the form of hunting or of animals attacking one another. Four known palettes contain images that can be read as clear expressions of human violence perpetrated against other humans. Additional fragments of palettes may have included further scenes of violence but are too fragmentary to be analyzed in depth. Of the known four, only the so-called Narmer Palette is of certain provenance; it was found in a deposit in the temple enclosure at Hierakonpolis. It is discussed below with Narmer's material (Figure 3.14).

The Battlefield Palette

An unprecedented image that combines death, destruction, and captivity decorates a palette known, for obvious reasons, as the Battlefield Palette (Figure 3.1).[11]

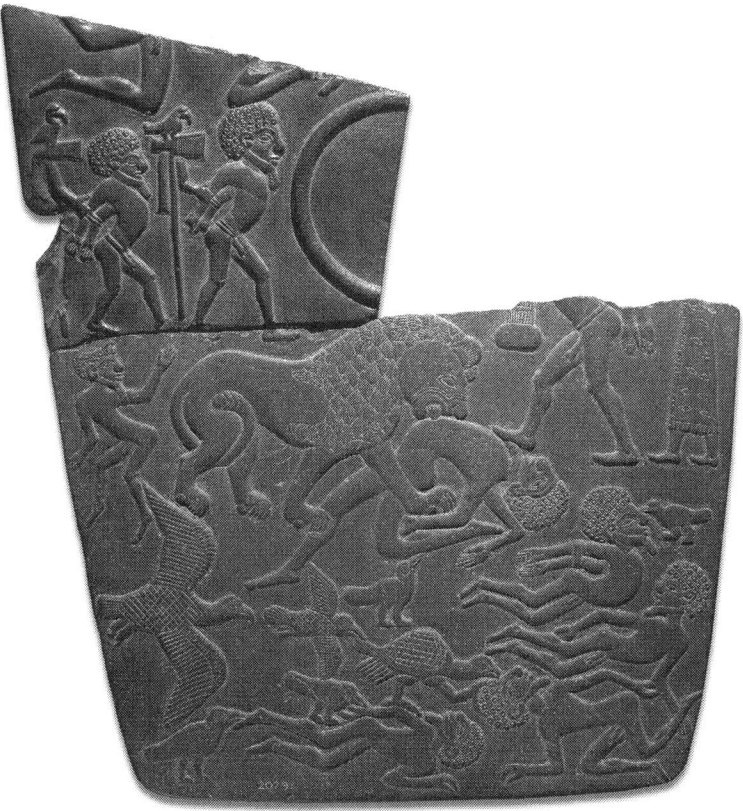

Figure 3.1 The Battlefield Palette, which shows a number of dead or captive people. A lion mauls the largest dead figure and carrion birds peck at others, while two bound captives are herded by standards. British Museum fragment dimensions: 19.6 x 28.7 cm, depth: 1 cm. Oxford fragment height: 13.2 cm.

There are two adjoining fragments of this palette, of unrecorded provenance.[12] One side of it is decorated with an apparently symmetrical scene of giraffes and a palm tree. The side with the round central space for grinding pigment has a variety of violent imagery.

All or part of 12 human figures are shown, as well as one lion and six carrion birds. The arrangement as a whole is disordered, and this chaos may be deliberately related to the meaning of the scene, which is one of domination and death. In the broken upper left are the bare legs and penises of two figures who are apparently sprawled on the ground, or at least are not standing or sitting in any ordinary manner. Beneath these, two adult men walk, bound, toward the central grinding space. These men are naked except for belts that possibly attach to penis sheaths. They have curly short hair and beards. They are shown in profile, striding forward.

Their arms are behind their backs, fists clenched, elbows bound together. They are held at the elbow by arms proceeding from stick-like standards topped with birds, in one case a falcon.

Beneath the central grinding space of the Battlefield Palette, a lion both treads upon and eats the belly of a man. This man has the same hair and beard as the bound, striding captives, but no belt. Above and to the right of this central scene are two partly preserved figures who walk to the left. The front is a man with a belt and possible penis sheath similar to the better preserved captives. He strides forward, one foot on the man being eaten by the lion. His hands are behind him, probably indicating that he, too, is bound at the elbows, though his elbows are missing. He is followed by a figure wearing a long garment, apparently a sort of dress. The garment is patterned and has a border, perhaps a fringe, along its bottom and front. A parallel for this garment, probably from a generation or two later, can be seen on a fragment of carved ivory from the tomb of Aha at Abydos. On that fragment the figure, who has a long beard and long hat or hairstyle, is in a bowed position and presents a plant.[13] What this robed figure does on the Battlefield Palette is unclear; it could be in control of the bound figure before it, or could itself be a captive. The remaining five human figures are curly-haired bearded men shown in various poses of disarray beneath and behind the lion. One of these figures is bound at the elbows, but the others have their arms free. None wears a belt, and the penises of all men are shown. Three of these figures are being pecked by the carrion birds. There are some differences in size between the human figures on the Battlefield Palette but they are not dramatic and appear to distinguish between importance of captives rather than between people of different factions. The figure being eaten by the lion is the largest; those scattered in disarray are the smallest.

The most obvious victor in the preserved part of the scene is the lion. The standards, with their hands, also clearly refer to captors, whether human or divine or some combination of the two, and the carrion birds also appear to be on the winning side or at least aiding and abetting the humiliation of the dead. None of the human figures can be certainly shown to be on the victorious side, and for this reason I suspect the figure in the long cloak is also to be understood as a victim rather than a dominator.

Clear abstractions in its iconography make the Battlefield Palette undoubtedly more than a simple illustration of an event. Lions do not conveniently prowl battlefields to eat deceased enemies, and captives cannot be marched forward by unaccompanied standards. Does this abstraction mean a single event is being interpreted in larger, more symbolic, terms, or that the image itself relates only to generalities about violence, not to an event at all? It is not possible to say, but the conclusion is unavoidable that these images, of lions and standards, of domination of a chaotic mass of defeated men, were understandable to their original audience because they represented an agreed role of violence in the working of the world. Such symbolism around violence argues for its relation to an institution. It is tempting to read the image of the lion as a representation of a king, but on the surviving pieces this is not a named king. Are we missing the part with a label, or should we understand this as a general and abstract reference to kingship, or is it more abstract even than that?

The Libyan Palette

An entirely different image of battle is found on the Libyan Palette. This palette, also sometimes called the Towns Palette, is known from a single unprovenanced piece from the lower part of the palette (Figure 3.2).[14] One side bears registers of animals separated by ground lines, with a bottom register of plants; on the very right of the bottom register are two signs that are usually read *Tjehenu*, hence the name "Libyan Palette."

The other side includes our violence. This, too, was evidently separated into registers, though only part of one line survives at the top right. On this are three human feet, all facing right, in an arrangement that is rather difficult to read; it looks as though the foot of one figure was between the striding feet of another. The bottom section of the palette shows seven different iterations of a related device. Roughly square enclosures with regularly spaced protrusions on their outsides surround a series of images, each different, including things such as birds, a plant, a building, and two men facing each other, possibly grappling with one another. All but the enclosure with the two men also include a number, not consistent across the group, of smaller solid squares. The images within the enclosures may represent labels; certainly they serve to distinguish between the seven examples, making clear that they are the same sort of thing but not, in some way, the same thing. These are usually read as the names of towns.[15] The heron is later associated with the town of Buto in the Nile Delta, and this may therefore indicate a set of Lower Egyptian places;[16] this is not necessarily

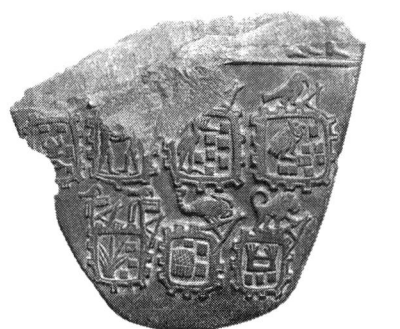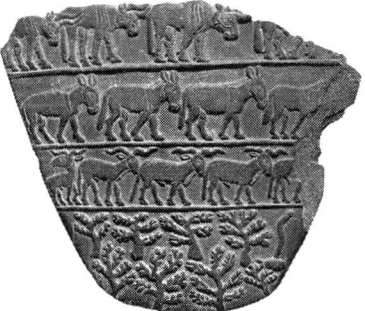

Figure 3.2 The Libyan Palette. One side of the fragment shows seven squares, usually interpreted as representing towns, being attacked by hoe-wielding animals and standards. The other side depicts rows of plants and animals and includes, at the lower right, the word usually read as "Libya". Dimensions: length 19 cm, width 22 cm.

inconsistent with *Tjehenu*, from the other side, as what we translate as Libya may have included the western Delta.

Where preservation allows us to see clearly, all of the enclosures are surmounted by further images, also unique to each. Various devices, mostly animals but in one case two standards with falcons on top of them, very like the standards seen on the Battlefield Palette, hold hoes and stick their points into the top or side of the enclosure. The animals depicted are a falcon, a lion, and a scorpion.

The abstractions on this piece are even more abstract than those on the Battlefield Palette, and they likewise must be understood as references to a codified relationship between institutions and symbols. There are only two human figures in the scene aside from feet in the register above. The preserved humans are those inside one of the towns, and they seem to serve as a label rather than as representations of humans acting within the scene. Despite this, the actions shown by non-human figures are clearly those of humans, with the animals and standards meant to represent either individual people or groups of people. The squares are almost certainly fortified places and the hoes are probably employed here as implements for destroying town walls, which were themselves presumably made of mudbricks, making an agricultural implement an excellent tool for the task.[17]

Even if we can be reasonably confident about the type of action depicted on the Libyan Palette, how to interpret it is still a real problem.[18] It seems highly likely that the squares represent named fortified places, at least some of which might be in the Nile Delta. Are we to understand them as all being attacked simultaneously, episodically in a sequence, or as part of different campaigns? It is not clear if they are meant to represent seven specific places as a list, or if they are meant rather to represent a totality of some sort, all the fortified places of a region perhaps. This is perhaps rendered less likely by the number—seven is not usually a number associated with plurality in Egypt, which is usually represented by three or by nine—but as the system of writing is still very much in development at this time, it might be a mistake to expect regularity in such a way.

The symbols on top of the fortified places are even more difficult to interpret than their interiors. All three of the visible attacking animals, and the two standards, appear relatively regularly in contemporary art. All are regularly associated with power in some way, and falcons and lions are certainly closely related to kingship in later times and perhaps at this time. The falcon is also closely associated with the city of Hierakonpolis in the Protodynastic Period.[19] The relationship between the falcon and kingship is in fact so close that it is the clearest way we can be confident that we have kings, thanks to its role in the *serekh*. As such, we may with some confidence assert that the attacking images on the Libyan Palette refer to accepted and previously defined aspects of a power structure, and at this time it seems appropriate to refer to that structure as kingship. But do these devices represent one king in different guises attacking seven places? Or seven kings?[20] Seven military divisions under one king? They do not help to clarify the degree to which this should be read as representative of a single military campaign, separate military campaigns, or violent control of places in general.

If we cannot say precisely what it represents, if in fact there is a great deal of ambiguity, it is still possible to advance some general conclusions about the Libyan Palette that allow it to sit in a more general discussion of the imagery of power. Notably, it is simultaneously by far the most specific document we have seen yet, and still in important ways reflective of generalizations. On the side of specifics, we seem to have individually labeled places. This is the first time we can really say that we have an image that purports to refer to a definable and bounded entity rather than a universal concept, the first time that specificity is embedded in the image itself rather than given by context. This specificity is apparently true of place, in the case of the towns, but rather remarkably it is still not clear that we have specificity of people on this fragment. *Tjehenu* on the opposite side may be an ethnic designation for a group. If we have references to kingship here, it is not clear at all that we have a labeled king—these are probably symbols of kingship, not of an individual king or kings. If this is the case, only the power of the office, not the power of the individual, can be said to be explicitly demonstrated in the surviving part of the Libyan Palette. That this might well not have been the case for the document as a whole can be demonstrated by a comparison to the Narmer Palette, where the bottom portion of one side also preserves an image of a powerful animal attacking a fortified place. That part of the image on the Narmer Palette is also not labeled with a king's name, but it stands at the base of a very labeled document that makes the association between the individual and the general notion of kingship quite clear. The same may be true of the Libyan Palette. In any case, the preservation of the general reference is certainly significant.

The Bull Palette

The Bull Palette is known only from a small fragment of the upper part of the palette (Figure 3.3).[21] The motifs preserved are all related to those seen on other palettes. At the top, a bull with lowered horns tramples and perhaps gores a flailing, prostate man. The man wears a belted penis sheath and has curly hair and a long curly beard, extremely similar to the victims on the Battlefield Palette. Beneath this trampling scene on one side are two images, only one largely preserved, of the same sort of device that is taken to represent a fortified town on the Libyan Palette. Within are a lion and a pot, most likely labeling the presumed town. The second town was also labeled. Neither preserves signs of being destroyed in the same way as the towns on the Libyan Palette. The other side of this fragment includes five semi-personified standards, whose arms grip a single rope. Below this are a leg and head of two different individuals; the position of the leg suggests that there may have been bodies in disarray similar to those on the Battlefield Palette. The head might belong to an upright figure. It has curly hair and a beard, again familiar.

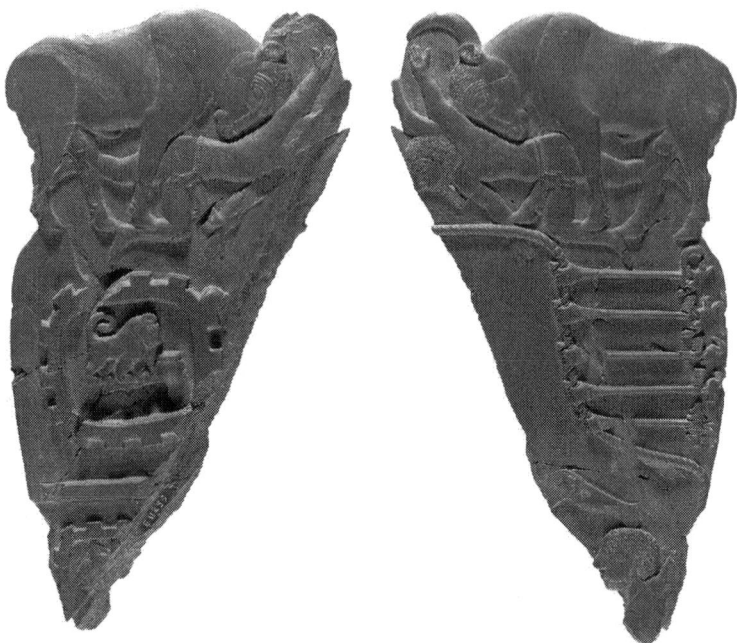

Figure 3.3 The Bull Palette. A trampling bull is preserved mauling a man who wears
a penis sheath; his beard is clear on the left. Personified standards and
representations of towns are elements shared with other palettes. Dimensions:
26.5 cm x 14.5 cm.

Ivory knife handles

Among the corpus of Protodynastic ivory knife handles, one preserves a clear scene of
captivity, a second may also show captives, and a third has an image of combat very
different from those seen on the palettes above.[22] These handles are of a standardized
form, all made to fit carefully knapped chert blades (see Figure 3.6). The handles were
typically provided with one smooth side and one side with a raised boss. It is assumed,
given the quality of the knives themselves and of the relief decoration on their handles,
that they were intended to be used for ritual purposes rather than mundane cutting.
Excavated examples of blades do show damage that suggests they were used.[23]

The two handles with possible scenes of captivity are poorly preserved, making
a reconstruction of their scenes problematic. The first, found in the Hierakonpolis
Main Deposit, has an image of captivity on its boss side (Figure 3.4).[24] Here five
captives are held by four captors. All the figures kneel, with captives having both
knees down and captors one knee up. The prisoners are bound at the elbow, with
leashes leading back to the hands of those who imprison them; the position of captivity, with elbows bound behind the back, is now unambiguous in form and meaning.
It is possible that two of the captives have beards, but the level of preserved detail is

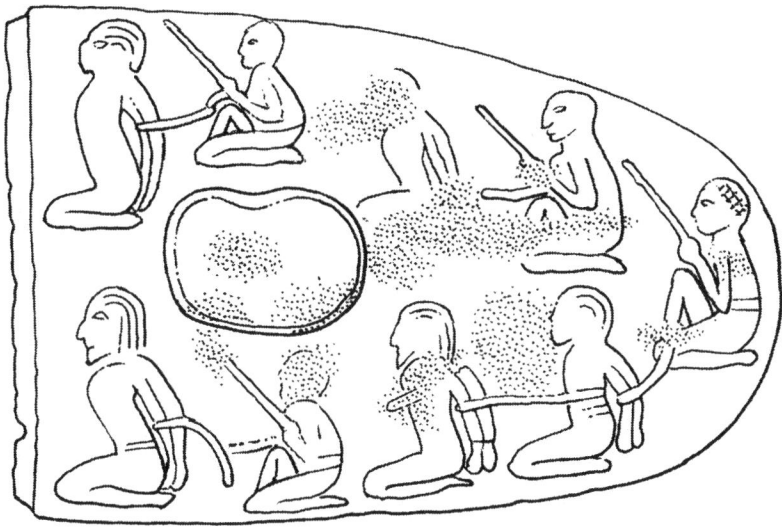

Figure 3.4 Oxford knife handle showing bound prisoners. Length: 9.5 cm.

not sufficient to be confident. There seems to be some distinction in hairstyle, with captors sporting shorter hair and captives longer. The captors all hold long sticks at an angle, but as their arms are held close to their bodies they do not actively threaten the prisoners. Notably, the figures are all roughly on the same scale, and if anything the captives are larger than those who control them.

Another knife handle that may preserve traces of a scene of captivity is in the Metropolitan Museum (Figure 3.5).[25] This handle is poorly preserved, and even those who have drawn the object have seen it quite differently. In Dreyer's reconstruction

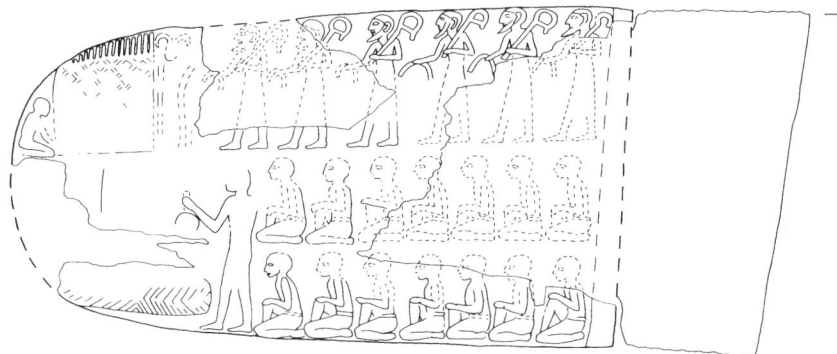

Figure 3.5 Metropolitan Museum knife handle, obverse, possibly showing domination at the lower left.

of the obverse, a standing figure in the lower left appears to clutch the hair of a head in front of him. Because of the oblong immediately beneath this head (if it is a head) and thus the lack of space to include an entire person, we may perhaps see this as a personified place. Dreyer has interpreted this as a royal smiting scene;[26] not enough is preserved of the striding figure, including an absence of headgear and of an upraised arm or weapon, for me to be confident in the reading, though it seems possible. On the other side of the handle, Williams and Logan interpreted rounded shapes in the upper left section of the reverse as heads of captives, bound with a rope held by a standard at the far left. If this is correct, then the captives are shown overlapping one another in a way that is atypical for images of multiple people in this period. The supposed standard is also of no recognizable form. On the other hand, the personified papyrus marsh behind the figures has an almost exact parallel on the Narmer Palette, where it is convincingly read as a reference to subjugated northerners. On the whole, the Metropolitan handle is too badly preserved to be of much use, but it may have both a smiting scene and a scene that includes, though is not centered on, captives. Either or both scenes might be given geographically specific labels.

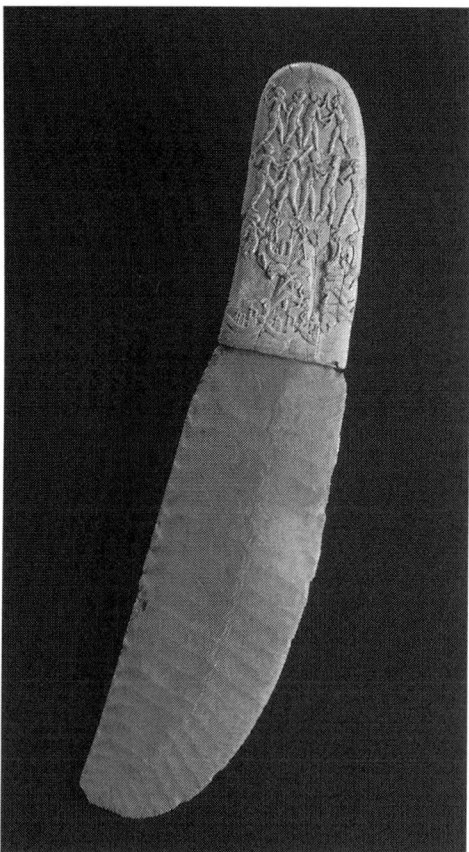

Figure 3.6 The Gebel el-Arak knife. Dimensions: height 28 cm; blade height 18.8 cm, handle height 9.5 cm.

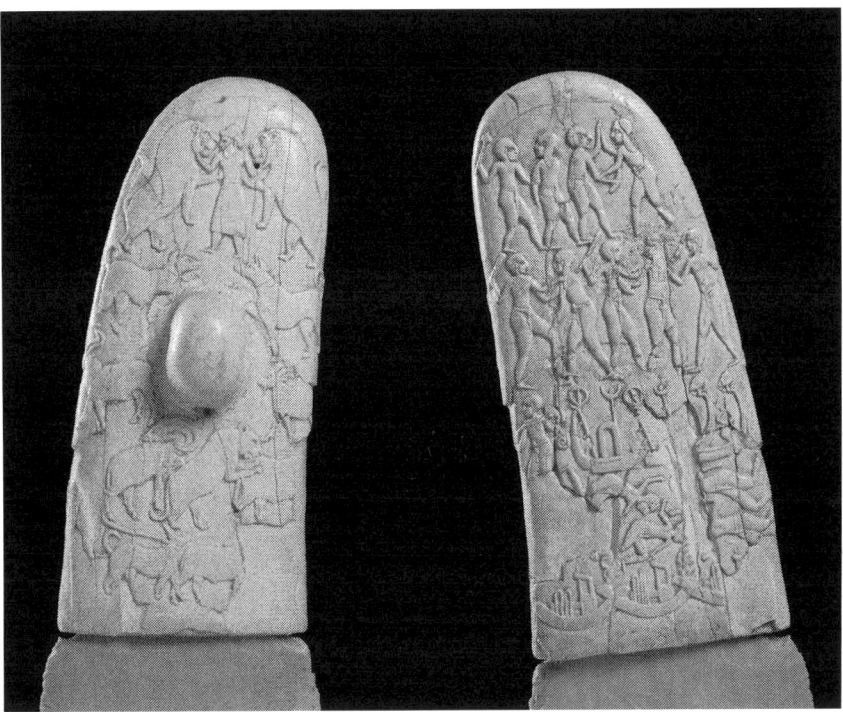

Figure 3.7 Detailed view of the two sides of the Gebel el-Arak knife handle. It is typical
for such relief carved ivory knife handles to have very different scenes on
either side. On the right are images of hand-to-hand fighting, boats, and dead
figures; on the left a single figure dominates animals.

The knife handle preserving a scene of combat is known as the Gebel el-
Arak handle after its presumed find-spot, though it was bought on the art
market (Figures 3.6 and 3.7).[27] Its scene of fighting is one of the best-known
images of violence from Predynastic Egypt; the imagery on the handle has also
received much attention because of its apparent iconographic relationship to
the Ancient Near East.[28]

The boss-side of the handle is primarily decorated with animals, some of which
are attacking one another, some of which are bound, and two of which—lions—
are shown in a heraldic pose flanking a man in Near Eastern style clothing who
holds them by their necks. The flat side of the knife handle is that preserving the
scene of human violence. The scene is divided into five registers, not separated by
ground lines. The top two registers show men engaged in personal combat. The
top row has two pairs of men, differently engaged. On the right the men face each
other, leaning in, grappling. They each have a hand in the air, in a gesture reminiscent of a high five. The man on the right uses his other hand to grasp the elbow
of his combatant, keeping at bay a weapon held at waist height that looks very
like the type of knife to which this handle belongs. Left of this pair are two others

in quite different attitudes. The man on the far left holds a mace aloft in his rear arm. His forward arm grasps the man in front of him at the elbow. These two are striding in the same direction, more captor and captive than combatants, though the man being held does turn to look at the threatening mace holder.

The posture of brandishing a long weapon in preparation for hitting an opponent is echoed three times in the register below. Here, however, the opponents fight back and the weapons are club-like, not maces with defined heads. To the left, two men with broad strides face each other, the man on the left with the raised club and his other hand grasping his opponent's hair near his throat. The opponent is apparently unarmed, but reaches toward his assailant with both hands. One hand may grasp the knee of his attacker. To the right three men are engaged. The one in the middle is unfortunately damaged, but the opponents on either side of him raise clubs (that in the hand of the right-most figure is slightly around the side of the knife handle and difficult to see in this view). Both these men also hold the middle figure, who himself is holding a knife toward the belly of the left opponent.

There are slight but clearly important differences between the combatants in these registers, who can be separated into two groups. All are the same size, all wear penis sheaths and nothing else. The only distinction is in hairstyle—three figures wear longer hair or wigs with lappets that fall over their shoulders; some remaining traces on the poorly preserved figure suggest he may have worn that as well. If so, all the combats are between a smooth-headed man or two, and a longer-haired man. All of the long weapons are wielded by smooth-headed people, who seem to be getting the best of the fight in three of the four vignettes, while the fourth is inconclusive. The knife appears a weapon available to all, being once held by a smooth-headed and once by a lappet-wearing figure.

The bottom half of this side of the Gebel el-Arak knife handle has rows of boats above and below, with a middle register of men lying prone, limbs splayed. The boats are not manned, and their relationship to the violence is unclear. To the left of the top row of boats stands a smooth-headed figure holding a rope; this may wrap around the side of the knife and bind an animal on the other side. Four of the men between the two registers of boats are preserved, though this area is broken and originally probably included five or six figures. The men appear as if they are swimming, but most probably are to be understood as dead. As this is a way of rendering dead people that is not necessarily related to water (see the Battlefield Palette, Figure 3.1), they may not be connected in any way to the boats. All the dead men wear penis sheaths and have smooth heads.

Much like the palettes discussed above, the fight side of the Gebel el-Arak knife handle combines a mode of visual representation that is similar to but not yet the same as pharaonic artistic conventions with a particular motif—hand-to-hand fighting—that has only scant precedent and that never achieved the prominence of, say, the smiting scene. The only extant fight scene before this was in Hierakonpolis Tomb 100 (Figures 2.9 and 2.11), which also focused on combats between individuals rather than ranks. The clear division of the scene on the knife handle into registers is an aspect of canonical art. The figures are for the most part shown as later figures will be, with faces in profile and eyes and torsos frontal, though two of the combatants in the fighting registers are shown with their shoulders to the viewer.

No single figure is given prominence on the fight side of the Gebel el-Arak knife handle. This was true, too, in the combat scenes of Hierakonpolis Tomb 100, and—perhaps surprisingly—continues to be true for all known images of combat before the New Kingdom. This fighting scene and its successors are not yet places for the display of individual kings' valor, and in fact never include anyone who can be recognized as a king. Groups can be identified on the basis of hairstyle and perhaps differences in boat type, though it is not clear which boats belong to whom. Even if we accept the hairstyle as distinguishing two groups, it remains impossible, when taking the composition as a whole, to say which is dominant—in the battle portions the long-haired men are apparently losing, while between the boats the smooth-headed have been killed. It is possible that the hair, the only distinguishing characteristic, was removed from the dead and that they were originally long-haired. Even if so, the failure to communicate this in the image itself leaves the modern viewer understanding this violence as essentially a draw; if this is reference to a specific battle with a known outcome then that knowledge was held by its original audience separate from the depiction. The point of the depiction thus appears to be the violence itself, not a record of the triumph of one group over another. This is in contrast to the scene on the other side, which shows a clearly singular figure in a pose of dominating the fiercest of animals. If the side with fighting is balanced chaos, the opposite side is pure control; even, perhaps, a hierarchy of control: a lion mauls some other quadruped and a human controls lions. It is in particular the differences between these two sides that highlight the absence of a dominant figure or group amid the fighting.

In addition to showing that a scene of violence could be utilized in a generalizing way, shown without resolution or victory, this knife handle demonstrates that the motion of smiting has not yet become canonical or associated with kings. Here the posture is utilized repeatedly, and once in conjunction with a mace. The striding, mace-wielding figure is included among a more general fight, is not distinguished from others, and is iconographically identical to the sprawling dead between the ships. The contrast with the pharaonic smiting icon, which would be codified only generations later, is stark.

Maceheads

The category of maceheads is arguably the most complex of these artifact types because maces are attested both in imagery, as we have just seen in the combat scene from the Gebel el-Arak knife, and archaeologically both as prosaic and ceremonial objects. Archaeologically, maces are present in Upper Egypt from the Naqada I Period onwards as a largely functional category, a type of weapon that was presumably actually used and is known to us from graves. The Protodynastic stone ceremonial examples, with their often elaborate carved scenes, are mostly known from the temple at Hierakonpolis. There is some temporal overlap in these functional and ceremonial uses, though maces as weapons are not known from Dynastic Egypt. We may have already seen maces in imagery, if the examples from Naqada I pottery, the Gebelein textile, and Hierakonpolis Tomb 100 are accepted as such. Naqada III images of maces are restricted in the type of mace— always pear-shaped—but quite varied in terms of use. Maces can be shown in (probably highly ceremonialized) hunting,[29] in hand-to-hand combat, and in ritual smiting by the king or by a more anonymous individual. The smiting motif is the most common and the only one that would persist, though it would in later periods be restricted to the king himself.

Only a small number of heavily decorated maceheads and fragments of them are known (see below, Figure 3.15, for a photograph of the decorated and undecorated maceheads from the Hierakonpolis Main Deposit). From our perspective they are a curious class of objects: while their very form makes them inherently related to violence, even to the type of ritual smiting that was at this time becoming a canonical image, their preserved imagery is almost never overtly violent. We have scenes of royal ritual that look very much like royal ceremonies (for instance the Narmer Macehead—Figure 3.16),[30] and scenes of royal agriculture, presumably also ritual (the Scorpion Macehead—Figure 3.8). We have buildings and animals and non-royal people. We have labels for some individuals, including the king and some who appear to serve roles in his court. But very few maceheads preserve what appear to be references to captivity or

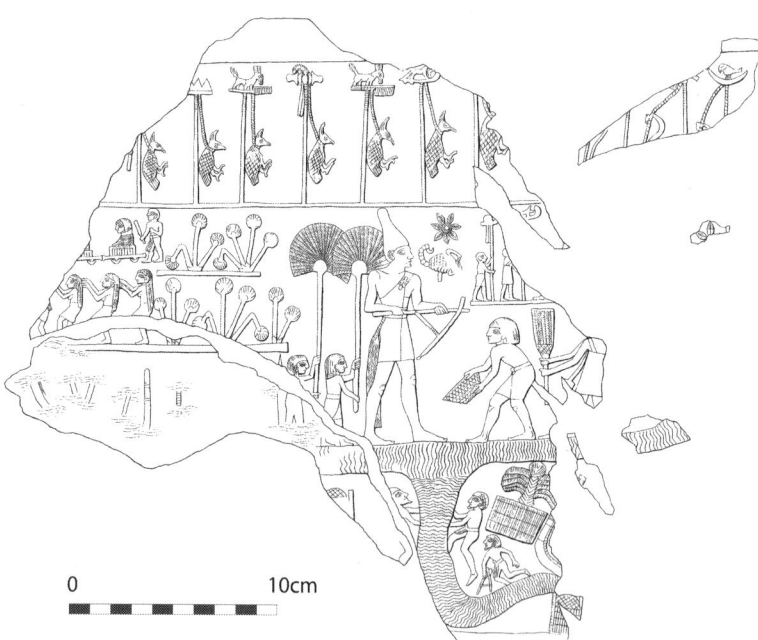

Figure 3.8 Drawing of the relief image on the Scorpion Macehead.

defeated enemies, and none to other types of violence. Captivity on the Scorpion Macehead is described here. The Narmer Macehead will be treated with his material, and a small ivory macehead with other carved ivory objects.

The Scorpion Macehead from Hierakonpolis has a complex scene in which the theme of captivity is present but does not appear to be dominant, rather framing an image in which the crowned king holds a hoe like those known from the palettes above and engages in presumably ritual agricultural activity (Figure 3.8).[31] It is incompletely preserved and much too large to have been used as a weapon. In the relief on the Scorpion Macehead, the king holds a plow and stands above a course of water. He is identified by means that are in line with pharaonic royal iconography—the White Crown and tail—as well as a rosette, which is a symbol of kingship that is only present in the few formative generations in Naqada III, between the Predynastic Period and the First Dynasty.[32] The top register of the macehead preserves a set of standards, probably representing places.[33] From them hang dead birds dangling from ropes tied around their necks. The use of this type of bird, called in Egyptian *rekhyt*, to symbolise the general population would become standard in later times. Here it may indicate that the people of these places had been violently subjugated and are now dead or subdued. Certainly places themselves appear to be distinguished and given specificity by use of the differentiated standards. While the king himself is not directly interacting with these figures, given his scale and the overall composition it seems reasonable to suggest that the subjugation of the birds/people is attributed to him. He, likewise, is given multiple layers of specificity, including his office and, if we are correct in our reading of the scorpion, his individual name. It has been suggested that an additional fragment of a macehead with a king in a Red Crown,[34] also from Hierakonpolis, may have been part of the Scorpion Macehead. A hypothetical reconstruction of the missing parts of the scene includes a falcon holding bound human prisoners;[35] whether or not this is true, the dangling birds can be used to make similar points about both captivity and the symbolizing of a person or people by means of an animal.

Additional ivory objects from Hierakonpolis

The Hierakonpolis Main Deposit contained a number of small ivory objects with relief decoration in addition to the knife handles; some of these retain scenes relating to captivity and smiting. One is dated to the reign of Narmer, therefore discussed below, and some others are probably roughly contemporary but include no royal name. The date of the deposit itself is almost certainly New Kingdom or later, making the dating of individual objects within it problematic.[36] Those discussed here can be reasonably attributed to the Protodynastic Period because these types of artifacts are not known later.

Several cylinders from at least two objects, perhaps cylinder seals or parts of scepters or mace handles, include smiting with a mace. Three of these are very similar and may come from the same object (Figure 3.9).[37] These have registers with the repeated motif of a man smiting another man. All the images are roughly

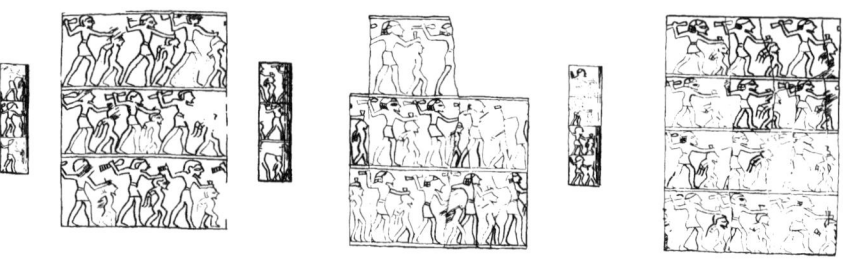

Figure 3.9 Three ivory cylinders, perhaps from a handle, from the Hierakonpolis Main
Deposit. The smiting motif is repeated, with no explicit indication that the
smiter is royal. Heights (in order shown): 10.5 cm, 11.4 cm, 11.4 cm.

the same. Both figures face to the right and both stride forward with their legs
apart. The smiting figure is behind and is substantially larger than the smitee. The
smiter reaches forth with one hand, which rests on top of the head of the smaller
figure. There is a small knob, perhaps representing grasped hair, in this forward
hand of the smiter. The back hand of the smiter is raised and grips a mace around
its middle. In one register the handle of the mace is composed of separate seg-
ments, perhaps much like the object on which this depiction is found. The smiter
always has a short beard and hair or a wig; on two of the cylinders it is clear that
the hair is a bit long in the back and composed of multiple sections. He wears a
short kilt. The smitee, who faces away from the smiter, is more sketchily drawn.
His arms are always bound at the elbow. He, too, has a short beard and hair on his
head, but wears no identifiable clothing.

The absence of any labels or distinct iconography makes it difficult to read
this image as even an oblique reference to a specific event or people, and this is
enhanced by the patterned repetition of the motif. Quibell called the image one
of a king smiting a prisoner,[38] but aside from the pose itself there is nothing to
identify the larger figures as kings; as we have seen on the Gebel el-Arak knife
handle, the pose and weapon alone cannot yet be confidently read as indications
of royal status. It is rather notable that, aside from size and the absence of clothing, there is really nothing to distinguish the smiter and smitee. This can only be
read as a very generalized image of physical power, both because of the lack of
distinguishing features on the figures shown and because of the repetition, which
makes any reference to a specific action highly unlikely. This generalization is in
contrast to the fourth ivory cylinder with a smiting scene from the Main Deposit
(Figure 3.17), which is exceptionally specific, including both Narmer's name and
a label for the captives. The contrast is the more striking given that the type of
object and context of discovery are the same.

A further object of interest from the Main Deposit is an ivory macehead with
three registers of marching captives (Figure 3.10).[39] Small votive maceheads are
known from other sites, too, and additional undecorated examples come from the
Main Deposit. This example, small and in a material that would have rendered

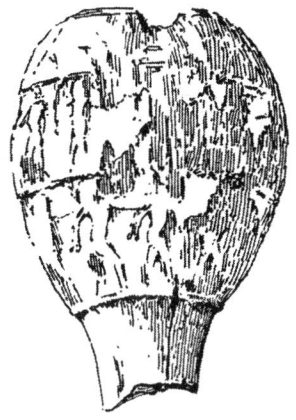
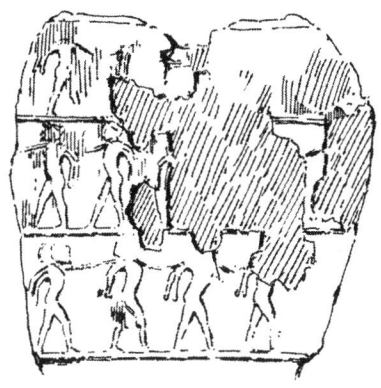

Figure 3.10 Ivory macehead from the Hierakonpolis Main Deposit. Height: 7.95 cm.

it impractical as a weapon, seems to stand somewhere between the usual plain votives and the large, royal, ceremonial examples discussed above. The preservation of the piece is poor, and it is not possible to see all of the original figures; however, it appears that all three registers contained files of captives, bound at the elbows and tied to one another by a leash that goes from neck to neck. The top and bottom files walk to the right, the center file to the left. No clothing is evident and the published drawing does not allow hairstyles or the presence or absence of beards to be determined. As the captives are tall enough to fill the height of each register, there is no room for a larger dominating figure. If any figure of any difference from the captives was once present, he is no longer visible. The patterning and the absence of a dominant figure make this image ahistorical, much like the ivory cylinders. One might argue that this image of only captives is apt for decorating a mace, with the dominator and the pose of smiting provided by whoever held the object.

These ivory objects from Hierakonpolis expand our understanding of the range of places in which imagery of bound captives and smiting could be found, but otherwise offer little elaboration on the themes examined on other types of objects. Their most distinctive characteristic is the use, on the relief carved pieces, of repetition to form patterns. In all of these cases we have a notable absence of specific references to events, but this should certainly not be pushed too far as the Narmer ivory cylinder is quite the opposite.

Captive figurines from temple deposits at other sites

While the Hierakonpolis Main Deposit is unique in its treasure trove of highly decorated royal objects, it is also part of a larger phenomenon of buried deposits of early objects in association with temples or shrines. These were probably collections of objects that had been dedicated as votives over generations, cleared at some later point but given an honored burial within the precinct.[40] Differences between assemblages at different sites presumably indicate differences of cultic requirements or foci of local cults, though they rarely if ever seem clearly related to a known god at any site. One example of such site-by-site differences is the absence of small votive maceheads in the deposits at Abydos.[41] Figurines are common in such deposits and were made in a variety of media, especially faience and ivory; they are generally under 10 cm in height and quite simple in nature. Representations include but are not limited to animals, boats, maceheads, and people. The whole corpus of figurines is notable for its variety of styles and depictions, making dating any individual piece extremely difficult. A small minority of human figurines from such deposits depict what may be captives; excavators tend to fall into two camps, either interpreting anything that might be a captive as certainly so, or not mentioning the possibility at all.[42] I consider it possible but not proven that captives were a category of figurines offered in early temples. As these are not direct depictions of violence I will not be comprehensive in gathering or discussing these pieces, but note a few examples from recent excavations to highlight issues of significance in trends of depiction of violence at the time.

One of the most extensive collections of figurines was recently discovered at the site of Tell el-Farkha in the eastern Nile Delta; three figurines from Farkha have been interpreted as captives (Figure 3.11).[43] The first is a faience figurine of a man in a crouching posture, not quite prostrate. His legs are tucked beneath him and his forearms rest on the ground. He has long hair, a beard, and perhaps

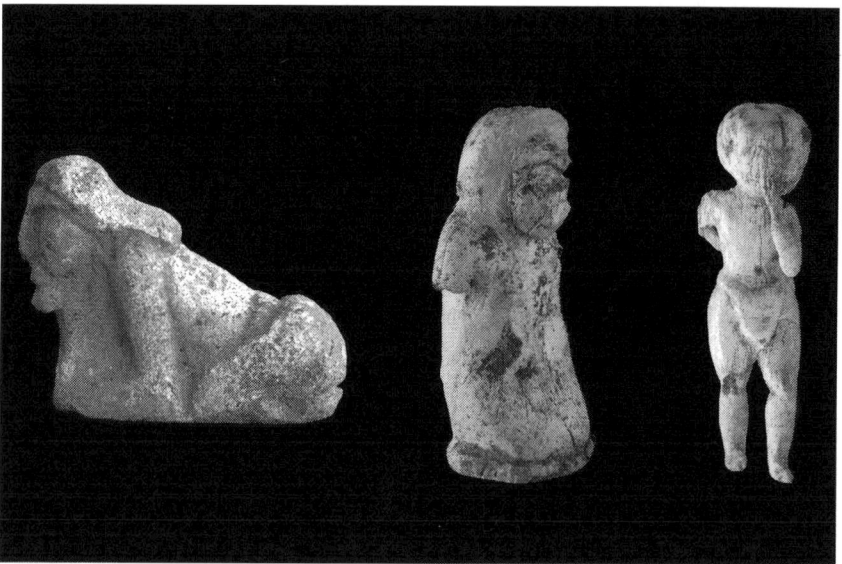

Figure 3.11 Three small figurines from temple deposits at Tell el-Farkha that have been interpreted as showing captives. The reading is uncertain.

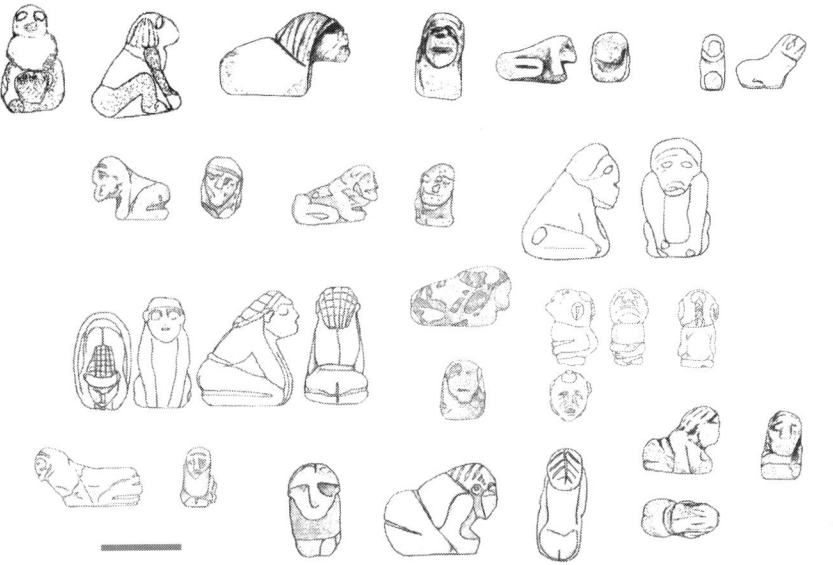

Figure 3.12 Figurines from Tell Ibrahim Awad in postures that may indicate captivity or submission.

the belt of an otherwise not visible penis sheath. It is not clear if his arms are bound, but his posture is one that can be associated with submission. The other two figures are carved in hippopotamus ivory. One kneels. His now broken arms may have been bound behind his back. The third figure holds one hand to his face, with the other arm behind his back; he wears an odd, diaper-like garment that has been called a type of penis sheath. The posture and proportions of this figure look more like a child than a captive, but the garment is confusing in either case.

A small and odd figurine from Tell Ibrahim Awad, also in the eastern Nile Delta, has its elbows drawn back in a position reminiscent of a captive pose (Figure 3.12, right, third figure from top).[44] The head is disproportionately large and ornamented with a single braided lock down the middle; the face is deeply lined. The legs are missing or truncated. Eleven other figurines of crouching humans have been found at Tell Ibrahim Awad (Figure 3.12),[45] recalling the first of the Farkha objects discussed above. Like that object, these are all in faience. In cases where the objects were detailed and the preservation sufficient to see, they wear long, striated wigs, and many have beards. At least one has a belt.

Additional captive figurines come from older excavations at Abydos and Hierakonpolis.[46] Finally, such figurines without certain provenance but possibly from Abydos were acquired for the private Kofler-Truniger collection in Luzern, Switzerland.[47] These examples fall into the same types as those from Farkha and Tell Ibrahim Awad: they are kneeling and supplicant or bound.

These small figurines are notable for their different postures and attributes. None of them are unambiguously representative of captivity, but they all have elements that have suggested it to some. They fit well with the general picture painted above, of a time of innovation and variety, even playfulness, in depictions of violence and captivity. No figures in poses of domination are known from these deposits and this should give us pause, though as we saw on the ivory macehead it is possible to have depictions of captives without captors. An understanding of why such objects might have been offered in temples of the Protodynastic Period rests on assumptions and analogies to later practice; it is reasonable to expect, but by no means certain, that they were dedicated by individuals as a way of asking a divinity for particular favors or protection. If this is the case, it is conceivable that figurines of captives could be related to pleas either to avoid captivity or to be protected from dangerous others. The latter has later parallels in the destruction of later execration figurines (see Chapter 7), but it is questionable if there was such a direct relationship between form and plea in the case of early votive figurines.[48]

Rock carving: the Gebel Sheikh Suleiman relief

An image that is probably roughly contemporary with the decorated objects discussed above is a rock carving from Gebel Sheikh Suleiman, near the later Egyptian fortress site of Buhen in Lower Nubia (Figure 3.13).[49] By and large I have chosen not to examine rock-cut images, though this is an area of current research for many scholars and there are images that may relate to the development of iconic representations of violence.[50] The reasons for my omission are related to problems in understanding them. The most fundamental difficulties are in dating rock art and in relating its iconography to images in other media, issues that have not always been adequately acknowledged in scholarship.[51] It has become common to speak of a direct relationship between rock-carved images and kingship; in my opinion this is writing history and assuming understanding at a level of specificity that the data will not bear.[52] The Gebel Sheikh Suleiman carving is chosen for inclusion both because it has been used in a variety of discussions of early royal ideology and because the divergent interpretations of it demonstrate why we must be cautious in looking at rock art alongside other media.

There are several components of the Gebel Sheikh Suleiman image, and neither their particulars nor their relationship is always clear. The techniques or styles of carving are different in different places, sometimes within one element of the tableau; interpretations of the discrepancies range from different phases, to different hands, to total bewilderment.[53] At the left of the scene is a *serekh*. The building is deeply incised; the falcon is more sketchily rendered, but its bottom part may also be damaged. In this case the *serekh* appears to be either anonymous or "plain"; anonymous *serekhs* are known on other media from only a few generations in the Naqada III Period and are one of the means of defining the Protodynastic Period in the reigns some generations before Narmer. "Plain" *serekhs* have longer currency, but the particularly dotted form that some have seen here has its closest

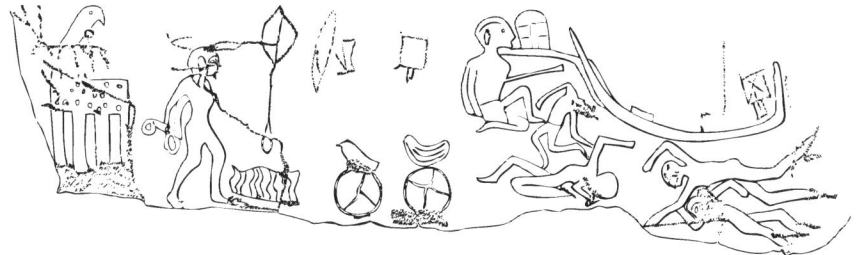

Figure 3.13 The rock carving at Gebel Sheikh Suleiman, after William Murnane.
Probably dating to the period of state formation and showing both defeated
dead and captured people, its interpretation raises problems that demonstrate
the difficulty of incorporating rock art into a more general description of
Egyptian art and history.

parallels from two generations after Narmer.[54] The *serekh* is the usual basis of
dating this relief, though given uncertainties that the relief as a whole—or even
the elements of the *serekh* itself—date to one episode of carving, the problems
thus raised should be clear.

Immediately to the right of the *serekh* is a large human figure, walking toward
the right, with his arms behind his back. He is well carved in raised relief. An
implement with curved ends at the level of his hands has been interpreted variously as a bow, perhaps identifying the man as coming from the border region
between Egypt and Nubia, or a rope binding his hands, or even a bow serving as
a binding mechanism.[55] The posture, with hands behind the back, is suggestive of
captivity. Details of this figure are very difficult to see, perhaps partly because of
damage but also because they seem not to have been indicated in the first place.
Neither clothing nor genitalia are evident. He appears to wear a short wig. If there
was a beard, it was small. Somaglino and Tallet have seen both an arm stretching
from the *serekh* to the head of this figure and an arm raised behind the Horus falcon, and thus interpret this scene as a smiting *serekh*;[56] this is not an interpretation
of the scene that has been seen by other epigraphers. In front of the walking, or
potentially smote, figure are several symbols including some that can be read by
analogy with later writing; these are a rectangle that is probably a pool of water,
and two circular emblems topped with falcons that are read as towns. These are
carved more lightly than the figure to their left.

The right part of the tableau consists of a largely empty boat and five figures
who are more clearly marked as defeated. The figures are once more well carved
in raised relief; this inscription is no quick graffito. The largest figure, on the left,
sits, resting on one knee with the other bent before him. His arms are behind his
back, in the position associated with captivity that would become standard and
that may have been already seen on the Gebelein textile and the smiting scene of
the Hierakonpolis Tomb 100 painting (Figures 2.8 and 2.10). A thick line going
from the neck of this figure to the boat on his right has often been read as a

leash binding him, but this is not immediately clear;[57] recent reassessment of the inscription by Bruce Williams has indicated it might instead be a line between strata of the rock itself and not carved at all.[58] The kneeling figure wears a short kilt, his hair is indicated by an additional line atop his head, and a squared chin might represent a short beard. The shaft of an arrow is sticking out of his chest. The four slightly smaller figures are shown strewn beneath the boat in postures of disorder, limbs splayed. Two of them are in the pose that so often looks like swimming. No details of dress or other iconography are visible.

In showing disordered dead strewn about, and in depicting the victims as human and the king as a symbol, the Gebel Sheikh Suleiman carving can be seen as parallel to the (known part of) the Battlefield Palette (Figure 3.1); the symbolic king is also parallel to representations of smiting *serekhs* from the reign of Narmer and his successors, more particularly so if the *serekh* here does indeed smite (Figures 3.17, 6.3, and 7.2). The problem of specificity with regards to the large captive has been noted above, but an equally important question is whether or not this *serekh* at Gebel Sheikh Suleiman was intended to refer to a specific king—as a smiting Narmer *serekh* clearly does—or to kingship more broadly, as might be suggested on the Battlefield Palette. Here in particular, since we seem to have the entire scene, it is notable that we cannot be confident that a specific king is referred to. This should make us very wary of assuming that it reports simply on a particular event; even if it does, it seems to deliberately distance itself from the specific to allow it to serve as a more general statement about kingship.[59]

Who would have seen the Gebel Sheikh Suleiman inscription? The great majority of depictions discussed in this chapter have been found in temple deposits, with elite tombs a poor second as a context for violent imagery. These contexts are inherently less accessible to a human audience than a rock drawing is (see Chapter 6). Should we assume that the Gebel Sheikh Suleiman inscription was intended to speak to passersby, to a less casual human audience, to a divine audience, or some combination of these? Many rock inscriptions in Egypt are in rather inaccessible places, which is one reason why they continue to be discovered regularly. In this case, the original location of the inscription was reasonably accessible from the Nile valley.[60] The "gebel" (mountain or hill) in question is a small sandstone hill about a kilometer west of Buhen south. Its visibility is not addressed by those who saw it in situ, but Arkell did note that it was extremely difficult to photograph, and thus perhaps to easily see.[61] It seems probable that an at least partly human audience was intended for this inscription; numerous graffiti and scratches indicate that there was in fact further interaction, perhaps over a very long time, with this image.[62] By whom or to what purpose, or even who carved the tableau originally, is not clear.

Depictions of violence in the reign of Narmer

The only heavily decorated artifacts from the Protodynastic Period that can be definitively associated with a specific, historically attested king are those with the name of Narmer on them.[63] Every king whose name we know prior to his is attested in inscriptions that are not on decorated objects. Kingship as labeled with a *serekh* exists before Narmer. Iconography that would come to be associated with kings also exists before Narmer, though kingship and its iconography are not fully formed by this reign.[64] But a picture of kingship with a connection to Horus, to niched façade architecture, to canonical art, to monumental building—these things we see brought together only from the reign of Narmer on.[65] The objects from his reign thus serve as a coda to a discussion of Predynastic art, the motifs of violence and subjugation, and their relationship to kingship within that art. While the Narmer Palette is undoubtedly the best known of these objects, it is one of many that together demonstrate the pivotal nature of this particular reign. Many but not all of the Narmer objects come from the Main Deposit at the Hierakonpolis temple. Narmer has known objects from most of the categories discussed above, excluding ivory knife handles and small figurines.

The Narmer Palette

The Narmer Palette is one of the most important and oft-discussed artifacts from any period of ancient Egypt (Figure 3.14).[66] It was found buried at the temple at Hierakonpolis, and is generally assumed to have been a dedication to that temple by Narmer himself, later buried when the temple was updated.[67] In basic form and function it is not dissimilar to other Naqada III decorated palettes, including the Libyan and Battlefield Palettes discussed above, but its preservation; its reference to a known, named king; the density of information contained on it; and its use of conventions of iconography and artistic canon related to later art mark

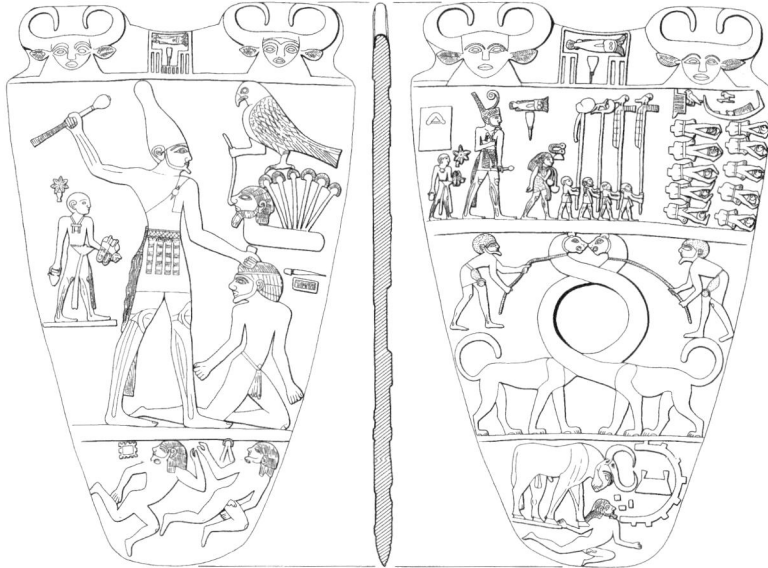

Figure 3.14 Line drawing of both sides of the Narmer Palette.

it as different from those palettes.[68] A full description of this object is not needed here, but several observations are relevant to a discussion of violence. Multiple images on the Narmer Palette are violent, in ways that are in most cases related to imagery we have already considered.

The largest scene on the Narmer Palette is a smiting scene, and here there can be no doubt that it deserves the name, that it is the icon familiar from later periods, and that parallels to the Islamic State beheading images can help us understand how such an icon functioned in the rapidly emerging Egyptian state. The smiting scene on the Narmer Palette occupies the majority of the non-grinding side. The king—identified as king by his wearing of the White Crown of Upper Egypt and as himself by his name above his head—stands in the approximate center of the scene. His well-muscled legs are apart, though he is not in an active striding pose; his right arm is raised behind his head, his left arm reaches before him. His right hand holds a mace around the middle of the handle; his left grasps the hair on top of the head of a captive. Narmer wears a short, elaborate kilt. A rather sketchily rendered sort of sash covers one shoulder and is tied on his chest. He also has a tail hanging from his waist and a short and narrow beard, possibly false.

The figure before the king is unbound, his arms on either side of his torso, his hands clenched. He kneels on the ground, with his knees down and well apart. His legs and body face the same direction as the king, to the right, but his head turns to look back toward the king. He is shown very nearly the same scale as the king, but because of his position, his head is at the height of Narmer's thighs. The captive's hair is elaborate, with a narrow fillet separating a wavy top portion from a tiered lower section. He wears a beard. Around his waist is tied a belt with a pendant front section, perhaps a loose penis sheath. Behind his head are two symbols, probably to label him either by name or by place of origin. Neither smiter nor smitee betray any emotion on their well-carved faces. Their impassive features are carved in canonical Egyptian style, completely in profile except for the eye, which is shown in full view.

The smiting scene is directly observed by figures on both sides, both of which seem to render the scene more ceremonial and less of an impromptu event. Behind the king and shown at a much smaller scale is an attendant bearing sandals and what appears to be a jar with a handle; he wears an elaborate garment. This attendant is labeled. In front of the king is a device consisting of a falcon, presumably representing the god Horus and thus in a sense another iteration of the king himself, pulling a rope that comes from the nose of a personified papyrus thicket. The hairstyle and beard of the head of this thicket are subtly but notably different than the head of the smote prisoner, directly below it; the thicket's head recalls the curly haired people on the Battlefield Palette. This may indicate that multiple types of enemies are being shown as subdued in the same larger image. In this image we have "realistic" and abstract references to domination in close combination.

Beneath the smiting scene, which takes place upon a groundline that serves as a register division, are two figures who appear to be sprawled with arms and legs apart. They may indicate dead people. Neither wears clothing, though only the one on the right has genitalia indicated. Both have tiered hairstyles that cover their shoulders and relatively full beards. Each has a different symbol before his head, perhaps labeling them.

The decoration on the other side of the palette focuses primarily on the central grinding area, which is encircled by the long and intertwined necks of two fantastical creatures. Their heads are bound and their leashes are held by human figures on either side. The top and bottom registers, above and below this central scene, both include elements of violence. In the top, the violence is in the past tense. Narmer, here wearing the Red Crown that in later tradition denotes Lower Egypt and carrying his mace at his side, along with a flail clutched to his chest, is part of a procession. The procession moves to the right, going toward an area where ten dead men lie in two neat rows. Violence perpetrated on them was ritual, though it may have followed death on the battlefield—they have been decapitated and castrated, with their heads and phalli placed between their legs, and their arms are bound at the elbow. Above them are signs that may represent place names.

The bottom register of the grinding side of the Narmer Palette has a scene of active but abstracted violence. Here a bull with lowered horns walks on a prone man whose posture is similar to the captive in the smiting scene on the other side, though this figure looks away from his tormentor rather than toward him. He wears no clothes and has his genitalia depicted. His shoulder-length hair is only striated, not tiered, and his beard is marked with detail. The bull's horns appear to be in the act of breaking down a town. This is indicated by a semi-circular wall with protruding bastions, much like the presumed towns on the Libyan Palette. As on that palette, a sign inside the town may label it, and small squares might indicate either bricks falling from the wall or buildings within the town. The violence here is shown in a notably static and impassive fashion, much like the smiting scene on the other side of the palette. The bull has all four hooves down, rather than moving at an active clip, and the face of the trampled man betrays no emotion. The bull is usually thought to represent the king.

The images of violence on the Narmer Palette have a combination of apparent references to specifics and to universals; some aspects, particularly images of the king, can be read as both simultaneously. One way we can trace specificity on this palette is through the use of writing, and another is through iconography. More ambiguously, differences in depictions between people can be argued to show them as distinct, either as individuals or as representative of types. The latter would itself be a combination of specificity and universality. The only word that can be read with complete confidence on the palette is the name of Narmer himself. This name appears three times on the palette: the niched façade building of a *serekh*, though without the Horus falcon, encloses the name on the top of both sides; the name, with no elements of a *serekh* whatsoever, occurs before the face of the king on the grinding side. The king is also identified by what he wears. Some elements of his depiction serve to distinguish him from other figures on the palette; notably, his elaborate kilt is unlike any other garment worn here. He is also the only one to wear a tail on this object. He is not the only one to wear a beard, and so neither its presence nor its form can be considered a mark that distinguishes him from the other figures. In subsequent periods a tail and false beard are certainly elements associated exclusively with kings and gods, but both of these—unlike the writing of a name in a *serekh*—have a prior history on figures that were not exclusively royal. The king is also the only figure to wear a crown, once the White and once the Red. The early history of these symbols is somewhat debated, but here they are clearly markers of kingship in the way they would continue to be for the rest of pharaonic history.[69]

Other figures also appear to be labeled. To understand the degree to which such labels can be read as elements of our specific/universal balance we would need to know if they are names or titles. In the case of the sandal bearer, it has often been suggested that the rosette is a symbol of the king and that the label—the same on both sides of the palette—beside this individual should most probably be read as a title on the lines of "royal something." Conversely, the two figures below the smiting scene, while rendered as more or less identical, are labeled differently from one another.

The relationship of the smiting scene to earlier images of captivity is important. Several elements of the scene are foreshadowed in White Cross-Lined Ware and Hierakonpolis Tomb 100, though the Narmer Palette also has notable differences from those images and they are not themselves entirely alike. Both the White Cross-Lined Ware images and the Hierakonpolis Tomb 100 scene show multiple captives at the same time. In both cases the captives appear to be bound and are shown at a distinctly smaller scale than their captors. In these ways, the Narmer Palette image is quite distinct from its predecessors. Like the White Cross-Lined Ware depictions and unlike the Hierakonpolis Tomb 100 scene, captor and captive on the Narmer Palette are distinguished by means of clothing and hair/crown. Here, however, the degree of specificity on the part of the dominating faction is greatly enhanced. We have not only distinctions between dominator and dominated, but also between king and multiple types of officials or courtiers who accompany him. The density of reference in this image is exponentially greater than was true of its predecessors. The Narmer Palette smiting scene is a pharaonic image on a Predynastic object, labeled in hieroglyphic writing, employing the conventions of pharaonic art with regards to profile/full view combinations and use of registers. It has some elements in common with earlier images, but those were not standardized. It has nearly everything in common with later images, which are standardized. It is a turning point.

The combination of specific and universal elements on the Narmer Palette is the underlying reason behind divergent interpretations of the object as recording historical "fact" or mythical kingship. Every one of the specifics is in some way shown as ritualized or abstract, meaning that it certainly is problematic to read the imagery as a straightforward depiction of a military action, even apart from the fact that Egypt was probably "unified" prior to the reign of this king. The dichotomy is probably a false one to begin with, as our notion of history and myth as separable entities has no apparent relation to how the Egyptians understood their world. Rather, as has been recognized by many recent commentators of this piece, all of whom pick up on different nuances of this complex relation, we are probably looking at the mythicized depiction of historical events that are folded into a concept of kingship as physically preeminent and responsible for the unity of Upper and Lower Egypt. It is interesting to note that, while both smiting and the unification of the Two Lands are of supreme importance to the concept of kingship from this point forward, and while both are represented by codified images that are ubiquitous in Egyptian art, there is only one other instance where the two are clearly combined into a single graphic icon (Figure 5.7).[70]

The Narmer Macehead

The Narmer Macehead, which was found in the Hierakonpolis Main Deposit, is a complete object. It is notably smaller than the Scorpion Macehead but still larger than an actual weapon would have been, larger than many of the undecorated maceheads in the Main Deposit (Figure 3.15).[71]

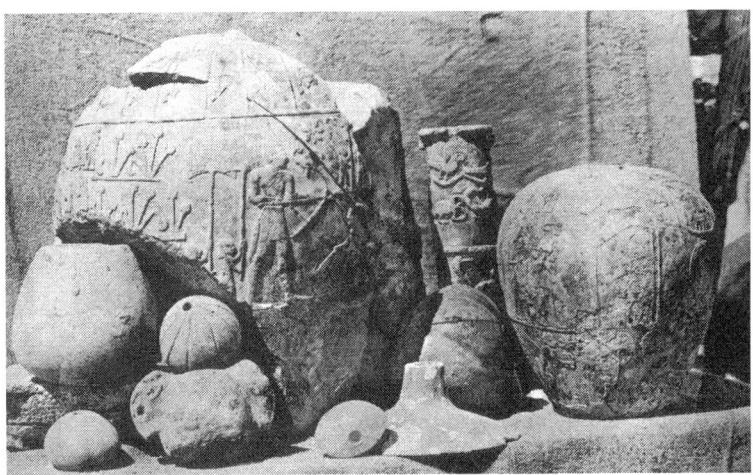

Figure 3.15 Maceheads from the Hierakonpolis Main Deposit. The Narmer Macehead is at the far right. The Scorpion Macehead is at the back left.

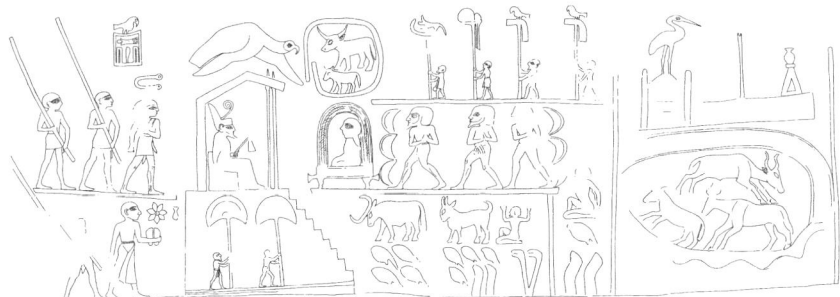

Figure 3.16 Drawing of the relief scene on the Narmer Macehead.

The main focus of the relief on the Narmer Macehead is, as was the case with the Scorpion Macehead, the person of the king, here wearing the Red Crown and sitting within a pavilion; figures of a captive or captives are a minor part of the decoration (Figure 3.16).[72] The king is clearly engaged in a ritual, quite likely an "Appearance of the King of Lower Egypt" as indicated both by his Red Crown and by the shrine associated with the town of Buto in the upper register.[73] Various other people appear in different guises both before and behind him, but all face the king. Three figures run between markers; their hands are clutched in front of them and it has been argued that they are bound, but this is unlikely.[74] A figure who is certainly bound is shown behind and beneath these runners, on the extreme right of the drawing. Only his legs, the lower part of his torso, and his arms remain, but the posture of both arms together behind his back is clear. Unfortunately, the damage to his head makes it impossible to say if he bore any distinguishing marks. He sits above the number 120,000. This may be a reference to numbers of subject people; this demonstrates the blurred line between image and text on such objects. Numbers in Egyptian ceremonial contexts seem unlikely to have been accurate in most cases, and the same is probably true here.

General and specific are both well represented on this macehead as a whole. Though the bound captive cannot be identified, he is probably to be understood as representing a much larger number of people such as himself. He, and the notion of subjugation, are thus made general. The king, as was true on the Scorpion Macehead, is identified both by references to general aspects of kingship—his crown and what we interpret as a recurring ritual occasion—and specifically by his name. The place Buto also seems to be specified. Both the Scorpion and the Narmer Maceheads seem to be primarily documents about ritual aspects of kingship. They connect individual kings to ceremonial actions. Though depictions of captivity are present in both, they are relatively minor in terms of the overall scenes, seeming to suggest almost off-handedly that domination is a part of kingship so basic as to be always present but not in need of shouting. It is well to remember, however, that the object type itself does certainly scream violence.

Ivory objects of Narmer

Two small ivory objects retain images of Narmer's name doing violence to prisoners who are identified as northern. In both cases the catfish of Narmer's name, which is not enclosed in a *serekh* though in each case is pictured close to a falcon, is personified by the addition of human arms. On an ivory cylinder from Hierakonpolis the catfish raises a stick in two arms (Figure 3.17).[75] He brandishes the stick toward three registers containing bound prisoners. The prisoners all face the angry catfish. They are kneeling, with their arms bound behind their backs. They are not visible in great detail, but have beards and hair or wigs. Beneath the stick-wielding name is a label almost certainly to be read as *Tjehenu*, the same word that gives the Libyan Palette its name. Specific with a vengeance. The departure of this scene from the smiting icon is notable. Given the absence of a human figure inflicting damage, the striding posture would be impossible. But the use of a stick held with two hands instead of a mace with one, and the fact that the

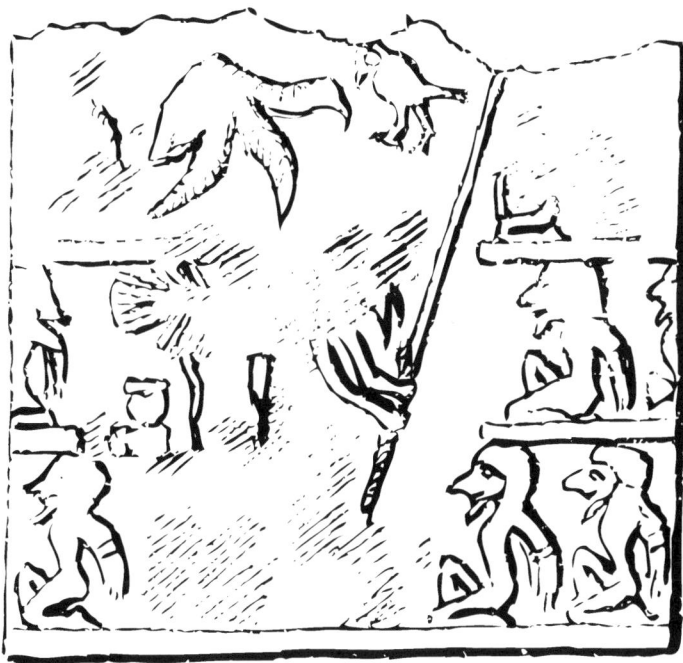

Figure 3.17 Ivory cylinder of Narmer from the Hierakonpolis Main Deposit, showing the king's name brandishing a stick at registers of bound captives.

prisoners are bound, which is unusual in iconic smiting scenes, demonstrate the creativity and flexibility present in images of violence in Narmer's reign.

The second artifact is an ivory tag, pierced in the corner to allow it to be tied to another object, probably one containing the oil referred to on the tag itself (Figure 3.18).[76] Here the catfish raises a mace in one hand, while the other hand reaches forward to grasp a single prisoner by the hair. This scene is thus much closer to the developing icon of smiting and shows that we can recognize it as such even absent the striding posture of an anthropomorphic king. The raised mace, unbound prisoner, and the forward hand of the king (or his name) holding on to that prisoner make this a smiting scene. Atop the head of the captive, who is not bound, is a papyrus plant; this presumably indicates that he represents people of the north. He is further labeled with a *nw* pot, perhaps an abbreviation for *Tjehenu*. If this is the case, given the papyrus on his head, *Tjehenu* seems likely to be a reference to people from the Nile Delta in this instance; this should caution us against thinking that terms we translate with geographic reference— such as "Libyan"—had the same fixed meaning in Egypt.[77] Narmer's *serekh* is to the right. In both of these cases we have an entirely specified king smiting a specified people. The distinction between them is visually extreme, as the king is represented not as a human but instead as a collection of symbols. Both of these objects lie at the intersection of image and inscription. Particularly on the tag,

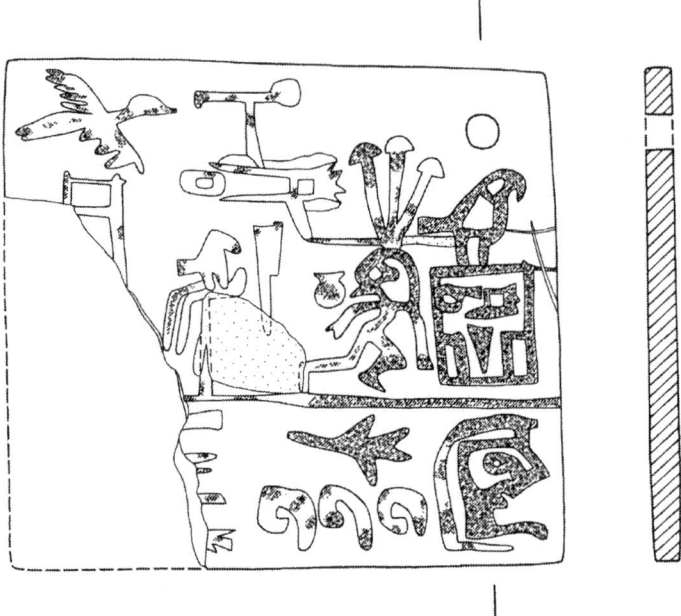

Figure 3.18 Ivory tag of Narmer, with the name of the king smiting a papyrus-headed captive.

a type of object often associated with year names, it is probable that a specific incident is being referred to. Nevertheless, the very nature of smiting prisoners, especially bound ones, is a ritual act rather than a battlefield necessity, and therefore connects these images to the timeless concept of coercive power.

The violent imagery from Narmer's reign is notable for its combination of older elements with radically new ones, and for the frequent use of the smiting motif, which from this point forward can reasonably be considered an icon. In the case of the ivory cylinder with the violent catfish (Figure 3.17) we can see the creative combining of elements that shows the flexibility and even playfulness of imagery in this reign: the binding and the difference in scale between dominator and dominated are old and familiar, and the hitting posture has some precedent, but the specificity—a name for the king, a label for the victims—is new. The palette combines smiting with other images of violence, as was also true in Hierakonpolis Tomb 100 but not elsewhere. Despite this, and though later kings would severely limit the range of ways in which smiting was depicted and the contexts within which it was found, the many iterations of Narmer smiting are for the most part recognizably variations of the same motif. It is the abundance of examples of this motif as well as its restriction to the king that make it so recognizably an icon from this period onwards. It acted to proclaim, presumably even to enable, the ability of the Egyptian king to violently dominate others. The others are variable, but not anonymous, as was the case earlier.

This underscores the ideological role of such imagery. Whether or not actual violent acts against multiple people are represented in such images, the depictions themselves can collectively be read as indicating royal dominion over a broad swath of people who represent larger groups.

The parallels between the Narmer smiting imagery and the Islamic State beheading pictures are numerous and instructive. In both cases the issue of a repeated motif that is recognizable despite differences is clear. Not all Islamic State images take place in the desert and not all victims wear orange, but enough is repeated time and again to link the corpus of images together. Each individual instance is more powerful because of the collective. Likewise, the Islamic State imagery deliberately uses individuals to represent groups, and by referring to a multitude of groups (Westerners, Egyptian Christians, "apostates" from Islam, etc.) makes an ideological claim for the dominance of the Islamic State over all. While the political aspect of the worldview demonstrated in such Islamic State imagery is not centered on a single ruler, as is the case for Narmer, it is notable that in fact one individual does seem to be prevalent though not universal as the beheader, especially in the more canonical of the desert beheadings. An ideological point is unquestionably made in the repetition of this individual, who has been identified as a British man.[78] Even the questions we ask about the historical versus ritual nature of the event shown can be seen as a parallel between these images. This is not immediately obvious—photographs, of course, are powerful in news media in part because they are understood to be, at least to some degree, "true" reports of a moment in time and space. The Islamic State imagery itself demonstrates how problematic this view is and how deliberately manipulated the shown moment was. One indication of this is the apparent rehearsing of the beheading so that, in the moment it actually happened, victims would not believe death to be imminent and would remain calm, serene as the eerily emotionless victims of Narmer's smiting.[79]

A final parallel of note may be seen in the timing of the increase of the use of such imagery. Beheading itself is not new, and images of beheading, particularly as a judicial punishment, were in circulation prior to the existence of the Islamic State.[80] As such, the Islamic State imagery draws on an existing motif. But much like Narmer, the increase in frequency and distribution of such images has been notable in 2014 and 2015, and its creation and dissemination have been deliberate in an unprecedented way. Such imagery in both cases has been central to a period of extremely fast development of a polity. In ancient Egypt such imagery would continue, but its period of most rapid innovation and most diverse use ended with the period of state formation. That this may also be the case for the Islamic State was suggested in 2016.

The transitionary period between the late Predynastic and the Early Dynastic Periods saw the development of many things we consider fundamental to pharaonic Egypt: increasingly standardized writing; monumental architecture; artistic convention; kings recognizable by name, their relation to Horus, their crowns and other attributes. While these elements were, as we have seen with the palettes and knife handles in particular, still capable of a notable amount of variety in the late Predynastic, this appears no longer true in the Early Dynastic. We see then a great restriction on the amount of imagery available and the contexts in which it is available. The most convincing explanation of this "evolution of simplicity" is Wengrow's suggestion that it represents the control of knowledge by the newly defined and empowered Egyptian kingship.[81] Gone are the palettes, gone are the knife handles. Gone are scenes of battle. Early Dynastic images of violence are more restricted in medium and in iconography. Only smiting scenes can be recognized as a distinct pictorial icon; other depictions are hard to separate from writing and even then are rare.

Continuity and discontinuity

Several patterns emerge when early images of violence, those discussed in both this chapter and the previous one, are looked at together. First, the paucity of such images for most of this time, with the exception of the transitional period of the Protodynastic, suggests that depicting violence was not at most times a major strategy of the display and maintenance of power, at least in the contexts we have recovered. Our understanding of the rise of social complexity and hierarchies of power is derived from other means. Depictions of dominance may occasionally have appeared as part of a local and particular way of documenting control—this may be the best way to read the Abydos Naqada I vessels—but violent iconography was not itself a defined structure used to support a static ideology. That does not mean at all that violence was not present, was not used as a means of aggregating power, or was not understood ideologically; it means only that violent imagery itself cannot yet be seen as a consistent tactic of domination. That can only happen once a scene is no longer just a picture, but is an icon. There are icons in Predynastic art, such as boats with figures with raised arms on Naqada II Decorated Ware (Figure 2.7). But I do not think we can demonstrate the presence of icons of violence prior to the reign of Narmer.

Another pattern of note is that scenes of control by captivity are earlier than scenes of control by direct violence, and always more common. In fact, if we leave out scenes of domination and discuss only those that depict moments when people inflict physical damage on other people, we have only Hierakonpolis Tomb 100 from before the Protodynastic Period. Are scenes of domination related to scenes of violence, or to scenes of control over animals, or to both? Hierakonpolis Tomb 100 would seem to suggest both, but again, their very paucity should give us pause before we assume that there was a standard set of meanings and concordances for violent imagery at this time.

The introduction of notable abstractions in images of violence belongs to the Protodynastic Period. A lion eats the fallen. Towns are destroyed by plow-wielding standards and animals. The king's name prepares to hit bound captives. In later material we will see that abstraction is utilized only in limited contexts. The most common is the king as a sphinx or griffin trampling enemies in his own mortuary complex (for example, Figure 4.10 from the Fifth Dynasty reign of Sahure). An exceptional example is the king, shown in human form and smiting plants, from a chapel at a divine temple in the Middle Kingdom (Figure 5.7).

A further pattern to emerge from the early material is that visual distinctions between actors are nearly ubiquitous, present from the start in both scenes of captivity and those of direct violence. These differences can be marked by clothing and/or hair, by size, by posture, or by a combination of these features; from the reign of Narmer onwards they are also marked by textual labels. That distinctions are made so consistently reinforces our understanding that these images always refer to oppositions, and that the oppositions are greater than simple historical battles: they refer on some level to what is right and proper, not just to what happened. This can be seen as notably in contrast to some battle scenes in private contexts of later periods, where there is no visible distinction between sides and no obvious resolution (see, for example, Figures 8.9–10). In the early Predynastic material the distinctions we see cannot clearly be understood as specifying individuals; rather, they seem to refer to groups. The emergence of particular individuals in the imagery is visible only in the period of state formation and should be understood as related to that. Kings are marked as kings in multiple ways: by the *serekh*, by their crowns, by the tails they wear, by the maces they hold. Some of these iconographic elements are new inventions of this period, such as the White Crown and the *serekh*. Some, such as the mace and tail, were present more broadly in earlier imagery but became exclusively royal prerogatives in the reign of Narmer or shortly thereafter.

The marking of difference between actors on the basis of size points to an important distinction between types of scenes that will be maintained until the New Kingdom. Scenes of domination often, though not always, include discrepancies of size. Combat scenes never do. Coupled with this is the failure in combat scenes to distinguish individuals at all, and even a rather surprising lack of clear distinction between victors and vanquished. While differences between actors in such scenes do sometimes mark groups, occasionally but not always recognizable groups, there is never a dominant figure, never an identifiable person. We will see this through the Middle Kingdom. Battle scenes are not yet the place for the king to romp in valor. His violent domination is only depicted elsewhere, in more ritualized scenes.

References to specific places in the imagery also seem to be products of the period of state formation and likewise should probably be read as related to the increasingly defined notion of kingship and a territorial Egyptian state. Place is a difficult topic in this material. With the exception of the Libyan, Bull, and Narmer Palettes, which include representations of walled and labeled towns and blur the line between writing and imagery, places themselves do not show up in the imagery. Rather, it is people of particular groups who are shown in a way that we often read as related to place. This is clearest when people and papyrus plants are combined in the documents of Narmer's reign. But even here this is a somewhat dangerous game—we read papyrus as symbolic of the geographical territory of the Nile Delta, which it certainly was in later times. But some of what we understand to be territorial terms, particularly *Tjehenu*, are better understood as ethnic designations, as demonstrated by the apparent combination of *Tjehenu* and papyrus to designate a captive on Narmer's ivory tag. It is still simplistic to say we then have "Libyans" in the Nile Delta. It is hard for us to leave behind our expectation of a relationship between places and people. We live in bounded nation-states, but this relationship between territory and polity and people was very new if present at all in the time of Narmer, and the ambiguities of place that we see in this material may reflect this. Here, perhaps a comparison to the Islamic State imagery is again revealing. That polity, too, is better defined ideologically than territorially, and complicates the relation between people and place. The iconic Islamic State videos are deliberately blank in landscape; this helps universalize their message. But they do use people to refer to an opposition that includes a geographic element as well as an ideological and political element: The Caliphate against The Outside.

The image from early Egypt that shares the most with the Islamic State beheading images is, as noted above, the smiting scene. It is similarly codified, uses the same repetition of elements that distinguishes recognizable figures, and allows for specific events or peoples to be tied into a larger ideological framework. That the smiting scene is an icon of supreme importance to pharaonic ideology is not in question. In its developed form the message of the smiting image is both simple and adaptable: the king is in control of people and, through them, of places. The control is total, is life and death, and is his alone. The icon is defined by a combination of consistent elements: the king, his posture, a mace, and the captive(s). All of these things can be found in pharaonic art in other types of depictions, meaning that it is the combination rather than the elements that constitute a smiting scene. For instance, the posture of striding, arm raised, can also be used for spearing fish in the marshes. The king can be shown doing a wide range of other things, some of which involve striding. Maces did become almost entirely royal, but kings carry them in contexts other than smiting.[82] Captives can be shown in a variety of situations and media.

That these elements need to be combined to constitute the icon of smiting also means that we cannot see the smiting scene as present in the early material simply because some of its elements are present. The depiction of smiting posture, maces, and captives have long Predynastic histories. But without the king these are not smiting scenes in the iconographic sense, as can be so clearly seen on the Gebel el-Arak knife. Depictions of kings recognizable as such are known only from the reign of Narmer on. From his reign on the smiting icon is a consistent element of pharaonic imagery.

To reject the idea that the smiting icon can be found in pieces, and that those pieces can be read separately as indicative of the presence of kingship, is not to reject that early images of domination and violence held symbolic power and were tied to tactics of power. That even very early imagery incorporates things such as weapons and captivity attests to the long-term development of the ideas behind royal domination in pharaonic Egypt and the importance of violence to the idea and maintenance of power. But ideas of domination and the imposition of order on chaos are so general that it makes no sense to view them as particularly Egyptian, let alone particularly pharaonic. The invention of Egyptian kingship in the Naqada III Period is still worthy of our awe. The development of the smiting icon—deeply ideological, extremely violent—was one of the ways in which

Egyptian kingship operated. Its dissemination in pharaonic Egypt is in many ways similar to the dissemination of Islamic State beheading images: a terrifying warning to those who exist outside the ideological framework it espouses, reassuring and glorious to those within.

This returns us to the always fundamental question of audience. Who would have seen these images? How did the images act? That they tell *us* much about the ideology of the early Egyptian state was certainly not their original purpose. All of the material of known provenance under discussion in this chapter was found either in tombs or in buried deposits at temples, principally that of Hierakonpolis. We do not know if such pieces were used in other contexts prior to their burial, but their find-spots suggest two fundamental things about the development of this imagery.

First, the contexts of these early images of violence mean that their known audiences were not, predominantly, living humans. Rather, such images communicated to the dead and to the gods. We cannot, then, understand such imagery as straightforward propaganda, intended to communicate about the power of a person or group over others as a means of reinforcing that power in a direct human way. We might ask if this is not a matter of bias in recovered contexts, if the Naqada I vessels might not have been used in contexts among the living that did utilize the imagery for the power of convincing. But in some cases this is clearly not the case. Hierakonpolis Tomb 100, for example, was never intended to be seen by a large living audience. The Narmer Palette is unlikely to have been used outside of the temple, and access to the temple was probably restricted. Thus, while it is possible that some of this imagery had now untraceable propagandistic value at some point in its use-life, it is also clear that the need to carry these messages of domination into other spheres—of the dead, of the divine—was a significant factor in their creation.

The second fundamental point is related: these images spoke to an audience that was already part of the worldview thus propounded. These two points are significantly at odds with the scene with which this chapter opened: a widely disseminated set of very similar images that are designed to evoke reactions from living audiences, particularly an audience of "others," those reactions to affect actions and policies. The development of the smiting scene, as far as we can see, occurred inside the elite contexts of Egypt, among those to whom it would have been right and proper, not terrifying. Its use in more public contexts where it might evoke other responses was a later adaptation.

Notes

1 Reyko Huang, "The Islamic State as an Ordinary Insurgency," *The Washington Post*, May 14, 2015, www.washingtonpost.com/blogs/monkey-cage/wp/2015/05/14/how-the-islamic-state-compares-with-other-armed-non-state-groups/?wpisrc=nl_cage&wpmm=1.
2 Lauren Williams, "The Ethics of Banning a Brutal Beheading Video," *ThinkProgress*, August 21, 2014, http://thinkprogress.org/world/2014/08/21/3473831/ethics-behind-blocking-foley-beheading-video/.

3 Identifying Menes with an historically attested king has proved an enduring sport in Egyptology, even as we have come to understand the process of political unification as having occurred over generations. He is usually thought to have been either Narmer or Aha, or perhaps a combination of the two. For a recent discussion, see Thomas C. Heagy, "Who Was Menes?," *Archéo-Nil* 24 (2014): 59–92.

4 For a recent overview of theories of state formation and the history of scholarship on this front, see Christiana Köhler, "Theories of State Formation," in *Egyptian Archaeology*, Ed. Willeke Wendrich (Chichester, West Sussex: Wiley-Blackwell, 2010), 36–54.

5 David Wengrow, "The Evolution of Simplicity: Aesthetic Labour and Social Change in the Neolithic Near East," *World Archaeology* 33, no. 2 (2001): 168–188; David Wengrow, *The Archaeology of Early Egypt: Social Transformations in North-East Africa, 10,000 to 2,650 BC* (Cambridge University Press, 2006).

6 Arguments about the specific date of both classes of artifact and specific examples continue, but are not particularly relevant here. That the densely decorated versions of these objects are in general later than their plainer cousins is well accepted, as is their disappearance in the Early Dynastic Period.

7 For a functional interpretation of the violent imagery on ceremonial slate palettes, see: David O'Connor, "Context, Function and Program: Understanding Ceremonial Slate Palettes," *Journal of the American Research Center in Egypt* 39 (2002): 5–25.

8 Willem van Haarlem, *Temple Deposits at Tell Ibrahim Awad* (Amsterdam: Van Haarlem, 2009); Günter Dreyer, *Elephantine VIII: der Tempel der Satet: die Funde der Frühzeit und des Alten Reiches* (Mainz: Philipp von Zabern, 1986).

9 The original discovery was announced by W.M. Flinders Petrie, "Excavations at Hierakonpolis: The Earliest Monuments of Egyptian History," in *Egypt Exploration Fund Archaeological Report 1897–1898*, Ed. Francis L. Griffith (London: The Egypt Exploration Fund, 1898), 6–10. The more complete early publication is in James Quibell and Frederick W. Green, *Hierakonpolis: Part II* (London: Bernard Quaritch, 1902). Brief bibliographies for individual pieces will be given below.

10 Somewhat earlier examples of plain palettes are also known from the Predynastic cultures of Lower Egypt, but these are not obviously related to the tradition that led to the late Naqada decorated tradition. The most comprehensive study of palettes is Krzysztof Ciałowicz, *Les palettes égyptiennes aux motifs zoomorphes et sans décoration: études de l'art prédynastique* (Kraków: Uniwersytet Jagielloński, 1991). More recent discussion can be found in Diana Craig Patch, *Dawn of Egyptian Art* (New York: Metropolitan Museum of Art, 2011).

11 British Museum EA20791; Ashmolean Museum AN1892.1171. Courtesy of the Trustees of the British Museum and with permission of the Ashmolean Museum, University of Oxford.

12 The smaller fragment is in the Ashmolean Museum (AN1892.1171), the larger in the British Museum (EA20791). A possible third fragment, which does not join the other two, is also known. It shows a quadruped with a bushy tail trampling a fallen man. It is not included here as it is not certain that it belongs to the same palette. James Harris, "A New Fragment of the Battlefield Palette," *Journal of Egyptian Archaeology* 46 (1960): 104–105; Béatrix Midant-Reynes, *The Prehistory of Egypt: From the First Egyptians to the First Pharaohs* (Oxford and Malden MA: Wiley-Blackwell, 2000), 243, fig. 20.

13 W.M. Flinders Petrie, *The Royal Tombs of the Earliest Dynasties: Part II* (London: The Egypt Exploration Fund, 1901), pl. 4.5.

14 Egyptian Museum, Cairo CG 14238. Photographed by Jürgen Liepe. Jacques de Morgan, *Recherches sur les origines de l'Égypte: ethnographie préhistorique et tombeau royal de Négadah* (Paris: Ernest Leroux, 1897), 264, pl. 3. See below notes 16 and 17 for several interpretive studies of this piece.

15 Wengrow, *The Archaeology of Early Egypt*, 208.

16 Fredrik Hagen, "Local Identities," in *The Egyptian World*, Ed. Toby Wilkinson (London and New York: Routledge, 2007), 244; Wolfgang Helck and Eberhard Otto,

"Buto," in *Lexikon der Ägyptologie, Band I*, Ed. Wolfgang Helck and Eberhard Otto (Wiesbaden: Harrassowitz, 1975), 887–889; Wolfgang Helck and Eberhard Otto, "Djebaut," in *Lexikon der Ägyptologie, Band I*, Ed. Wolfgang Helck and Eberhard Otto (Wiesbaden: Harrassowitz, 1975), 1098–1099. The heron's association with Buto from before the Protodynastic Period may be indicated by a tag from Tomb U-j at Abydos. Günter Dreyer, *Umm el-Qaab I: das prädynastische Königsgrab U-j und seine frühen Schriftzeugnisse* (Mainz: Philipp von Zabern, 1998), 130, fig. 80, Tafelchen 127, 128; Francis Breyer, "Die Schriftzeugnisse des prädynastischen Königsgrabes U-j in Umm el-Qaab: Versuch einer Neuinterpretation," *Journal of Egyptian Archaeology* 88 (2002): 56.

17 Marc Etienne, "À propos des représentations d'enceintes crénelées sur les palettes de l'époque de Nagada III," *Archéo-Nil* 9 (1999): 149–163. It has also been proposed that the image shows the foundation of towns: Antonio Pérez Largacha, "The Libyan Palette: A New Interpretation," *Varia Aegyptiaca* 5, no. 3 (1989): 217–226. While the use of the hoe for non-destructive royal action is found on the Scorpion Macehead, this explanation is, on the whole, less satisfying than the explanation that here they represent destruction.

18 Krzysztof Ciałowicz, *La naissance d'un royaume. L'Egypte des la période prédynastique a la fin de la 1ère dynastie* (Kraków: Jagiellonian University, 2001), 180–182; Whitney Davis, *Masking the Blow: The Scene of Representation in Late Prehistoric Egyptian Art* (Berkeley, CA: University of California Press, 1992), 229–233; Breyer, "Die Schriftzeugnisse des prädynastischen Königsgrabes U-j in Umm el-Qaab," 53–65; Kurt Sethe, "Zur Erklärung einiger Denkmäler aus der Frühzeit der ägyptischen Kultur," *Zeitschrift für Ägyptische Sprache und Altertumskunde* 52 (1914): 55–59.

19 Renée Friedman, "The Early Royal Cemetery at Hierakonpolis: An Overview," in *Recent Discoveries and Latest Researches in Egyptology: Proceedings of the First Neapolitan Congress of Egyptology. Naples, June 18th–20th 2008*, Ed. Francesco Raffaele et al. (Wiesbaden: Harrassowitz Verlag, 2010), 70.

20 Dreyer, *Umm el-Qaab I: das prädynastische Königsgrab U-j und seine frühen Schriftzeugnisse*, 173–180.

21 Louvre E 11255, unprovenanced, possibly Abydos. Léon Heuzey, "Un prototype des taureaux de Mycènes et d'Amyclées (Pl. I)," *Bulletin de correspondance hellénique* 16, no. 1 (1892): 307–319; Ciałowicz, *La naissance d'un royaume*, 179–180, fig. 27; Etienne, "À propos des représentations d'enceintes crénelées sur les palettes de l'époque de Nagada III," 149–163.

22 Decorated knife handles probably start somewhat earlier than this, but those with motifs of violence all seem to date to the Naqada III.

23 Diana Craig Patch, "Early Dynastic Art," in *Dawn of Egyptian Art* (New York: Metropolitan Museum of Art, 2011), 155; Winifred Needler, *Predynastic and Archaic Egypt in the Brooklyn Museum* (Brooklyn: The Brooklyn Museum, 1984), 270, 272.

24 Ashmolean Museum AN1896–1908.E497. © German Archaeological Institute Cairo. Helen Whitehouse, "A Decorated Knife Handle from the 'Main Deposit' at Hierakonpolis," *Mitteilungen des Deutschen Archäologischen Instituts, Abteilung Kairo* 58 (2002): 425–446, fig. 1; pictures: pl. 46 a–b.

25 Metropolitan Museum of Art 26.241.1. The drawing here was provided to me by Günter Dreyer, and is the one on display beside the object in the Metropolitan Museum; he is working on publishing this object and has found what he calls a mistake in the reconstruction of the other side (Günter Dreyer, personal communication). A previously published drawing of both sides can be found in Bruce Williams, Thomas J. Logan, and William J. Murnane, "The Metropolitan Museum Knife Handle and Aspects of Pharaonic Imagery before Narmer," *Journal of Near Eastern Studies* 46, no. 4 (1987): 245–285, figs. 1–2.

26 Günter Dreyer, personal communication; I am grateful to him for discussing a piece he is still in the process of publishing.

27 Louvre E 11517. Georges Bénédite, "Le couteau de Gebel el-'Arak: étude sur un nou-vel objet préhistorique acquis par le Musée du Louvre," *Monuments et mémoires de la fondation Eugène Piot* 22 (1916): 1–34; Krzysztof Ciałowicz, "Le manche de couteau de Gebel el-Arak: le problème de l'interprétation de l'art prédynastique," in *Essays in Honour of Prof. Dr. Jadwiga Lipińska*, Ed. Joanna Aksamit et al. (Warsaw: National Museum in Warsaw, 1997), 339–352. The knife has occasionally been thought to be a forgery but this is unlikely, as has been shown by Rainer Boehmer, "Gebel-el-Arak und Gebel-el-Tarif-Griff: keine Fälschungen," *Mitteilungen des Deutschen Archäologischen Instituts, Abteilung Kairo* 47 (1991): 51–60; and Uwe Sievertsen, "Das Messer vom Gebel el-Arak," *Baghdader Mitteilungen* 23 (1992): 1–75.

28 See especially, Holly Pittman, "Constructing Context: The Gebel el-Arak Knife. Greater Mesopotamian and Egyptian Interaction in the Late Fourth Millennium B.C.E.," in *The Study of the Ancient Near East in the Twenty-First Century: The William Foxwell Albright Centennial Conference*, Ed. Jerrold Cooper and Glenn Schwartz (Winona Lake, IN: Eisenbrauns, 1996), 9–32; Ciałowicz, "Le manche de couteau de Gebel el-Arak," 339–352.

29 This is visible on the Hunter's Palette: Davis, *Masking the Blow*, 99. The argument that depictions of hunting in Predynastic Egyptian art are always ceremonial has been made on the grounds that hunting itself was not an important part of the agricultural economy of the time, only an elite pastime. See recently Stan Hendrickx and Merel Eyckerman, "Continuity and Change in the Visual Representations of Predynastic Egypt," in *Recent Discoveries and Latest Researches in Egyptology: Proceedings of the First Neapolitan Congress of Egyptology. Naples, June 18th–20th 2008*, Ed. Francesco Raffaele et al. (Wiesbaden: Harrassowitz Verlag, 2010), 126.

30 See Chapter 2 for caution about interpreting early ceremonies as *heb-seds*.

31 AN1896–1908 E.3632. Mace-head of Scorpion King © Ashmolean Museum, University of Oxford. James Quibell, *Hierakonpolis: Part I* (London: William Clowes & Sons, 1900), 8, pl. 26; Ciałowicz, *La naissance d'un royaume*, 197–202; Patrick Gautier and Béatrix Midant-Reynes, "La tête de massue du roi Scorpion," *Archéo-Nil* 5 (1995): 87–127, fig. 15. Line drawing: Nicholas Millet, "The Narmer Macehead and Related Objects: [Correction]," *Journal of the American Research Center in Egypt* 28 (1991): 223–225, fig. 2.

32 Alain Anselin, "Le scorpion et la rosette: essai de lecture des deux sémogrammes nagadéens," *Apuntes de Egiptología* 1 (2005): 15–33; Thomas Schneider, "Das Schriftzeichen 'Rosette' und die Göttin Seschat," *Studien zur Altägyptischen Kultur* 24 (1997): 241–267; Harry Smith, "The Making of Egypt: A Review of the Influence of Susa and Sumer on Upper Egypt and Lower Nubia in the 4th Millennium BC," in *The Followers of Horus: Studies Dedicated to Michael Allen Hoffman*, Ed. Renée Friedman and Barbara Adams (Oxford: Oxbow Books, 1992), 244.

33 Wengrow, *The Archaeology of Early Egypt*, 213; Patch, *Dawn of Egyptian Art*, 142.

34 UCL 14898; Quibell, *Hierakonpolis: Part I*, pl. 26a; Barbara Adams, *Ancient Hierakonpolis* (Warminster: Aris & Phillips, 1974), 3, pls. 1–2; Krzysztof Ciałowicz, *Les têtes de massues des périodes prédynastique et archaïque dans la Vallée du Nil* (Warsaw: Nakładem Uniwersytetu Jagiellońskiego, 1987), 41–43.

35 Ciałowicz, *Les têtes de massues des périodes prédynastique et archaïque dans la Vallée du Nil*, 41–43.

36 Elise Baumgartel, "About Some Ivory Statuettes from the 'Main Deposit' at Hierakonpolis," *Journal of the American Research Center in Egypt* 7 (1968): 7–14.

37 Not all of the excavated examples were illustrated in the published report on Hierakonpolis. Line drawings in Quibell and Green, *Hierakonpolis: Part II*, 37, pl. 15.1, 15.2, 15.4. The possibility that this type of object is a mace handle was briefly explored by Helen Whitehouse, "The Hierakonpolis Ivories in Oxford: A Progress Report," in *The Followers of Horus: Studies Dedicated to Michael Allen Hoffman*, Ed. Renée Friedman and Barbara Adams (Oxford: Oxbow Books, 1992), 78.

38 Quibell, *Hierakonpolis: Part I*, 7.

39 Quibell, *Hierakonpolis: Part I*, 7, pl. 12.4–12.6.
40 Votive deposits in early temples were a particular focus of Richard Bussmann's *Die Provinztempel Ägyptens von der 0. bis zur 11. Dynastie* (Leiden: Brill, 2010). Discussions of this phenomenon at specific sites, but including comparison to such deposits elsewhere, can be found in Dreyer, *Elephantine VIII: der Tempel der Satet*, 37–54; and van Haarlem, *Temple Deposits at Tell Ibrahim Awad*, 76–85.
41 van Haarlem, *Temple Deposits at Tell Ibrahim Awad*, 80.
42 Ciałowicz at Farkha falls into the former category, and van Haarlem's publication of the Tell Ibrahim Awad material follows the later tactic. Krzysztof Ciałowicz, "Early Egyptian Objects of Art," in *Tell el-Farkha I: Excavations 1998–2011*, Ed. Marek Chłodnicki, Krzysztof Ciałowicz, and Agnieszka Mączyńska (Kraków: Institute of Archaeology, Jagiellonian University, 2012), 201–244; van Haarlem, *Temple Deposits at Tell Ibrahim Awad*.
43 Courtesy of the Polish Archaeological Expedition to the Nile Delta. First figurine: Ciałowicz, "Early Egyptian Objects of Art," 206–207, fig. 8; second figurine: Ciałowicz, "Early Egyptian Objects of Art," 209–210, fig 13.
44 van Haarlem, *Temple Deposits at Tell Ibrahim Awad*, no. 20. The drawing and description do not match one another for this item, which is listed as "lower legs fragment . . . quite damaged"—the drawing makes clear it is not. The dimensions are also apparently for a different piece, and so I am not certain about the material, which is listed as ivory.
45 van Haarlem, *Temple Deposits at Tell Ibrahim Awad*, nos. 64–75; he identifies these as crawling figures rather than captives.
46 Richard Bussman, *Die Provinztempel Ägyptens von der 0. bis zur 11. Dynastie*, 242, 250, 294.
47 Dreyer, *Elephantine VIII: der Tempel der Satet*, 54–58; van Haarlem, *Temple Deposits at Tell Ibrahim Awad*, 82–83. Hans Wolfgang Müller and Ernst Kofler-Truniger, *Ägyptische Kunstwerke: Kleinfunde und Glas in der Sammlung E. Und Kofler-Truniger, Luzern*, Münchner Ägyptologische Studien 5 (Berlin: Verlag Bruno Hessling, 1964).
48 Harco Willems, "The Social and Ritual Context of a Mortuary Liturgy of the Middle Kingdom (CT Spells 30–41)," in *Social Aspects of Funerary Culture in the Egyptian Old and Middle Kingdoms*, Ed. Harco Willems (Leuven: Peeters, 2001), 318ff; Georges Posener, *Cinq figurines d'envoûtement* (Cairo: Institut français d'archéologie oriental du Caire, 1987). Richard Bussman illustrates the dangers of such an assumption with the case of crocodiles, *Die Provinztempel Ägyptens von der 0. bis zur 11. Dynastie*, 215–17.
49 This carving has been the subject of extensive and ongoing study and debate. Arkell published the first photographs of the inscription. Murnane published a new drawing of it that has been the basis of most subsequent discussion. A more recent redrawing was undertaken by Xavier Droux and Renée Friedman; their revisions and comments upon them were the subject of a paper presented in 2014 at the Fifth Origines Conference in Cairo, but have not yet been published. Friedman and Bruce Williams are currently undertaking a new study; Bruce Williams, "A New Collation of the Gebel Sheikh Suleiman Monument" (paper presented at the annual meeting for the American Research Center in Egypt, Atlanta, Georgia, April 16, 2016), and personal communication. The preliminary conclusions of Friedman and Williams are not entirely in line with another recent interpretation based on first-hand observation by Somaglino and Tallet: Claire Somaglino and Pierre Tallet, "Gebel Sheikh Suleiman: A First Dynasty Relief after All," *Archéo-Nil* 25 (2015): 122–134. Anthony Arkell, "Varia Sudanica," *The Journal of Egyptian Archaeology* 36 (1950): fig. 1, 28, pl. 10; William J. Murnane, "The Gebel Sheikh Suleiman Monument: Epigraphic Remarks," in Bruce Williams and Thomas J. Logan, "The Metropolitan Museum Knife Handle and Aspects of Pharaonic Imagery before Narmer," *Journal of Near Eastern Studies* 46 (1987): 282–285.
50 Predynastic rock and cave art was the focus of *Archéo-Nil* volume 19, 2009: "L'art rupestre des déserts égyptiens."

51 Riemer's work is an example of conscientious treatment, but his conclusions are correspondingly broad and therefore unsuited to use in a study that depends on a relatively tight chronology. He acknowledges the problems of dating and iconographic comparison to other media. Heiko Riemer, "Prehistoric Rock Art Research in the Western Desert of Egypt,"*Archéo-Nil* 19 (2009): 33. For a general critique of approaches to rock art in Egyptology, see Wengrow, *The Archaeology of Early Egypt*, 111–114.

52 For example, John Darnell writes of a rock-carved image of a man following a boat that "[t]he cosmographic imagery employed to represent royal power during the late Naqada II Period gives way to a depiction of royal power as a suitable vision of cosmic stability." John C. Darnell, "The Wadi of the Horus Qa-a: A Tableau of Royal Ritual Power in the Theban Western Desert," in *Egypt at Its Origins 3: Proceedings of the Third International Conference "Origin of the State. Predynastic and Early Dynastic Egypt," London, 27th July–1st August 2008*, Ed. Renée Friedman and Peter Fiske (Leuven: Uitgeverij Peeters en Departement Oosterse Studies, 2011), 1179–1180. This statement may very well be true, but it rests on a series of unprovable assumptions about who the figure is, what the image as a whole shows, what the specific date of the image is, and what its relationship to a series of other examples with equally grey representations and dates is.

53 Murnane, "The Gebel Sheikh Suleiman Monument: Epigraphic Remarks," 283.

54 Somaglino and Tallet, "Gebel Sheikh Suleiman: A First Dynasty Relief after All," 127. However, Köhler has noted that the *serekh* with the dotted name section has parallels to potmarks on large storage vessels in this period, which may help to date the inscription to the era of Narmer. E. Christiana Köhler, "History or Ideology? New Reflections on the Narmer Palette and the Nature of Foreign Relations in Pre- and Early Dynastic Egypt," in *Egypt and the Levant: Interrelations from the 4th through the Early 3rd Millennium BCE*, Ed. Edwin C.M. van den Brink and Thomas E. Levy (London and New York: Leicester University Press, 2002), 502.

55 The most usual interpretation has been of a bow. Murnane questioned this reading on the assumption that the inscription was probably near the place it referred to, and Gebel Sheikh Suleiman is not really in "bow land" as usually understood. See Murnane, "The Gebel Sheikh Suleiman Monument: Epigraphic Remarks," 282, n. 5. I do not think this issue can be resolved; neither the geographic specificity of the association with bows nor the expectation that the inscription is explicitly historical and would need to be near the place of a victory thus commemorated can be demonstrated. That the presence of a bow might indicate an A-Group rather than Egyptian authorship for the carving has also been suggested but is not widely accepted: Bruce Williams, "The Lost Pharaohs of Nubia," *Archaeology* 33, no. 5 (1980): 19.

56 Somaglino and Tallet, "Gebel Sheikh Suleiman: A First Dynasty Relief after All," fig. 5.

57 Arkell, "Varia Sudanica," 29; Murnane, "The Gebel Sheikh Suleiman Monument: Epigraphic Remarks," 283.

58 Williams, "A New Collation of the Gebel Sheikh Suleiman Monument."

59 The possibility that anonymous *serekhs* are such generalized symbols in other contexts has been recognized. See Stan Hendrickx, "Arguments for an Upper Egyptian Origin of the Palace-Facade and the Serekh during Late Predynastic-Early Dynastic Times," *Göttinger Miszellen* 184 (2001): 94–95; Mariusz A. Jucha, "New Protodynastic Serekhs from the Nile Delta: The Case of Finds from Tell el-Farkha," *Polish Archaeology in the Mediterranean (Research 2009)* 21 (2012): 638. This reading disagrees with the specifically historical interpretation offered by Somaglino and Tallet of a war fought by the First Dynasty king Djer, which relies not only on the form of the *serekh* and boat, but also on proposed readings of several hieroglyphs, some of which other scholars have thought to be later additions to the inscription. It is not so much that I think Somaglino and Tallet are wrong as that their conclusions are not, from my point of view, provable, and that I am more comfortable seeing the ambiguity as a potentially intended part of the record. Somaglino and Tallet, "Gebel Sheikh Suleiman: A First Dynasty Relief after All."

60 It has now been moved to the National Museum in Khartoum as its original location was flooded when the Aswan High Dam was built.

61 Arkell, "Varia Sudanica," 28.
62 Nearby inscriptions include one in Karian, left by a first millennium BC mercenary; the image under discussion here was also partly defaced by graffiti dated to the Middle Kingdom. Arkell, "Varia Sudanica," 28.
63 The closely contemporary Scorpion Macehead may fall into the same category, but as "Scorpion" is written without a *serekh*, and as a king Scorpion from this time is not otherwise definitively attested, the artifact raises more questions than it answers. It would in any case be the exception that proves the rule, as Narmer has numerous artifacts with scenes of violence and his name written in an unambiguous manner. As noted above, some other objects such as the Libyan and Battlefield Palettes that show animals associated with kings may simply be missing inscriptions, and therefore may refer to specific kings rather than generalized notions of power and/or kingship.
64 The impulse to teleologically interpret early art, which I have tried to work against throughout this book, is particularly strong for the reign of Narmer. For discussions of some of its problems and bibliography, see David Wengrow, "Rethinking 'Cattle Cults' in Early Egypt: Towards a Prehistoric Perspective on the Narmer Palette," *Cambridge Archaeological Journal* 11, no. 1 (2001): 95.
65 Here I agree with Toby Wilkinson, who has seen this reign as a defining moment in the creation of Egyptian kingship: Toby Wilkinson, "What a King Is This: Narmer and the Concept of the Ruler," *The Journal of Egyptian Archaeology* 86 (2000): 23–32. I disagree, however, with Wilkinson's contention that this involved a discarding of older traditions. Rather Narmer's reign seems to me to mark the consolidation of older ideas, the bringing of universal ideas under the heading of kingship, and the beginning of the restriction of the display of such images to the royal sphere itself. How much monumental building is present in the reign of Narmer is still a matter of debate. It seems likely that he built a temple at Abydos for his own cult. Laurel Bestock, "Brown University Abydos Project: Preliminary Report on the First Two Seasons," *Journal of the American Research Center in Egypt* 48 (2012): 35–79.
66 Line drawing by Barry Kemp.
67 James Quibell, "Slate Palette from Hierakonpolis," *Zeitschrift für Ägyptische Sprache und Altertumskunde* 36 (1898): 81–84; Quibell, *Hierakonpolis: Part I*; and Quibell and Green, *Hierakonpolis: Part II*. The bibliography on this object is extensive and continues to grow. Two recent treatments, with extensive bibliographies, can be found in David O'Connor, "The Narmer Palette: A New Interpretation," in *Before the Pyramids*, Ed. Emily Teeter (Chicago, IL: The Oriental Institute of the University of Chicago, 2011); and Maria Michela Luiselli, "The Ancient Egyptian Scene of 'Pharaoh Smiting His Enemies': An Attempt to Visualize Cultural Memory?," in *Cultural Memory and Identity in Ancient Societies*, Ed. Martin Bommas (London and New York: Continuum International, 2011).
68 Erik Iversen, *Canon and Proportions in Egyptian Art*. 2nd ed. (Warminster: Aris & Phillips, 1975). This is rebutted by Gay Robins, *Proportion and Style in Ancient Egyptian Art* (Austin, TX: University of Texas Press, 1994).
69 The early history of the crowns of Egypt is not particularly well understood. The first instance of something shaped like a Red Crown is a raised decoration unassociated with a human figure on the shoulder of a pot dated to the Naqada I. Joan Crowfoot Payne, *Catalogue of the Predynastic Collection in the Ashmolean Museum* (Oxford: Clarendon Press, 1993). The crown or something like it is also known as headgear on human figures from rock drawings that have sometimes been dated to the Predynastic Period, including three figures in different tableaux near the Wadi Hammamat, noted by Hans Alexander Winkler, *Rock-Drawings of Southern Upper Egypt* (London: Egypt Exploration Society, 1938), pls. 13–14; discussed recently by Stan Hendrickx et al., "A Lost Late Predynastic–Early Dynastic Royal Scene from Gharb Aswan," *Archéo-Nil* 19 (2009): 173–174. Dating these closely is not possible, and it is thus uncertain if they predate the reign of Narmer (Hendrickx et al., "A Lost Late Predynastic–Early Dynastic Royal Scene," 174).
70 The binding of the Two Lands has its own icon, the *sema-tawy*, in which the heraldic plants of Upper and Lower Egypt are tied around one another. This is not a violent

icon, and is known first in the Old Kingdom. It is perhaps surprising how *rarely* icons of unification and physical domination were condensed into one.

71 Quibell, *Hierakonpolis: Part I*, pl. 25.
72 AN1896–1908 E.3631. Macehead of King Narmer © Ashmolean Museum, University of Oxford. Line drawing: Millet, "The Narmer Macehead and Related Objects: [Correction]," fig. 2.
73 Millet suggested this was more likely than the more common interpretation of a *heb-sed*, and his reasoning is convincing: Nicholas Millet, "The Narmer Macehead and Related Objects," *Journal of the American Research Center in Egypt* 27 (1990): 56.
74 Millet examined the piece and produced a new drawing: Millet, "The Narmer Macehead and Related Objects"; Millet, "The Narmer Macehead and Related Objects: [Correction]." He rejected the contention by Helck that the wrists of these men were bound, and indeed it would be an otherwise unattested type of binding. Millet, "The Narmer Macehead and Related Objects," 55, note 5.
75 Ashmolean Museum E3915. Quibell, *Hierakonpolis: Part I*, 7, pl. 15.7.
76 The use of such ivory, bone, or wood labels to label commodities was already ancient; such tags from tomb U-j at Abydos offer our first extant evidence of writing from Egypt. © German Archaeological Institute Cairo. Günter Dreyer et al., "Umm el-Qaab: Nachuntersuchungen im frühzeitlichen Königsfriedhof: 9./10. Vorbericht," *Mitteilungen des Deutschen Archäologischen Instituts, Abteilung Kairo* 54 (1998): 113–145; fig. 29; Ilona Regulski, "Scribes in Early Dynastic Egypt," in *Zeichen aus dem Sand: Streiflichter aus Ägyptens Geschichte zu Ehren von Günter Dreyer*, Ed. Eva-Maria Engel, Vera Müller, and Ulrich Hartung (Wiesbaden: Harrassowitz, 2008), 581–611. They probably always served both an administrative function with regard to commodities and an ideological function, with representations related to royal ritual. See Lisa Mawdsley, "Two Labels of Aha: Evidence of a Pre-Mortuary Administrative Function for First Dynasty Potmarks?," *Cahiers Caribéens d'Egyptologie* 15 (2011): 53; Alejandro Jiménez-Serrano, *Royal Festivals in the Late Predynastic Period and the First Dynasty* (Oxford: Archaeopress, 2002), 20–24.
77 Dreyer et al., "Umm el-Qaab: Nachuntersuchungen im frühzeitlichen Königsfriedhof: 9./10. Vorbericht," 138–139, fig. 29.
78 Souad Mekhennet and Adam Goldman, "'Jihadi John': Islamic State Killer Is Identified as Londoner Mohammed Emwazi," *The Washington Post*, February 25, 2015, www.washingtonpost.com/world/national-security/jihadi-john-the-islamic-state-killer-behind-the-mask-is-a-young-londoner/2015/02/25/d6dbab16-bc43-11e4-bdfa-b8e8f594e6ee_story.html.
79 Rebecca Ratcliff, "Isis Tricked Victims into Appearing Calm with Beheading Rehearsals," *The Guardian*, March 10, 2015, www.theguardian.com/world/2015/mar/10/isis-tricked-victims-into-appearing-calm-with-beheading-rehearsals.
80 An example is a widely circulated image of a Saudi beheading, one iteration of which can be found illustrating an article in an English language Egyptian newspaper about executions in Saudi Arabia from March 2013: "Saudi Arabia May Stop Beheading Due to Swordsmen Shortages," *AhramOnline*, March 10, 2013, http://english.ahram.org.eg/News/66531.aspx. Images of this particular execution have been used to illustrate a range of news articles about different beheadings, and so its relation to a specific event has largely been lost. Beheadings for judicial purposes are not generally reported on with imagery in a systematic way, demonstrating the difference between those images that do exist and the very calculated making and distributing of Islamic State beheading videos.
81 Wengrow, "The Evolution of Simplicity," 168–188; Wengrow, *The Archaeology of Early Egypt*.
82 Maces are shown on some Middle Kingdom private coffins, but there they are not held by people.

4   To live forever

The decoration of royal mortuary complexes

Eugene Delacroix painted *La Liberté guidant le peuple* (Figure 4.1) in 1830.[1] The central figure is a woman, distinguished from all others in the scene by her sex, her stature, her pallor, the icon of the tri-color flag she brandishes, the clarity with which we can see her, the bright cloud of smoke that serves as a nimbus behind her head. The diagonal line of the flagpole in her raised hand is echoed in the rifle with a bayonet she holds in her other hand. There is an exceptional amount of movement in the painting, from the flapping flag and ribbons of Liberty's dress to the boy at her side waving two pistols, to the man in the crowd behind her with a sword above his head. This movement is in contrast to the stasis of the foreground, where figures lie dead. One in particular seems to mirror Liberty.

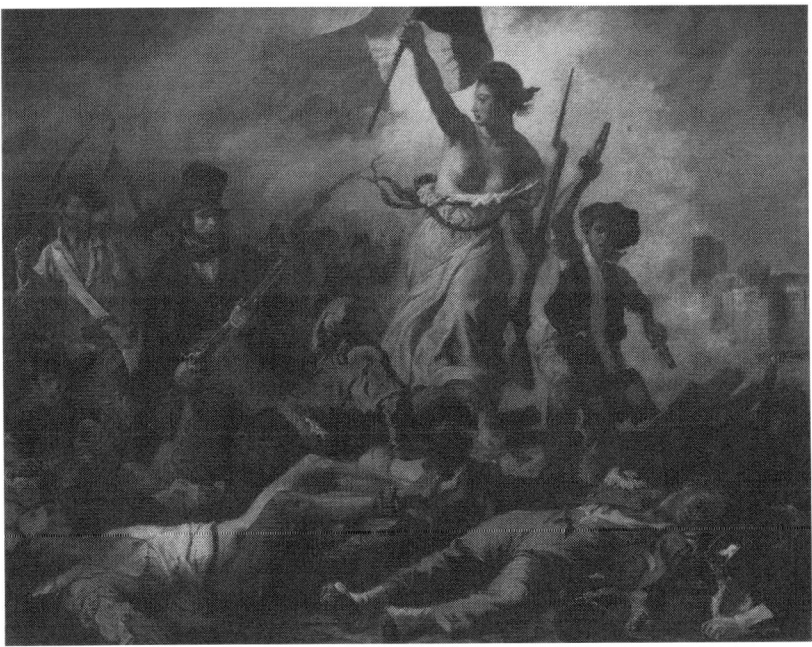

Figure 4.1 La Liberté guidant le peuple, oil on canvas, Eugene Delacroix.

He, too, is half-undressed; he, too, has pale skin and clothes. But he has been killed, and she must lead the populace to victory. The image is extremely violent, though the particular moment shown is rather in between actual moments of destruction. The pile of dead serves as a pedestal for Liberty, who leads her ragtag but heavily armed cohort on to further action. The city burns in the background.

Liberté presents us with a concept that has been shown as a living woman, placed within the framework of an actual historical event. This elevates the event to the level of ideology, of being a demonstration of the proper functioning of the world. The figures are not at all equal: the protagonist is large and well lit, while those who might be considered ordinary people are subordinate to her; there is no preeminent human. The prominence of a youth to the right of Liberty seems to highlight that the people are varied and not hierarchical—there is room for multiple entwined ideals here, even if one is central. The violence of the image serves to underline the difficulty and importance of the concept at stake: it is an ideal not only worth fighting for, but also worth dying for. The specific moment is connected to past historical events—an audience would be forgiven for thinking it refers to the Revolution of 1789 instead of the overthrow of a tyrant in 1830—and this, as well as the embodied ideal of Liberty, allows it to serve as a general moral statement.

At its most basic level, then, Delacroix's painting conflates an actual event with a cosmic narrative, and does so with an image that is highly unlikely to have been anything one might actually have observed on the battlefield. The 1830 revolution was right and proper because it was connected to a larger historical trajectory in which France violently upheld its ideals. Those ideals would triumph—perhaps inevitably, in the view of the painting, since they are led by such a symbol—but they had to be fought for, and fought for repeatedly.

The ways in which an image can bridge ideal and real, event and ritual, symbol and history, form the backbone of the following consideration of violence in Egyptian kings' tombs and in the contexts that follow in subsequent chapters. In the Egyptian royal tomb, the concept at stake was kingship, but this was every bit as much an ordering principle of the universe as Liberty was and is in France. Like Liberty, kingship had to be upheld through repeated violence, and the depiction of that violence was more than a passive reflection of ideology or a report on events. It also convinced its audiences in ways that made image and audience complicit in upholding the right working of the universe.

The royal tomb complex is the most consistent and best represented type of context in which images of violence occur in the Old and Middle Kingdoms; it also preserves the largest variety of such images. Most of the tombs in question, with the exception of that belonging to king Nebhepetra Mentuhotep of the Eleventh Dynasty, are pyramids. By the time images of violence begin to decorate royal tombs, the elements of a standard Old Kingdom pyramid complex had been set (Figure 4.2 shows a plan of Sahure's Fifth Dynasty pyramid complex as an example).[2] In addition to the pyramid itself, which housed the burial chamber, there was a temple abutting the pyramid on its east side (variously called a pyramid temple or a mortuary temple in scholarly literature; I will use the term

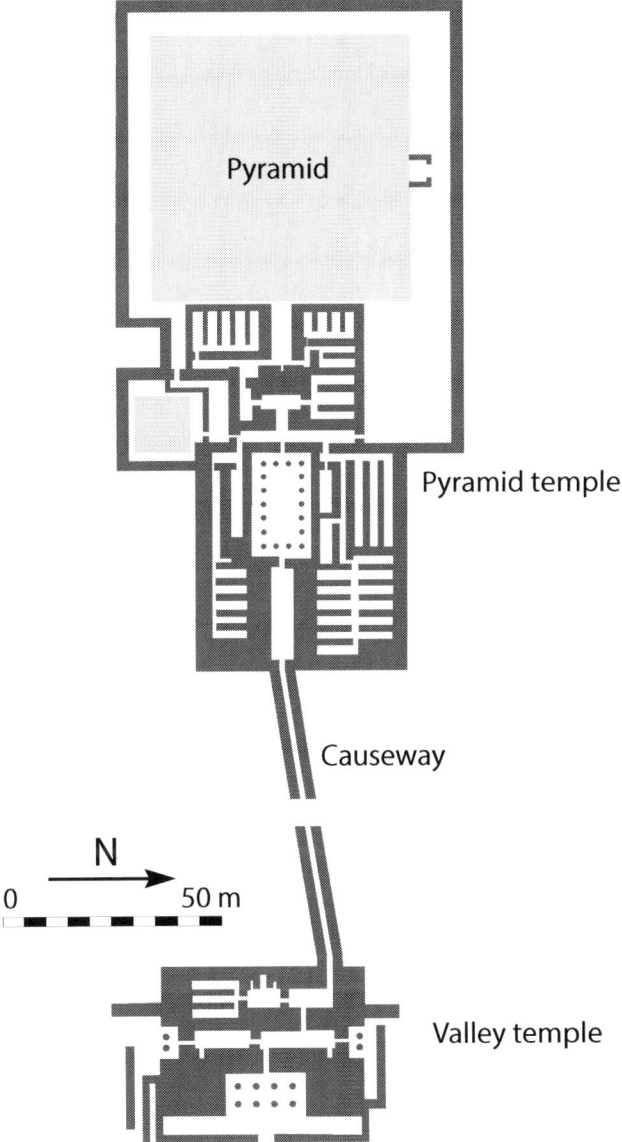

Figure 4.2 Schematic plan of the pyramid complex of Sahure at Abusir, Fifth
Dynasty. While proportions and details of pyramid complexes changed
dramatically, all of the Old Kingdom complexes discussed here had the
same essential elements and arrangement, with the pyramid itself on the
west and the temples and causeway on the east. All scenes of violence, as
all scenes of any sort from these complexes, are found inside the temples
and causeway.

pyramid temple as that is descriptive, while mortuary temple involves a level of interpretation); a long causeway running east-west, enclosed by high walls and usually covered; and what we call a valley temple on the east. Less standardized elements included additional small pyramids, an enclosure wall around the main pyramid, and boat burials. Only the interior walls of the temples and causeway were decorated with relief scenes.

Pyramids were built in the low desert to the west of the cultivated land that was annually flooded by the Nile, and the valley temples were often near or even imme-diately adjacent to the line of the flood. All of the Old Kingdom pyramids are in necropoleis near the then capital of Memphis. At the very beginning of the Middle Kingdom, Nebhepetra Mentuhotep built his tomb as an unusual terraced structure in and in front of the cliffs at Thebes, in the south; many parts of this were carved with relief scenes, including ones of battle. His successors in the Twelfth Dynasty returned to building pyramid complexes in the north; these were less standardized than their Old Kingdom predecessors in location and layout, but retained many of the same elements. At no point were the interior parts of pyramid complexes, includ-ing the elements that received decoration, public monuments. As such, the principal audiences for the imagery discussed here are likely to have been the deceased king himself, as well as the divinities with whom he associated in the afterlife.

Violence of all types—smiting, trampling, battle—was a regular and perhaps even required part of the decorative program of royal tomb complexes from quite early in the history of the Old Kingdom, almost as early as decorative relief programs for such monuments started existing at all. Smiting scenes we have encountered previously; they are present in this context in much the same iconic form already seen on the Narmer Palette (Figure 3.14). Trampling scenes involve the king as a fantastical leonine beast, either a griffin or a sphinx, treading on helpless enemies. Battle, which in this context is seen only between ordinary soldiers and certainly never involving the king, is represented both by massed soldiers acting in unison and by hand-to-hand combat. While the royal tomb complex consistently employed violent themes among its imagery, violence does not ever appear to have been the most prominent or profuse pictorial element in this context.

This chapter will address all examples of images of violence decorating royal tomb complexes of the Old and Middle Kingdoms known to me, particularly looking for patterns and shifts that speak to an understanding of the role of depicting violence in royal ideology. Some attention will also be paid to scenes of bound captives under control of people or gods, as these are important for understanding the development of visual ethnic stereotypes. The great majority of the material gathered here consists of fragments of painted raised relief on limestone. Seven kings of the Old Kingdom and three of the Middle Kingdom have extant remains of violent reliefs from their mortuary complexes. Relief scenes are presented here chronologically, with brief additional descriptions of statues of captives found in royal tombs.

Preservation of the relief programs from these monuments is in all cases poor. It is also often not possible to tell precisely where in a given complex a scene might have been placed. When the original location is known or reasonably reconstructed,

I present the evidence in the order the deceased king himself would have encountered it when leaving his burial in the pyramid: first the pyramid temple, then the causeway, and finally the valley temple. The state of preservation also affects our ability to date some fragments, particularly those in reused contexts. Dating of fragments without royal names on them relies on stylistic comparison to a very limited body of securely attributed reliefs; dates are changed in publication regularly, which demonstrates the difficulty of such attributions. In general I have not engaged in the battles about date, but have arranged things according to the most recent scholarly consensus. Finally, because the material is in all cases fragmentary, it is always impossible to say how many such scenes a particular king had, or to suggest that a king had none when none are preserved.

Despite the problems of preservation, provenance, and date, I offer a few observations and numbers before diving into the evidence in hopes that they will help to situate the reader. Seven Old Kingdom kings have preserved remains of violent scenes from their mortuary complexes. This includes one Fourth Dynasty king, four Fifth Dynasty kings, and two Sixth Dynasty kings. The Middle Kingdom mortuary complexes in general are even more poorly preserved. Our evidence of this type of scene from the Eleventh Dynasty reign of Nebhepetra Mentuhotep is very good; more fragmentary bits are known only from the reigns of Senwosret I and III (the latter only from his monument at Dahshur, not his Abydos burial complex). Within this group of ten kings from both Kingdoms, eight have known smiting scenes, three have trampling scenes (plus an additional one if jewelry is added into the mix),[3] and four have battle scenes. Smiting is thus the most commonly represented type, and two kings in this group have remains of smiting scenes but no other violent motifs (Userkaf and Pepy I). This is probably due to preservation; it is by far the most common for kings to have multiple of these scene types, and when we can tell they seem to have been present in multiple areas of the pyramid complex. A particular subset of triumphant scenes deserves special mention from the start: the so-called Libyan Family Scene, in which the king despatches a Libyan leader while a Libyan woman and two Libyan children watch in distress, is present in at least three and possibly as many as seven complexes.[4] In two of the certain cases this is a smiting scene, in one a trampling scene. The specificity of the Libyan Family Scene raises issues of historical accuracy that will be addressed in the conclusion to this chapter.

The presence of the Libyan Family Scene also points to one of the major concerns with this material: visual ethnic stereotypes are frequently employed to mark and define foreigners and victims of this violence. The Libyan stereotype is extremely consistent. A stereotype of "Asiatics," sometimes further differentiated by inscriptions and perhaps by purposeful alterations of distinct iconographic details, is also quite consistent. Both Libyan and Asiatic stereotypes come in male and female versions. Most kings who have violent scenes at all include both of these peoples within them, but differently. Both, for instance, can be victims of smiting or trampling (men only, in both cases). Only Asiatics are shown as victims of battle (only men in combat itself, but women can be shown as suppliants or captives).

Another visual ethnic stereotype that is consistent through the Fifth and Sixth Dynasties, but not before or after, is harder to pin down but is usually assigned to people from the south; they appear as both Puntites and Nubians in the scholarly literature.[5] In these two Dynasties it is regular to find in reliefs, only as victims of triumph or in captivity, men wearing chevron-shaped armbands; hair fillets—thin headbands tied around the forehead and hair; and usually three longer locks of hair draped over their shoulders beneath their more regular hairdos. The skin of such people, when color is present, is red-brown. I have found only three possible and imperfectly parallel contemporary images with labels that might help us determine the ethnic or geographic designation of such a stereotype. Three men with related attributes are shown as small relief figures in two tombs at Giza. All three are labeled as Nubians. In one tomb, a man wears three (?) locks of hair slightly separate from the wig at the shoulder. In another both of these locks and a fillet are present on one Nubian, and the fillet alone on another. None wear chevron armbands.[6] A visual ethnic stereotype of Nubians in a form more familiar from later examples is clearer in material from other contexts, but does seem to have been used in Middle Kingdom royal tomb complexes: both Nebhepetra Mentuhotep and Senwosret III have fragments of dark-skinned archers.

The Old Kingdom

The Fourth Dynasty

It is not known precisely when images of violence were first added to the growing repertoire of pyramid complex scenes, but it can be located with some confidence in the early Fourth Dynasty. Suggestions that Snefru had smiting scenes are unprovable,[7] and in fact smiting scenes are not preserved from any of the Fourth Dynasty pyramid complexes. While Khufu is known to have had a relatively extensive relief program in his pyramid temple, and perhaps in his valley temple, there are no extant violent images.[8] Khufu's successor, Khafre, is probably the first king for whom we have evidence of the utilization of violent or related motifs, which are present on two fragments whose dates have been the subject of some debate. No later Fourth Dynasty evidence remains.

A limestone block with relief found in association with Khafre's complex, though of uncertain precise provenance, includes an image of a bound prisoner facing another man; this, then, is not precisely violence but rather a representation of the aftermath of domination (Figure 4.3).[9] The preserved piece shows two heads and torsos. On the right, a figure with red-brown skin and very short black hair faces to the left, his left hand raised to his mouth. He wears crossed straps on his chest. His right hand is unfortunately in a poorly preserved section, but that arm is reached out toward the second figure, who faces him. This facing man has both arms raised, his elbows painfully tied together with a rope and held over his head while his useless hands flop to the sides. He has long hair, yellow skin, and a short pointed beard that crawls up his cheeks, all features associated with stereotyped images of "Asiatics."[10] They are slightly different in details but still

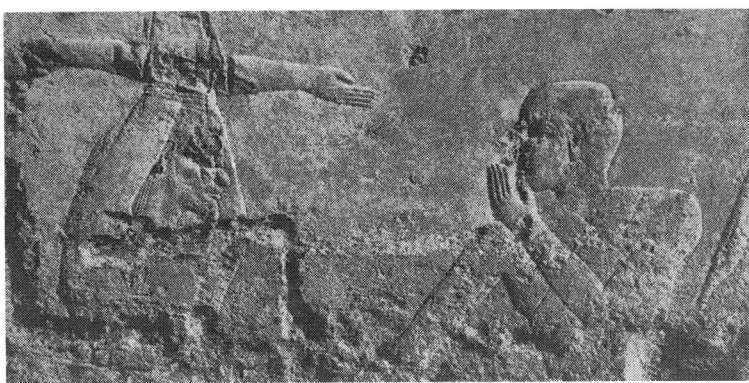

Figure 4.3 Detail of relief on a limestone block found at the pyramid complex of Khafre
at Giza. On the right is an Egyptian, not the king; on the left is a prisoner with
bound arms raised above his head. His short beard and long hair are visual
stereotypes usually associated with the depiction of Asiatics. Dimensions of
whole relief: 50 × 70 cm.

recognizably similar to some of the features of the man being smote by Den on an
earlier label from Abydos, where the inscription makes clear that he is from the
east (see Figure 7.3).

The two figures on Khafre's relief may have been part of a larger vignette
showing conflict and its aftermath. To the right of the Egyptian can be seen the
tip of a shallow-bladed axe; this is at the height of his shoulder, making it difficult to understand what role it plays in the composition. On the same block,
not visible above, is preserved the bottom part of a register above that with the
bound prisoner.[11] Here are the legs of four figures, two on each side, facing one
another. The leftmost figure wears a calf-length kilt. Having groups of figures of
the same size facing one another is relatively unusual and could indicate oppos-
ing forces. The long kilt in that case might be an ethnic marker. Oppenheim has
noted that this scene is remarkable not only for being the first known depiction
of a foreigner in a royal pyramid complex but also for being, in conjunction with
the following piece, the first time a "fleeting moment" rather than a "frozen,
timeless" ritual scene is shown.[12]

The second fragment with violent imagery dated stylistically to the reign of
Khafre and thus probably originally from his mortuary complex, though it was
found at Lisht, comes from a scene showing a rank of massed archers, their bows
drawn (Figure 4.4).[13] The clean-shaven men with slightly hooked noses have red-
brown skin. Their black hair is cropped close to their heads. They wear thick
white straps crossed on their torsos. Each grasps three arrows, fletched with feathers and with slightly broadened, blunt tips. One arrow is held against the taut
bowstring, the other two in the hand grasping the bow, ready to reload. The bows
do not appear to be fully drawn; they are nearly straight, curved only at their ends,

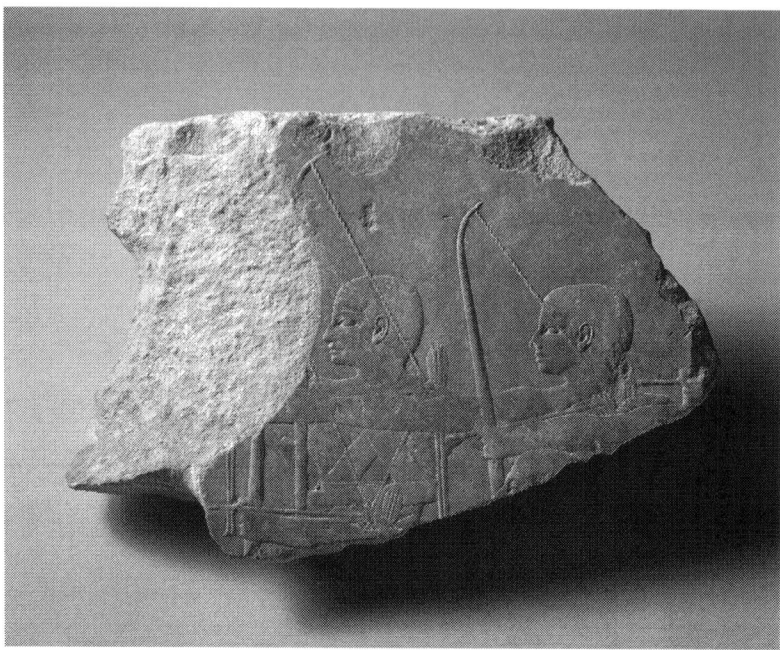

Figure 4.4 Relief fragment showing archers firing in unison, probably from the pyramid complex of Khafre at Giza, Fourth Dynasty. Found reused at Lisht. Dimensions: 25.4 × 37.5 cm.

and the hands pulling the arrows and bowstrings back are clutched in front of the men's chests rather than pulled back entirely.

Two men at the top of the fragment have their faces entirely preserved, as well as parts of their torsos. They stand at the same level as one another. A third archer at this level is preserved only in his bow-holding, outstretched arm. Part of the head of a fourth archer is visible to the lower right; he indicates that there was a second row of archers, perhaps kneeling. These two rows of bowmen act together but show subtle differences, such as the angle at which the bows and arrows are pointed, which make the scene more than just a tessellation of repeated shapes. The impression conveyed is both one of military precision, with ordered ranks acting in unison, and one of slight variation that makes the soldiers somehow more human and the moment more momentary, and less timeless.

There is little doubt that this is an image of military combat (or less likely, training). The crossed chest straps worn by the figures are often (though not always) worn by archers, and the preparation to fire in rank and unison distinguishes the scene from a hunt. The object at which the arrows are fired is unclear and cannot be reconstructed by analogy to better preserved scenes. Other images of battle show either hand-to-hand fighting or attacks on fortified places.

While the latter can include multiple men of the same army firing bows at the same time, archers are never again depicted in ranks in this overlapping way. This is true for both royal and private contexts.

The Fifth Dynasty

The Fifth Dynasty is the high point for numbers of preserved reliefs showing violence in royal tombs, with a plethora of examples and a variety of types from several pyramid complexes located at both Saqqara and Abusir. From later in the Dynasty it is clear that images such as smiting scenes were incorporated into larger tableaux that included many standardized elements. Because of this, though the earliest Fifth Dynasty fragments preserve only the non-violent elements of these larger scenes familiar from somewhat later depictions, it seems quite probable that the smiting scene itself was in use as part of the relief program from at least the beginning of the Dynasty, and that its use was a standard and fairly static element of the relief program. The same can also probably be said of other military elements, such as scenes involving running troops and ships; because such scenes do not show violence directly, they are not considered here. Since the only preserved battle scene comes from the last reign of the Dynasty, it is not clear if this was a regular element of the decoration.

Userkaf

The earliest hint of a smiting scene comes from the badly disturbed mortuary complex of Userkaf at Saqqara. All that remains of this image is a depiction of the goddess Seshat and a bit of a caption mentioning *seqer*: smiting. The fragment is probably from the pyramid temple, and is thought to have come from either the transverse corridor or the pillared hall before the statuary niches.[14] Despite its small size, this fragment can be interpreted as depicting the goddess recording booty and accompanying a smiting scene that is witnessed by a family, based on analogy to a better preserved scene of Seshat from the pyramid temple of Sahure at Abusir (see below, Figure 4.5) as well as later Old Kingdom examples.[15] In later examples the combination of these elements becomes regular and defines what can be called the Libyan Family Scene.

Sahure

The reign of Sahure is much better represented in remaining reliefs than that of his predecessor, and it includes more complete examples of scenes of and relating to violence than any other king's reign. Sahure was buried in a pyramid complex at the site of Abusir, an area not previously used for royal burials, which lies between Saqqara and Giza. Sahure's scenes of violence make it clear that this theme is folded into large and complex tableaux. The relations between different parts of these scenes are not always clear, however. Violent elements found in the decoration of Sahure's mortuary complex at Abusir include a

Libyan Family Scene of smiting; the king as a sphinx trampling his enemies, a scene not attested earlier; archers; and gods with bound prisoners. Related scenes not addressed here include running soldiers and ships bringing both goods and people from foreign lands to Egypt. Most of these reliefs are in Berlin, though this pyramid complex is the subject of ongoing excavation and new fragments have been recently discovered.

The tableau that once included the king smiting a Libyan chieftain is represented now by a block from the west end of the south wall of the columned hall of Sahure's pyramid temple (see Figure 4.2 for a plan of the temple and Figure 4.5 for the relief).[16] The block includes several different elements. Only a very small portion of the smiting scene itself remains—only the elbow of a raised arm of a prisoner—but its reconstruction at the leftmost part of the relief is secure. The accompanying inscription reads "smiting the chief of the *Tjehenu* (Libyans)."[17]

In the much better preserved portion that accompanied the smiting, Seshat is seated on a throne to the upper right. She has scribal palettes over each shoulder and writes on a board in front of her. The text before her specifically states that she records the number of captives brought from all foreign countries, though only the west is represented in the reliefs. In front of her are three registers of people, including men, women, and children. All of the adults kneel and face to the left, most with their hands raised in supplication. They wear crossed and decorated straps across their chests, as well as elaborate necklaces or ties that hang down their torsos. The men have small, pointed beards and penis sheaths. The women also appear to have a sort of hanging element at the waist; these are indistinguishable in the relief from the men's penis sheaths. Both men and women have semi-circular elements at their hips. All of the adults and perhaps some of the children appear to sport forehead ornaments that look similar to Egyptian uraei. All of these are attributes of the visual ethnic stereotype of Libyans. Beneath Seshat and the Libyans are four registers, each with a different and numbered type of livestock. The use of labels and numbers gives an aura of both specificity and historicity to this scene; this is both magnified and to a degree called into question by the presence of Seshat. Yes, here a goddess of writing is making a documentary record of what is happening. On the other hand, her very divine nature places the scene firmly within the ritual sphere.

This divine/historic combination is maintained throughout the rest of the relief. The bottom register is divided in two. To the right stand two divinities connected via inscriptions with western lands: Ash, Lord of *Tjehenu*, and the Goddess of the West. The Goddess specifically says she is offering to the king the chief of the *Tjehenu* (Libyans). To the left are three Libyans: two children and one woman. They are dressed identically to the Libyans above, but they are standing, facing left, each with one arm raised. They are provided with their names. This is evidently the family of the Libyan chief, who is presumably about to be smote by the king in the now missing left portion of the scene. The scene as a whole is one of carefully recorded living booty, some of which will soon be dead, facing the smiting king. Even gods labeled in a way that connects them to the subjugated people participate in offering the captives to the king.

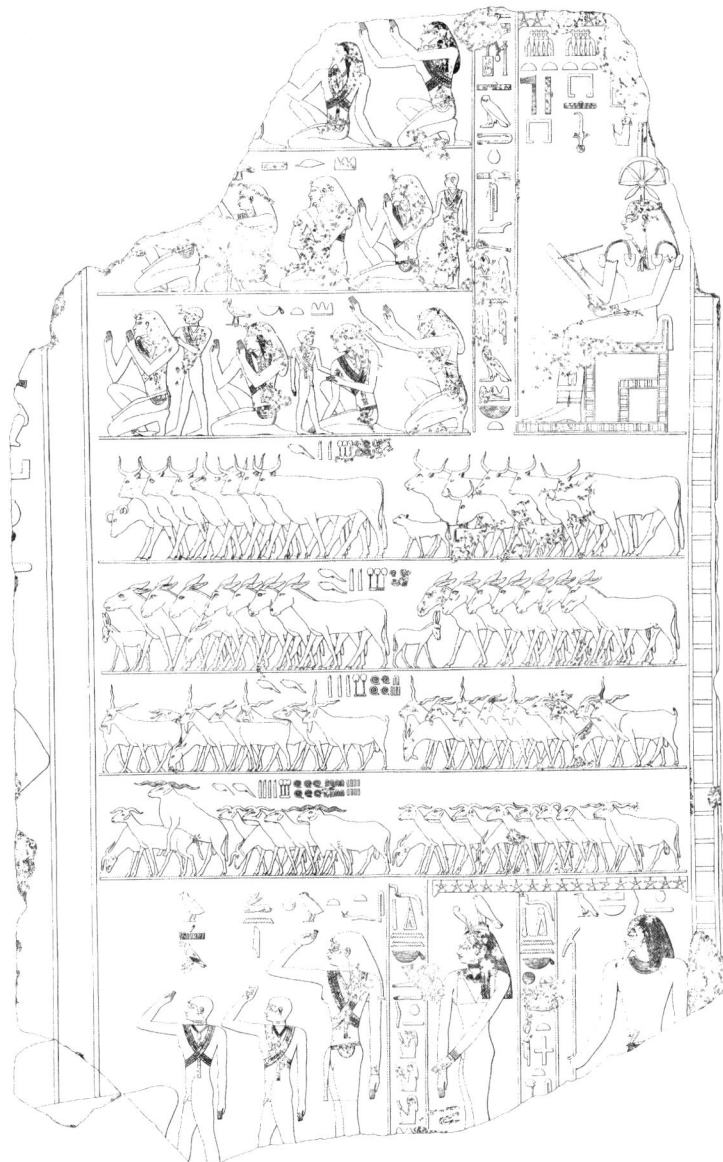

Figure 4.5 Relief from the pyramid temple of Sahure at Abusir. The goddess Seshat records booty, including humans and animals from Libya. At the bottom, two children and a woman raise their hands to their heads in apparent dismay; they look toward the almost entirely destroyed image of the smiting king. This "Libyan Family Scene" became codified, even down to the names of the watching family. Dimensions: 87 × 57 cm.

Additional fragments from the pyramid temple are too small to read with certainty, but suggest at least another smiting scene (the hand of the king holding a mace faces the wrong way to have been part of the known Libyan Family Scene).[18] Another fragment shows another family with raised hands; it includes two adults behind the children, and so likely comes from an expeditionary scene rather than a smiting scene. A better-preserved relief does show eight ships with not only Egyptian soldiers but also Asiatic men, women, and children with arms raised in supplication. It has been suggested that there might have been an Asiatic family/smiting/booty scene parallel to that of the Libyans, but this is not definitively attested elsewhere and so is less certain.[19]

If the possible "Asiatic Family Scene" and the Asiatic expedition really belong together, it would be a juxtaposition of "good foreigner/bad foreigner" themes that are rarely quite so overtly contrasted in Egyptian art, though both are common. Whatever their relationship to one another, the presence of violent scenes and "good foreigner" scenes in Sahure's pyramid temple demonstrates that, ideologically if not actually, it is not just the *action* of subduing foreigners that is proper to the king. On the contrary, the *state* of being acknowledged as overlord by foreigners—and Egyptians—who pose no violent threat is also conventional.

The causeway of Sahure's pyramid complex at Abusir preserves a large number and variety of scenes with violent motifs, but very few that are explicitly violent. Related scenes include ships returning from an expedition, captive foreigners, soldiers on the march, and troops in training. Of particular note in the causeway are the variety of peoples shown as well as the variety of poses and relations articulated. Because these scenes are not explicitly violent, I will not address them comprehensively and will instead highlight only those most useful for shedding light on the themes considered in this chapter.

One of the most remarkable and well-preserved scenes from the entire mortuary complex of Sahure shows registers of bound prisoners, their binding ropes held by gods (Figure 4.6).[20] The position of some of the captives, with arms above their heads, is reminiscent of the relief from the complex of Khafre (Figure 4.3), though in that case an Egyptian directly faces the bound man; this is not the case in the Sahure composition, which has a very formal arrangement. The block with this scene was originally from the east end of the north wall of the causeway, thus close to the valley temple.[21] It was part of a larger scene that once presumably included the king on the left. Four registers containing figures are partially preserved on this relief. The top and third rows contain deities who hold ropes; the ropes lead to the human figures, all adult males, in the second and fourth rows, who are bound and controlled by the gods. The gods are labeled but the prisoners are not, though they are rather distinguished by the use of detailed visual stereotypes. The top row of gods is badly preserved, but was probably fronted by Horus, by analogy to Seth in the first position of the third row.[22] Behind him comes a goddess, then a god, then another goddess. Only two gods of the second row are preserved: Seth and the "Lord of the Hill Countries," Sopdu, represented here with the pointed beard that is often a stereotypical attribute of an Asiatic. All of the deities grasp *Was*-scepters in their right hands, and in their left hold *ankh*s and

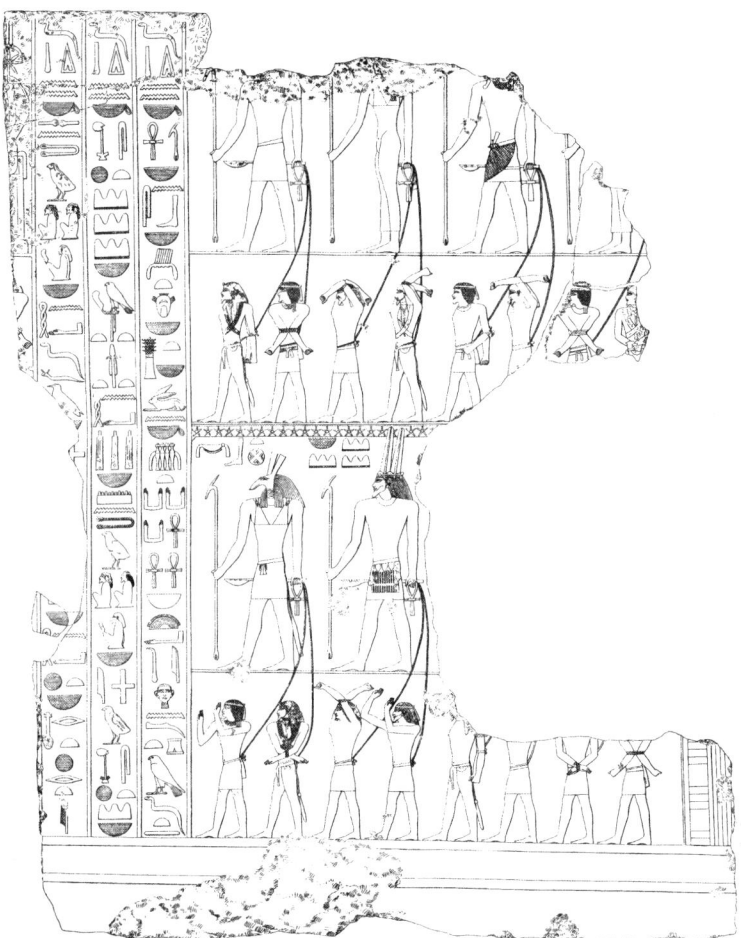

Figure 4.6 Gods hold ropes leading to bound prisoners of various ethnicities in the registers below them, from the causeway of Sahure's mortuary complex at Abusir. Not all of the captives are of identifiable ethnicity, and some may represent Egyptians. Dimensions: 54 × 43.2 cm.

the ropes that bind the captives below them. The male deities also hold axes with arced, fenestrated blades in their left hands.

The prisoners below the gods are shown at a smaller scale than their captors. They are differentiated from one another by their hair, clothing, and position. Most have their arms bound at the elbow, either behind their backs or above their heads, but two in the bottom row have their hands free to raise in supplication to the king; these two are certainly still captive as shown by the ropes attached to their waists. This is the first preserved scene that allows for a detailed and comparative study of the iconography of visual ethnic stereotypes in Egypt.

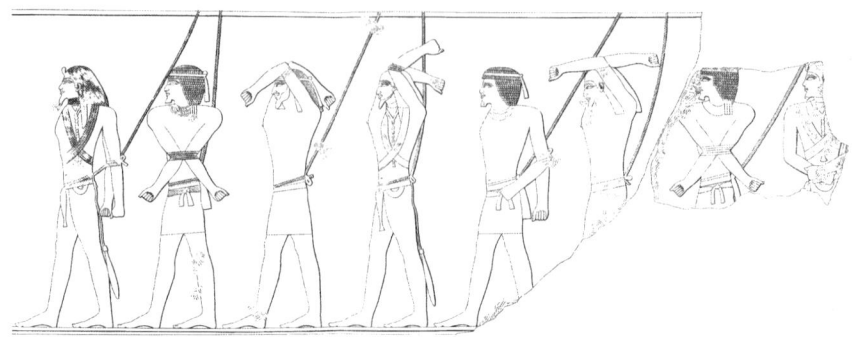

Figure 4.7 The upper register of bound captives from Sahure's causeway, showing
details of the visual ethnic stereotypes present in the scene as a whole. The
fifth figure from the left may be Egyptian. Dimensions: 10 × 26.4 cm.

Some of the prisoners are Libyan, shown with the same stereotypical attributes as the Libyan men in the Libyan Family Scene from this complex. Other
men, with pointed beards and fillets, are shown in the same way as the Asiatics
from the ships mentioned above; this stereotype, too, has been substantially
codified by this point. Some figures appear at first quite similar to Egyptians
but are distinguished by three small locks hanging from their wigs over their
shoulders, by fillets in their hair, by a somewhat odd form of belted kilt, and
by chevron-shaped armlets on their upper arms.[23] These are our probable southerners. However, not all human figures perfectly match any of the three types
defined by these attributes. Borchardt, who excavated the relief, suggested that
additional foreign lands might be represented in the imagery alongside the traditional three.[24] One, the fifth man in Figure 4.7,[25] might even be Egyptian. It is
in any case likely that some ambiguity or at least blurred distinctions between
peoples are deliberate factors in this scene of captives differentiated by such
attributes, as is the decision not to label them. This has the effect of suggesting a
generalized "all" as the subject of captivity here.

The accompanying inscription to the left consists of speeches of the gods,
who tell the king that they bring him foreign peoples belonging to three specified groups. While the words used for the peoples involved are not entirely
straightforward, it is clear that they specify people from the east and west. Clearly
identifiable people from the south are absent in the inscription.[26] That some of
the figures cannot be confidently identified according to ethnic stereotypes, and
that one of the gods who holds the ropes binding captives is explicitly a god
from beyond the bounds of Egypt, as indicated both by his name and his depiction, makes it impossible to read this image as a straightforward statement about
Egyptian control of foreigners.

Recent discoveries have provided additional fragments of imagery related
to violence from Sahure's causeway, in most cases giving additional examples

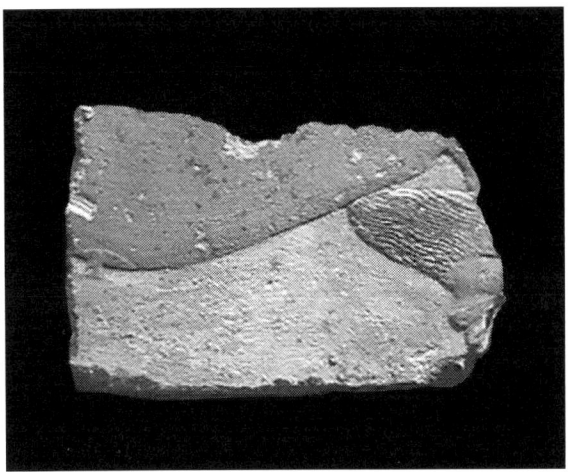

Figure 4.8 A small fragment from Sahure's causeway showing the pointed beard of an Asiatic in a painful posture that suggests victimhood, perhaps as part of a trampling scene.

of types of scenes already known from elsewhere in the complex. For instance, a small fragment with the chest and bearded chin of a presumed Asiatic in an uncomfortable position was excavated near the eastern end of the causeway (Figure 4.8).[27] This is in the same vicinity as Borchardt's discovery of the scene of gods leading bound prisoners. The neck of the Asiatic is bent forward at an angle that makes him unlike the bound prisoners; it is possible that he was a victim in a trampling scene, though once more the parallels are not perfect. He may also have been shown with his arms bound behind his back.

Finally, the recent causeway excavations of Sahure's mortuary complex have uncovered a block with a type of scene not previously known here: the king's nautical crews undergoing various sorts of military training.[28] This block has five registers of which the top three contain training and contests. The top register shows an archery lesson with four different scenes, each with two figures (Figure 4.9 shows one of these groups).[29] These are perhaps the same two figures—in each case an instructor and trainee—shown at different stages of the lesson. Both have similar characteristics, with close-cropped hair and bare chests; the instructors wear kilts while the archers wear aprons. The archer in each case stands facing right with bow drawn, ready to loose his arrow at a target that has already been shot multiple times. As was the case with Khafre's archers, the shape of the bow and the position of the archers' hands are not really accurate representations of what shooting looks like. In these vignettes, the instructor stands behind the archer, arms on his shoulders, the two of them clearly looking together down their shoulders and straightened arms along the length of the bow. Inscriptions accompany the scenes, with the instructor giving different advice each time.[30]

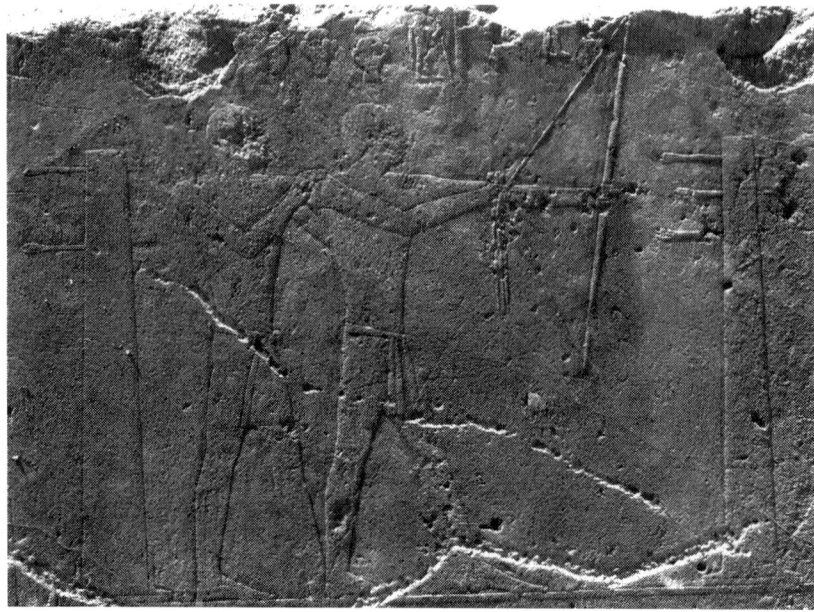

Figure 4.9 One of several vignettes showing archery target practice from the causeway
      of Sahure's mortuary complex at Abusir.

Arrows stuck in the target are all over the place; this guy needs all the advice he
can get, and quite a bit more practice.

   The second register of the block that shows archery practice contains images
of stick fighting, again with instructors giving a hands-on lesson with advice and
exhortations to fight.[31] These men wear simple kilts with no aprons. The third register shows six wrestling contests labeled as occurring between the crew and workers,
who all wear aprons. The wrestlers are in different positions in each case and one
set of them is observed by a referee who is dressed similarly to the instructors in
the top registers. The advice in this case, if given, has not been preserved.[32] These
scenes are remarkable for showing troops that are not in formation, in contrast to
the more common images of men running together, and for showing what could be
considered a "before." This is very rare with images of violence but not unusual in
other types of scenes, where, for instance, the bringing of columns for construction
or the fashioning of a statue are familiar motifs. The juxtaposition of wrestling with
military scenes can be seen in private tombs at Beni Hasan (Chapter 8).

   The valley temple of Sahure's pyramid complex has a range of scenes of or
related to violence, including one of the most spectacular trampling scenes
known from ancient Egypt, and military personnel in more pacific pursuits.
In the trampling scene, the king is pictured as a winged feline, most often called
a griffin (Figure 4.10).[33] Three of his legs, shown with exquisitely modeled mus-
culature, his tail, and part of his winged back are preserved. That it is the king,

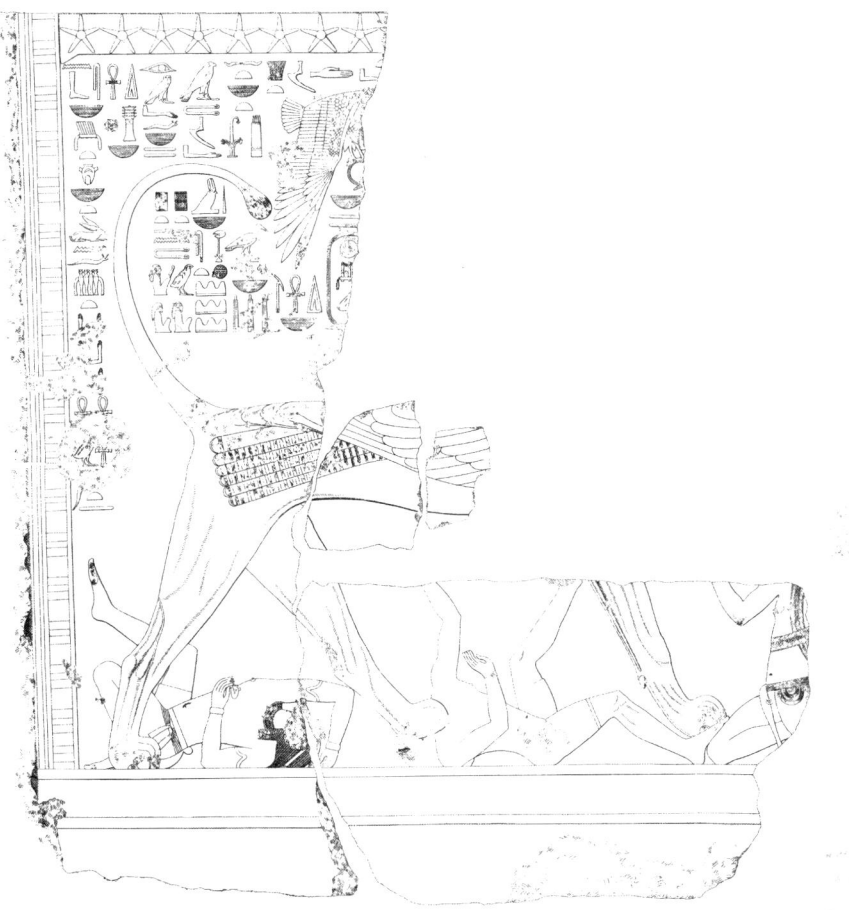

Figure 4.10 Sahure as a griffin tramples three people with different attributes in his
valley temple at Abusir, Fifth Dynasty. Dimensions: 61.2 × 54 cm.

specifically as an incarnation of the god Horus, is evident from the inscription
above him. At the bottom of the scene are three helpless enemies. On the left lies
a contorted man with one leg bent in the air and one arm thrown above his head.
He wears a short kilt and a collar, bracelets and chevron-shaped armlets. His
left hand is held to his chest where it touches an *jb* sign, presumably representing his heart. His head is partly destroyed, but he wears a wig with ringlets and
a fillet. This figure certainly bears the same stereotypical markers as the least
identifiable of the marked people in the scene of gods leading prisoners from the
causeway (see above Figures 4.6 and 4.7).

The middle figure is pinioned by two paws of the trampling king, one of
which obscures the face of the victim and one of which holds down his right foot.

His left foot is in the air, as are both of his hands. This figure wears a garment that clings to his thighs, similar to modern bicycle shorts, but presumably representing a split kilt. The paw of the king would have always obscured most of the figure's head, though there is also some damage at this point. There are no obvious ethnic markers on this figure, which thus might be read either as a generic enemy or as an Egyptian.

The third figure, on the right, is only partially preserved but is clearly dressed in the same fashion as the Libyans discussed above in the scene with Seshat; his fancy crossed chest straps and penis sheath are unmistakable. This Libyan is kneeling rather than stretched out on the ground. He raises his front hand and faces the king. It is likely that the king's front paw either held or swatted this figure. All three victims are clearly subjugated by the feline king in quite painful fashion. The trampling king faces to the right, heading out of the temple.

There are preserved parts of an inscription to the upper left of the trampling scene, partly enclosed within the curled tail of the violent king. The inscription makes clear that this is Horus Sahure doing the trampling: Horus, strong of arm, who acts with his own arms. The king is also called "he who tramples the *Senetiu*"—that word, best translated as rebels or enemies,[34] is written with three different foreign peoples as determinatives, ideographic signs at the end of a word that are not pronounced. These three figures all have long hair. One balances a feather on his knee, one wears a fillet, one or more may have beards. Their iconography is thus not precisely the same as that of the trampled victims, but it might be said to convey the same message of plurality and difference. The inscription also refers to the binding together of the bows—the bows, while not specified in number in this case, are a reference to the totality of Egypt's enemies, often represented as the Nine Bows.[35] In this inscription it is thus the state of the peoples—as enemies or rebels—rather than specific geographic associations that is stressed.

The trampling scene is allegorical. It cannot relate to any particular action, historical or ritual. The king might metaphorically be said to rage on the battlefield like a griffin; we might even connect this to the image of a lion tearing out the chest of a fallen enemy on the Battlefield Palette (Figure 3.1). But no texts or images ever indicate a single battle against such a diverse set of enemies, nor is it easy to imagine how one could have occurred. To trample them simultaneously while in the form of a griffin is an expression of the ideological role of the king as physically dominant; it has nothing to do with historical action, and does not try to suggest that it does. This is thus a different type of scene than seen previously, and not only because it employs a new motif. However, particularly in light of observations about other scenes from this complex, we must once more pause to ask about whom precisely the king is shown to dominate. Here the middle victim is the most interesting. Why has he no visible attributes of origin? From consideration of the pyramid complex as a whole, we would perhaps expect Libyans, Asiatics, and our presumed southerners to be shown. Two of these are here, but an Asiatic is missing. If the artist needed to include an Asiatic, why did he obscure the parts of the body—chin and hair—that would make him most obviously so (as was indeed the case with the small fragment from the causeway, Figure 4.8)? This figure may have been painted yellow, now faded, but even that would not have differentiated between an Asiatic and a Libyan. Given, too, that the inscription is not specific about the peoples trampled, I am most comfortable seeing this figure as intentionally ambiguous, the best way of making sure that this allegorical scene could cover all possibilities and was not limited by its own narrow references.

Not only content but also location within the pyramid complex perhaps illuminate the functions of Sahure's images of violence. They are found in a limited number of areas. The most violent images are the trampling scenes and the smiting scene; there are no known battle scenes from this complex. The trampling scene found by Borchardt came from the valley temple, probably at the point of transition to the causeway. It is linked with a scene of the king's ship and running soldiers. An additional fragment of a trampling scene was found near the causeway, very close to the valley temple; it may originate from that temple. The smiting scene is found in the columned hall of the pyramid temple on the west side, again at a point of transition to a different element of the complex. These two types of violent scenes do not represent conquest itself; if they are to be read as related to combat at all, they represent its aftermath. The same can be said of the scene of gods presenting bound prisoners to the king and of the ships returning from Asia with un-bound but still presumably subject foreign people. The latter images, the least obviously related to violence, come from the interior part of the pyramid temple and from the causeway.

On the whole, it seems that images related to violence were utilized somewhat differently in different parts of the complex; were located primarily at points of transition within the pyramid complex; and were particularly prevalent on the eastern sides of each of the three decorated elements of the complex. What might differences between their placement in the pyramid temple, causeway, and valley temple tell us? The causeway has only one small fragment from a triumph scene, and what might be termed the most informal depictions seen here—the training scenes. These are informal in composition and, when compared to ritual smiting or allegorical trampling, informal in terms of depicted events. Does this reflect the fact that the causeway is a passage, and probably not the location of ritual actions as specifically as either of the two temples?

What does the apparent emphasis on the east mean? Geographic references in Egyptian architecture can be very specific, and perhaps we should read this as indicating a particularly hostile relationship with the east. This is at odds, however, with the content of the images preserved, in which the east is only one focus, with the west being at least as prominent. The apparent focus on points of transition may be the most intriguing element of location, as well as that which is easiest to be confident about given the vagaries of preservation and the difficulty of arguing from negative evidence. In later periods, images of violence could play a protective role, guarding, for instance, the outer doorways of temples. It is possible that this was already the case, though the inclusion of violence on interior walls suggests that the decorum of such protection changed notably over time.

Niuserra

The next king with preserved relief fragments of violence is Niuserra. From his complex at Abusir we have multiple examples of the smiting scene, as well as a fragment of a trampling scene. As was the case with Sahure, there are no battle scene fragments known from the complex of Niuserra.

From the pyramid temple of Niuserra come many small fragments from a smiting scene or scenes that, for the first time since Hierakonpolis Tomb 100, include a group of captives bunched together (Figure 4.11; it is of course possible that the earlier Libyan Family Scenes discussed above included captive groups, though the preserved elements do not allow us to know).[36] This is made clear by the repetition of four feet on tiptoe, all in a close-packed row, and by another fragment where four elbows are similarly together. These are given different colors. The very close repetition of these body parts in these poses is not known from anything other than a smiting scene, making their identification likely despite the small size of the fragments. This, if it really represents a shift, is important both in terms of the visual pattern created by the repeated body parts and because smiting multiple people is different than smiting one. It is not physically possible to grasp

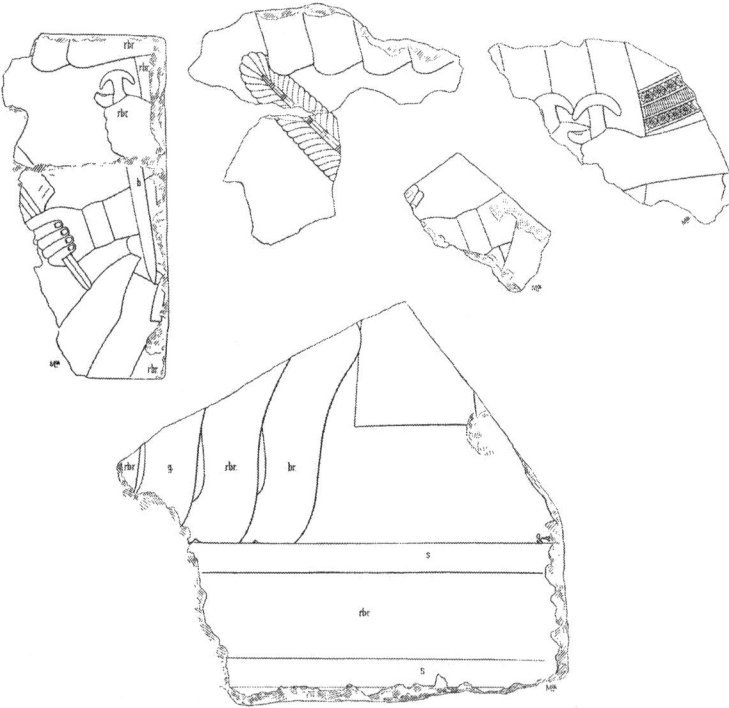

Figure 4.11 Fragments of smiting scenes with multiple victims from the pyramid temple of Niuserra at Abusir, Fifth Dynasty.

four people by the hair at once and despatch them with a mace-blow, making a scene with multiple prisoners more obviously emblematic and less seemingly reportorial than a smiting scene with a solitary enemy. That skin color suggests diversity among the group further removes it from looking like a simple historical action. Additional small fragments from the same area retain images of hands, three of which clutch daggers, and two of which hold feathers. The feathers and daggers may be ethnic markers. We have at least two smiting scenes represented in these fragments, and possibly more.

From the causeway of Niuserra's complex come many fragments from what appear to have been a number of different trampling scenes.[37] These were present on both the north and the south walls, and were clustered at the end of the causeway nearest to the valley temple, again a place of transition. The repetition of this motif is as noteworthy as its elements, and there are subtle differences from Sahure's trampling scene in both details and location. Two clear and one probable trampling scene are shown in Figure 4.12.[38]

From the south wall of the east end of the causeway is a partially preserved relief that may be either a smiting/captive family scene or a trampling scene with an integrated family (Figure 4.12, top row). Only the lower parts are preserved. To the right are the bent knee and foot, and the trailing hand, of a captive; the trailing hand would be less usual in a smiting scene, leading to the suggestion that it is instead trampling; given the very small number of well-preserved smiting

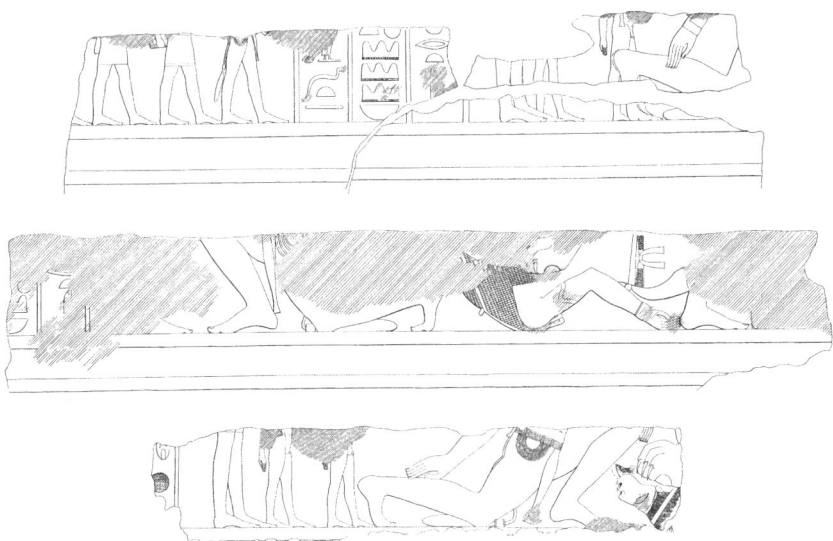

Figure 4.12 Several fragments from trampling scenes found at the causeway of the pyramid of Niuserra at Abusir, Fifth Dynasty. The inclusion in two cases of one adult and two juvenile bystanders links these reliefs to the Libyan Family Scene.

scenes from this time, this is said with real caution. Behind the captive's foot and overlapped by it stands a naked child, whose elbows appear to be bound behind his back. The feet and lower legs of another child and an adult are behind this; this may suggest a scene of a mother and two children watching a leader being despatched by the Egyptian king. Here the family is carefully integrated into the scene, even overlapped by the smitee, and bound. These fragments may thus demonstrate the development of the trampling scene from previously separate motifs. The earlier Libyan Family Scene of Sahure has a vertical band separating the violence done to the leader and his watching family, and the children in that case are not bound. The earlier trampling scene, from the reign of Sahure, did not include family at all as far as can be seen.

Further innovation is shown by the postures of the figures in the middle row of Figure 4.12, which cannot be entirely matched to postures seen elsewhere. In this scene, which is without question a trampling scene, we see the penis sheath of a Libyan who has one knee down on the left. To the right we see the back of the head of one of our possible southerners, with the hair fillet, locks, and chevron armband clear. The paw of the king is visible on his throat, showing that the king faced to the left. Left of the trampled enemies can be seen the remains of a single foot, possibly suggesting a solitary bystander for this violence.

In the bottom block shown on Figure 4.12, the main visible figure is identifiable as a Libyan based on his garments. He is shown with one knee bent to the ground, the other knee bent and raised before him. One hand trails along his back leg. Beneath his fore-shin we see the upside-down head of an Asiatic, identifiable by his pointed beard and hair fillet. His eye, once inlaid, has been gouged out. The cheek of this victim is held by the extended claws of a lion's paw. It is clear that this paw is part of an image of a leonine form of the king who faced to the left, toward the Libyan, and that the semi-prostrate Libyan abases himself before this menacing might. This scene is thus closely parallel to that known from the valley temple of Sahure, where the king as a griffin tramples two enemies while a semi-prostate Libyan is before him. The most notable difference, of course, is that here the Asiatic identity of the enemy beneath the front paw of the king is visually emphasized. Once more, two bound children precede one adult, facing the trampling, and the similarity to the Libyan Family Scene is unmistakeable.

A small fragment found in the valley temple of Niuserra retains one of the more interesting smiting scenes of the Old Kingdom (Figure 4.13).[39] The fragment shows an arm that is over-life-sized and green, indicating it is that of Osiris or perhaps a fecundity figure.[40] The arm wears a bracelet that has a miniature image of a smiting king. Here the king wears the Red Crown and faces to the left. He grasps the standing prisoner—who strides away from the king and is too small to be identifiable by any visual ethnic stereotype—by the hair and prepares to administer the classic mace-blow. A winged falcon protects the king from above. This image is, of course, an image of an image. It is an indication of one context in which imagery of violence may have been common but is now lost to us; indeed, in the Middle Kingdom and later we have examples of royal jewelry bearing the smiting scene (see Chapter 7). I take its presence in the pyramid temple

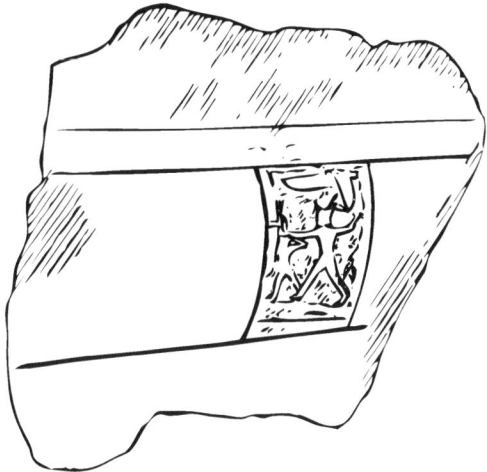

Figure 4.13 A fragment of relief from the valley temple of Niuserra showing an arm wearing a bracelet. On the bracelet is an image of the king in the Red Crown smiting. Abusir, Fifth Dynasty.

of Niuserra to be essentially secondary. The large and green figure himself, and presumably his relationship to the king, was the focus here—not royal violence. Too little is preserved to tell what the position of the green figure was.

On the whole, the relief fragments of Niuserra at Abusir demonstrate a continuing interest in and perhaps expansion of the use of violent scenes, but it is not possible to be quite so suggestive of their specific uses as it was in the case of Sahure. Here we certainly have images of violence—violent violence—from the causeway as well as the pyramid temple and, in an itty-bitty way, the valley temple. Trampling scenes continue to show a variety of peoples at once, and this may also now be true of smiting scenes, which certainly are of multiple people in this case. The watching family has now been integrated into both scene types; given the inherently allegorical nature of the trampling scene, this integration of what we have read elsewhere as an historicizing element of specificity should give us pause about reading family in any case as explicitly referring to a particular event. It does also mean that the repetition of a watching family was not simply thoughtlessly copied, but was rather part of a dynamic reconfiguring of elements of violent scenes that was clearly thoughtful and meaningful.

Unis

The last king of the Fifth Dynasty, Unis, has bequeathed us a range of images of violence and related topics from his mortuary complex at Saqqara. Most of his themes are familiar from his predecessors, but blocks attributed to this complex also take up the depiction of battle that has not been attested since the Fourth

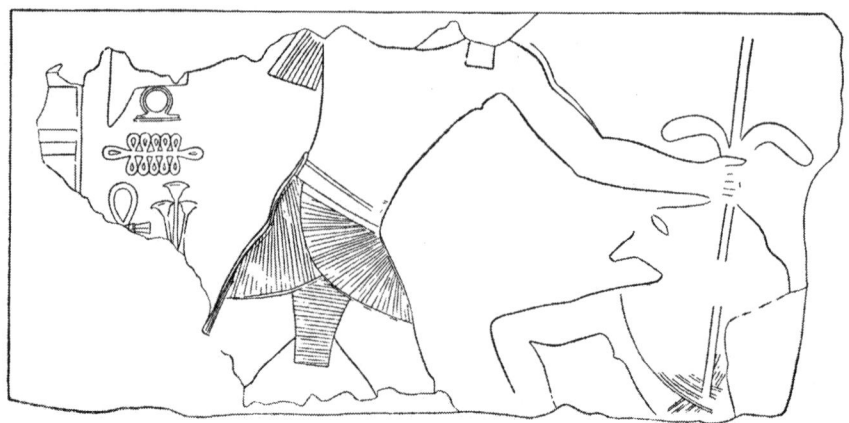

Figure 4.14 Unis smites a Libyan, from his pyramid temple at Saqqara, Fifth Dynasty.
Dimensions: 50 × 150 cm.

Dynasty and offer our first definitive images of combat between Egyptians and those depicted with stereotypical attributes of foreigners.

Blocks and fragments found near the pyramid temple of Unis depict a variety of familiar image types. One is a classic smiting image (Figure 4.14).[41] The king is preserved from his chin to his knees. He strides in a wide stance on the left side of the block. He wears a *shendyt* kilt, a tail, and a false beard. His left hand is extended before him, grasping by the hair an enemy with pointed

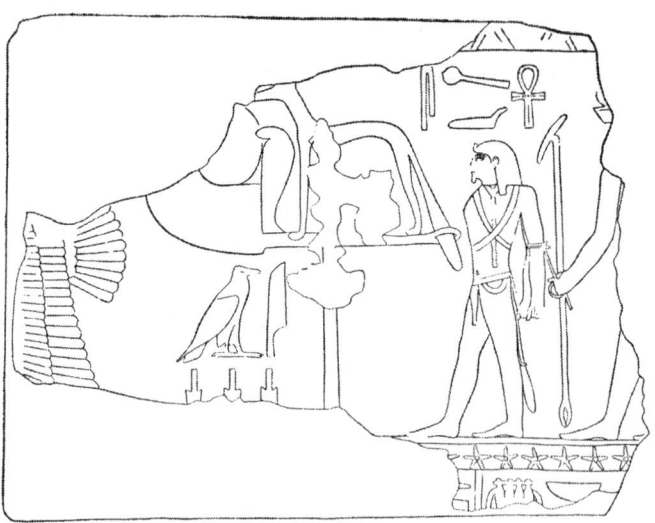

Figure 4.15 A bound Libyan is herded by a god holding a *Was*-scepter. Pyramid temple of Unis, Saqqara. Dimensions: 67 × 90 cm.

beard and crossed chest straps—a Libyan. The long stave commonly found in the king's grasping hand is here, too. The mace-holding arm is missing, but the pose is unmistakable.

From the same area comes a block with an image of a god leading a bound captive (Figure 4.15);[42] this is a small-scale part of a much larger scene. The god is largely missing, but walks from the right to the left. His hand holds a *Was*-scepter and a rope that is attached to the bound elbows of a Libyan prisoner with all of the standard stereotypical ethnic attributes. Above the head of the prisoner is the caption "captive"—a compound word made of the verb *seqer*, smite, plus the word for life, *ankh*; before him is a very large standard of the god Wepwawet. A caption in the register below this may relate to Seshat's recording of booty.[43] This is rather different from Sahure's scene of gods with bound captives, with the god and the prisoner standing on the same register, though again not quite at the same scale.

Another block from the pyramid temple preserves two registers of prisoners (Figure 4.16).[44] In the top register a man of indeterminate origin kneels and raises his hands in supplication. Behind him stands a naked male child, also with a hand

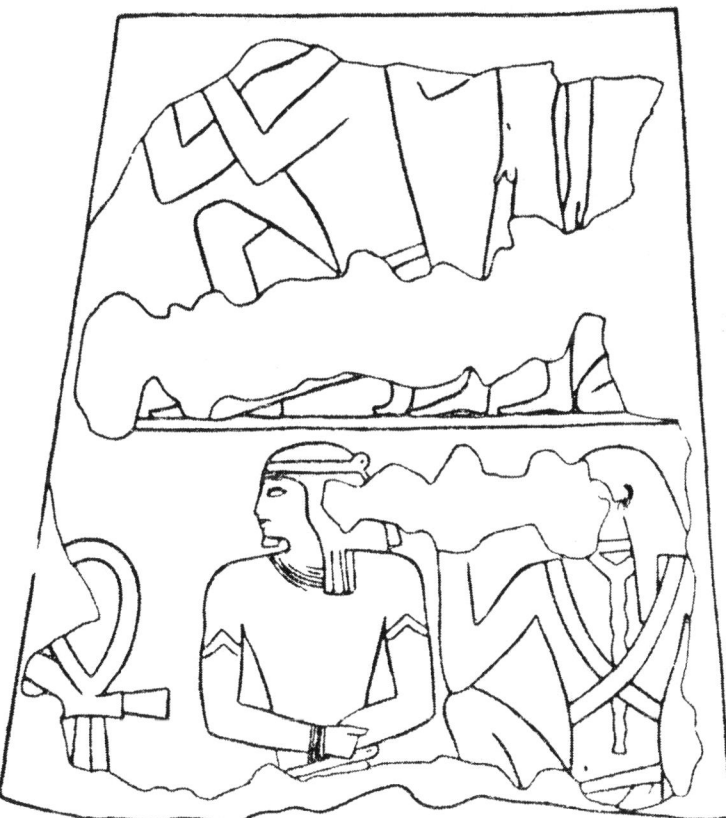

Figure 4.16 Bound prisoners beneath unbound supplicants, from the pyramid temple of Unis at Saqqara. Dimensions: 43 × 35 cm.

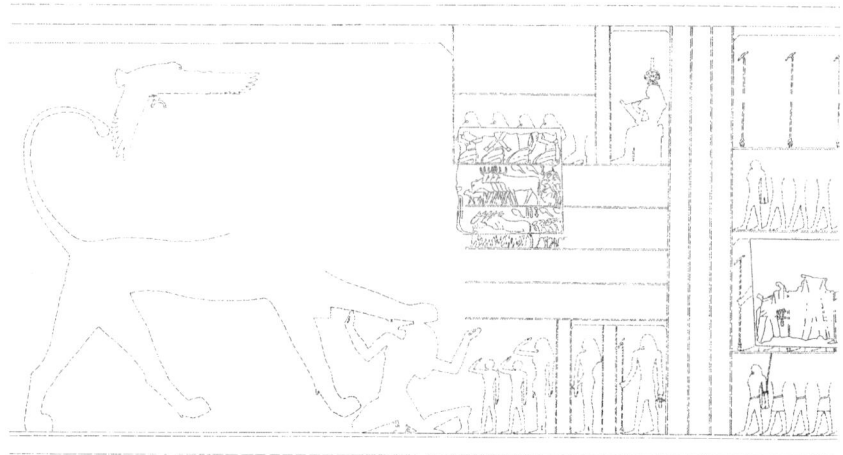

Figure 4.17 Reconstruction of a scene from the causeway of Unis at Saqqara. Only small
fragments are extant (shown in solid lines). While the reconstruction as a
whole is plausible, and all of its elements are known from Old Kingdom
pyramid complexes, the combination of elements in this way is not certain.
The fragmentary nature of reliefs from royal tombs is a major impediment
to understanding what was shown, how it was shown, and how these images
functioned. Dimensions of reconstruction: 220 × 410 cm.

raised, and behind him is the knee of a third figure. The bottom register has two
kneeling prisoners facing left. The first has the familiar fillet and armbands, and
his wrists appear to be bound in front of him. The second is a Libyan, with crossed
chest straps and a necktie; he raises one hand. Other very small fragments from
the pyramid temple include two with images of unidentifiable bound prisoners
and one with the toes of two parallel feet that stand on point and must be the
remains of a scene with multiple smitees.[45]

The causeway of Unis' complex retains fragments of a range of violent
images, or hints that they were once there. The corpus of causeway reliefs presents difficulties, not least in that probably less than half the total of originally
excavated fragments has been recorded and published.[46] Furthermore, the recovered remains are in most cases very fragmentary, and the tendency to reconstruct
whole scenes on the basis of scant remains is problematic—published reconstructions should be treated with extreme care. For instance, Labrousse and
Moussa reconstruct fragments into a tableau that they think decorated the north
side of the end of the causeway adjacent to the valley temple (Figure 4.17).[47]
The reconstruction shows the king as a griffin or sphinx trampling a Libyan
enemy, while the family of the stricken enemy watches. Above this are registers
of livestock and bound prisoners, their numbers recorded by a seated Seshat.
Behind her, further registers of striding gods hold ropes leading processions of
bound prisoners.[48] The scene as reconstructed contains elements that are now

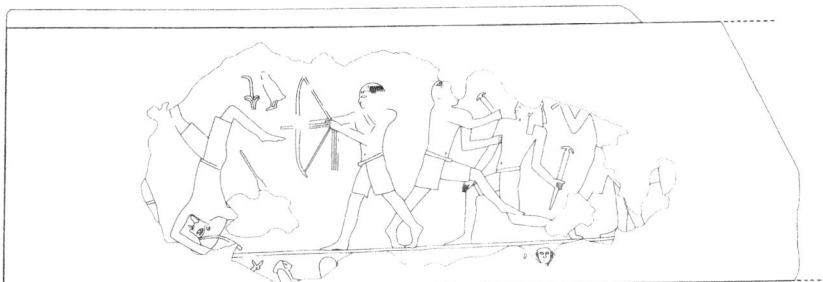

Figure 4.18 A battle scene from the causeway of Unis at Saqqara. Egyptians with
bows and daggers attack and get the best of Asiatics in individual combat.
Dimensions: 51 × 150 cm.

familiar; the trampling leonine king, for instance, is clearly related to the Sahure
image of trampling from an analogous location in his mortuary complex. But
only two fragments are used in this reconstruction. The first is a badly damaged
block showing divinities holding *ankhs* and scepters and possibly ropes leading
to bound prisoners. The second has parts of two registers of animals beneath
a register of kneeling, bound captives, their arms in a range of uncomfortable
positions.[49] Seshat, the trampling king, and the mourning Libyan family are all
assumptions, and Niuserra showed us that there was variability and innovation in
the way these elements could be combined.

The best-preserved examples of battle scenes from an Old Kingdom royal
mortuary complex come from the causeway of Unis. Two damaged blocks with
this theme remain, as well as fragments of others. The first has parts of seven
figures, five of which are reasonably well preserved and two of which are just
leg fragments (Figure 4.18).[50] The action is shown as individual combats, always
between two armed figures. On the left an upside-down kilted man with his legs
waving in the air is being shot at by another. The ethnic stereotypes of these two
are clear: he on the left has a pointy beard and a fillet around his hair and looks
like an Asiatic; he on the right wears a kilt, has a short wig with tiers of curls and
straps across his chest, and is Egyptian. The Asiatic has lost his weapon, maybe
a stick or a mace, which is shown falling through the air. The Egyptian faces to
the left; his bow is threaded with a blunt-tipped arrow and drawn back. He holds
three other arrows in his left bowstring hand. The Egyptian's back leg crosses
with the leg of one of his compatriots, who faces to the right. This man, who
leaps through the air with only one foot on the groundline, is in the act of plunging a dagger into the shoulder of another man. The ethnic identity of this man
is harder to determine, but he is probably also an Asiatic. He may have a beard,
and certainly wears a somewhat longer wig or hairstyle with a fillet tied around
his forehead—the tail can be seen dangling at the back of his head. He grasps a
dagger similar to that of his attacker. Both of these daggers have moon-shaped
ends to their hilts. The warriors clasp their daggers around what appears to be the

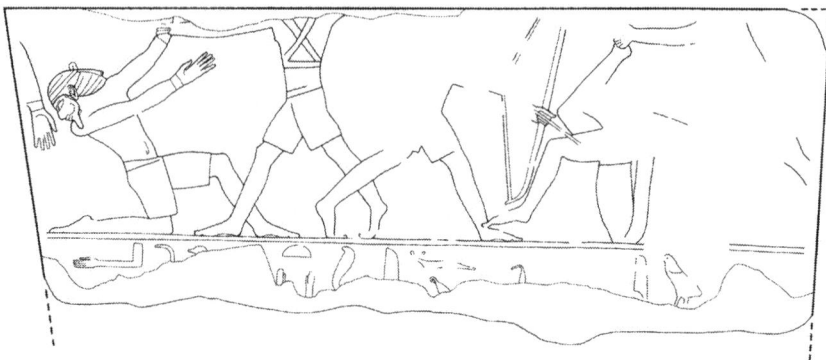

Figure 4.19 Another battle scene from the causeway of Unis at Saqqara. Once more we
see individual combats, with an Asiatic getting the worst of it. Dimensions:
36.5 × 92 cm.

middle of the blade, raising questions about the type of weapon. To the right, a
less well-preserved figure strides toward the right with an upraised arm. He is in
the act of swinging a long weapon, though whether it is an axe, stave, or mace
is unclear. This scene is notable for its dynamic activity, the range of positions
(nothing is repeated on the available fragment) and weapons, and the proximity
of the protagonists to one another—they are all engaged in hand-to-hand combat.
All of these things are in stark contrast with the sole earlier example of a battle
scene: the fragment with massed archers shooting in unison, attributed to the
mortuary complex of Khafre.

The second battle scene block from the causeway of Unis has similar characteristics to the first (Figure 4.19).[51] Parts of six figures are present. The four in the
middle are the best preserved and form two groups of combatants. On the left, an
Asiatic is on one knee, with his arms raised in front of him and his head turned
to the side. A man (his head is missing but the crossed straps on his chest are like
those of the Egyptian in the above-mentioned block) striding toward him grasps
one of his hands. The striding figure appears to have his other arm raised, ready
to bring a weapon down on the head of the Asiatic. To the right of these figures
another combat ensues. A head- and torso-less figure with a bow aims downward
toward a figure, also unidentifiable, who sprawls with one leg in the air. The bow
is much larger than the bow in the previous relief. The unfortunate victim in this
case appears on close inspection to be headless, with his shoulders resting directly
upon the register line. The leg he throws in the air may be caught at the ankle by
the largely destroyed figure on the far right, indicating perhaps that not all combats were one-on-one.

Smaller fragments from the Unis causeway preserve additional examples of
battle scenes that appear similar to those described above, particularly in showing
opposed pairs of combatants. They may well be parts of the same larger scene

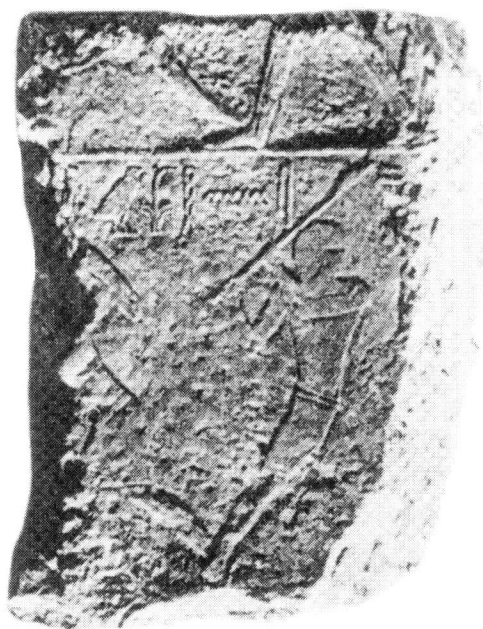

Figure 4.20 An axe-swinging soldier, with his back to another attacker, from the
causeway of Unis at Saqqara.

or scenes. A small piece shows an Egyptian vigorously swinging an axe with
a curved blade (Figure 4.20).[52] His enemy is not preserved. To the left of this
combat, another partly preserved figure is in a pose suggestive of attacking a
fallen or falling enemy. The register above has the feet of two opposed figures
in active poses, also likely engaged in a struggle, and the leg of another. Another
block shows an Egyptian attacking an upside down figure, whose head is missing
(Figure 4.21).[53] The arm of the Egyptian hits the enemy at about his knees. To the
right is the limb of another person, in a different duel, and to the left an Egyptian
from a third combat. A final fragment, not pictured here, depicts two sets of two
people, with only their legs remaining.[54] It is not clear if they are engaged in
armed combat or wrestling. Černy additionally recorded but did not draw small
fragments from the causeway, which have subsequently been lost, showing two
archers and two combatants.[55]

These scenes are the antithesis of most other depictions of soldiers in royal
mortuary contexts. Those show ranks of soldiers doing the same things, and
usually running. While the patterns are always subtly broken, the overwhelming
impression is always one of order. This is chaos. The only other un-ordered
depiction of military personnel we have seen was the image of archery training
from the reign of Sahure. That, too, came from the causeway. In addition to their

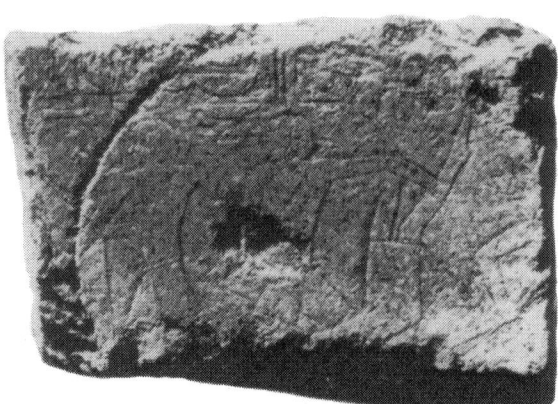

Figure 4.21 More one-on-one combats, increasing the variety of poses known from such
scenes, from the causeway of Unis at Saqqara.

playful variety of poses showing a type of activity otherwise not well represented
in pyramid complex remains, these personal combats from the causeway of Unis
are notable for their inclusion of inscriptions with the violence portrayed. These
are preserved at the head level of combatants on 4.18, 4.20, and probably 4.21;
in 4.19 this part of the register is missing. These appear not to be long inscriptions at all, though those were clearly present elsewhere attached to these scenes,
but rather short captions of the sort also present with Sahure's archers receiving
instruction (Figure 4.9). While the evidence is very scanty, it should be noted
that the king himself is not known to have been present at all in these less formal
scenes.

A final fragment from the causeway that may represent a battle scene, now lost
but recorded in Černy's notebooks, possibly shows an attack on a fortified place;
if it does, it is unique in the corpus of extant royal reliefs of the Old Kingdom. The
tiny fragment, of which only Černy's rough sketch remains, seems to show a part
of a curved wall with a rounded bastion on its exterior. On the inside of the curve
are lines that appear to show the knee and elbow of a prostrate individual. Espinel
has shown that this may parallel the lower left corner of the siege of an Asiatic
town as depicted in the private tomb of Inti at Deshasha (see Figure 8.3).[56] The
representation of a walled town in this manner, as a plan, has antecedents dating to
the Naqada III palettes; it is notably different from the side-view of fortifications
that became standard in early Middle Kingdom depictions of such attacks.

One causeway fragment that is rather difficult to read may show ranks of
troops in combat (Figure 4.22).[57] With one exception, only the legs of the figures
are preserved. All wear similar split kilts of the sort worn by the combatants in the
battle scenes. On the left side of this block, six men (one almost entirely missing)
run to the left. The first four are in tight formation, but the last two are rather farther apart; all have their legs in the same positions. On the right side of the block,

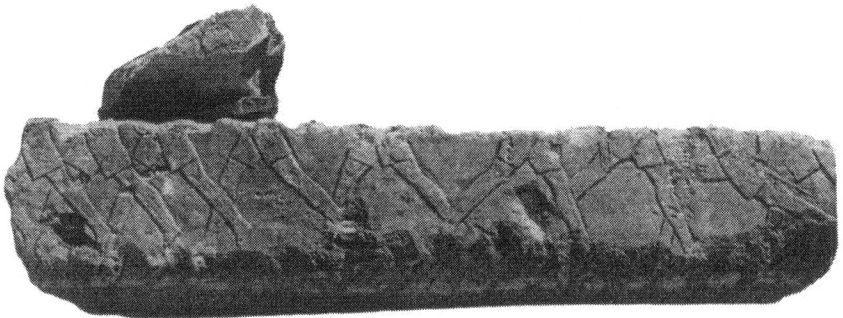

Figure 4.22 Running troops who seem to be colliding with other running troops, and thus engaged in battle, from the causeway of Unis at Saqqara.

toward the center, two men run toward the right. The hind leg of the leftmost of these figures crosses the hind leg of the last left-running man. But facing these two figures on the far right of the block are two kilted men. Their front knees are much more sharply bent than those of the other running men; they appear somewhat as though they are leaping. The end of a stick—whether a stave or axe is unclear—is visible between these two men. The first of them may hold a sword. No other weapon can be seen in the preserved part of this relief, but it is difficult to see what else it could depict instead of a clash between ranked troops and in place of individual combats. In this respect it is more reminiscent of Khafre's archers than the above combat scenes were, though unlike that earlier example we do not have overlapping rows suggesting a particularly tight formation.

The valley temple of Unis is not well preserved. It seems to have had scenes similar to the ship of state from the valley temple of Sahure, now represented by tiny fragments with standing oarsmen; one possibly shows a bound prisoner lashed to the deck.[58] These fragments do not materially aid our understanding of Unis' complex.

The Sixth Dynasty

The Sixth Dynasty pyramid complexes were quite standardized. However, while their images of violence are largely as would be expected, they do preserve some points of particular interest, including in what is missing. Only two complexes, those of the Pepys, have fragmented remains of violent scenes—and these include only triumph and no battle depictions.

Pepy I

The pyramid temple of Pepy I at Saqqara has fragments of a smiting scene that, while incomplete, is at least better preserved than many from other royal pyramid complexes (Figure 4.23).[59]

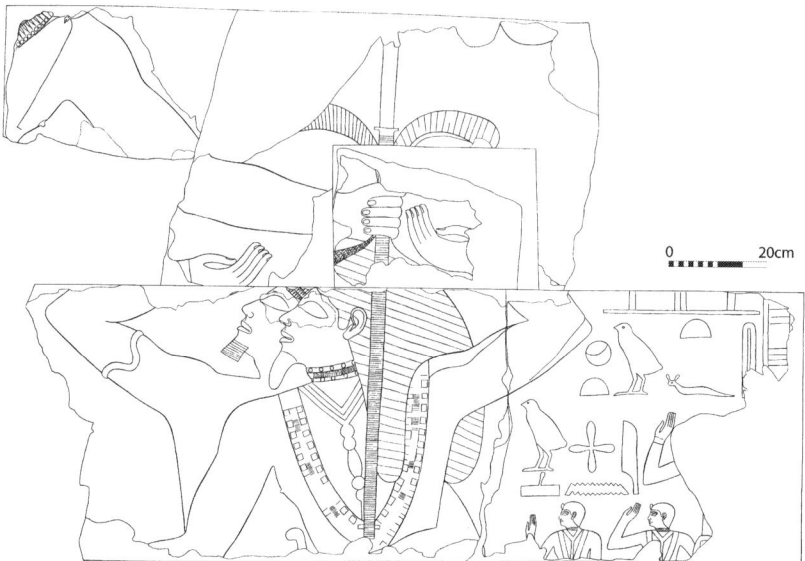

Figure 4.23 Pepy I smites a southerner and a Libyan at the same time, while watched by the typical Libyan Family. Dimensions: 155 × 175 cm.

At the right, fragments of three watching figures remain, their arms raised toward the smiting. The two children at the front have short hair, forehead ornaments, and elaborate straps crossed over their chests. An adult behind them is mostly missing but can be seen to wear a bracelet. These three characters are labeled with personal names; they are the same names as those of the Libyan family from the pyramid temple of Sahure, but are written slightly differently. The grieving family here is not separated from the smiting scene by a band of text. Unlike the case at Sahure's temple, here part of the smiting scene itself is preserved. The king is mostly gone, except for his advanced left arm and a small bit of his pectoral-clad chest. He grasps an elaborate long instrument and the hair of not one, but two captives. These two largely overlap one another. The front enemy has a rounded beard, long hair, a choker, and two different types of elaborate crossed straps on his chest. He is the very picture of a Libyan. The man behind him has hair in a tiered pattern, a short, square beard, and a bent armband around his raised biceps. He is the very picture of a presumed southerner. There are thus two elements of this scene that make it impossible to accept as a simple historical record of triumphant despatch of the enemy after a battle: the repetition of the names of the Libyan family from an earlier context, and the inclusion of enemies from such different places (the latter may also have been originally true at Sahure's). While the Sixth Dynasty kings were across the board less innovative in their pyramid complexes than their predecessors had been, I am still reluctant to see the use of this strangely historicizing but not historical scene as just a "cliché."[60] The combination of precision and inaccuracy must be meaningful.

Pepy II

The last major royal mortuary complex of the Old Kingdom was built by Pepy II at Saqqara. The relief decoration from Pepy II's complex as a whole is notable for being exquisite, extensive (though fragmentary), and more or less monotonous. None of its themes are surprising. In general, not only in its violent scenes, there is less narrative and less experimentation than previously. Given the large amount of surviving relief fragments, it seems unlikely that this is simply a matter of preservation.

From the mortuary complex of Pepy II come a number of smiting scenes, including both an iteration of the Libyan Family Scene and a scene that has been hypothetically reconstructed to show the king smiting an animal (not shown here). Additionally, there are trampling scenes and a presentation of foreign captives. All of these scenes are fragmentary, and while the reconstructions are given below, due caution should be taken to note which pieces are actually extant and the degree to which these drawings represent plausible rather than demonstrable scenes.

The Libyan Family Scene from the pyramid temple of Pepy II cannot be fully reconstructed; the clearest element is the family itself (Figure 4.24).[61] Here once more we see two children followed by a woman, all holding one hand before them. They wear chest straps, not as complicated as in the analogous scene of Pepy I, and the woman has a forehead ornament, a chevron-shaped choker, and wears a penis sheath. Their names are written above them—the familiar names. The scene is not precisely the same as that of Pepy I: a band of text separates the mourners from the smiting, and the smiting itself—poorly preserved except for its very base, which is sufficient in this case—has only a single victim. The remaining bit of text calls Pepy lord of the foreign lands. To the left can be seen four feet

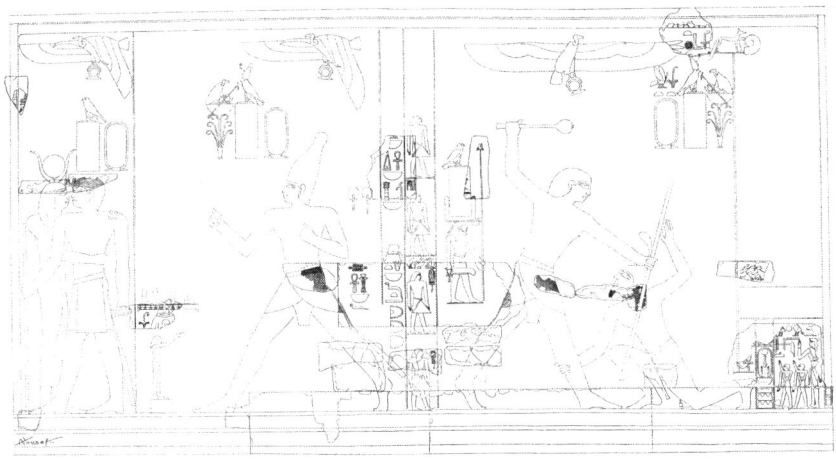

Figure 4.24 A reconstructed Libyan Family Scene from the pyramid temple of Pepy II. The family itself, visible at the lower right, is the best-preserved part of the scene.

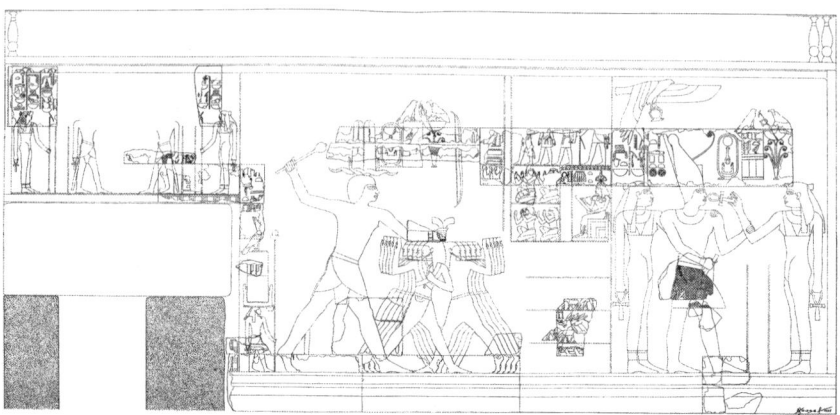

Figure 4.25 Pepy II smites a multitude.

and one knee in the unmistakable postures of smiting and being smote. Between the knee and front foot of the smitee hang the end of a tail and a penis sheath: Libyan, as expected. Further fragments that do not adjoin this scene but presumably come from it include pieces of the king's legs and kilt, and the beard, collar, and lappet of the Libyan. A staff crosses his hair.

Another well-represented smiting scene from the vestibule of the pyramid temple of Pepy II shows the king smiting a large group of standing prisoners (Figure 4.25).[62] Once more the bottom of the scene is the only part continuously preserved. It shows the king on the left, legs spread and striding. To his right are the feet and lower legs of ten captives: five on the left stride right, five on the right stride left. In the group on the left, where their kilts can be seen, the first figure has a tail hanging down his thigh and between his legs. This probably makes him a Libyan and certainly indicates that there was differentiation of ethnic stereotypes on the basis of iconography within this group: it is an "all."[63] Another piece from this vicinity shows the king's wrist, wearing a beaded bracelet, well-manicured hand grasping the barely visible remains of his victims' hair. Also reconstructed as parts of the same large scene are fragments related to smiting, including numbered donkeys and goats.

One block (Figure 4.26)[64] has at the bottom right the crown of Seshat. In front of her can be seen two figures, unbound, with hands raised in supplication. The one in the rear wears a fillet. Before him a better-preserved man has a fillet, a short, square beard, and bracelets. The register above this includes the lower parts of three bound prisoners herded by a *Was*-scepter holding god. The three are differentiated from one another but held by the same rope, which binds their elbows in three different painful positions and then ties them all together. In the rear is a man with a dagger stuck through his belt. Before him is another figure with a fancy belt and bracelets; by analogy with the depiction of the presentation of prisoners in the causeway (see Figure 4.30), this man would also have been wearing

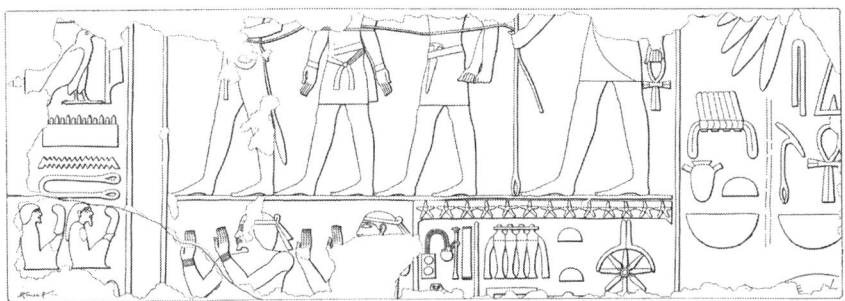

Figure 4.26 A god leads bound prisoners above Seshat (only her crown is visible), from the pyramid temple of Pepy II at Saqqara.

chevron-shaped armlets and so should be understood as a probable southerner. Before them comes a man with the penis sheath of a Libyan.

A particularly beautiful fragment of captive foreigners (Figure 4.27)[65] from the vestibule of the Pepy II pyramid temple shows how exquisite the carving was here. At first glance it appears to be a single man, looking slightly upward, his hand raised to implore mercy, his lips slightly parted. He has a somewhat hooked nose and a short, square beard. But there are three shoulders present, the foremost with fingers wrapped around it, once more indicating a multitude. Once thus alerted, we notice the traces of a second pair of lips and chin, this one beardless. A horizontal line at throat level suggests that the three are bound. This piece cannot be certainly connected to the other scenes that can be more broadly reconstructed. Familiar as they all are, the fragments from Pepy II's pyramid temple are also not precisely like either one another or previous attestations of the motif.

The causeway of Pepy II has both an impressively large presentation of bound prisoners scene and an exceptional variety of trampling. The trampling scenes from Pepy II's causeway (Figures 4.28 and 4.29),[66] unfortunately from our perspective but perhaps not from that of their intended audience, preserve more details of the magnificent and deadly, if somewhat stiff-legged, king than they do of the hapless foes he tramples.

There are four such scenes; we can be certain because parts of the back of the king are present from each. Two face in each direction, and presumably these flanked the end of the causeway as it led into the pyramid temple. In two cases the king seems to have been a human-headed sphinx, indicated by the remains of a beard on one fragment, and in the other two a griffin, shown by the feathers of his wings. In only two cases do fragments of the trampled foes survive. One has a foot and bits of two other limbs. Their posture is one of disarray. The other is more helpful, showing the claws of the king's paw on the throat of a man lying on his back. His knees are up, his arms thrown in the air on either side of the leg of the king. No remaining indications of ethnic markers can be observed.

The presentation of foreigners probably occupied four registers and stood originally closest to the causeway's outside entrance (Figure 4.30).[67] The top

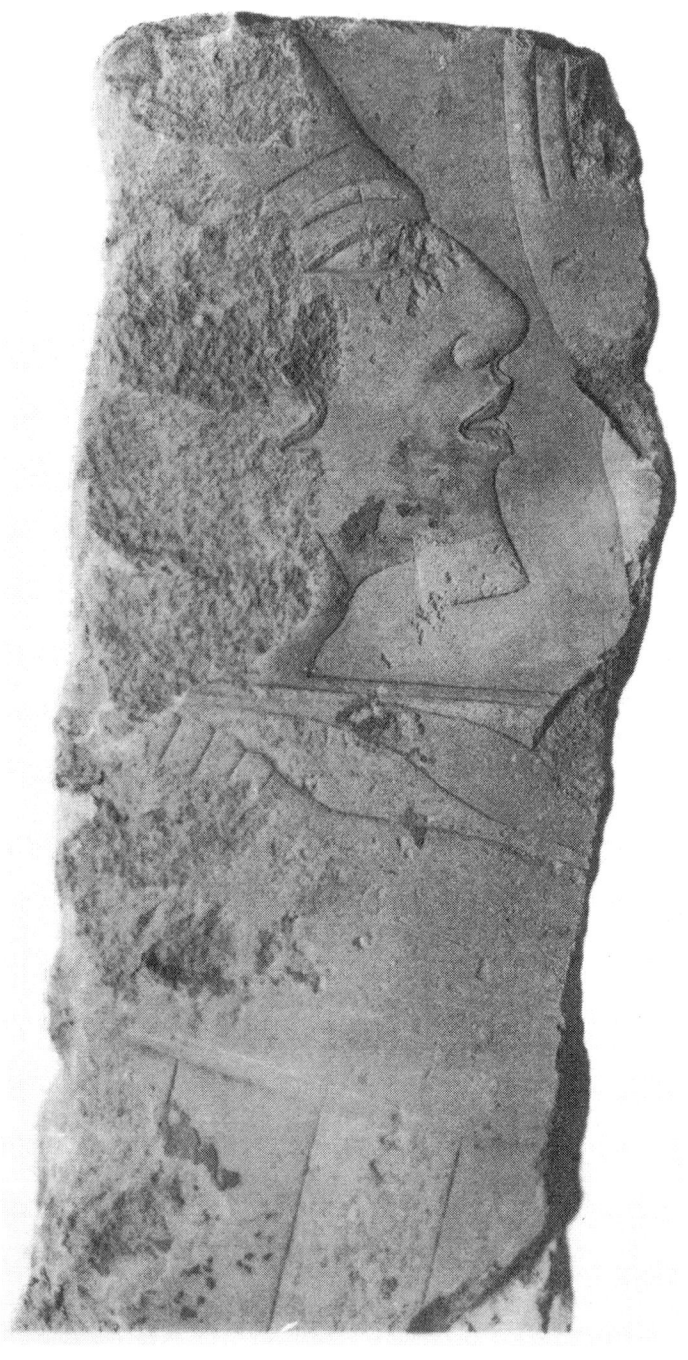

Figure 4.27 Three prisoners, bound at the neck and raising their hands, from the pyramid temple of Pepy II at Saqqara.

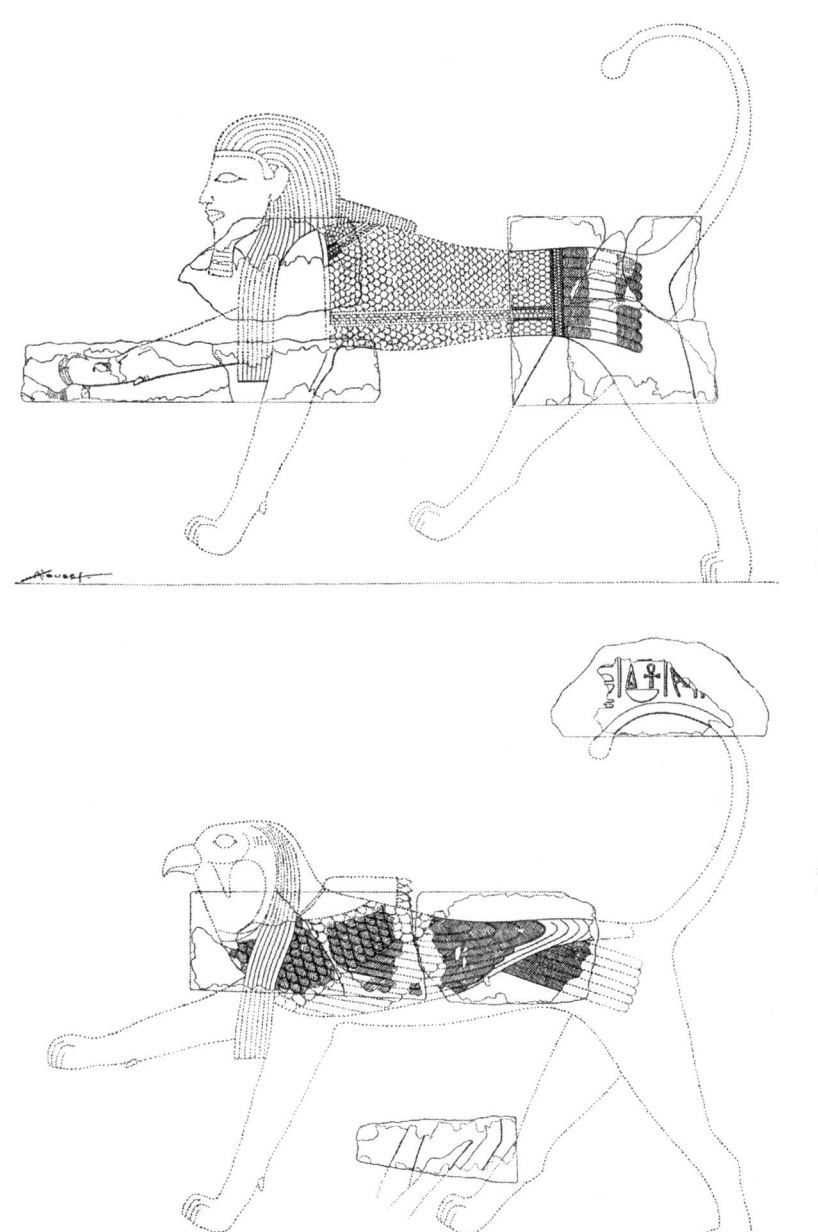

Figure 4.28 Pepy II as mythical animals trampling enemies, from his causeway at Saqqara.

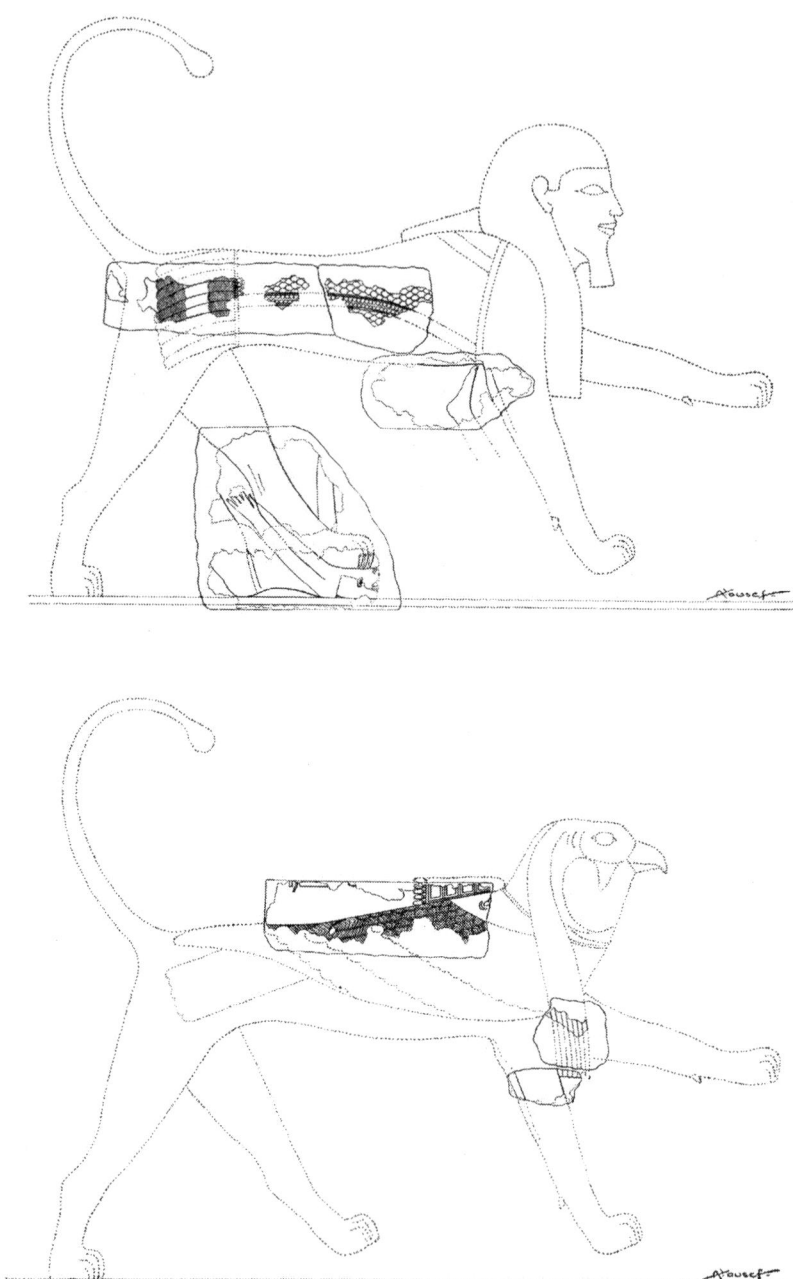

Figure 4.29 Further iterations of a trampling Pepy II from his causeway at Saqqara.

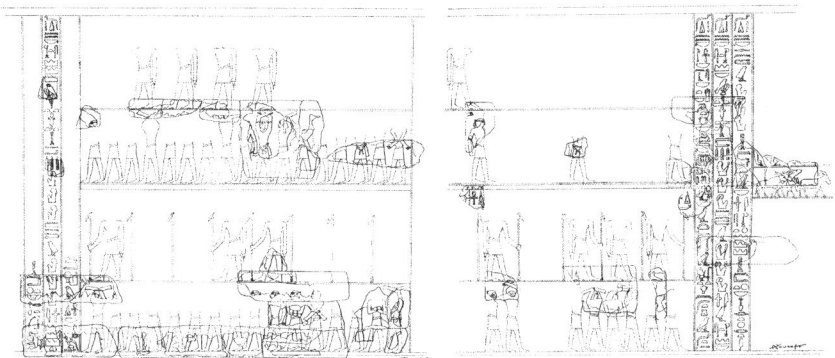

Figure 4.30 The presentation of typical foreigners from the east end of the causeway of
Pepy II, Saqqara.

and third registers, which have been reconstructed as slightly taller than the second and fourth, held gods. Nothing but feet remain of any of the gods; the base
of one *Was*-scepter survives between two of them.[68] Slightly more extensive
fragments remain of the prisoners. Unsurprisingly, they are bound in a variety
of painful positions. All preserved fragments show men. It is clear that they
represent the familiar mix of Asiatics, Libyans, and presumed southerners. One
well-preserved fragment with a southerner, identified on the basis of his chevron-
shaped armlets, shows him wearing a complicated belt, a short beard, and a fillet
around his chin-length hair. While the scale of these figures is quite small, it
would seem here that the identifiers of this ethnic type have shifted somewhat
over the preceding centuries. This is less true of the Libyans; one of these is
clear here from the semicircular object hanging from his belt, his narrow crossed
chest straps, and the very top of what was probably a penis sheath.[69] Enough
paint is retained on these fragments for Jéquier to have noted that skin color
ranges from orange to dark brown, with color apparently chosen more for artistic
alternation than for specific reference to ethnicity.[70] One man has a dagger stuck
through his belt. None of the preserved chins from this relief are beardless, and it
is not possible to say if Egyptians might have been included among those herded
by the gods. On none of these fragments is there a preserved rope leading from a
god to a prisoner, nor anything to suggest one, and so it appears that the leashes
in this case are at most implied. A second tableau, understood by its excavators
to have been next to the bound prisoners scene, has left us a fragment of Seshat
recording war booty.[71]

Pepy II's valley temple has preserved fragments of what was almost certainly
a smiting scene (Figure 4.31).[72] The only tolerably well-preserved part is the bottom right of the scene, where two feet and the waist of a kneeling figure can be
seen. As reconstructed, the two feet belong to a single individual, with another
suggested on the basis of a hand fragment on a block that also includes the shin

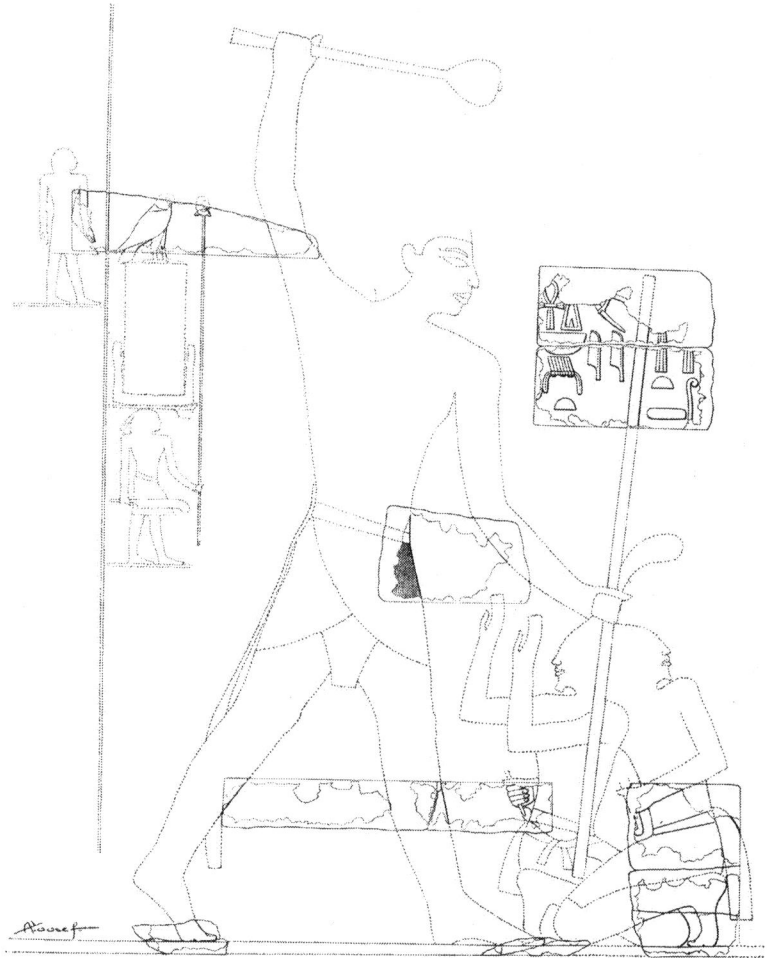

Figure 4.31 Pepy II smiting multiple captives from his valley temple at Saqqara.

of the king. In other cases, such as at Niuserra's pyramid temple smiting scene, multiple feet in the same position clearly belong to separate individuals. Traces on this block indicate that the foremost figure wore a sort of tailed belt hanging behind his kilt and clutched a narrow implement that ended in a curl. Insufficient amounts remain to really understand this scene in terms of the precise number or identity of its victims, but its basic nature seems clear. The slightly angled, long implement that runs across the fragment with the inscription is good corroboration of the smiting nature of the scene, assuming these fragments belong together.

Statuary from Old Kingdom pyramid complexes

Statuary from late Old Kingdom mortuary complexes adds an additional type of evidence for our understanding of imagery of royal violence, though it does so obliquely. From six pyramid complexes come remains of statues, somewhat less than life-size, of bound prisoners. To us, and presumably to the Egyptians, these statues recall relief scenes of captivity, though the pose is in fact a rare one in relief. The statues will be treated summarily here, rather than comprehensively, as they do not directly show violence. These images raise issues of ethnic stereotyping in particular, however, which makes them relevant to the discussion here.[73]

Examples of bound prisoner statues are known from the reigns of Raneferef, Niuserra, Djedkare Izezi, and Unis in the Fifth Dynasty, and from the two Pepys of the Sixth Dynasty. It seems therefore reasonable to assume that such statues were regular features of pyramid complexes from the middle of the Fifth Dynasty through the Sixth, despite some differences over that span of time. No complete statue of this type has been found; all have had their heads severed from their bodies, and in the case of the statues from the pyramid complex of Pepy I, this was apparently intentional. The statues may thus be understood as including a performative element, though the most recent study of the figures suggests that this was not smashing them on the head in a reenactment of smiting but rather careful chiseling in a more measured, but still presumably ritual, destruction.[74]

None of the statues is inscribed. The variety of their physical characteristics is quite breathtaking. While this is easiest to catalog in terms of hair—there are smooth wigs and wigs with tiered curls, wigs with vertical striations, wigs with center parts—it is even more striking in terms of facial characteristics. These statues have an individualism that is rarely found in Egyptian art, being most notable in the corpus of Fourth Dynasty sculptures called reserve heads.[75] Chin treatment is another location for variety—there are smooth chins, squared goatees, longer squared beards, rounded but still narrow beards. The most pressing question raised by this variety of features is who is represented in this corpus.

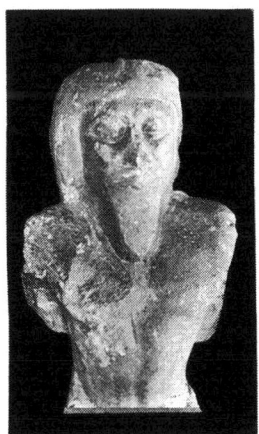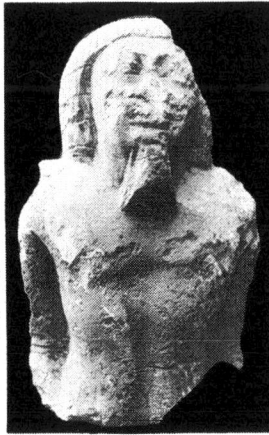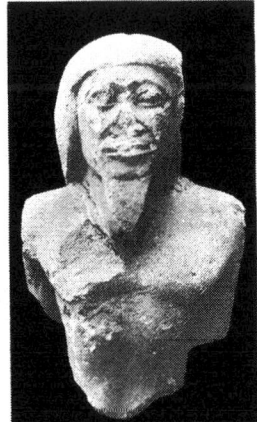

Figure 4.32 Examples of the many bound prisoner statues from the pyramid complex of Pepy II. Expressions of ethnicity are both probable and difficult to read on these sculptures, and some may represent Egyptians.

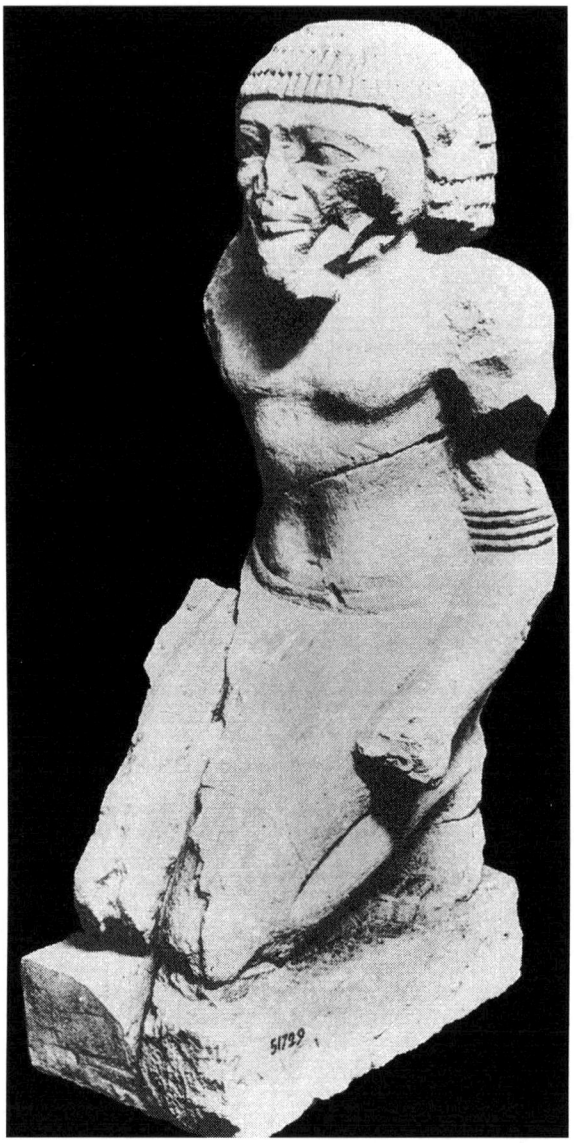

Figure 4.33 Sculpture of a bound prisoner—an Egyptian?—from the pyramid
complex of Pepy II.

The iconography of visual stereotypes is substantially less present or easily dis-
entangled in this corpus than is true in reliefs. No distinctions are made with clothing
or jewelry. Hairstyles and beards do differ, but these are not the most straightforward markers even in the reliefs. Some hairstyles that do appear to be consistent in

reliefs, such as the correspondence between fillets with three locks on the shoulder and the presence of chevron armlets, are not represented in the statues. In the end, only the rather pointed beard (see, for example, Figure 4.32)[76] seen on a few of the statues might be considered a marker, though even that shows up on different group types in relief: Libyans and Asiatics. It is certainly at least as important that markers on the whole are omitted from such a clearly meaningful category of statues. I think this ambiguity must be intentional, and perhaps should be read as deliberately allowing a multiplicity of identities to be grafted onto a single statue.

That such an ambiguity allowed association of bound prisoner statues with Egyptians seems likely. Borchardt noted this in discussing one of the sculptures he excavated at the complex of Niuserra at Abusir.[77] Other examples, apparent images of Egyptian elites with their tiered wigs, except for the fact that they are bound, are known from Pepy II (Figure 4.33).[78]

There are notable differences between these statues and the smiting scenes that might at first glance appear to be their close cousins. Differences include pose, the often highly individualized faces of the statues, and their previously mentioned performative role—particularly if the performance was not in fact smiting. The postures of the smitees in relief are themselves varied, but are without exception quite active—smitees stride, or kneel with legs apart and reach forward. It is very rare to show bound captives in such scenes.[79] In contrast, the late Old Kingdom statues are entirely static, in postures representative neither of movement nor of the capability of movement; they have an air of resignation. The variety of facial features makes the statues seem more representative of individual than stereotyped peoples, but their lack of identifying inscriptions makes even that individuality suspect. They suggest that statuary of domination worked quite differently than relief decoration of domination.

The Middle Kingdom

The kings of the Middle Kingdom continued the Old Kingdom tradition of incorporating elements of violence into the relief programs of their mortuary complexes, including both triumph scenes and battle scenes. Because the material is even more fragmentary than that of the Old Kingdom, it is difficult to draw concrete conclusions from it. However, it will be noted that the introduction of scenes of attacking fortifications shown in side-view and of dark skin as an ethnic marker, as well as the absence of preserved attestations of the previously common Libyan Family Scene, are apparent departures from the Old Kingdom.

The Eleventh Dynasty

Nebhepetra Mentuhotep

The first Middle Kingdom king to use martial imagery in his tomb complex was Nebhepetra Mentuhotep in the middle of the Eleventh Dynasty. Universally regarded as the first king of the Middle Kingdom and an important reunifier of the country after a period of political fragmentation, there is no reason to doubt that he was an active military campaigner. That he fought wars within Egypt and against Egyptians as well as campaigns abroad, and that he left the most substantial body of remaining Middle Kingdom images of violence, make this king arguably the most important one for assessing the ideological role of images of violence in Egypt. He will be critical to this study in Chapter 5 as well, as he also utilized violent motifs in divine settings.

Nebhepetra commissioned a mortuary monument at Deir el-Bahri in Thebes that was in many ways innovative, combining some aspects of the local type of tomb his predecessors—the First Intermediate Period Theban dynasts—had used, with some elements from Old Kingdom royal mortuary monuments and some entirely new elements. His tomb was not a pyramid but rather a chamber accessed by a sloping passage that leads deep beneath the cliffs of the western desert. The tomb chamber has no proper superstructure aside from the cliffs themselves, but is accessed through and marked by a collonaded, terraced temple that sits at the back of the bay of cliffs of Deir el-Bahri. The mortuary complex was built over the course of a long reign, has multiple elements including chapels for royal women, and was highly decorated.[80] The style of reliefs exhibits a great range and this is usually understood to be a deliberate attempt to use style to communicate different messages at different parts of the reign, first connecting Nebhepetra with the rise of the Theban Eleventh Dynasty and then, when he could more reasonably claim to control all of Egypt, with the Old Kingdom past and Memphite style. Because of this, style has been used to date aspects of the relief program even when they are broken and cannot be connected with certainty to specific locations.[81]

While the relief program of Nebhepetra's mortuary complex is fragmentary, enough has been found of images of war and triumph to make it a very valuable document for our purposes. As was true in the Old Kingdom, there are images of soldiers engaged in more pacific pursuits as well as images of actual combat; because we have only fragments, it is not always possible to say if a soldier was engaged in one or the other. None of the remaining fragments definitively include the king himself participating in violence.[82]

Because we have only fragments, the nature of the war compositions as a whole is impossible to reconstruct; they are striking, however, for the variety of people and poses employed and the apparent attack on a fortified place.[83] People who are shown with elements of stereotypical representations are common, particularly with those already seen as characteristic of "Asiatics," but we also see the dark skin of a Nubian. Attributes of visual ethnic stereotyping are not utilized entirely consistently, and particularly given the fragmentary nature of the reliefs it is not possible to say entirely what was meant. Descriptions below are from a representative selection of the preserved fragments, most of which are at the British Museum, but are not comprehensive.

The most dramatic fragment of violence from this complex retains a number of people shown with yellow skin, fancy kilts, and in the case of the preserved head,

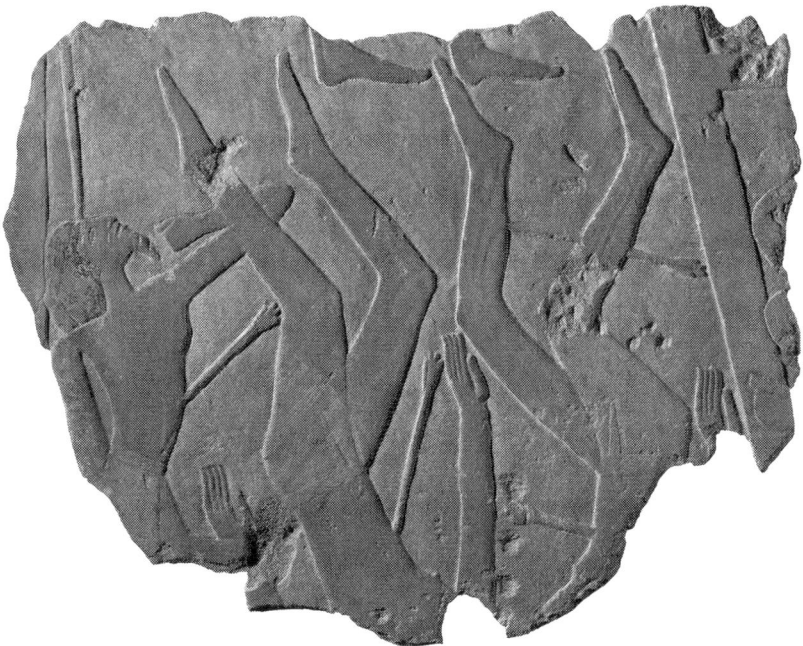

Figure 4.34 Yellow-skinned figures fall in the space between a wall, just visible
                on the left, and a ladder leaning against that wall. They are stuck with
                arrows. Another figure climbs the ladder, with his head, shoulder, and
                the head of his axe barely visible on the right. From the lower colonnade
                of the mortuary complex of Nebhepetra Mentuhotep at Deir el-Bahri.
                Dimensions: 60 × 66 cm.

a fillet around the hair and a rather pointed, rounded beard (Figure 4.34).[84] This
fragment, the right part of a block, preserves traces of five different figures. To the
far left is a vertical line; this almost certainly represents the wall of a fortification.
On the extreme right is an angled line—this is the side of a ladder, as shown by
one of the rungs barely visible at the top. A better-preserved analogy is found in
the contemporary private tomb of Intef, also at Thebes, allowing quite a bit of
confidence in the reading of the Nebhepetra fragment (see Figure 8.7). In this
fragment, the back of the head, shoulder, and axe of a man climbing this ladder
are preserved. Between the ladder and the wall are four men. At the top we see
only two feet, right side up,[85] but the other three men are more complete and are
in a state of complete disarray. The two on the right are head down, limbs loose.
Each has an arrow stuck in his chest, and the man on the right has an additional
arrow going all the way through his muscled calf.[86] He wears a spotted kilt; the
other wears a striped one. To their left is another man with an arrow protruding
from the base of his ribcage. His head is up but he is clearly not in good shape.

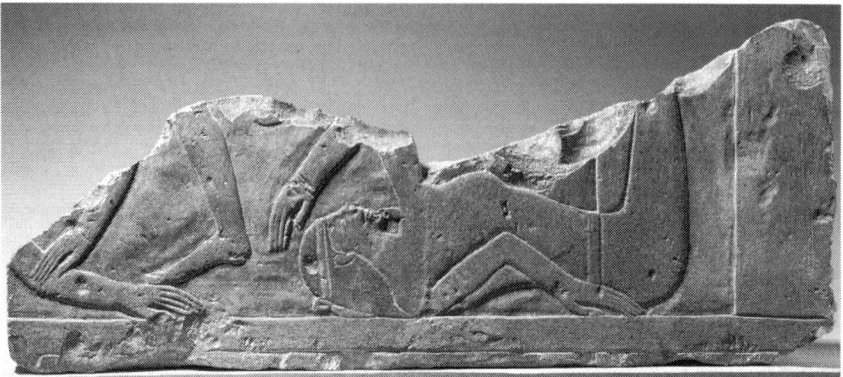

Figure 4.35 A woman wearing a hair-fillet lies in distress at the base of a wall,
disordered limbs behind her suggesting another victim of the violence.
Dimensions: 25.5 × 68.8 cm.

He raises a fist toward his bearded chin, his red-haired head is thrown back, and
another arrow has hit him smack between the eyes. His head is pressed against
a wall behind him. If there was a feather in his hair, which is possible, it was
smashed against the wall and is now largely missing. Little does his fancy kilt
avail him. This is the first unambiguous representation of an attack on a fortified
place in a royal context.

Quite possibly from the same scene comes another fragment showing pieces
of two or three people (Figure 4.35).[87] The reason for suggesting it is the same
scene is the presence, on the right, of a straight element that looks quite like
the edge of a fortress wall, if the fortress were shown in side-view. At the
base of this wall, next to it rather than overlapping it, is a woman, legs in the
air, lying on her back, one hand raised to her forehead in apparent distress.
Perhaps she has fallen off the fortification wall. She wears what looks like a
belted long skirt, and has a fillet tied around her hair. Behind her head are two
arms and a leg in disarray; if they belong to one person, this person is in an
extremely uncomfortable position. If they belong to two, they are not in much
better shape.

Two fragments preserve images of the active firing of bows. One shows a
single archer (Figure 4.36).[88] Facing to the left and wearing crossed chest straps, a
kilt with a sash or belt wrapped several times around the waist, and a sporran, he
clutches a sheath of arrows and fires the one fitted to his bow. He is clean-shaven
and his hair is not visible. Whether he is Egyptian or Nubian is uncertain.[89] This
archer's foe is also not visible.

The second archery fragment has remains of three bowmen firing in formation
(Figure 4.37).[90] It is reminiscent of the scene from Khafre's much earlier reign.
Two men, beardless heads largely preserved, face to the right. They both have
short hair with a fillet; a feather sticks up from the back of the fillet. The patterning

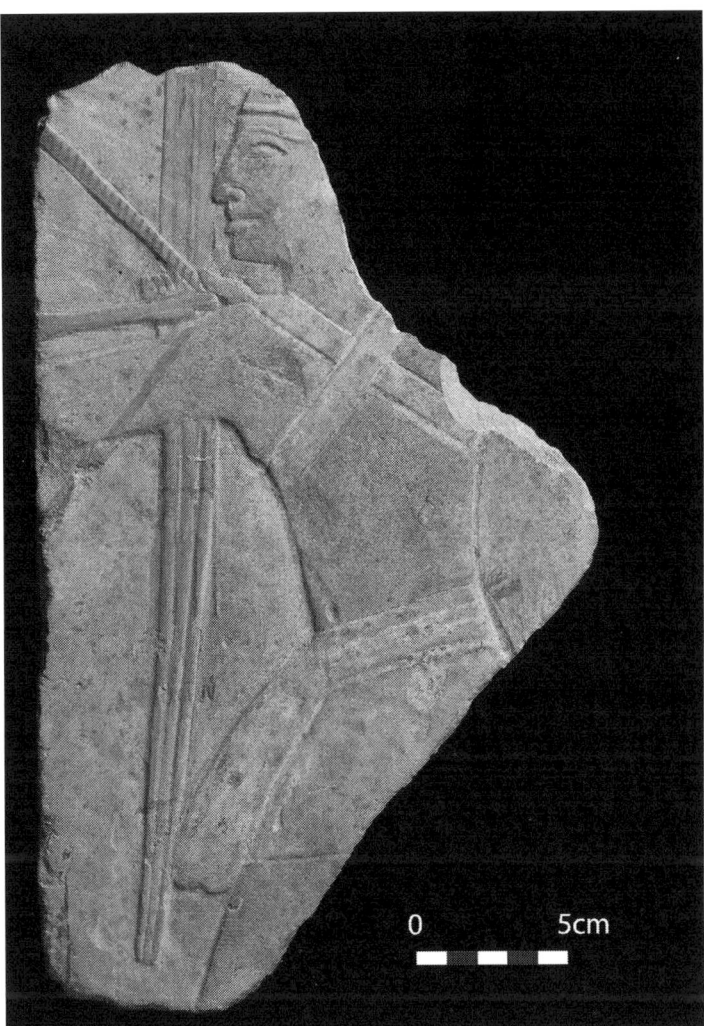

0   5cm

Figure 4.36 An archer firing his bow, from the mortuary complex of Nebhepetra
        Mentuhotep at Deir el-Bahri. This figure is a good illustration of how
        complicated assigning ethnic identity can be; Fischer first identified him
        as Nubian and subsequently changed his mind, calling him Egyptian.
        Dimensions: max. height 31 cm.

of the piece is deliberate and quite lovely, with the feathers fitting nicely into the
upper angle of each drawn bow. A third bow indicates a now missing archer. The
bows are held at the same angle, their fitted arrows angled slightly up.

    Hand-to-hand combat is preserved on two fragments in which men wear-
ing crossed straps on their chests hold on to parts of enemies. One, wearing

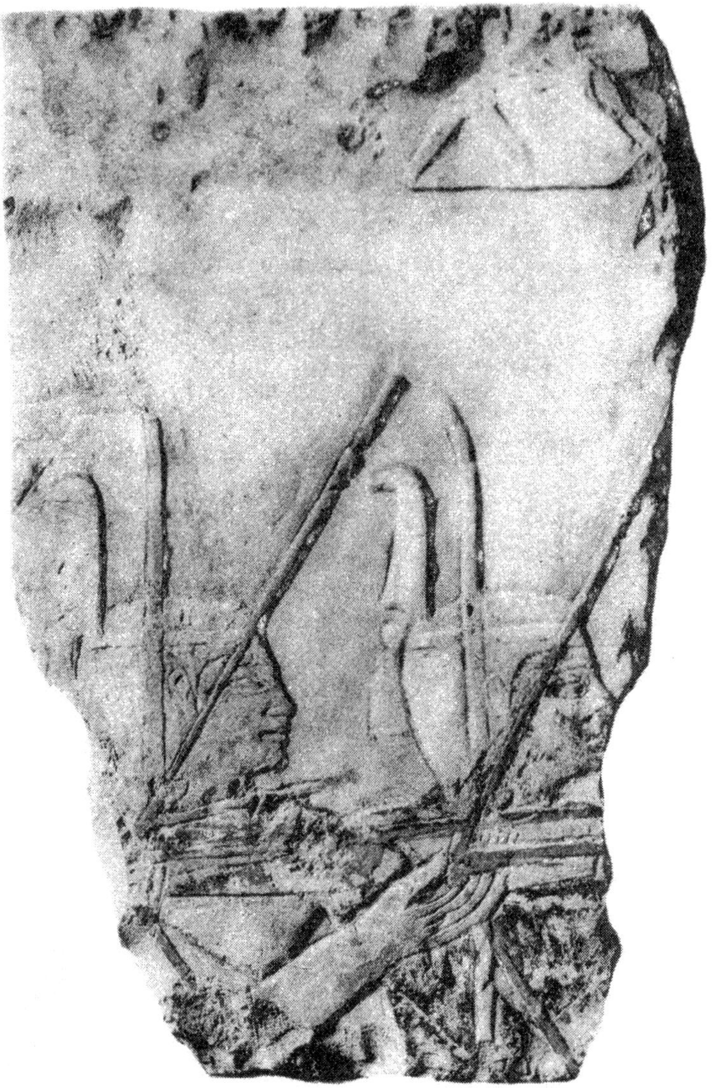

Figure 4.37 Archers firing in unison, from the mortuary complex of Nebhepetra
Mentuhotep at Deir el-Bahri.

an elaborately curled short wig and crossed chest straps, holds an ankle and
prepares to strike his yellow-skinned enemy (Figure 4.38).[91] This enemy is
clearly in disarray, his hand thrown in the air and his leg in a position entirely
incompatible with standing or offering defense. The bottom of the haft of a
weapon is visible at the upper right, and this and the pose of the striking soldier

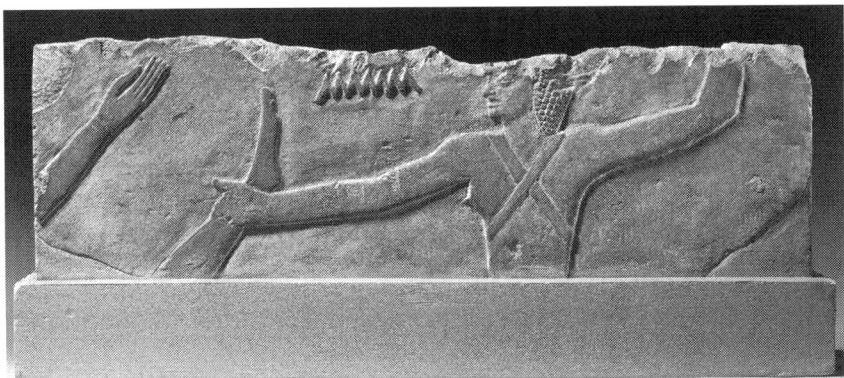

Figure 4.38 A soldier with straps crossed on his chest holds the ankle of a yellow-skinned opponent and prepares to strike him. While it cannot be read, it is clear that an inscription accompanied this image. From the mortuary complex of Nebhepetra Mentuhotep at Deir el-Bahri. Dimensions: 19 × 62.5 cm.

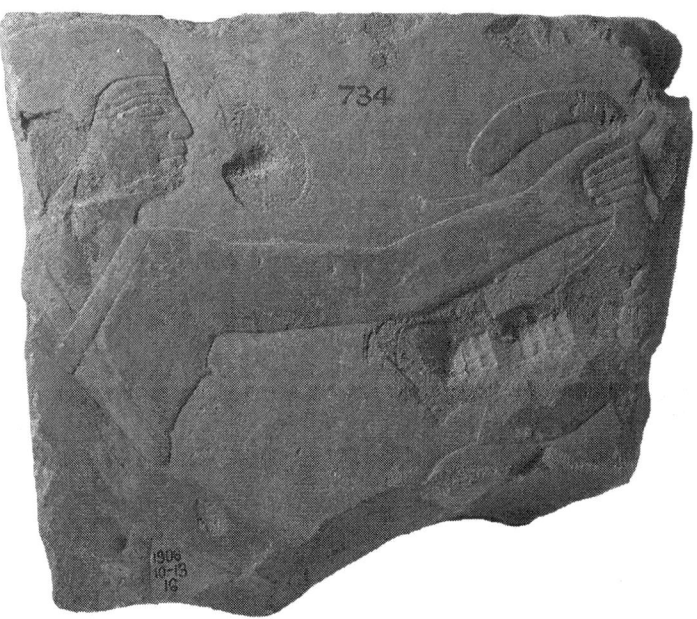

Figure 4.39 Another soldier from the mortuary complex of Nebhepetra Mentuhotep prepares to despatch a captive victim in hand-to-hand fighting. Grasping of the hair in this way is more usually associated with the king smiting, but the lowered arm of the perpetrator, and the fact that the victim does not turn to face him, separate this vignette from that classic icon.

are certainly reminiscent of the classic smiting scene, though the pose of the victim is different.

The other image shows the combatant holding the hair of his enemy, again an element related to smiting imagery though the scene as a whole is quite different, in part because the victim is in the wrong position, facing away (Figure 4.39).[92] Here the aggressor has plain hair. His second arm is held low, as though to thrust a dagger into his victim, who is too badly preserved to say much of, apart from that he wore his hair longer than he might have wished for the event in question.

A fragment with figures not opposed to one another but perhaps acting in concert shows people with different attributes (Figure 4.40).[93] On the left is the face, shoulder, and arm of an Asiatic, identified by his pointed beard and yellow skin. He grips a small rectangular shield with flared corners, which we see from the back. In front of him and with his head at a higher level, which makes their relative position somewhat difficult to understand, is a kilted man with a bare

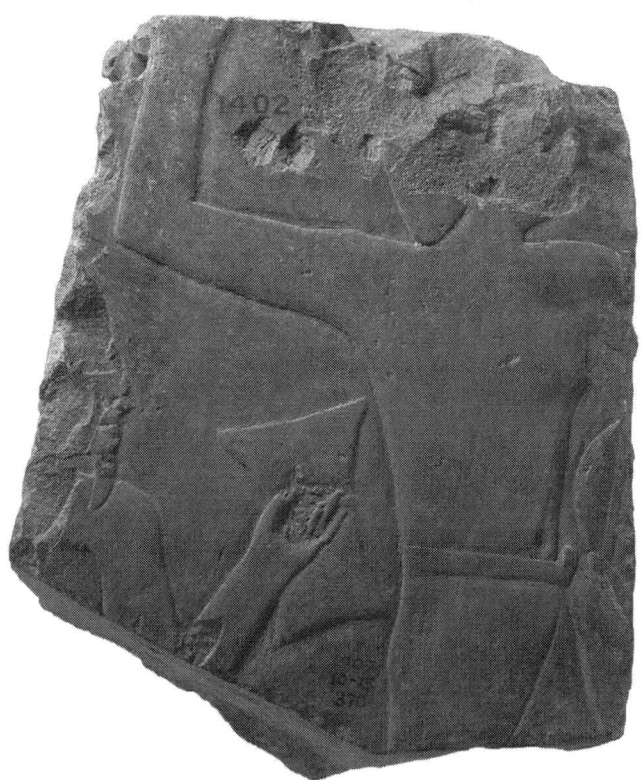

Figure 4.40 Parts of warriors. He on the left has the beard of an Asiatic as well as an unusual shield type. He on the right, with his arm raised, bears no notable stereotypical features and may be Egyptian. Dimensions: 33 × 20 cm.

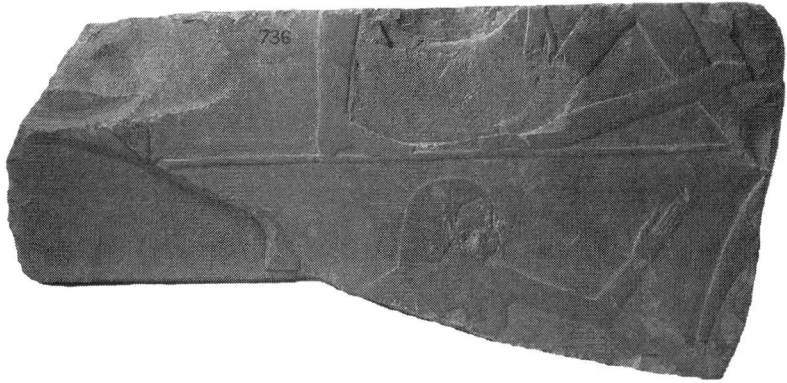

Figure 4.41 Parts of two registers, the top of which appears to show someone in the process of being slain, and the bottom surrendered females. Dimensions: 26 × 54 cm.

chest who raises his rear arm, presumably to strike a blow with a weapon that is now missing. He might be Egyptian; no ethnic attributes remain. What might be an axe blade can be seen before his torso, but I cannot determine with confidence how it works with the two warriors on the left.

Yet another fragment that appears to belong to this group has parts of two registers preserved (Figure 4.41).[94] In the upper one we see three legs, an additional foot, and a hand. The hand and right two legs are in a position suggesting their owner is being felled. The left leg, which is notably yellow in color, probably belongs with the foot that can just be seen behind the knee of the falling person. In this case, it appears that we might have a yellow-skinned person despatching a foe. The bottom register has the torso of a woman who raises her hands on either side of her in apparent submission. She wears no fillet in her hair and cannot be obviously associated with the visual stereotypes present on so many of these fragments. She seems to walk behind another woman, visible only from her wig.

A tiny but significant fragment preserves only the forearm, bow, and arrow of a single archer (Figure 4.42).[95] The importance of this piece lies in its paint. Not only are details of the bowstring picked out, but the skin of the archer is also very definitely dark brown. We should probably understand this person as a Nubian, making it the first clear use of part of what would become the standardized visual ethnic stereotype of southern people.

A final victim is shown on a small fragment that demonstrates some of the limits of our understanding of visual ethnic stereotypes. A line that looks much like the shaft of a weapon protrudes from his shoulder, and a similar line leads to his head (Figure 4.43).[96] This man wears a short beard, cut straight across the bottom and thus different from the usual beards of the "Asiatics" here, and a fillet in his shoulder-length hair. There is a feather stuck in the back of the fillet. The feather

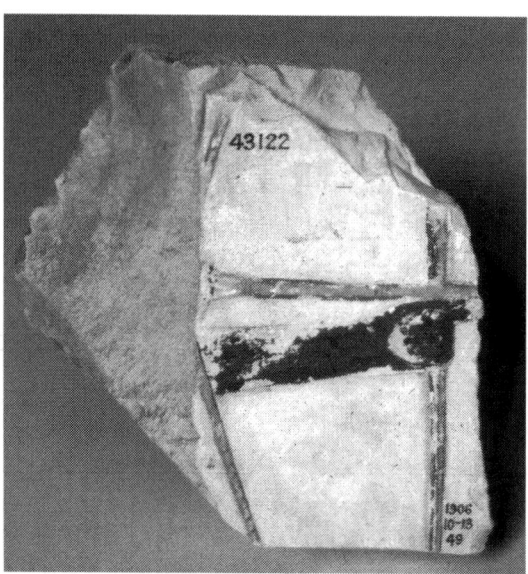

Figure 4.42 This fragment preserves only the arm and arrow of an archer, who is notable for his dark skin. This presumably indicates that he is Nubian and is the earliest known use of skin color to distinguish people from the south in a royal monument. From the mortuary complex of Nebhepertre Mentuhotep at Deir el-Bahri, Thebes. Dimensions: 14 × 15 cm.

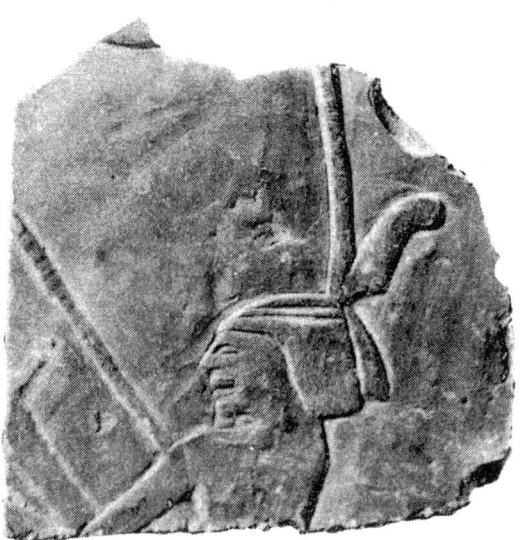

Figure 4.43 A fillet- and feather-wearing victim, chin bedecked with a square beard, with an arrow or spear protruding from his shoulder. From the mortuary complex of Nebhepetra Mentuhotep.

and fillet look much like those of the archers firing in unison above, though those are clean-shaven.

In addition to combat itself, this complex seems to have shown something of its aftermath, first hinted at with the woman with upraised arms shown above. One fillet-wearing bearded man kneels and reaches forth his arms; he may represent a prisoner. Clearer evidence comes from fragments with children. In one case a small child is held at waist height by a woman who is followed by an archer who holds his bow in a relaxed pose (Figure 4.44).[97] The bow crosses the wig of the woman; he appears to be herding her before him. She is not represented with a clear ethnic stereotype. The archer has red-brown skin and apparently a red apron in front of his kilt. The presence of children in scenes of triumph has already been seen, but the inclusion of captives at all, let alone the inclusion of women and children, has not been seen in the earlier small fragments of battle. Given the state of remaining fragments, it is impossible to say if this is a new feature or not.

Finally, while much less represented than the combat scenes, images of triumph are likely from the mortuary complex of Nebhepetra Mentuhotep. Extant fragments include overlapped faces, including probable Nubians, that likely come from a smiting scene as well as pieces showing the king as a trampling sphinx.[98]

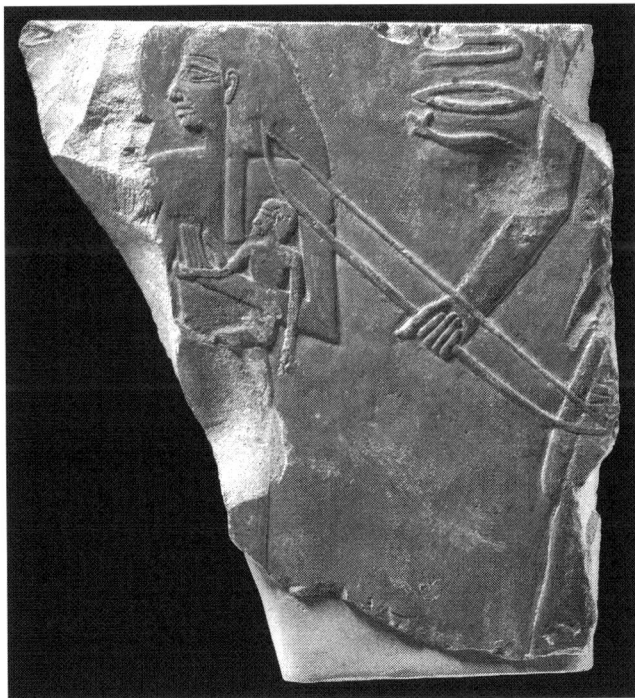

Figure 4.44 In a fragment apparently showing the aftermath of a successful battle against a place with families, not just an army, an archer herds a woman and child. From the mortuary complex of Nebhepetra Mentuhotep at Deir el-Bahri. Dimensions: 25.5 × 25.5 cm.

Representations of ethnic stereotypes are rife in these fragments. The undoubted presence of people with yellow skin and fancy clothes, stuck with arrows and falling from a place against which a ladder leans, does strongly suggest a battle against an Asiatic foe. Other fragments suggest this theme as well, though Asiatics in other cases, such as the shield holder, are not so clearly enemies. That Nebhepetra Mentuhotep here claimed to have fought against peoples of the northeast may be corroborated by a similarly damaged inscription from the same part of the complex, which appears to mention names of two such peoples.[99] This might account for the differences in iconography in apparent Asiatic victims. We also appear to have a Nubian archer. In no preserved trace from Nebhepetra Mentuhotep's mortuary complex is an Egyptian clearly shown as the victim of violence. However, even the preserved fragments suggest caution in interpreting ethnicity as directly linked to "sides" and victory in combat; we have, for instance, the same markers of fillet and feather given to the archers firing in unison, who show no signs of being beaten, and to the last victim shown above. The latter wears a short square beard and slightly longer hair. What among these attributes should be taken as definitive markers of ethnicity, and what combinations must we see to be confident of the ethnicity expressed? I do not think the surviving evidence permits us to know with precision.

In addition to the use of stereotyped images, perhaps even so precise as to differentiate between different groups of Asiatics, the scenes of war from the mortuary complex of Nebhepetra Mentuhotep are noteworthy for their inclusion of captioning inscriptions, though we cannot usually read them. There also appear to have been longer documentary inscriptions included on the same walls, some of which may refer to campaigns.[100] These two types of inscriptions in conjunction with the imagery argue for a much greater level of specificity than has previously been seen in battle pictures from any royal mortuary context in Egypt. While that specificity certainly makes the reliefs look historical to a much greater degree, the fact remains that Nebhepetra's battles that are attested from other sources were within Egypt; we are not really so certain how much control he had in the north of Egypt itself, and therefore what kind of access he would have had to the northeast outside of the territory of the Nile. This makes it almost funny to try to read historical events from these depictions: we have something we're not sure about, and are missing what we are quite confident in. It is tempting to say that this is a simple substitution, that it was less taboo to depict battle against "others" than against Egyptians, and so what were really wars within Egypt were simply switched around a bit in this very charged context. Royal mortuary pictures of war against Asiatics had a nice pedigree, after all, as shown for instance in the reliefs from Unis's causeway (Figures 4.18 and 4.19 above). On the other hand, we have seen that earlier royal mortuary complexes might have allowed for Egyptians to be victims, and in other contexts Nebhepetra showed himself smiting Egyptians (see Chapter 5). In the end, I do not think we can say with any confidence whether these battle scenes are supposed to represent real events and, if so, which ones; simply by virtue of being included here we must understand their purpose as essentially ideological even if they did incorporate historical occurrences.

While there is no doubt that Deir el-Bahri is a royal mortuary complex, it also for the first time raises fairly serious questions about the division between royal and divine temples, and thus the inclusion of martial imagery in each. There is debate about the degree to which Nebhepetra himself was actually deified during his lifetime,[101] but that this monument is tied into the divine cultic landscape of Thebes in a way that is larger than just the king's mortuary cult is beyond doubt. As such, for our purposes, the designation of Nebhepetra's Deir el-Bahri temple as a royal mortuary complex is somewhat problematic: the reliefs in this temple might have been seen during rituals associated with the gods of Thebes as well as those associated with the king himself. This foreshadows what will become standard in the New Kingdom.

The martial relief scenes of Nebhepetra Mentuhotep's mortuary complex are especially interesting in contrast to those known from other monuments he built. The inclusion at Deir el-Bahri of many lively, individualized scenes of various aspects of combat is not like his utilization of the ancient and static smiting scene in other contexts (see Chapter 5). While the division between royal and divine is more problematic for this king than it has been at any previous point, the discrepancy in the usage of this type of imagery in different contexts is notable.

The Twelfth Dynasty

Amenemhat I

A small number of fragments from the pyramid complex of Amenemhat I at Lisht contain elements that, while not directly showing violence on a scale we can be certain of, are together strongly suggestive. In particular these include a Libyan captive with bound wrists, a child carried on the back of an adult, a sheaf of arrows grasped in a hand, and—most telling of all—a tiny fragment of a head with two feathers, from which a shaft that might be an arrow protrudes.[102] The relationship of these fragments to those found at Deir el-Bahri from the reign of Nebhepetra Mentuhotep is clear, and can be taken as likely indicating the presence of at least one battle scene. The specific location of the scene(s) from which these fragments came within the pyramid temple complex cannot be reconstructed.

Senwosret I

The first Twelfth Dynasty mortuary complex certain to have held images of violence belongs to Senwosret I at Lisht.[103] Only fragments remain, and not all of them published, but they demonstrate the presence of at least three smiting scenes, a combat scene, and bound prisoners from the pyramid temple.[104]

A fragment from Lisht currently in the Royal Ontario Museum in Toronto shows the outstretched left hand of the king clutching the hair of five captives (Figure 4.45).[105] Slight variation in the color of the hair of the captives might be

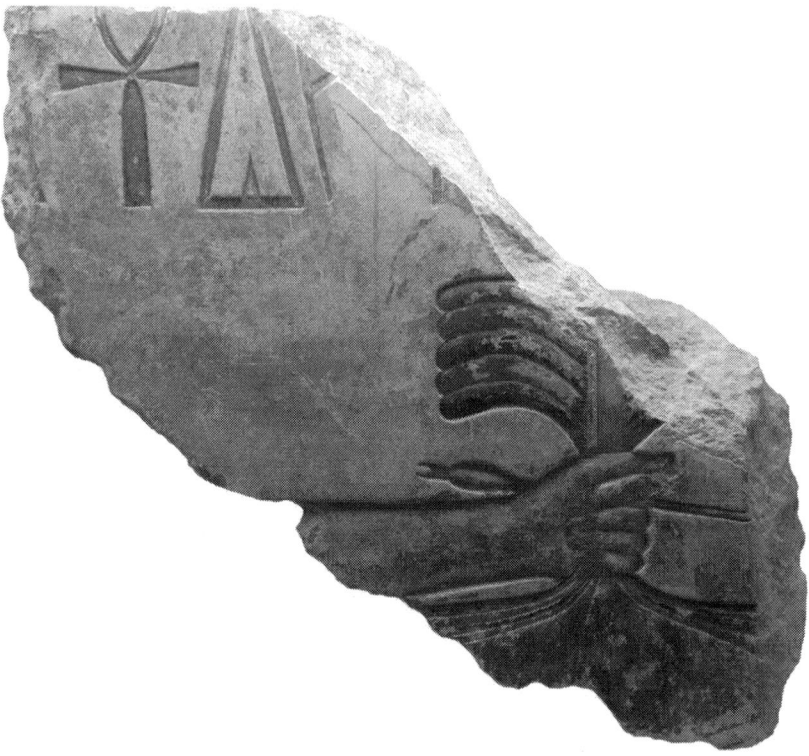

Figure 4.45 Senwosret I grasps the hair of what appear to be five people, presumably to
             smite them. The inclusion of an arrow in the king's hand is unusual. From
             his pyramid complex at Lisht.

just a visual effect or might indicate that the victims are of different ethnicities. In
addition to a segment of what is presumably a long staff, the king holds a fletched
arrow. This is the first time I know of when a king is shown in a way that indicates
he might be shooting an arrow in a scene other than hunting. In fact, the elements
of this scene—hair of smitees, arrow apparently fit to a bow string (though that
is not shown, at least not by the bottom of the king's hand)—do not make much
sense together either visually or in terms of meaning. I know of no previous smiting scene where the king holds an arrow, but the combination might be seen as
foreshadowing some of the more baroque combinations that will come in the New
Kingdom, such as Seti simultaneously strangling a Libyan with a bow while preparing to smite him with a sword from a moving chariot.[106]

Fragments of two other smiting scenes are also known from Lisht, almost certainly associated with the pyramid of Senwosret I. One currently in Princeton is
similar to the above scene, with the king facing to the right and clutching the hair
of five overlapping captives. Here the king's long staff crosses the hair of his

victims, and there is no arrow in the picture. The final known Senwosret I smiting scene is represented on two fragments in Cairo.[107] In this case, two tufts of hair are present in the king's hand, and we have the preserved face of one of his victims: lifted to face the king, furrowed brow giving more pathos to the scene than is usual. Because we have the king's hand and the hair tufts in all three cases, we can be confident that they belong to different iterations of the smiting scene. A separate fragment with Seshat making a record, with foreigners of different types as determinatives to the inscription in front of her, might have belonged to one of these smiting scenes or another.[108]

That a combat scene once graced the complex of Senwosret I is clear from a single fragment that preserves the torso of a spear-throwing foreigner (Figure 4.46).[109] His curly hair, puffy on top of his forehead, is previously unattested in this corpus, but his rather yellow skin and his pointed beard mark him as an Asiatic. The edge of his shield can be seen to the left; it appears to be the same sort held by the Asiatic on a fragment from the mortuary complex of Nebhepetra.

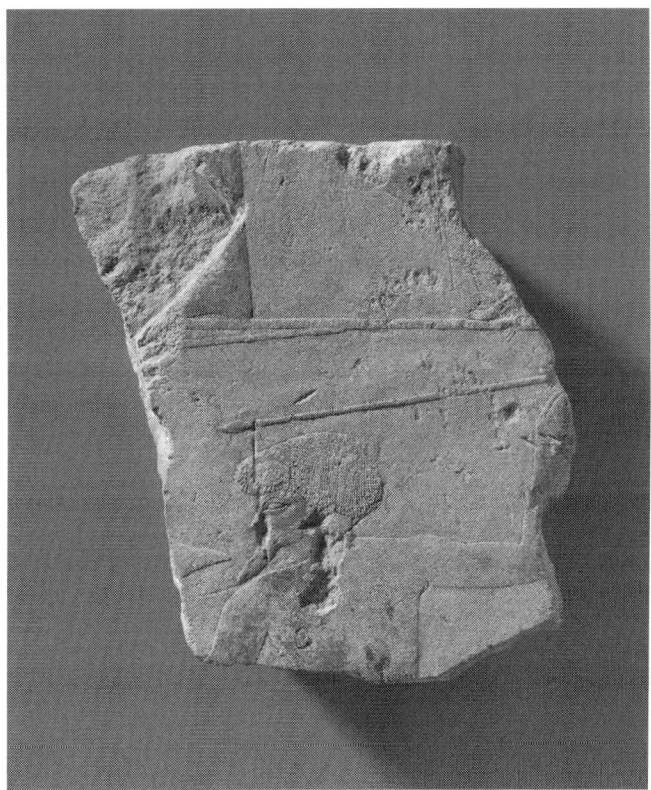

Figure 4.46 A foreigner with an unusual hairstyle, but a beard that may indicate he is Asiatic, hurls a spear. From the pyramid temple of Senwosret I at Lisht, Twelfth Dynasty. Dimensions: 22 × 22 cm.

The angle of the spear is slightly down, and it may be that this figure stood atop a fortification. Two feet and a knee from the register above are shown in a position of action that suggests battle also occupied that register.

One small fragment from Senwosret I's causeway appears to show two men grappling with one another but is too fragmentary to allow us to be certain of either their actions or their ethnicities, though they do seem to be differentiated and one may be a Libyan.[110]

Senwosret III

The relief decoration from the mortuary complex of Senwosret III at Dahshur yielded multiple fragments with violent imagery. The so-called South Temple, an enigmatic structure without close precedent in other pyramid complexes, is the location of an image of the king bending to smite a group of captives.[111] In it, four elbows of different colors are all that remain of the captives, who seem to be raising their hands in plea; the king's navel can be seen to the left. A different block has the remains of parallel bent legs of prisoners from the same type of scene, possibly the same scene, and a separate fragment shows a bound Libyan captive. Egyptian troops are also represented in the fragments, including one with running archers[112] and a second with the head of an archer.[113]

While these demonstrate the continuation of broader military themes from the Old Kingdom, they do not add to our understanding of direct violence. The temple attached to the pyramid has no such images, and the reduced size of this temple has suggested to Oppenheim that it played a changing role in the dynamic royal cult of the time.[114] None of these fragments present unexpected themes, though details of the king's dress in the smiting scene and a feather visible below the elbows suggest something might have been a bit unusual here. The archer has been called Nubian but the grounds for this identification are not really clear; his hair, and that he is an archer, might be suggestive but are hardly definitive, particularly given the presence of archers who do not appear marked for ethnicity from the same complex.

Additional hints of violence have been excavated from the causeway of Senwosret III. Fragmentary bits include dark-skinned men with various weapons, including bows and arrows, sometimes in active postures. In one case we have bits of two registers, with the top showing walking feet and the lower showing feet in the air, presumably representing dead or dying victims in a battle. While it cannot be ruled out that these fragments come from a battle against Nubians, it seems on balance more probable, when considering the whole corpus of violent imagery, that Nubians and Egyptians fight together against a common enemy here. Representations of Asiatics as personified places on fragments from the causeway suggest who that enemy was.[115]

Aside from demonstrating that triumph and battle scenes, with actors differentiated on the basis of visual stereotypes, continued into the Twelfth Dynasty in the context of the royal tomb, the complexes of the Twelfth Dynasty do not add much to our knowledge of this motif.

Interpreting imagery of violence from royal tombs

Violent scenes from kings' mortuary complexes include images of the king smiting captives, of the king trampling enemies, and of battle. As the collection of these images demonstrates, themes ranging from scene type to ethnicity were moderately consistent across the Old and Middle Kingdoms, with some innovations but no major ruptures seen over time. In these concluding remarks I will address some aspects of what these images might have communicated to whom, and how they functioned. To do this I will briefly examine their audience, followed by a discussion of historicism in the corpus, and then ideology. Collectively I think they argue for a relatively simple vision of kingship, one in which historical specificity, nuance, and personality are elided in favor of timeless themes of domination. They represent, then, the theory of kingship rather than its practice, as is befitting their context: their essential purpose was to permit the king his proper afterlife in a rightly functioning cosmos, not to record mundane events.

Audience

All of the relief images appear to have been on the interiors of the buildings. It is not clear how accessible the interior or even the exterior of mortuary monuments of kings would have been to a living human audience, but the answer probably lies somewhere in between "not very" and "almost not at all." Some parts of the complex were clearly intended to allow for the ritual feeding of statues of the king, which we know involved groups of priests.[116] But perhaps surprisingly, some aspects of the complex seem to have been totally inaccessible; notably, the causeways of several kings were permanently blocked off at times when cult activity was still going on in the associated temples, meaning that these causeways were not only passages for living priests between these temples.[117] At least some of the imagery was thus not accessible even to the limited human audience that was allowed in parts of the complex. Lack of accessibility, even of light, suggests that the chief audience for the images was the deceased king himself and the gods; a human audience was rather subsidiary, and any view of these relief cycles as propagandistic communication to a general public about the role of the king is misplaced.

Gods themselves are, of course, sometimes an audience to the violence portrayed even within the images themselves. That the divine cared about the king smiting is absolutely certain: there is Seshat, writing down the numbers. But that the audience within and of the pictures is not entirely the same is also quite clear, and this reminds us forcefully of the difference between violence itself and pictures of it as tactics of royal power. Seshat might see the inside of a pyramid complex, but no Libyan family would have.

Historicism

Do all or some of the violent moments in time captured in relief, displayed for gods and dead kings, depict events that actually happened? The answer to this question certainly has consequences for our use of such scenes to understand Egyptian history, but does it affect our interpretation of the scenes, their role within royal mortuary complexes, and their relationship to royal ideology? I would suggest that (a) not all of the scenes can reflect events, but some might; (b) that some of those events must have been ritual in nature even if they did really occur; and (c) that in any individual mortuary complex it is relatively unimportant if an event depicted took place at all or in the reign of that king, but that, on the whole, the prevalence of violent imagery is so pervasive as to demonstrate that violent domination is fundamental to royal ideology. This is hardly a revolutionary conclusion. It does seem likely to me that this ideological role was grounded in ongoing actual violence on the part of Egyptian kings, not only historical memory or rituals that offered substitutes for violence, but this is in the end pure speculation.

It is highly unlikely, if not impossible, that all images of violence from royal mortuary complexes are directly related to particular violent actions. The best example of this is the trampling scene, which cannot easily be read as anything other than symbolic, both because of the form of the king and because of the mixture of enemies in individual tableaux. The latter point also applies to smiting scenes, but here the issue is murkier and has received much attention, particularly with regard to the Libyan Family Scene. In that scene, the combination of extremely specific details—the names of the family—along with repetition across reigns leads to the impression that it is *supposed* to look like a particular historical event, the killing of a particular chief after a battle, but that it cannot be. The kings who have the scene cannot all have fought historical battles with enemies with the same names.

It might be too simple to laugh at the kings copying from one another to claim an event they had no right to, or unthinkingly repeating a cliché. In the first place, the scenes are not copies of one another, exhibiting even within the preserved fragments some notable differences. Furthermore, in at least one case the king smites people of different ethnicities while watched by the Libyan family; this, then, does not purport to be a simple post-battle historical triumph. If repetition keeps us from seeing this as historical, and the multiplicity of enemies in one case cautious us against seeing it as a claim to be historical, can we at least imagine other types of reality to which it might refer? Might there have been a more ritual action than a historical one? Smiting, after all, is never shown in connection with battles in this corpus that we can see—it does not lay visual claim to be culmination of actual war. Might smiting the foreigners have been a royal ceremony enacted independent of war? In this case, we might draw an analogy to drama, and suggest that a repeated ceremony might have required the playing of named roles, different actors with the same names reign in and reign out. The performance of a dramatic script is itself both grounded in time and meaningful because of its connection to repetition. Whether or not smiting itself was repeated or only the carving of it on walls, to think of it in terms of drama reminds us not to be contemptuous of repetition, of variations within that repetition, of the celebration of artistry even inside a determined framework, of the need, each time, to convince an audience that *this* instance matters even if they already know the plot.

Our third type of scene, the battle scene, would appear to have the most obvious capacity for historical accuracy. Unfortunately we have very few of these scenes, and none of them are labeled. However, some aspects of them point to a function that is less universalizing and less obviously related to kingship, and that therefore might have left scope for inclusion of historical events in a way the more formal scenes of triumph did not. There are no preserved examples of the king engaged in battle, and given the types of scenes we have of battle—hand-to-hand combat and archers firing in unison—it is not clear how he could have been incorporated without violating the decorum of royal depictions. In this regard, the adoption of the chariot by New Kingdom kings was not only an innovative weapon of war but also something that allowed for a real change in imagery, providing a way for the king to be simultaneously engaged in battle and separate from it, still unique. I think it is unlikely that the king was depicted in battle prior to that, and that his absence here is not simply a matter of poor preservation.

If I am correct, the apparent absence of the king from battle scenes prior to the New Kingdom suggests that they were not used to make straightforward points about royal valor or domination. What do they do? All remaining battle scenes from royal mortuary complexes where the combatants can be sorted into sides show Asiatics as victims of Egyptian soldiers. That there might be some Asiatics also fighting on the side of Egyptians does not negate the fact that victims are restricted to this group, rigorously identified by means of the now-codified visual stereotypes. Triumph scenes show no such particularity, regularly including not only Asiatics but also Libyans, people presumed to be from the south, and even on occasion apparently Egyptians. It is tempting to read this as representing episodes in a broad historical pattern in which Egypt fought more wars to the northeast than to the west or south, in contrast to a more ideological and universalizing significance for the triumph scenes. The problem, of course, is that the scenes still do not look convincingly like actual battles in which we can be confident. Only Nebhepetra Mentuhotep has enough preserved for us to get much sense of the picture of a battle as a whole, and we are not certain he fought people from the northeast at all.

That battle scenes, even if they pictured historical battles, were not intended to give a complete record of wars fought by the kings who commissioned the pictures seems likely. This is seen most clearly again with Nebhepetra Mentuhotep, whose numerous fragments of battle include none that look like the civil wars we know he fought and that were also important to his brand of legitimacy. This does mean that even if history is an element, the utilization of battle scenes as a whole was curated in a way where accuracy was second to ideology, and that not all elements either of violent history or violent ideology were appropriate for visual expression in all contexts.

In the end, while we ourselves wish to know how accurate these scenes of violence are and how much we can read of real violence from them, I think the question of history misses the point. The corpus cannot be understood without attending both to its insistence on specificity and to the ways it distances itself from specifics. Allegory, repetition, impossible combinations, lack of details, unpictured wars—all not only work against historical readings, but must also be understood in their own right as deliberate choices designed to make the images effective at what they *were* intended to do. What they were intended to do was to connect particular kings with an ideology of kingship.

Ideology

The ideology argued for by violent images in royal mortuary complexes is not subtle. Triumph scenes in particular offer a picture of dominant kingship that is absolute. They do not seem nuanced in any way, though as all are fragmentary it is likely that we are missing some elements, such as crowns, which might deepen the picture at least a bit. As extant, they offer a sustained argument that the ideal king is violently dominant over all peoples. Those peoples are represented quite consistently and clearly refer to geographic regions outside Egypt; with somewhat less certainty I have suggested that Egyptians are also in the mix. It is the peoples, not the lands they come from, who are dominated in the visual imagery. The king himself is present in greater variety, being both human and mythical beasts.

There is no clear indication in this material that either foreigners or violence are elements of chaos; in fact, while the king as dominator of foreign peoples is certainly a main point, the relationship if any that such domination had to keeping order is not obvious unless we ourselves read it into the scenes. To my mind, and recognizing the very limited amount of evidence and the problems of arguing from silence, the separation between triumph and battle scenes and the absence of the king from the latter even speaks against a reading of violent motifs in this context as inherently and always reducible to the royal imposition of order on chaos. If triumph is a thing the king does, battle is a thing that happens; its relationship to kingship as anything other than background noise is not immediately obvious from the preserved fragments.

If the purpose of the relief program as a whole was to demonstrate to the gods that the king was worthy of maintenance in this life and the next,[118] then it seems reasonable that his domination over all be one focus of the program and the main import of violent scenes. It also seems reasonable that particular events, both ritual and historical, played a role, if a secondary one. The king must be an exemplar of kingship. Being an exemplar required both that he act individually and that those actions be proper within a universal framework of kingship. Scenes of violence in royal mortuary complexes must have been deeply reassuring to their audience, proving that the king in question was doing what he should. But for precisely that reason, we should not expect that a focus on the particular was likewise a need for accuracy. It is quite possible, even probable, that the king practiced violence both by ordering wars and engaging in violent rituals, but we cannot do more than speculate on the relationship between any such actions and pictures of them on royal tomb walls. In such a context, to produce such an outcome, the theory of kingship was more important than the reality of a king's reign. And so we return to Delacroix's striding Liberty: a scene no time-traveling photographer could have captured, it is successful both because it references specific events and because ideology is triumphantly ascendant, treading on those events in glory.

Notes

1 The painting is oil on canvas and measures 260 × 325 cm. It was first exhibited in the 1831 Salon; it now hangs in the Louvre: R.F. 129. Masterpics/Alamy Stock Photo.
2 Map by the author.
3 See Chapter 7 for imagery of violence on portable objects, including jewelry.
4 Dagmar Stockfisch, "Bemerkungen zur sog. 'Libyschen Familie,'" in *Wege Öffnen: Festschrift für Rolf Gundlach zum 65. Geburtstag*, Ed. Mechthild Schade-Busch (Wiesbaden: Harrassowitz, 1996), 315–325; Jean Leclant, "La 'famille libyenne' au temple haut de Pépi IER," in *Livre du centenaire 1880–1980*, Ed. Jean Vercoutter (Cairo: Institut français d'archéologie orientale du Caire, 1980), 49–54. The Twenty-Fifth Dynasty King Taharqa also had two Libyan Family Scenes as part of his iconographic program at the Temple T at Kawa, in Nubia. László Török, *The Image of the Ordered World in Ancient Nubian Art: The Construction of the Kushite Mind* (Leiden, Boston, MA: Brill, 2002), 93–94; M.F. Laming Macadam, *The Temples of Kawa II: History and Archaeology of the Site* (Oxford: Oxford University Press, 1955), pl. IX.
5 Ludwig Borchardt identifies men with armbands pictured as enemies in Sahure's reliefs as Puntites: *Das Grabdenkmal des Königs S'aḥu-Re (Band 2): die Wandbilder: Text* (Leipzig: J.C. Hinrichs'sche Buchhandlung, 1913), 18–23. However, other scholars seem to generally disagree with this identification; Leclant, for example, identifies a smote enemy with the armband as a Nubian: Leclant, "La 'famille libyenne' au temple haut de Pépi IER," 50. Others prefer to be more general and identify such peoples as either Puntite or Nubian, or simply as southerners: Henry George Fischer, "Varia Aegyptiaca," *Journal of the American Research Center in Egypt* 2 (1963): 34–39; Thomas Schneider, *Ausländer in Ägypten während des Mittleren Reiches und der Hyksoszeit. Teil 1: die ausländischen Könige* (Wiesbaden: Harrassowitz, 1998), 17.
6 Hermann Junker, *Giza II: Grabungen auf dem Friedhof des Alten Reiches bei den Pyramiden von Giza: Band II: die Maṣṭabas der beginnenden V. Dynastie auf dem Westfriedhof* (Wien and Leipzig: Hölder-Pichler-Tempsky, 1934), fig. 28 (right side); Hermann Junker, *Giza III: Grabungen auf dem Friedhof des Alten Reiches bei den Pyramiden von Giza: Band III: die Mastabas der vorgeschrittenen V. Dynastie auf dem Westfriedhof* (Wien and Leipzig: Hölder-Pichler-Tempsky, 1938), fig. 27 (right side).
7 Tarek El Awady, *Abusir XVI: Sahure—The Pyramid Causeway: History and Decoration Program in the Old Kingdom* (Prague: Charles University in Prague, 2009), 59.
8 Adela Oppenheim gives a discussion of the Khufu program in "Decorative Programs and Architecture in the Pyramid Complexes of the Third and Fourth Dynasties," in *Structure and Significance: Thoughts on Ancient Egyptian Architecture*, Ed. Peter Jánosi (Vienna: Austrian Academy of Sciences Press, 2005), 464–468,
9 Georg Steindorff, "Die übrigen Fundstücke," in *Das Grabdenkmal des Königs Chephren*, Ed. Uvo Hölscher (Leipzig: J.C. Hinrichs'sche Buchhandlung, 1912), 110–111, fig. 163. Steindorff attributed the piece to the Fifth Dynasty on the basis of the fine carving and the iconographic similarity of the bound prisoner to reliefs from the pyramid complex of Sahure (see Figures 4.6 and 4.7). More recently, it has

been argued that a Fourth Dynasty date is more probable: Oppenheim, "Decorative Programs and Architecture in the Pyramid Complexes of the Third and Fourth Dynasties," 470 and notes.

10   Steindorff, "Die übrigen Fundstücke," 111.

11   Visible in Steindorff, "Die übrigen Fundstücke," 110, fig. 162.

12   Oppenheim, "Decorative Programs and Architecture in the Pyramid Complexes of the Third and Fourth Dynasties," 470.

13   Metropolitan Museum of Art 22.1.23; www.metmuseum.org. The dating of this piece has been the subject of discussion. Its most recent attribution, to Khafre, has been proposed by Dorothea Arnold: Dorothea Arnold, Christiane Ziegler, and Krzysztof Grzymski, Ed., *Egyptian Art in the Age of the Pyramids* (New York: Metropolitan Museum of Art, 1999), 264–267, cat. no. 66; Hans Goedicke attributed it to Khufu in *Re-Used Blocks from the Pyramid of Amenemhet I at Lisht* (New York: Metropolitan Museum of Art Egyptian Expedition, 1972), 74–77.

14   Audran Labrousse and Jean-Philippe Lauer, *Les complexes funéraires d'Ouserkaf et de Néferthétepès. Volume 1* (Cairo: Institut français d'archéologie oriental du Caire, 2000), 111–113; Audran Labrousse and Jean-Philippe Lauer, *Les complexes funéraires d'Ouserkaf et de Néferthétepès. Volume 2* (Cairo: Institut français d'archéologie oriental du Caire, 2000), figs. 228–232.

15   Userkaf had other reliefs that showed military personnel in non-violent tableaux, including two of running troops and one of runners and rowers on a ship: Arnold, Ziegler, and Grzymski, *Egyptian Art in the Age of the Pyramids*, 319, cat. nos. 103–104; William Stevenson Smith, *The Art and Architecture of Ancient Egypt: Revised with Additions by William Kelly Simpson* (New Haven, CT and London: Yale University Press, 1981), 128–129, fig. 122. The association of running troops and ships is a particular theme that is found in other pyramid complexes and in private tombs of the Old Kingdom.

16   Figure 4.5: Borchardt, *Das Grabdenkmal des Königs S'aḥu-Re (Band 2): die Wandbilder: Abbildungsblätter*, pl. 1.

17   While only a bit of this is preserved, the reading seems secure. Kurt Sethe, "Die Inschriften," in *Das Grabdenkmal des Königs S'aḥu-Re (Band 2): die Wandbilder: Text*, Ed. Ludwig Borchardt (Leipzig: J.C. Hinrichs'sche Buchhandlung, 1913), 72.

18   Borchardt, *Das Grabdenkmal des Königs S'aḥu-Re (Band 2): die Wandbilder: Abbildungsblätter*, pl. 2.

19   Andrzej Ćwiek, "Relief Decoration in the Royal Funerary Complexes of the Old Kingdom: Studies in the Development, Scene Content and Iconography" (PhD diss., Warsaw University, 2003), 201–202.

20   Borchardt, *Das Grabdenkmal des Königs S'aḥu-Re (Band 2): die Wandbilder: Abbildungsblätter*, pl. 5.

21   Borchardt, *Das Grabdenkmal des Königs S'aḥu-Re (Band 2): die Wandbilder: Abbildungsblätter*, pl. 5.

22   Borchardt, *Das Grabdenkmal des Königs S'aḥu-Re (Band 2): die Wandbilder: Text*, 19; Sethe, "Die Inschriften," 83.

23   Borchardt, *Das Grabdenkmal des Königs S'aḥu-Re (Band 2): die Wandbilder: Text*, 19–20.

24   Borchardt, *Das Grabdenkmal des Königs S'aḥu-Re (Band 2): die Wandbilder: Text*, 21.

25   Borchardt, *Das Grabdenkmal des Königs S'aḥu-Re (Band 2): die Wandbilder: Abbildungsblätter*, pl. 6.

26   Sethe, who first published the inscription when the original excavation was done, suggested that this may have reflected an historical reality, with Sahure including here only peoples over whom he had had success. Sethe, "Die Inschriften," 82.

27   Awady, *Abusir XVI*, 116, fig. 67a.

28 Zahi Hawass and Miroslav Verner, "Newly Discovered Blocks from the Causeway of Sahure," *Mitteilungen des Deutschen Archäologischen Instituts, Abteilung Kairo* 52 (1996): 184; Awady, *Abusir XVI*, 206–211.

29 Awady, *Abusir XVI*, 207, fig. 94.

30 Awady, *Abusir XVI*, 206–208.

31 Awady, *Abusir XVI*, 208–210.

32 Awady suggests that this shows a real wrestling match as opposed to training: Awady, *Abusir XVI*, 210–211.

33 Borchardt, *Das Grabdenkmal des Königs S'aḫu-Re (Band 2): die Wandbilder: Abbildungsblätter*, pl. 8.

34 Adolf Erman and Hermann Grapow, *Wörterbuch der ägyptischen Sprache, Band 3* (Leipzig: J.C. Hinrichs'sche Buchhandlung, 1929), 462.

35 The first reference to the symbol of the Nine Bows in its fully developed form is on the base of a statue of Djoser of the Third Dynasty: Eric Uphill, "The Nine Bows," *Jaarbericht van het Vooraziatische-Egyptisch Genootschap Ex Oriente Lux* 19 (1967): 394. Possible precursors of the concept and symbolism of the Nine Bows might date as far back as the Gebel Sheikh Suleiman relief, but this is uncertain: Panagiotis Kousoulis, "Egyptian vs. Otherness and the Issue of Acculturation in the Egyptian Demonic Discourse of the Late Bronze Age," in *Athanasia: The Earthly, the Celestial and the Underworld in the Mediterranean from the Late Bronze and the Early Iron Age*, Ed. Nicholas Chr. Stampolidis, Athanasia Kanta, and Angeliki Giannikouri (Herakleion: University of Crete, 2012), 130.

36 Berlin 16110/11/15, No. 17922. Ludwig Borchardt, *Das Grabdenkmal des Königs Ne-user-Re'* (Leipzig: J.C. Hinrichs'sche Buchhandlung, 1907), 86, fig. 64.

37 Borchardt, *Das Grabdenkmal des Königs Ne-user-Re'*, 47.

38 Berlin No. 17919. Borchardt, *Das Grabdenkmal des Königs Ne-user-Re'*, pl. 11.

39 Berlin No. 17910. Borchardt, *Das Grabdenkmal des Königs Ne-user-Re'*, 38–39, fig. 19.

40 Ćwiek suggested that this was the arm of the king. Ćwiek, "Relief Decoration in the Royal Funerary Complexes of the Old Kingdom," 202.

41 Audran Labrousse, Jean-Philippe Lauer, and Jean Leclant, *Mission archéologique de Saqqarah II: le temple haut du complexe funéraire du roi Ounas* (Cairo: Institut français d'archéologie orientale du Caire, 1977), 88–90, fig. 65, pl. 32.

42 Labrousse, Lauer, and Leclant, *Mission archéologique de Saqqarah II: le temple haut du complexe funéraire du roi Ounas*, 91, fig. 66, pl. 32.

43 Ćwiek, "Relief Decoration in the Royal Funerary Complexes of the Old Kingdom," 203.

44 Labrousse, Lauer, and Leclant, *Mission archéologique de Saqqarah II: le temple haut du complexe funéraire du roi Ounas*, 92, fig. 67, pl. 32.

45 Labrousse, Lauer, and Leclant, *Mission archéologique de Saqqarah II: le temple haut du complexe funéraire du roi Ounas*, 93–94, figs. 69–71, pl. 32.

46 Andrés Diego Espinel, "Blocks from the Unas Causeway Recorded in Černý's Notebooks at the Griffith Institute, Oxford," in *Old Kingdom, New Perspectives*, Ed. Nigel Strudwick and Helen Strudwick (Oxford and Oakville, ON: Oxbow Books, 2011), 52.

47 Audran Labrousse and Ahmed Moussa, *La chaussée du complexe funéraire du roi Ounas* (Cairo: Institut français d'archéologie orientale du Caire, 2002), 19–20, 135, fig. 15.

48 Labrousse and Moussa, *La chaussée du complexe funéraire du roi Ounas*, 19–20, 134–135, fig.14–15.

49 Audran Labrousse and Ahmed Moussa, *Le temple d'accueil du complexe funéraire du roi Ounas* (Cairo: Institut français d'archéologie orientale du Caire, 1996), 96–99.

50 Labrousse and Moussa, *La chaussée du complexe funéraire du roi Ounas*, 136, fig. 16.

51 Labrousse and Moussa, *La chaussée du complexe funéraire du roi Ounas*, 136, fig. 17.

52 Boris de Rachewiltz, "Scavi sulla via sacra di Unis," *Archivio Internazionale di Etnografia e Preistoria* 2 (1959): pl. 5, fig. 10. Every effort was made to contact the publisher for permission to publish this image (and 4.21, 4.22) with no success.

53 de Rachewiltz, "Scavi sulla via sacra di Unis," pl. 6, fig. 12.

54 Labrousse and Moussa, *La chaussée du complexe funéraire du roi Ounas*, 137, fig. 20.

55 Espinel, "Blocks from the Unas Causeway Recorded in Černý's Notebooks at the Griffith Institute, Oxford," 60–61.

56 Espinel, "Blocks from the Unas Causeway Recorded in Černý's Notebooks at the Griffith Institute, Oxford," 61, fig. 9.

57 de Rachewiltz, "Scavi sulla via sacra di Unis," pl. 5, fig. 11.

58 Labrousse and Moussa, *Le temple d'accueil du complexe funéraire du roi Ounas*, 80–1.

59 Leclant, "La 'famille libyenne' au temple haut de Pépi IER," pl. 2.

60 Leclant, "La 'famille libyenne' au temple haut de Pépi IER," 52.

61 Gustave Jéquier, *Fouilles à Saqqarah: le monument funéraire de Pepi II. Tome II: le temple* (Cairo: Institut français d'archéologie oriental du Caire, 1938), pl. 8.

62 Jéquier, *Le monument funéraire de Pepi II. Tome II: le temple*, pl. 36.

63 See Jéquier, *Le monument funéraire de Pepi II. Tome II: le temple*, pl. 37 for detail.

64 Jéquier, *Le monument funéraire de Pepi II. Tome II: le temple*, pl. 38 bottom.

65 Jéquier, *Le monument funéraire de Pepi II. Tome II: le temple*, pl. 40.

66 Gustave Jéquier, *Fouilles à Saqqarah: le monument funéraire de Pepi II. Tome III: les approches du temple* (Cairo: Institut français d'archéologie oriental du Caire, 1940), pls. 15 and 16.

67 Jéquier, *Le monument funéraire de Pepi II. Tome III: les approches du temple*, pl. 12.

68 Jéquier, *Le monument funéraire de Pepi II. Tome III: les approches du temple*, pl. 13, upper right.

69 Jéquier, *Le monument funéraire de Pepi II. Tome III: les approches du temple*, pl. 14.

70 Jéquier, *Le monument funéraire de Pepi II. Tome III: les approches du temple*, 10.

71 Jéquier, *Le monument funéraire de Pepi II. Tome III: les approches du temple*, 10.

72 Jéquier, *Le monument funéraire de Pepi II. Tome III: les approches du temple*, pl. 36.

73 The bound prisoner statues are the focus of a current PhD dissertation study by Tara Prakash at the Institute of Fine Arts, New York University: "Statues of the 'Other': An Examination of Three-dimensional Representations of Foreigners in Ancient Egypt." Anticipation of her much more thorough study is another reason why these are treated summarily here.

74 Tara Prakash, "Shoulders, Knees, and Toes: The Bodies of the Prisoner Statues from Pepi I's Pyramid Complex" (paper presented at the annual meeting for the American Research Center in Egypt, Atlanta, Georgia, 2016).

75 For a review of past interpretations and new suggestions regarding the meaning and function of reserve heads, see: Massimiliano Nuzzolo, "The 'reserve Heads': Some Remarks on Their Function and Meaning," in *Old Kingdom, New Perspectives: Egyptian Art and Archaeology 2750–2150 BC*, Ed. Nigel Strudwick and Helen Strudwick (Oxford: Oxbow Books, 2011), 200–215.

76 Jéquier, *Le monument funéraire de Pepi II. Tome III: les approches du temple*, pl. 48.

77 Borchardt, *Das Grabdenkmal des Königs Ne-user-Re'*, 42, fig. 24.

78 Jéquier, *Le monument funéraire de Pepi II. Tome III: les approches du temple*, pl. 47.

79 An exception is an ivory cylinder of Narmer in which the king's name prepares to smite three registers of bound captives—Figure 3.17; even here, however, they do not rest on both knees but rather have one raised, and this example is of course from a transitional period.

80 Edouard Naville, *The XIth Dynasty Temple at Deir el-Bahari* (London: The Egypt Exploration Fund, 1907); Dieter Arnold from the notes of Herbert Winlock, *The*

Temple of Mentuhotep at Deir el Bahari (New York: Metropolitan Museum of Art Egyptian Expedition, 1979).

81 See Elisa Fiore Marochetti, *The Reliefs of the Chapel of Nebhepetre Mentuhotep at Gebelein* (Leiden, Boston, MA: Brill, 2010), 17–20 for a discussion of "pre-" and "post-unification" styles and for a list of other relevant sources.

82 A figure of a soldier with crossed straps across his chest, clutching a bow and sheath of arrows in one hand and an axe in the other, is labeled "son of Montuhotep" (without a cartouche). This figure stands behind a larger figure, of whom only a fragment of leg is preserved. Naville considered this likely to be an image of the king and a prince engaging in battle: Naville, *The XIth Dynasty Temple at Deir el-Bahari*, 7, pl. 12.B. Robert Ritner has claimed that there is a Libyan Family Scene of Nebhepetre Montuhotep, which clearly would show the king practicing violence. It is not known to me if this scene is supposed to come from this monument or on what grounds it is argued for, and as publication of the scene is still intended no further information was available. Robert Ritner, "Libyan vs. Nubian as the Ideal Egyptian," in *Egypt and Beyond: Essays Presented to Leonard H. Lesko upon His Retirement from the Wilbour Chair of Egyptology at Brown University June 2005*, Ed. Stephen E. Thompson and Peter Der Manuelian (Providence, RI: Brown University, Department of Egyptology and Ancient Western Studies, 2008), 305.

83 Many fragments are grouped onto pls. XIV and XV of Naville, *The XIth Dynasty Temple at Deir el-Bahari*, and are briefly described on 68–69.

84 British Museum EA732. © The Trustees of the British Museum. Photography by Anna Kellen/Imaging Department, The Metropolitan Museum of Art; Naville, *The XIth Dynasty Temple at Deir el-Bahari*, pl. 14.D.

85 A reconstruction of this scene that includes three fragments, not certainly part of the same tableau but possibly so, would have this figure stuck through the knee with an arrow. See David O'Connor, "An Expanding Worldview: Conquest, Colonization, and Coexistence," in *Ancient Egypt Transformed: The Middle Kingdom*, Ed. Adela Oppenheim et al. (New Haven, CT and London: Yale University Press, 2015), 164, fig. 79.

86 I cannot help but note the discrepancy between the shapely legs of these victims and the rather horrifying cankles of the statuary of Nebhepetra Mentuhotep himself from the same temple. I am put in mind of the Lyle Lovett lyric "He's got skinny legs/like I always wanted."

87 British Museum EA735. © The Trustees of the British Museum. Photography by Anna Kellen/Imaging Department, The Metropolitan Museum of Art.

88 Division of Anthropology, YPM 6776. Courtesy of the Peabody Museum of Natural History, Yale University, New Haven, CT. Photographed by Nathan Utrup. Henry George Fischer, "The Nubian Mercenaries of Gebelein During the First Intermediate Period," *Kush* 9 (1961): 68–70, fig. 9; Henry George Fischer, "Eleventh Dynasty Relief Fragments from Deir el Bahri," *Yale Art Gallery Bulletin* 24, no. 2 (1958): 32, 37, fig. 4.

89 Fischer, "The Nubian Mercenaries of Gebelein During the First Intermediate Period," 68–80.

90 Courtesy of the Egypt Exploration Society. Naville, *The XIth Dynasty Temple at Deir el-Bahari*, pl. 15.C.

91 British Museum EA731. © The Trustees of the British Museum. Photography by Anna Kellen/Imaging Department, The Metropolitan Museum of Art.

92 British Museum EA734. © The Trustees of the British Museum. Naville, *The XIth Dynasty Temple at Deir el-Bahari*, pl. 15.H.

93 British Museum EA1402. © The Trustees of the British Museum.

94 British Museum EA736. © The Trustees of the British Museum.

95 British Museum EA43122. Courtesy of the Trustees of the British Museum.

96   Courtesy of the Egypt Exploration Society. Naville, *The XIth Dynasty Temple at Deir el-Bahari*, pl. 14.A.
97   British Museum EA738. © The Trustees of the British Museum. Photography by Anna Kellen/Imaging Department, The Metropolitan Museum of Art. An additional fragment with a child carried by a man who wears a long kilt and also apparently holds a bag of goods is EA739.
98   Metropolitan Museum of Art 2003.434; Dieter Arnold, personal communication.
99   Naville, *The XIth Dynasty Temple at Deir el-Bahari*, 5.
100 Naville, *The XIth Dynasty Temple at Deir el-Bahari*, 5.
101 Habachi was the first Egyptologist to suggest that Nebhepetra Mentuhotep was deified in his lifetime: Labib Habachi, "King Nebhepetre Menthuhotp: His Monuments, Place in History, Deification and Unusual Representation in the Form of Gods," *Mitteilungen des Deutschen Archäologischen Instituts, Abteilung Kairo* 19 (1963): 16–52. The evidence for such an assumption has been more recently reviewed by other scholars and revolves around his relief program and use of iconography to emphasize his divine origin and status: David O'Connor, "The Dendereh Chapel of Nebhepetre Mentuhotep: A New Perspective," in *Studies on Ancient Egypt in Honour of H.S. Smith*, Ed. Anthony Leahy and John Tait (London: Egypt Exploration Society, 1999); Ludwig D. Morenz, *Die Zeit der Regionen im Spiegel der Gebelein-Region: kulturgeschichtliche Re-Konstruktionen* (Leiden: Brill, 2010), 146, 150–152, 602–605.
102 Peter Jánosi, *The Pyramid Complex of Amenemhat I at Lisht: The Reliefs* (New York, New Haven: Metropolitan Museum of Art, Yale University Press, 2016), 72–75, pl. 75.
103 It has been suggested that the causeway of Amenemhat I held combat scenes but this cannot be verified. The basis of the assertion seems to be one small and unpublished fragment showing the presentation of "tribute of conquered foreign nations." William C. Hayes, *The Scepter of Egypt: A Background for the Study of the Egyptian Antiquities in The Metropolitan Museum of Art. Vol. 1, From the Earliest Times to the End of the Middle Kingdom* (New York: Metropolitan Museum of Art, 1978), 173.
104 I am grateful to Adela Oppenheim of the Metropolitan Museum of Art, who took the time to gather and show me a number of archival photographs of unpublished fragments from this complex. I would not have known of their existence without her. Much in this section owes to her help, and while I cannot illustrate all the fragments here, my observations are based on the photographs she was kind enough to let me see.
105 Royal Ontario Museum 958.49.6.A. I am grateful to Krzysztof Grzymski for giving me the provenance information on this fragment, which was excavated by the Metropolitan Museum expedition.
106 The Epigraphic Survey, *Reliefs and Inscriptions at Karnak, Volume 4: The Battle Reliefs of King Sety I* (Chicago, IL: The University of Chicago, 1986), pls. 27–28.
107 Cairo Museum JdE 63943a and b.
108 Brooklyn Museum 52.129.
109 Metropolitan Museum of Art 13.235.3; www.metmuseum.org.
110 Fischer, "The Nubian Mercenaries of Gebelein During the First Intermediate Period," 71, fig. 10a.
111 Adela Oppenheim, "Appendix: Relief Decoration of the King's Temples and Queens' Chapels," in *The Pyramid Complex of Senwosret III at Dahshur: Architectural Studies*, Ed. Dieter Arnold (New York: The Metropolitan Museum of Art, 2002), 143, pl. 163c.
112 Cairo Museum JdE 51978; Gustave Jéquier, *Douze ans de fouilles dans la nécropole memphite 1924–1936* (Neuchatel: Secrétariat de l'Université, 1940), 136–137, fig 39.
113 Oppenheim has referred to this figure as Nubian. Oppenheim, "Appendix: Relief Decoration of the King's Temples and Queens' Chapels," 143, pl. 163b.

114 Adela Oppenheim, "Aspects of the Pyramid Temple of Senwosret III at Dahshur: The Pharaoh and Deities" (PhD diss., New York University, 2008), 636. Oppenheim's exhaustive study of the relief fragments showing the king and gods includes 457 plates, and none of them feature imagery of violence, at least none that can be identified due to their fragmentary nature. There are plates that refer to Senwosret III's dominion over foreign lands: pls. 311 (right side of the S tympanum), 326 (right side of N tympanum), 333 (left side of N tympanum), 334 (left side of N tympanum).

115 Once more I express my gratitude to Adela Oppenheim for showing me these unpublished fragments.

116 The Abu Sir Papyri make this abundantly obvious for the period in question. Paule Posener-Kriéger and Jean Louis de Cenival, *The Abu Sir Papyri, Hieratic Papyri in the British Museum. Fifth Series* (London: Trustees of the British Museum, 1968).

117 Awady, *Abusir XVI*, 107.

118 As argued, for instance, by Awady, *Abusir XVI*, 45.

5   Uniter of the two lands

Images of violence in divine temples

Four men, all in perfect profile. To the left, an elaborately costumed figure stands, his feet spread and heels turned in toward one another. In addition to a decorated kilt and tunic, his costume includes a plumed headdress and a mask—his own

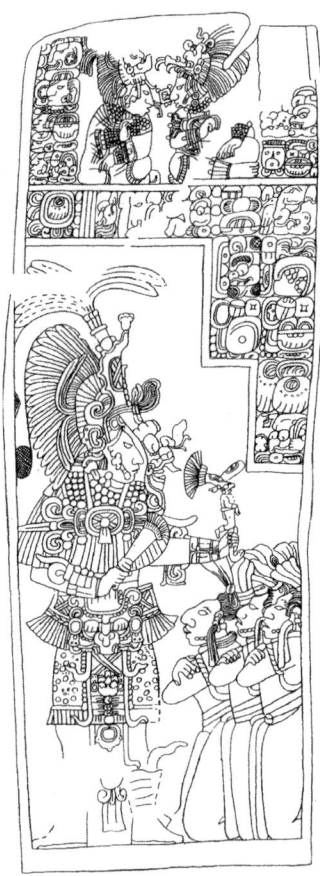

Figure 5.1 Relief carving. Late Classic Maya Stela 11, Yaxchilan, Chiapas, Mexico. Eighth century CE.

face is shown behind another, more abstract, face. The standing figure's right arm is bent at the elbow, his hand holding a truncheon-like implement in front of his body. His left hand stretches forth to grasp an elaborate anthropomorphic figurine above the heads of three kneeling captives.

The captives overlap one another and are similarly but not identically shown, creating a scene that is both patterned and broken, reminiscent of the victims of Egyptian smiting scenes that include overlapping victims. They wear thick belts around their waists, long earrings, and long hair tied in tails above their heads. Three dots decorate the side of each of their chins. Their forearms are bound, their arms crossed before their chests, their right hands visible clasping their upper left arms. The figure in front has his lips slightly apart and the fingers of his hand slightly spread on his arm, the only signs of visible distress. The scene is surmounted by an inscription and an image of two smaller seated figures in plumed headdresses facing one another.

The tall standing stone that carries this image stood between two others on the path to a religious structure, one stela among many that marked the dynastic splendor of Late Classic Maya Yaxchilan in eighth-century CE Chiapas, Mexico (Figure 5.1).[1] The stela has deeply carved relief on both sides; the one facing the temple provided the scene shown above. This image is not a picture of violence in action, and the objects held are not immediately recognizable as weapons. However, the hierarchy and subjugation that are expressed make it clear that the image is one of power, and the potential for ritualized violence was inherent in Maya power relations. The similarity to the Egyptian smiting scene, even down to the impassivity on the faces of its protagonists, is remarkable.

Maya stelae provided a nexus for the interaction between kingship, the divine, and time. The Maya concept of time was complex and detailed, marking different cycles of time and situating events within the framework of cosmic temporal periods. Stelae, with their often self-referential inscriptions, were erected especially at ends of cycles or sub-cycles of time. The Yaxchilan Stela 11 is simultaneously a very explicitly historical document grounded in a specific day and a monument that portrays the timeless nature of kingship and the importance of subjugation to kingship. It does this within the setting of a divine temple, in a location where its audience was not simply a human one.

There are reasons beyond the basic similarity of a physically dominant ruler shown at a divine temple that make this stela an appropriate one for raising points about not only the art of violence, but also how we study it in Egypt. The Maya, like the Egyptians, utilized primarily iconic images of domination rather than narrative depictions of battle; when the latter occur their departures from the iconic images indicate that they operate differently.[2] Furthermore, assumptions about the actual practice of violence on the basis of imagery—our best-preserved source of evidence but also hardly a straightforward one—are as rife in the scholarship of the Maya as in Egyptology.[3] A final point that will be critical to the Egyptian images of violence from early temples can be raised on the basis of the Yaxchilan stela, though it is not a point of direct comparison: unlike in Egypt, Maya culture and Maya political structures did not have similar geographic bounds—violence in Maya culture was largely *between* Mayans. The images we have from early

Egyptian temples, in stark contrast to later temples and contrary to what we often think of as the central reason for showing royal violence in Egypt, sometimes depict the Egyptian king perpetrating violence against Egyptians.

Egyptian temples as a context for imagery

Nothing better illustrates the need to see Egyptian material culture and ideology as dynamic and audience-dependent than an attempt to discuss violent imagery in divine temples in Egypt. The basic nature of a temple in Egypt is a home, a sanctuary in the most literal sense, for a god manifest in a statue.[4] At its most elemental level, divine cult in Egypt took the form of giving food to gods in their homes. This was the job of the king himself, deputized to priests. State temples, those commissioned by kings, were built to accommodate the giving of offerings—in essence, meals—and not as places of public worship. Imagery in pharaonic divine temples, of which we have large amounts only starting in the New Kingdom, is overwhelmingly dedicated to showing the interaction between the king and the gods for their mutual benefit.

This essentially domestic function of divine temples means that, much like royal mortuary complexes, imagery *within* them cannot have been intended to communicate primarily to a broad public audience. Imagery on the *exterior* of Egyptian temples might well have played a more public role. The great New Kingdom cycles of violent imagery, such as Qadesh, are known from the most accessible, least sacred parts of temples; we are rarely sure from which part of a temple earlier images came, and are unsure if their exteriors were decorated at all. At least one example discussed below was interior.

Our understanding of how temples functioned prior to the New Kingdom is poor because little is preserved, and this lack of evidence extends to the preservation of images of violence. Only three Egyptian monuments have preserved violent wall relief over the course of the millennia covered by this book, and a small handful of objects from temples include references to violence that straddle the line between text and image. The architectural decorations are all problematic or atypical in one way or another, and both the architectural examples and the objects are limited to two widely separate reigns: Khasekhem of the Second Dynasty and Nebhepetra Mentuhotep of the Eleventh Dynasty. Both of these kings were important architectural innovators, and their decoration of architecture must thus be seen within the broader context of experimentation. Both are also thought to have fought civil wars—generally considered to have been rare in Egypt, and not part of the canonical ideal of kingship over a united Egypt. That Khasekhem and Nebhepetra Mentuhotep thus may have had a relatively unusual relationship to both architecture and warfare must be taken into account when examining the evidence from their reigns. That visual references to Egyptians as enemies are dependent on context as well as on history is suggested by a comparison to Nebhepetra's mortuary complex, where it was noted that the *failure* to portray Egyptians as enemies requires some explaining (see Chapter 4); they are present here, unambiguously.

In addition to the possibility that violence in temple decoration may thus be related to historically rare types of events, the scarcity of material to consider from this context is not limited to this motif: we have relatively little extant material evidence of divine temples at all before the New Kingdom. What we do have suggests that there may have been major changes in the form of the divine temple and in its relation to kingship and to the administrative functions of the state over the course of Egyptian history, with the clearest shift occurring in the early New Kingdom.

Changes in the ways divine temples functioned as parts of royal Egyptian ideology and even economy can best be indicated by looking at trends in the total building program of kings across time. In general, remaining evidence suggests that Egyptian kings before the New Kingdom focused most of their building activity on monuments connected to their own cult—there is a reason why Chapter 4, on royal mortuary complexes, is a whopper. Even remains with royal inscriptions and decoration at provincial divine temples from the periods under consideration here are most often interpreted as chapels associated with offerings to the king himself rather than to the god. Royal patronage of local divine cults and the knitting of those gods and their cults into a more or less systematic religious framework that connected ruler, divinities, land, and taxes was a process that took millennia and did not proceed in a linear fashion. Moreover, divine temples seem to have been very conservative in their locations, meaning that later iterations of a divine temple often obliterated traces of earlier structures to the degree that we do not even know if there was a standard architectural plan for temples before the New Kingdom.[5] Because of the state of the evidence, there is no possibility to arrive at a reasonable understanding of the role or roles that images of violence played in divine temples before the New Kingdom. This chapter thus serves to raise questions about the relationships between those few preserved images and other images occurring in other contexts and periods, and the observations and conclusions offered here are limited.

The Early Dynastic Period: Khasekhem

King Khasekhem reigned at the end of the Second Dynasty, a period for which we have very scant historical information. His immediate predecessor seems to have been a king called Peribsen, who took the unparalleled decision to write his *serekh*, the heraldic device enclosing one of the names of a king that developed during the Protodynastic Period, topped by the god Seth instead of the traditional Horus. It is often thought that this change represents a major rupture in government. Khasekhem topped his *serekh* with Horus, but from the late Second Dynasty we also have a king named Khasekhemwy whose *serekh* had both Horus and Seth. The usual interpretation of these *serekh* shenanigans is that there was a rupture under Peribsen, Khasekhem fought a civil war, and on winning it he changed his own name and claimed a relation with both of these titular gods for himself.[6] Some or perhaps all of the imagery of violence from the reign of Khasekhem

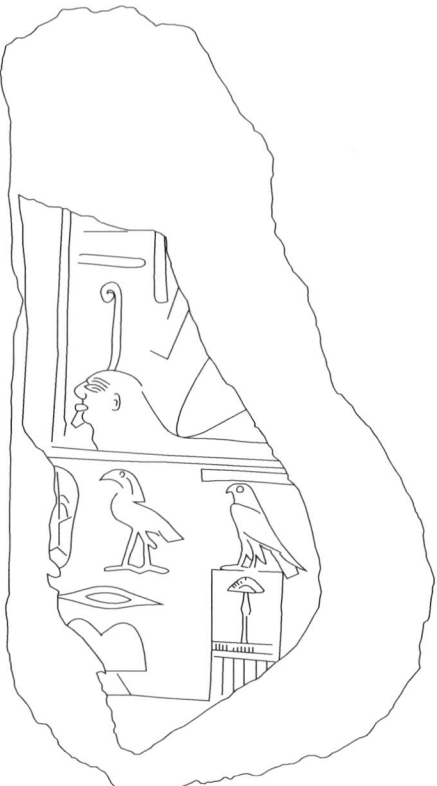

Figure 5.2 Relief decoration on an architectural fragment found in a deposit at the temple at Hierakonpolis. The inscription names King Khasekhem of the late Second Dynasty. The lightly incised scene above his name shows a human-headed tract of land labeled with a bow; the knee of a captor pins this personification to the ground.

seems to reflect an internal conflict. From this reign we have one relief fragment and two statues that show images or texts about war; all were found in association with the temple at Hierakonpolis. Since the chief divinity of Hierakonpolis was Horus, the titular god of kingship, separating royal from divine at this site is particularly problematic.

An architectural relief that appears to picture violent domination was found in a storeroom at the main temple at Hierakonpolis, and thus in a context similar to the Main Deposit discussed in Chapter 3. The fragment is of a hard stone incised in simple low relief; it comes from a corner and is thought to be part of a door jamb (Figure 5.2).[7] The remaining bit is divided into two registers. The lower contains the name of the king in a *serekh* and a short inscription, which cannot be translated with total confidence but that certainly indicates action against foreign lands.[8]

Above, a schematic representation shows a flat object, probably the sign for land, with a human head growing from its left. The head appears to be bearded, has a hooked nose, and on its top balances an image of a bow. The hair of this personified device slopes to the right, and the whole is pinned to the ground by a bent knee— the only part left of a human figure. A square-ended long feature at an angle before the knee may be the end of some implement—it could be the end of a staff held by a smiting king, similar to that seen both earlier and later in several contexts (for example, Figure 5.6, Figure 7.3, and most of the images from Chapter 6). The end of an inscription to the left may read *ta*, "land." That the human figure kneels suggests he might be a captive in a smiting scene, though in no other known case does the captive kneel *on* something. Does the kneeling figure himself dominate the personified bow land, or is he labeled by that land? If he dominates the land, does that mean the kneeling figure is himself the king, or that we have a sort of nested hierarchy of domination shown in a smiting scene?

This scene recalls the personified papyrus thicket dominated by a falcon on the Narmer Palette (Figure 3.14). The reference is presumably also similar: the king (whether that is his knee or he is smiting the kneeler) was shown physically domi- nant over a device that contains a combined reference to a place and its people. The bow as a geographic designation is not particularly specific, a problem we already ran into in interpreting the Gebel Sheikh Suleiman rock carving in Chapter 3. *Ta-seti*, the land of the bow, was a term used to refer both to southern- most Egypt and to northern Nubia, and later texts certainly speak of bowmen from other areas as well, including especially to the northeast of Egypt, in the Sinai or the Levant.[9] Whether in this image this was intended to be ambiguous and thus generalizing, or rather specific and easily understood, is unknowable. However, the very fact that the captive is shown as an abstraction removes this image from the possibility of being a simple visual report and shows us the familiar workings of an ideological statement that may or may not be built upon an actual historic event. While the image can be read with reasonable certainty as an image of royal triumph, it has no known close parallel. The abstract device of a personified tract of land, while it has the precedent of Narmer, never became canon. And kneeling on things is not otherwise either a posture of domination or something done by submissive captives. These unusual aspects may be related to the transitional and experimental time period from which this relief comes.

Two statues of Khasekhem further suggest a combination of royal ideology, events, and imagery in temples in this reign, once more in ways that are not par- alleled from other periods. These were found in deposits at Hierakonpolis and show the king in a completely static pose, but include imagery of completed violence on their bases. These are the earliest well-preserved royal statues from Egypt and are quite similar, though the one in Oxford is carved from limestone (Figure 5.3)[10] and the one in Cairo from siltstone. In both, the king sits on a block throne, legs together, wearing a calf-length robe with a rolled collar. On his head is the White Crown. His right arm stretches out on his right thigh; his left arm crosses his waist, his fist held at the opposite elbow. Around the bases are crudely carved scenes that fall somewhere between inscriptions

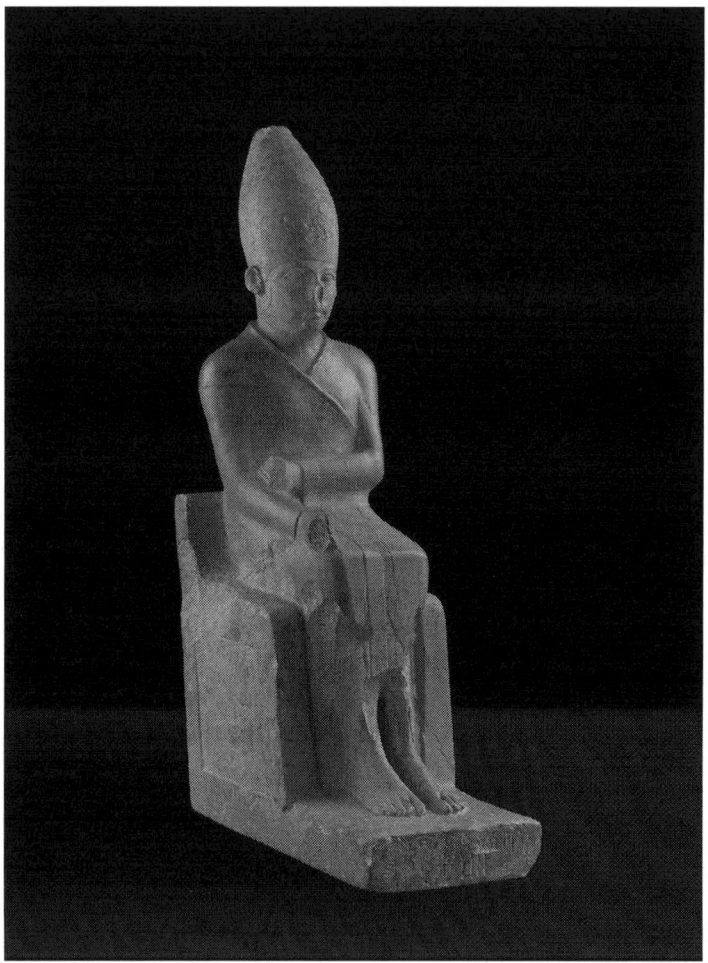

Figure 5.3 Limestone statue of Khasekhem from Hierakonpolis, Second Dynasty.

and images (Figure 5.4).[11] A number of bodies, roughly scratched rather than carefully carved, are shown in a range of contorted and painful positions. All are probably to be understood as dead.

On the front in each case we see some dead people in combination with a number—47,209 on the limestone statue and 48,205 on the siltstone one—and a distinguished dead figure. This man is shown lying on his belly, arms bound behind his back, short beard on his chin. The better-preserved image on the limestone statue shows a papyrus thicket growing from this figure's head, presumably indicating that he represents Lower Egypt, and a stick—an arrow or a mace?—protruding from his face.

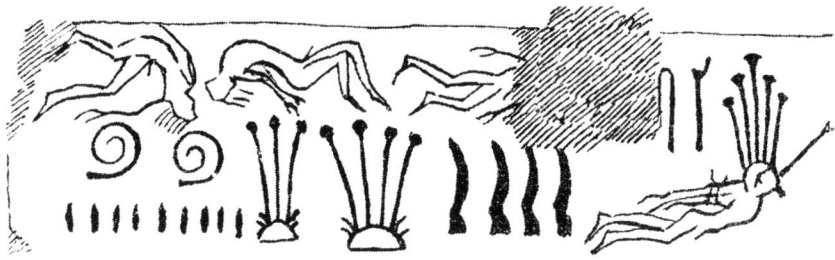

Figure 5.4 The front of the base of a limestone statue of Khasekhem showing three dead people above the number 47,209. To the right is an apparently bound captive with a beard; the papyrus growing from his head suggests that he is from, and presumably representative of, Lower Egypt.

The image of a static king sitting on a throne but simultaneously in domination is a common one from Egypt and can be used to show the king in control of both Egypt and foreign lands. The former is usually accomplished by the inclusion of a *sema-tawy* device on the side of the throne; this iconic image shows the knotting together of a papyrus plant and a lotus flower, emblems of Lower and Upper Egypt respectively, which are inextricably entwined. Enthroned kings dominate foreign lands by stepping on nine bows,[12] representing the totality of the king's enemies (including Egyptians). Both of these generalized images of royal dominion are extremely common starting in the Old Kingdom, but are not explicitly violent. Khasekhem's statues differ from them both in their inclusion of killed people as part of the imagery of domination and for their inclusion of a very specific number—an apparent historicizing detail. This unique image sits somewhere between other statues of enthroned kings, images of royal triumph over pictured human enemies, and scenes of war with dead littering the battlefield.

The apparent historicism of the Khasekhem statues can be compared to images we saw in royal mortuary complexes that sometimes, in their very precision, raised our eyebrows about their accuracy. If in the Libyan Family Scene it is the repetition of names across generations that first suggested caution, here it is both the numbers themselves—unbelievably high and impossibly precise—and the fact that they differ. Do these doubts mean that we should think twice about whether or not Khasekhem really fought northerners? Probably not—the references are consistent, including vessels also found at Hierakonpolis that include inscriptions about the year of fighting northerners, and they really do help to explain the *serekh* problems of the later Second Dynasty.[13] What we should rather see is that once more we have evidence that historicism is more important than historical accuracy, and that events are being treated in royal discourse as simultaneously having occurred in real time and as being representative of bigger truths about the role of the king. The imagery was not a report.

The Eleventh Dynasty: Nebhepetra Mentuhotep

Aspects of the career of Nebhepetra Mentuhotep were discussed in Chapter 4. This important king was maybe not quite so clearly the reunifier he has historically been considered, but he certainly presented himself as such. This self-presentation is as critical as the historical reality for our understanding of his monuments and in particular his imagery of violence in divine settings. Nebhepetra built a number of small provincial chapels at sites throughout Upper Egypt, with a new one discovered as recently as 2014.[14] The nature of these chapels is not entirely consistent from place to place, but all linked the king to local cults in some way. Of these chapels, two, from Gebelein and Denderah, preserve images of violence. The preserved images—smiting scenes—differ notably from those of the same king preserved in his mortuary complex.

The Gebelein chapel is dated on stylistic grounds and based on the form of the king's titulary to the "time of the wars," prior to reunification; it appears to relate the cult of Hathor of Denderah to royal ceremonial themes that are largely in

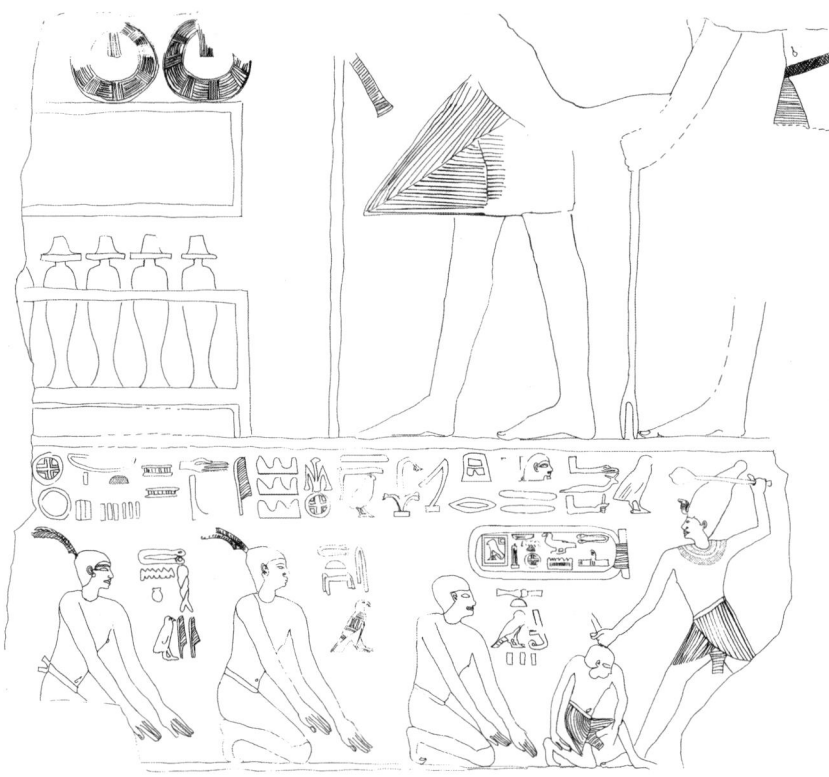

Figure 5.5 Nebhepetra Mentuhotep on a relief fragment from Gebelein. The king smites an Egyptian, while people from other places watch and perhaps await their turn.

keeping with Old Kingdom notions of kingship.[15] Only fragments of relief remain, representing a small percentage of the original program, and their relationship is not usually clear. The overall decoration included processions of personified provinces bearing goods and probably fecundity figures. The two preserved smiting scenes are both relatively small and in registers below much larger figures, including divinities and in one case the king; this is in contrast to the Denderah chapel discussed below, where smiting was the central motif.

A limestone block now in Cairo preserves an unprecedented smiting scene from Gebelein that also has its unusually clear labels preserved (Figure 5.5).[16] The top register of this block has the lower part of two figures who approach offerings on tables, including jewelry and ceremonial vessels. The front figure wears a kilt and carries both a staff and what appears to be a mace, though only its handle is preserved. This is presumably the king, who is followed by a second male figure who holds a scepter. The hierarchy of scale makes the smiting scene below visually subordinate to the serene scene of king and god consecrating offerings above, though the presence of a mace in each connects them.

The lower register, which is approximately half the height of the register above it, has five figures. On the right the king strides, facing left, mace raised in the classic smiting pose. He is labeled by a cartouche in front of him that encloses not just his name but also an epithet: "Mentuhotep, Son of Hathor, Lady of Denderah." He wears a pleated kilt, a collar, and the White Crown with a uraeus on his brow. The handle of the mace crosses in front of the crown, with the pear-shaped macehead directly above the uraeus. The king's outstretched arm grasps the hair of a cowering figure.

There are notable ways in which this smitee does not fit the ordinary mode of the victim. He does not raise his hands. He is curiously hunched, head bowed forward. This posture does not work well with Egyptian artistic conventions, but even this awkwardness emphasizes the abject nature of the man—a departure from the usually emotionless smiting scene, despite the still impassive face of the victim. His kilt is identical to that of the king, a pleated *shendyt* kilt that is far from a generic piece of clothing, and in fact there is no reason whatsoever to think he is anything other than an Egyptian. He is unlabeled while every other preserved figure in the scene is labeled. Is this because he needs no label—he is immediately recognizable without explanation as Egyptian, perhaps even a rival Egyptian ruler in the civil wars—or because a level of ambiguity is deliberately maintained? What few examples of Egyptians as victims we have seen in other contexts were more ambiguous than adjacent references to others, but in this case the *shendyt* suggests we are not looking at an everyman.

The remaining three preserved subject figures are a bit larger. These are all shown in the same position: kneeling, facing to the right, and observing the smiting immediately before them, with both hands reaching toward the ground in front of them: hands open, palms down. This pose is unique in representations of subject peoples. These figures are labeled in front of their faces, with general terms rather than individual names. They are probably to be read as, in order from the front, (a type of) Nubian, (a type of) Asiatic, a Libyan. The Nubian wears a simple kilt and has very short hair or a cap. He is not given any identifying marks aside from the label before him. The Asiatic and Libyan are wearing similar kilts, the only difference being a tab on the Libyan's back. Both of these figures wear tall feathers in their hair. It is quite probable that there were originally more than these three, indicated by a number of fragments of people reaching their hands out in similar positions.[17] The use of labels without clear visual iconographic stereotypes makes this image remarkably different from what we are familiar with from royal mortuary contexts, though in those cases, too, we saw that it is possible for the king to smite a group of different people at once. A depicted internal audience for smiting has been seen previously in the Libyan Family Scene, but this mixed cocktail of adult male subjects is unprecedented.

The scene as a whole is surmounted by an inscription that is more closely related to the scene itself than we have often seen before. It reads "subduing the chiefs of the Two Lands, reorganize Upper and Lower Egypt, the foreign lands, the two banks, the nine [bows], the towns."[18] In this inscription, as in the scene below it, the emphasis is on Egyptians, though foreign lands are mentioned. That all are present together, however, makes the image much less historical and more of a general statement about the violent dominance of the king.

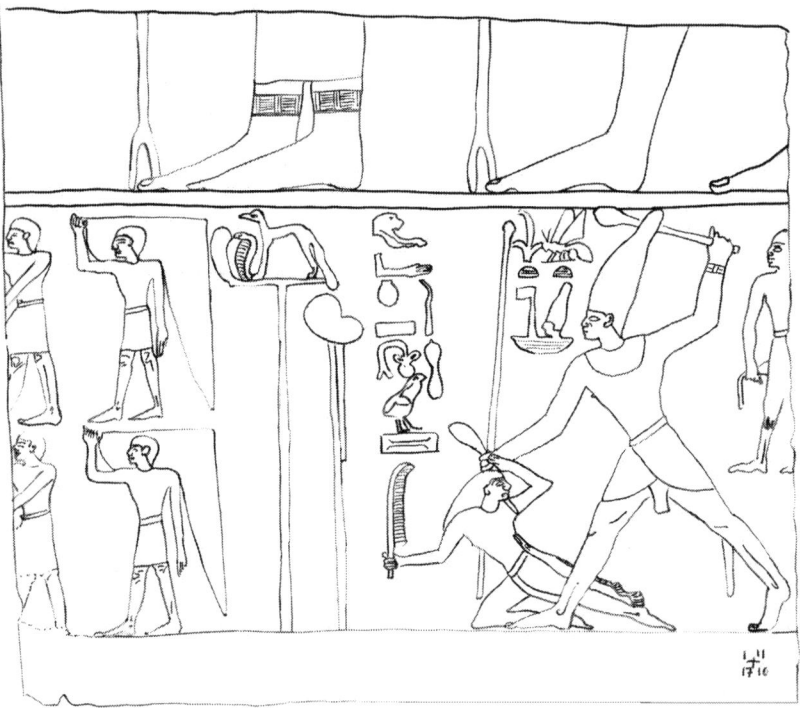

Figure 5.6 Nebhepetra Mentuhotep on a relief from Gebelein. The king smites a Libyan, who is both labeled and shown with some aspects of visual stereotypes.

A second block with relief from Gebelein bears another smiting scene (Figure 5.6).[19] This is once more the lower register of a larger composition, with feet belonging to a goddess and a male figure, either a god or the king, at a much larger scale in the register above. The lower register contains multiple figures engaged in different activities. To the left, four men carry objects, perhaps parts of the temple itself.[20] Behind them are two standards, connecting Wepwawet to the scene, and behind these the king smites an enemy. The king wears the White Crown and *shendyt* kilt and brandishes a mace. His front arm reaches out to grasp the hair of his victim, as well as a long and almost upright staff. An inscription in front of the king's face names him first with the title *nsw bit*, usually translated King of Upper and Lower Egypt, and then with the name "Divine one of the White Crown," which is the second form of this king's Horus name, prior to his adoption of the name "He who unites the two lands."[21] The victim is in a pose of action, hand to his head, one leg extended behind him and one knee bent. He turns to face the king. He wears a beard, a long fish tied as a tail behind him, and what may be a penis sheath. His second hand clasps a feather. The inscription above him confirms the identification: he is a Libyan. The king is somewhat larger in scale than his victim, though both are larger than the other figures in the register. Behind the smiting scene, another smaller figure floats with no groundline and clutches an unidentifiable object in his hand. One is reminded a bit of the sandal bearer behind Narmer smiting on his palette (Figure 3.14). The violent episode on this relief is almost jarring in its inclusion in a composition that as a whole looks ritual, perhaps a foundation ceremony.

In Denderah, Nebhepetra Mentuhotep built a small chapel, which is still well preserved, that contains a unique smiting scene. The chapel is likewise dated to the middle part of his reign, when he used the second of his three titularies.[22] Both the chapel itself and its smiting scene have received attention disproportionate to their size. The chapel was small, measuring only 1.45 m wide and 2.3 m long on the inside of its single chamber. The doorway faced east. The entirety of the interior was decorated with relief scenes and inscriptions, and the inscriptions make it clear that the chapel was intended to house a statue of the king named "Horus beloved in Denderah" and "Horus living forever," and to serve as a *ka*-chapel for the king.[23]

From our perspective, the most interesting scene is that at the very back (Figure 5.7).[24] Here Nebhepetra is depicted in the classic striding pose of a smiting king, facing to the left. He wears a *shendyt* kilt and the Double Crown; his upraised left arm is broken off at the hand. His right hand clenches an emblem about which there has been some disagreement. Is it entwined stalks of papyrus and lotus plants, an elongated *sema-tawy* of sorts, shown more traditionally below?[25] Or a papyrus stalk wound around the *renpet* sign, which means "year"?[26] The latter seems the more likely reading to me, as one of the stalks is entirely straight, not twined. The straight stalk ends in only a slight curve, whereas the entwined stalk ends in a full curve and a bud. However one reads the smote device, Nebhepetra is shown in this relief panel as violently controlling an emblem of Egypt, rather than Egyptians themselves. Whether he is smiting all

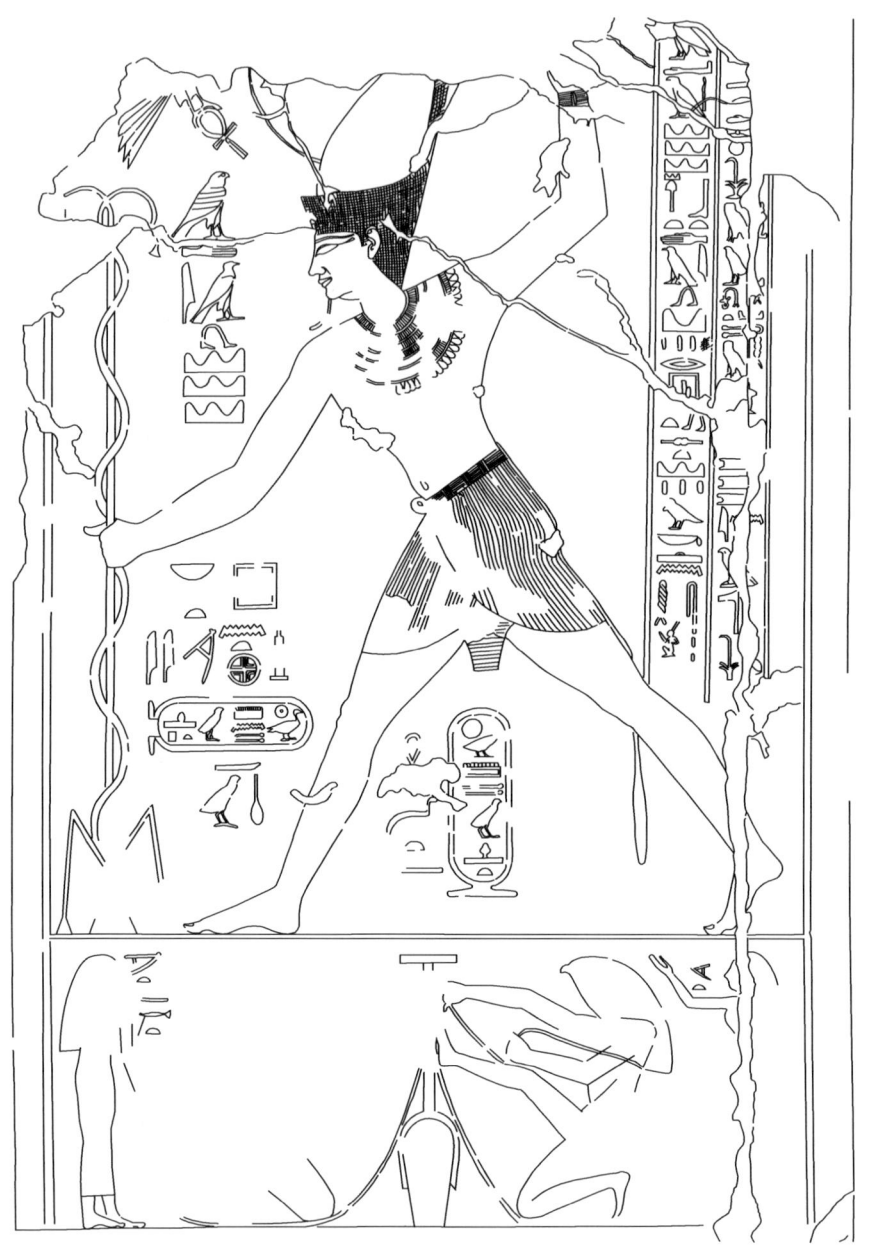

Figure 5.7 Nebhepetra Mentuhotep smites an abstract emblem, from a chapel at Denderah, Eleventh Dynasty.

of it or half of it is not entirely clear but also perhaps not entirely relevant. If the device depicts a *renpet* sign, then the whole can be read almost as a year label from the First Dynasty (for example, Figure 7.3) would be: the year of smiting Lower Egypt. This has less the effect of defining a year on the basis of the event than the effect of defining the king on the basis of that year.

That the image is best understood as underlining the violent domination of the king more generally, rather than taking a solely historical focus to the events of his reign, is also suggested by the mismatch between the image itself and the accompanying texts. The immediate label for the king in this image calls him "Horus who subdues the hill/foreign countries." Elsewhere in the chapel the texts highlight military successes of the king in both Egypt and against others, including the territory Wawat, in Lower Nubia, and peoples labeled here *Medjayu* and *Tjehemu*.[27] This, of course, is similar to what we saw with the scene at Gebelein where Nebhepetra smites an Egyptian, foreigners watch submissively, and the overlying inscription records domination broadly. Both are notable for their inclusion of Egypt among the dominated, but both do so within a context that is more general.

In addition to its unusual depiction of the king smiting an emblem representing Egypt, this relief is noteworthy for its precise location within the chapel. Egyptologists are accustomed to reading smiting scenes from temples as providing a protective shell around ritual spaces: chaos—controlled by the king—floating around the outside of the calm and ordered center. This is an appropriate expectation for New Kingdom imagery. Such a view is so prevalent that when relief fragments of violence are found without secure provenance, they are assumed to have been on the outside of monuments.[28] At Denderah the image of smiting is on the inside, and presumably directly behind the king's statue. There is no holier or, by the usual logic, more dangerous place. Why is it there? It is possible that our logic is faulty or else does not apply in all cases, and that images of violence were either not inherently chaotic or that cult statues did not always need to be protected from chaos. It is also possible that the very peculiarities of this scene or context render it other than threatening, despite its subject matter. Perhaps the use of an emblematic plant rather than a depiction of a human enemy nullifies the threat, or perhaps the fact that the statue in question was of the king makes an image of royal domination acceptable.

The location of the Denderah smiting scene, in a small dark shrine behind a statue, would also have rendered it almost totally invisible to human eyes. The chief audience for the scene would seem to be the statue itself. The placement of the smiting scene at Denderah thus suggests it is less about creating a protective apotropaic shell around the shrine or about convincing an audience, and more about enshrining one of the actions that made Nebhepetra a legitimate and effective king. In this sense the image works well with the reliefs on the interior side walls of the same chapel, which show the king largely in relation to various gods in activities that may be read as underlining his legitimacy.[29]

The Nebhepetra violent scenes from divine contexts are difficult to interpret because of the lack of comparanda and the historical peculiarities of his reign.

They date to midway through that reign. There are important differences between these scenes and the smiting scenes known from royal mortuary complexes. The smiting of Egyptians is a clear example, but the quite different use of visual ethnic stereotypes more broadly is also notable, including the apparent use of an abstract symbol to represent a place. Perhaps the use of labels rather than imagery and the use of that abstract symbol suggest that, unlike his predecessors, Nebhepetra Mentuhotep used the smiting scene to emphasize domination over places more than over peoples. Are these differences due to context or history, or are they a personal quirk? Without more divine temple imagery to compare, we cannot answer this question, but addressing the ways history and/or historicity are employed does at least demonstrate some of the ideological messages contained in these reliefs.

In the smiting of an Egyptian at Gebelein, it seems somewhat unlikely that our image of violence is a simple representation of a triumphant conclusion to a historical war. Reasons for doubt are present both within the image itself and within a broader consideration of the sources we have—extremely fragmentary and difficult to interpret though they are—about fighting in the late First Intermediate Period and early Middle Kingdom.[30] Within the image itself, our Egyptian is being smote in front of representatives of a range of places; either they are waiting their turn under the mace or the subject world is observing the king's control of his territory. This cannot be a simple historical record of triumph after a war against everyone any more than a smiting scene with victims of different ethnicities could in a mortuary context. The degree to which Nebhepetra actually fought peoples either inside or outside Egypt is irrelevant here. This is a ritual scene, with peoples from different places playing different roles in the scene. Egypt is up first, the only one we know for certain is going to get hit.

At Denderah it is hard to read the smiting as referring to anything other than violent domination of the king over Egypt, and the possibility that this is in essence a large year label may suggest a greater degree of historicism. Nonetheless, the image is uniquely abstract in showing a non-human victim and the inscription makes the totality of violent references in the scene clearly generalizing and not relegated to one episode.

In neither the Second nor the Eleventh Dynasty was violence against Egyptians a taboo topic within divine spaces. This tends to emphasize the closeness of the king to the gods, rather than to paint him as the first among Egyptians. While the ideal state of the universe may have been a unified Egypt dominant over its neighbors, a reality in which Egypt was itself in need of being violently repressed not only could be acknowledged up front, but was also an appropriate theme. To me, this suggests that the triumph of subduing Egyptians is much more important to the king and gods than is the fact that the rebellion itself is threatening. The triumph is something to boast of to the divine; it is a demonstration of the fitness of the king to rule. Here it is particularly notable (with all due caveats about the amount of surviving evidence) that we have only smiting scenes, never battle scenes, from this context. These images only acknowledge discord at the end point, and the only active participant is the king. There is no question of who is dominant.

The victims do not represent an actual threat to the order personified by the king, but rather their very abjectness emphasizes the totality of royal power. Despite their probable reference to historic civil wars, these depictions are still rhetorical statements about the theory of kingship. They are also, perhaps more so than is usually the case in other circumstances, reports on its practice.

Finally, perhaps we should even consider if these fragments speak to the role of imagery in divine temples at all. It is the case that the few examples considered here come from temples that are not attached to the king's mortuary establishment. But Khasekhem's pieces all come from a temple peculiarly associated with divine kingship—Horus the god being inseparable from the reigning, living king. Is Hierakonpolis a divine temple at all, or a temple to the divine king? The chapels of Nebhepetra at Gebelein and Denderah were certainly associated with divine temples, but should we really consider them part of the temple proper or rather attached locations where cult was fundamentally for the king himself? In fact, it seems better to regard these examples as related to royal cult, though not necessarily mortuary cult. They point to the inextricability of divinity and royalty, at least in royally commissioned monuments, but also to the primary role of the king in that relationship even within the context of the god's home. The smiting motif would be used by New Kingdom kings to adorn the exteriors of their temples, divine and mortuary. But aside from the continuity of that icon, a consideration of violent imagery in pre-New Kingdom divine temples does more to support an argument that temples themselves changed—and that we are not really looking at divine temples at all in the later sense, here—rather than to suggest a precedent for the much better preserved monumental scenes of subsequent times.

Notes

1 JM01600. Stela 11, back. Drawing © 2000 John Montgomery.
2 Andrew Finegold, "Battle Murals: Violence, Representation, and Time in Epiclassic Mesoamerica" (paper presented at the conference The Art of War at Brown University, Providence, Rhode Island, November 7, 2015).
3 Donald McVicker, "Images of Violence in Mesoamerican Mural Art," in *Latin American Indigenous Warfare and Ritual Violence*, Ed. Richard J. Chacon and Rubén G. Mendoza (Tucson, AZ: The University of Arizona Press, 2007), 73–90.
4 For a discussion of the functions and meanings of temples that demonstrates how much more complex they were than this most basic function, see: John Baines, "Temples as Symbols, Guarantors, and Participants in Egyptian Civilization," in *The Temple in Ancient Egypt: New Discoveries and Recent Research*, Ed. Stephen Quirke (London: British Museum Press, 1997), 216–241.
5 Competing theories on this front have fueled an important debate, with Kemp arguing that earlier temples were "preformal"—not standardized in plan and reflective of local traditions—and O'Connor suggesting that at least some of them were rather quite regular and much like their successors: David O'Connor, "The Status of Early Egyptian Temples: An Alternative Theory," in *The Followers of Horus: Studies Dedicated to Michael Allen Hoffman*, Ed. Renée Friedman and Barbara Adams (Oxford: Oxbow Books, 1992), 83–98. For a discussion of Kemp's classification system and its application to the analysis of different early temples, see: Barry Kemp, *Ancient Egypt: Anatomy of a Civilization*, 2nd Revised ed. (London: Routledge, 2006), 112–135. More recently, Richard Bussmann has added nuance to Kemp's argument, showing that not

all "preformal" temples reflected solely local cultures free from royal engagement: *Die Provinztempel Ägyptens von der 0. bis zur 11. Dynastie* (Leiden: Brill, 2010), 115–155; and "Local Traditions in Early Egyptian Temples," in *Egypt at Its Origins 3: Proceedings of the Third International Conference "Origin of the State: Predynastic and Early Dynastic Egypt," London, 27th July–1st August 2008*, Ed. Renée Friedman and Peter Fiske (Leuven: Peeters, 2011), 747–762.

6 See Toby Wilkinson, *Early Dynastic Egypt* (London and New York: Routledge, 1999), 89–92, for an analysis of the evidence traditionally used to substantiate this theory and additional sources associated with it.

7 Cairo Museum JE 33895. Drawing by the author, based on James Quibell and Frederick W. Green, *Hierakonpolis: Part II* (London: Bernard Quaritch, 1902), 47–48, pl. 58. They call it part of a stela, but this is unlikely. Another architectural fragment with a picture of a bound prisoner but no royal name may date to this reign as well. Bussmann, *Die Provinztempel Ägyptens von der 0. bis zur 11. Dynastie*, 51.

8 Petrie read it as "humbling the foreign lands" in Quibell and Green, *Hierakonpolis: Part II*, 48. Other scholars have come up with alternative interpretations, which have been outlined by Gérard Godron, "À propos d'une inscription de l'Horus Khâsékhem," *Chronique d'Égypte* 43, no. 85 (1968): 34–35.

9 Ogden Goelet gives a brief discussion and bibliography on the use of the term *ta seti* in "Kemet and Other Egyptian Terms for Their Land," in *Ki Baruch Hu: Ancient Near Eastern, Biblical, and Judaic Studies in Honor of Baruch A. Levine*, Ed. Robery Chazan (Winona Lake, IN: Eisenbrauns, 1999), 24–25. Miroslav Bárta discusses the use of the term "bowmen" to refer to eastern bedouin in "Borderland Dynamics in the Era of the Pyramid Builders in Egypt," in *Understanding Life in the Borderlands: Boundaries in Depth and Motion*, Ed. William Zartman (Athens, GA and London: The University of Georgia Press, 2010), 33.

10 AN1896–1908 E.517 © Ashmolean Museum, University of Oxford. Carved limestone statue of King Khasekhem seated. Only the limestone example currently in the Ashmolean Museum is illustrated here. Hermann Junker, "Die Feinde auf dem Sockel der Chasechem-Statuen und die Darstellung von geopferten Tieren," in *Ägyptologische Studien*, Ed. Otto Firchow (Berlin: Akademie-Verlag, 1955), 162–75; Quibell, *Hierakonpolis: Part I*; Quibell and Green, *Hierakonpolis: Part II*. The other, which is siltstone, is in Cairo (JE 32161). A fragment of the base of the Cairo statue is currently in Liverpool. Barbara Adams, "A Fragment from the Cairo Statue of Khasekhemwy," *Journal of Egyptian Archaeology* 76 (1990): 161–163.

11 James Quibell, *Hierakonpolis: Part I* (London: Bernard Quaritch, 1900), pl. 40.

12 See Chapter 4, note 35.

13 For images and descriptions of the vessels, see: James Quibell, *Hierakonpolis: Part I*, pls. 36 (top right) and 37 (center right, bottom); and David P. Silverman, Ed., *Searching for Ancient Egypt: Art, Architecture, and Artifacts from the University of Pennsylvania Museum of Archaeology and Anthropology* (Dallas, TX: Dallas Museum of Art, 1997), 94, cat. no. 24. One of them is in the Cairo Museum (CG 14724).

14 Josef Wegner, "A New Temple: The Mahat of Nebhepetre at Abydos," *Egyptian Archaeology* 46 (2015): 3–7. The newly discovered chapel is located some distance away from the main Osiris temple, but its connection to the Osiris cult is made clear by its inscriptions. A list of the chapels known as of 2010 is in Richard Bussmann, *Die Provinztempel Ägyptens von der 0. bis zur 11. Dynastie*, 476–477; more detailed descriptions of the contents of these chapels can be found on pgs. 480–481.

15 Elisa Fiore Marochetti, *The Reliefs of the Chapel of Nebhepetre Mentuhotep at Gebelein* (Leiden, Boston, MA: Brill, 2010), 17, 23.

16 Cairo J.E. T.R. 24/5/28/5. Marochetti, *The Reliefs of the Chapel of Nebhepetre Mentuhotep at Gebelein*, 50–52.

17 Marochetti, *The Reliefs of the Chapel of Nebhepetre Mentuhotep at Gebelein*, 53.

18 Marochetti, *The Reliefs of the Chapel of Nebhepetre Mentuhotep at Gebelein*, 52.

19 Cairo J.E. T.R. 1/11/17/10. Marochetti, *The Reliefs of the Chapel of Nebhepetre Mentuhotep at Gebelein*, 57–61.

20 There is debate about what these objects are; Jéquier, for example, thought they represented half of the sign for sky: "Les talismans *ankh* et *shen*," *Bulletin de l'Institut français d'archéologie orientale* 11 (1914): 141. For a summary of other theories, see: Marochetti, *The Reliefs of the Chapel of Nebhepetre Mentuhotep at Gebelein*, 57–58.

21 Claude Vandersleyen, "La titulature de Mentouhotep II," in *Essays in Egyptology in Honor of Hans Goedicke*, Ed. Betsy Bryan and David Lorton (San Antonio, TX: Van Siclen Books, 1994), 317–320.

22 Labib Habachi, "King Nebhepetre Menthuhotp: His Monuments, Place in History, Deification and Unusual Representation in the Form of Gods," *Mitteilungen des Deutschen Archäologischen Instituts, Abteilung Kairo* 19 (1963): 16–52; David O'Connor, "The Dendereh Chapel of Nebhepetre Mentuhotep: A New Perspective," in *Studies on Ancient Egypt in Honour of H.S. Smith*, Ed. Anthony Leahy and John Tait (London: Egypt Exploration Society, 1999), 215–220; Georges Daressy, "Chapelle de Mentouhotep III à Dendérah," *Annales du Service des antiquités de l'Égypte* 17 (1917): 226–236.

23 O'Connor, "The Dendereh Chapel of Nebhepetre Mentuhotep: A New Perspective," 217.

24 Line drawing by the author, based on Habachi, "King Nebhepetre Mentuhotp: His Monuments, Place in History, Deification and Unusual Representation in the Form of Gods."

25 Habachi, "King Nebhepetre Menthuhotp: His Monuments, Place in History, Deification and Unusual Representation in the Form of Gods," 21; Daressy, "Chapelle de Mentouhotep III à Dendérah," 227–228; Wolfram Grajetzki, *The Middle Kingdom of Ancient Egypt* (London: Duckworth, 2006), 19.

26 O'Connor, "The Dendereh Chapel of Nebhepetre Mentuhotep: A New Perspective," 218.

27 O'Connor, "The Dendereh Chapel of Nebhepetre Mentuhotep: A New Perspective," 219.

28 Marochetti, *The Reliefs of the Chapel of Nebhepetre Mentuhotep at Gebelein*, 31. O'Connor attempts to have his cake and eat it too, noting how unusual the interior smiting scene is but comparing it to a pylon behind a monumental statue in the New Kingdom and suggesting that the rear wall "radiat[es] protection out onto the court, which would be 'linked' to the scene as soon as the *ka*-chapel door was opened for cult purposes." (O'Connor, "The Dendereh Chapel of Nebhepetre Mentuhotep: A New Perspective," 210). I find this unconvincing and prefer to highlight the unique nature and placement of this scene.

29 O'Connor, "The Dendereh Chapel of Nebhepetre Mentuhotep: A New Perspective," 219.

30 Evidence for the continuation of war into the Twelfth Dynasty comes most dramatically from the so-called Slain Soldiers, a mass burial of about 60 men who clearly died in battle and were buried at Thebes. This appears to date to the Twelfth Dynasty. See Carola Vogel, "Fallen Heroes? Winlock's 'Slain Soldiers' Reconsidered," *Journal of Egyptian Archaeology* 89 (2003): 239–245. Ongoing research into desert rock graffiti also supports the conclusion that the wars of reunification were not quick or limited to the reign of Nebhepetre. Examples of such research include: Harco Willems, "The Nomarchs of the Hare Nome and Early Middle Kingdom History," *Jaarbericht Ex Oriente Lux. Jaarboek van het Nederlands Instituut Te Leiden* 28 (1985): 80–102; John C. Darnell, "The Rock Inscriptions of Tjehemau at Abisko," *Zeitschrift für Ägyptische Sprache und Altertumskunde* 130 (2003): 31–48.

6 The preservation of order

Images in the landscape

The straight lines of the spears drive, horizontal, across the rock. What could be more immobile than the face of a cliff? What could better capture movement than an image of a spear thrust from the back of a galloping horse into a falling enemy? The paradox of this combination of kinetic and static helps give the relief of Hormizd II at Naqsh-e Rustam its particular power (Figure 6.1),[1] but it is the fact that the relief is one of many that imbues the place itself with such meaning.

In this relief, we see three human figures and two horses. On the very left a man stands, helmeted, facing right, holding a T-shaped standard from which ornaments hang. To his right, occupying the most prominent part of the composition, are a horse and a rider. The current ground line is the ground itself, but the horse does not touch it.[2] His forelegs are thrown out in front of him, nearly horizontal.

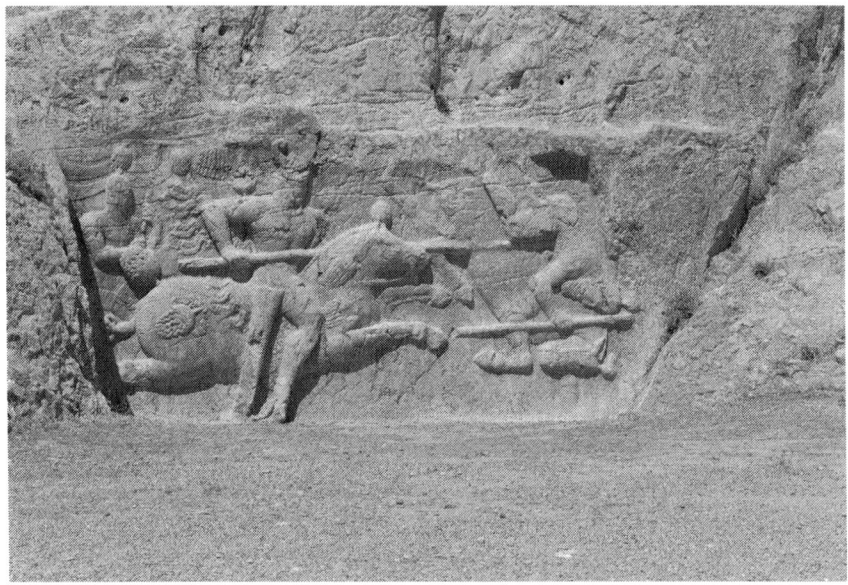

Figure 6.1 Hormizd II spears a falling enemy. Sasanian rock relief at Naqsh-e Rustam, Iran.

His hind leg, too, is extended; its hoof is not shown, not contained within the frame of the relief. The rider, sporting impressively muscled legs and a posture of pure power, holds the spear whose line defines the center of the whole relief. The rider is partly eroded, but appears to have long hair, armour, and elaborate headgear; though the latter is partly destroyed, it can be seen by analogy to portraits on coins to have included an eagle with a curled tail and a pearl in its beak. It is on the basis of this crown that the warrior can be identified as the Sasanian king Hormizd II (302–309 CE).[3] A well-preserved quiver hangs beside his leg. The composition plays with the spear, held in the near hand of the king but passing behind the head of his horse. Horse and rider are heavily decorated, with numerous tassels attached to the rich fittings of the horse, and an impressive fringe flying in the wind from the garment of the rider.

His victim is in distress, an image different from the uncompleted violence of an Egyptian smiting scene. He and his horse tumble, heads to the ground and legs in the air. The line of his own clutched weapon parallels that of the king, but he cannot use it: Hormizd's spear pierces his belly and death is presumably at hand.

When Hormizd's relief was carved, Naqsh-e Rustam was already an ancient place, already defined by royal monuments and carvings. The burial place of earlier Achaemenid kings, their tombs also carved into the cliff face (Figure 6.2),[4] the site in the Sasanian Period was used for reliefs that depicted events in different levels of specificity. The most famous is that of Sharpur defeating the Roman emperors, but in some cases, including here, we cannot be sure of the particular enemy or battle. The reliefs of Naqsh-e Rustam collectively do not tell a sustained narrative history of the Sasanian kings, but do make a sustained argument about

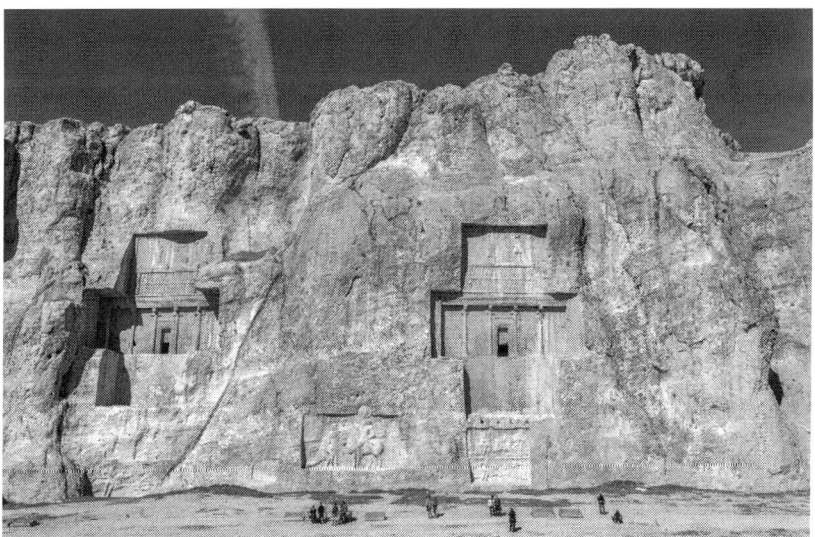

Figure 6.2 The relief of Hormizd II killing an enemy on horseback is situated directly beneath the earlier rock-cut façade of an Achaemenid royal tomb.

various elements of Sasanian kingship, including both violence and a relationship with the past. The very fact of carving them here, in a place already strongly associated with kingship and where other royal events had been previously carved by other kings, tied Hormizd's particular besting of an enemy into cosmic narratives about kingship. It is the imagery itself, the accessibility of that imagery, and the repeated use of one location that gives these pictures their power.

Egyptian images of violence in the landscape are surprisingly rare and exhibit both meaningful similarities to and notable differences from the Sasanian images at Naqsh-e Rustam. The most obvious similarity is the repeated return to a site on which to carve images of violent kings. In the Egyptian case this is restricted to one site during the time covered by this study—it is not a central or ceremonial site but rather a peripheral one, in the Sinai, associated with mining. Despite this, the violent images are all of kings and almost every relief from this site that has any pictorial representation at all, not just text, has a smiting scene. As in Iran, the multiplicity of images as well as their immobile presence on living rock create a sense of permanence. Since the images could have been experienced collectively, the sense they attain together is as critical as the sense conveyed by any single image.

Rock faces in the desert were locations for Egyptian art since great antiquity. However, as noted in Chapters 2 and 3, their date and relation to both political and artistic developments in the Nile valley are difficult to assess prior to the inclusion of inscriptions. The example of the tableau at Gebel Sheikh Suleiman discussed in Chapter 3 points out the innovative nature of the period of state formation more than it demonstrates a stage of development of a coherent tradition of rock art. That there was a coherent tradition, and that its earliest attestations are nearly contemporary with Gebel Sheikh Suleiman, shows that there were multiple reasons for drawing on rocks in ancient Egypt and reminds us to be at least somewhat wary of rigid categorization. The particularly royal tradition of images on living rock, in which we sometimes find images of violence, is much more restricted in amount and location than prehistoric and Predynastic imagery in the landscape; pharaonic pictures on rocks are found predominantly in connection with quarry and mine sites and the routes leading to them. In most cases, human conflict is not a theme in pharaonic rock art, early or late. The exception comes from a series of smiting images in the Sinai dated to the Early Dynastic Period and Old Kingdom.

The specific location, not just the labeling of the landscape, is critical in this context. The Sinai Peninsula was a place of turquoise and copper mining for Egypt and probably supported a small nomadic or semi-nomadic indigenous population, which may have fluctuated over time. Pharaonic interactions with the Sinai began as early as the Protodynastic Period, and the first kings did carve their names on rock faces in the Sinai; three early kings in four carvings include smiting, and their images serve as a bridge between the earliest inscriptions and the smiting scenes that follow. From the Old Kingdom, nine recorded carvings show the king in human form smiting captives, in many cases identifiable iconographically or by inscription as people from east of Egypt. While pharaonic activity in the Sinai continued in the Middle Kingdom and rock cut inscriptions were still made, the smiting scene disappears then.

Both the presence of the smiting scene in the very early Old Kingdom and its cessation before the Middle Kingdom are in contrast to the use of similar imagery elsewhere, particularly in royal tomb complexes. It may be that this is because the image played an historically specific role with regards to interactions between the Egyptian state and the people who might reasonably oppose Egyptian state activities. Those people may well have included both local populations and members of the mining expeditions. Favoring a reading that is time, place, and even politically specific is the fact that no similar images were made to the south, where Egypt also engaged in the acquisition of resources outside its traditional borders and where rock faces were also available to be carved.[5] When Sinai smiting images cease, we must assume that the relationship between place, people, and message had changed. In the Middle Kingdom, from which no such images are known, Sinai rock inscriptions rather record the glory of expedition leaders and even staff instead of kings themselves. The context ceased to be a place where the primary import of rock carving was royal ideology.

The Early Dynastic Period

The first smiting scene known from the landscape is a somewhat abstract one, dated to the First Dynasty King Djer (Figure 6.3).[6] The location of the image is a site called Wadi Ameyra in the south Sinai, about 30 km from Wadi Maghara, where the later images are clustered. The location had already been, for generations, a place where the Egyptian kings of the Protodynastic Period and earlier First Dynasty had carved their names, frequently in connection with boats.[7] The rock faces utilized were not vertical but rather gentle slopes, and the images were made by pecking and are not true reliefs.

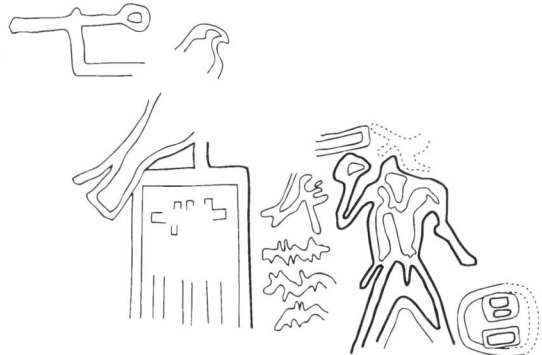

Figure 6.3 The *serekh* of Djer smites a captive, on a rock face at Wadi Ameyra in the south Sinai. Dimensions: 45 × 65 cm.

The inscription of Djer differs from its predecessors in having no boat, in including a human figure, and in showing smiting, though the king is present as a *serekh* with his name rather than in human form. The inscription is not well preserved and can be more clearly illustrated with a drawing than with photographs. The *serekh* is on the left. The rear talon of the Horus falcon is shown as a human arm, raised behind the head of the bird and brandishing a mace horizontally, grasped in its middle.

The second figure in the image is difficult to see clearly. Separated from the *serekh* by a partly missing inscription, he appears to have a male human form. Both his head and his legs below the knees are missing, and it is unclear if he was shown striding or kneeling. The position of his arms shows that he faces away from the *serekh;* he appears to wear a belted garment, perhaps a kilt. His forearm is slightly flexed and held before his body while his rear arm is raised toward his head. The discoverers of the inscription thought it possible that he represents the divinity Ash on the basis of traces of a caption.[8] Either the smiting king has no depicted victim, or the god himself is the victim; either would be without parallel. The direct connection between the figures is not preserved, but it seems unlikely that the falcon directly grasped the figure in front of it. The remnants of the possible Ash inscription are directly behind the head, where a hand would have to be.

The closest parallels for this image come from near-contemporary objects from kings' tombs, on which we also see the name of the king smiting (Figures 3.17, 3.18, 7.2). The visual problem created by needing too many limbs for a falcon who must both perch atop a *serekh* and smite a captive was not successfully resolved, and one wonders if this was a reason the motif was discontinued.

Three further images from the First Dynasty are known in the Sinai: two from the reign of king Den and one of uncertain attribution but possibly from the reign of king Semerkhet, penultimate king of the Dynasty.[9] These inscriptions are located at Wadi el-Humur, 25 km north of the main concentration of Old Kingdom reliefs at Maghara. All three are on a single rock face and so anticipate the creation of place on the basis of a collection of images over time. In a number of other ways, these images also foreshadow the coming Old Kingdom reliefs in their particular details; they are much more like what follows than what preceded them, though the inclusion of the god Ash connects them, too, to the preceding example.

The topmost relief on the rock at Wadi el-Humur belongs to Den and shows four figures plus a standard of the god Wepwawet (Figure 6.4),[10] a regular feature of later Sinai smiting images. On the right is the god Ash, labeled, shown with plumes on his head and a staff. Before him is the standard, clutched by the prone smitee, who has one knee down and the other raised and bent. The position of his head is not entirely clear, but he appears to look backwards and to the left, over his shoulder, toward the king who grasps his hair and prepares to smite him. The prisoner is clothed in a kilt with a tab and perhaps has a beard. The king wears the White Crown and a kilt with an apron or central tab; his raised arm holds what may be a stick or a mace. His *serekh* is in front of his face, above the head of his victim. Behind him and at a much smaller scale can be seen an

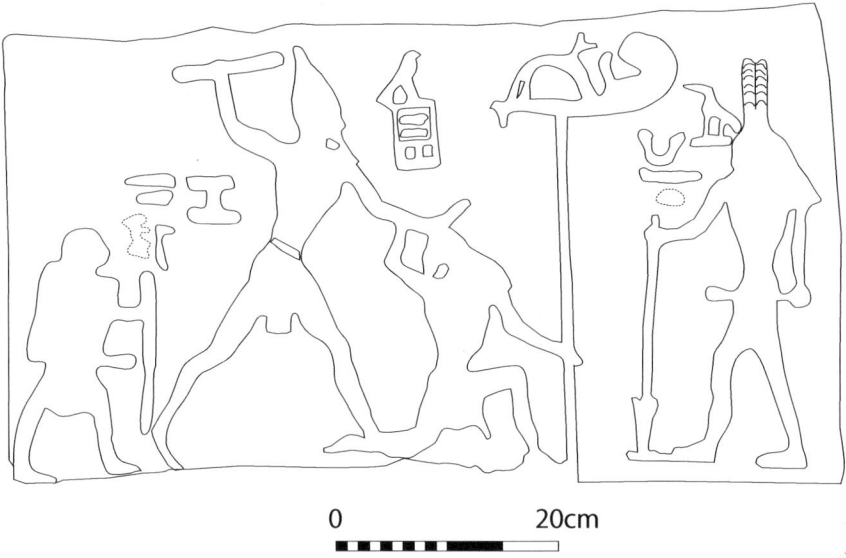

0   20cm

Figure 6.4 Den, a king of the mid-First Dynasty, smites a captive on a rock face at Wadi el-Humur. His victim clutches the base of a Wepwawet standard. On the right the scene is watched by the god Ash, while on the left an official at a smaller scale looks on. Dimensions: 35 × 60 cm.

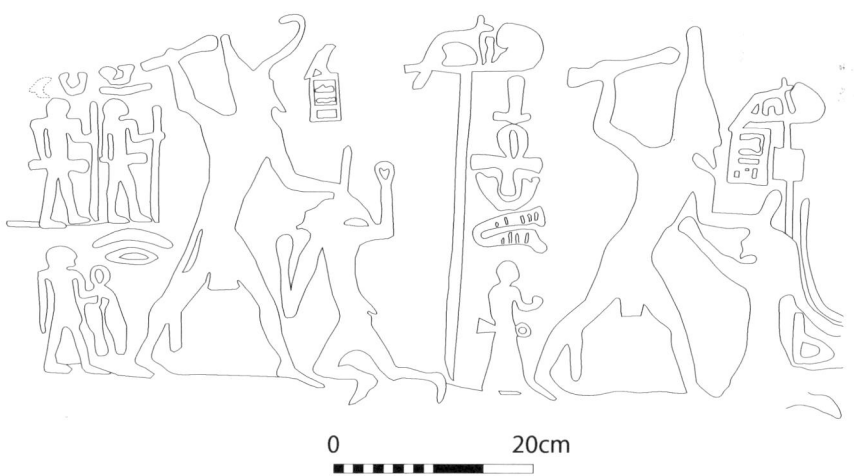

0   20cm

Figure 6.5 Den smites again, once more watched by officials. This double scene, separated by the standard of Wepwawet, is below that shown in the previous image on the rock face at Wadi el-Humur. Dimensions: 35 × 80 cm.

official striding and holding a long staff; he appears to wear a camping backpack, but this is presumably a result of the quality of the stone and carving.

Below this is a double vignette with two smiting scenes of the same king separated by a Wepwawet standard (Figure 6.5).[11] On the right, Den in the Red Crown again grasps a captive by the hair and prepares to hit him, this time clearly with a small-headed mace. The tail of the king here hangs just off his back leg, and the beard of his prisoner, who faces him, is clear. An inscription to the right perhaps mentions the east.[12] An official behind the king is labeled with a title and a personal name, the latter of which is well attested from other sources during the reign of Den.[13]

On the left of this double vignette, the king wears the Red Crown while smiting his bearded captive and is watched by three officials on two registers. The lower of these officials holds sandals, much as the person behind Narmer does on his palette (Figure 3.14). In the upper register, the two officials hold long vertical staffs and shorter horizontal implements, which might be maces.[14]

The final smiting scene on this rock face is the lowest of the vignettes. In it, a Red Crown-wearing king faces to the right and smites a kneeling captive who faces him (Figure 6.6).[15] The spaghetti-legs of the captive are unusual, but the

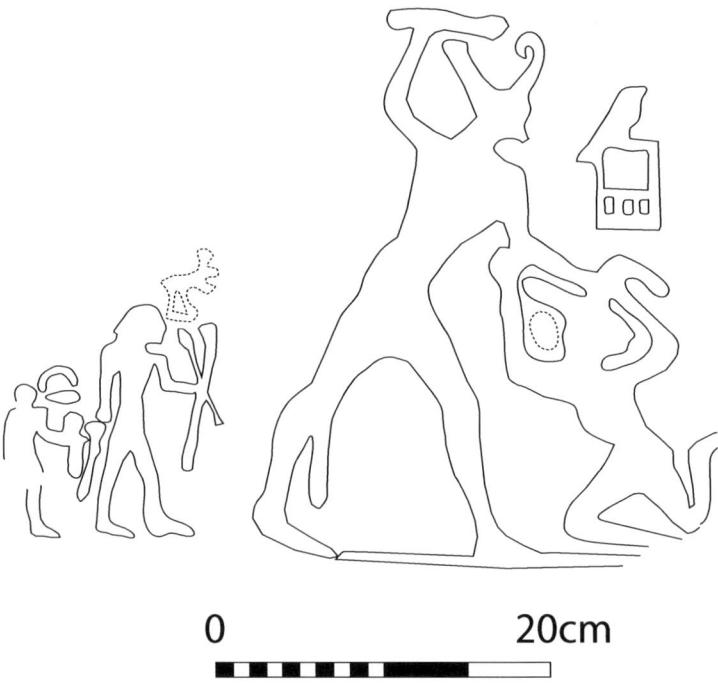

0   20cm

Figure 6.6 A king in the Red Crown smites a captive, Wadi el-Humur, Sinai. The name in the *serekh* cannot be reliably read, but it probably dates to the First Dynasty (as do the smiting scenes above it on the same rock face). Two officials but no Wepwawet standard grace this scene. Dimensions: 35 × 50 cm.

amount of detail is minimal and little can be said about him aside from that his hair is long enough to grasp and may also have a protruding tuft—a feather?— below the forearm of the king. The king's tail is visible between his legs, and his *serekh* is before him. This is not really legible but may belong to the late First Dynasty king Semerkhet, or perhaps to a king of the Second Dynasty.[16] The scene is once more watched by two non-royal figures, here shown at different scales not only from the king and smittee but also from one another. The taller, in front, appears to carry a bow and arrow. The figure behind him also grasps something, perhaps sandals.

These recently discovered scenes do much to show the continuity of this type of image in this type of context from the earliest period of Egyptian history. That the very early images regularly include officials, combining images of kings and humans in a way that is unique for most of the periods under consideration in this book, must raise further questions. Is this a holdover from earlier practice, as suggested by the parallel to the Narmer Palette, reminding us that the First Dynasty was still a transitional period for the use of imagery at all? Or does the inclusion of officials here speak to the audience for the image, as well as that which the image showed? Officials could look at these. Might it even be indicative of who commissioned these pictures? I do not think we can answer these questions for the First Dynasty, but indications that these monuments were commissioned by officials and were not, in that sense, royal pictures at all will grow in the following dynasties.

The Old Kingdom

The remaining known smiting scenes from the Sinai date to the Old Kingdom and are notable for starting early and for being clustered in a small area at Wadi Maghara; the continuity, from the period of state formation into the Old Kingdom, of place and image type in this case is much, much greater than with any other context we have.[17] Also to be noted with the Old Kingdom reliefs is their size: most are quite large, often well over a meter in length. The smiting icon was a regular element in the landscape before it was a regular element in the royal tomb. The earliest known such depiction from Maghara dates to Djoser, the first king of the Old Kingdom, who we know did not have smiting images among the well-preserved scenes at his mortuary complex. Likewise, many of his successors smite in the Sinai, including two from the Third Dynasty, which is in general poorly represented in the Nile valley. The first two kings of the Fourth Dynasty are also represented in the corpus, after which this type of image becomes somewhat rarer in this Dynasty. There are several Fifth Dynasty examples, and one from the Sixth, which is the latest yet known.

The area of the inscriptions is concentrated near the remains of huts for mine workers. The huts are concentrated on a hill; the smiting scenes, though somewhat dispersed, are largely on a hill to the west, facing the huts with a wadi between the two.[18] The space between the two is generally over 100 m, rendering the specifics of the images invisible from the area of occupation.

However, that the images defined the hill on which they were carved, and that the hill itself was a constant visual presence for those living and working in the vicinity, seems clear.[19]

The Third Dynasty

Djoser was the first king of the Third Dynasty, best known for the Step Pyramid at Saqqara, which inaugurated the era of pyramid building in Egypt. The name Djoser itself is not attested in contemporary documents, which give us his Horus name: Netjerikhet. In his inscription at Maghara, the king's *serekh* with the name Netjerikhet is at the far right, facing the tableau to the left (Figure 6.7).[20]

The central element of the scene is the king, facing right, in an active posture of smiting. His legs are spread, his back heel raised, and his front knee slightly flexed. His front arm stretches out to grasp his captive, while his rear arm is raised and gripping a mace. The mace is not particularly well defined and looks rather more like a golf club than a standard piriform mace; strangely, the maceheads in the Sinai images are notably small in many cases.

The king wears a *shendyt* kilt, identifiable by the flap hanging between his legs, a tail, a beard, and a headdress that has a uraeus at its brow. The captive is shown at a somewhat smaller scale than the king. He kneels—only one leg is clearly distinguishable—and looks back over his shoulder toward his smiter. One arm is on his knee and the other raised toward his head, perhaps grasping the wrist

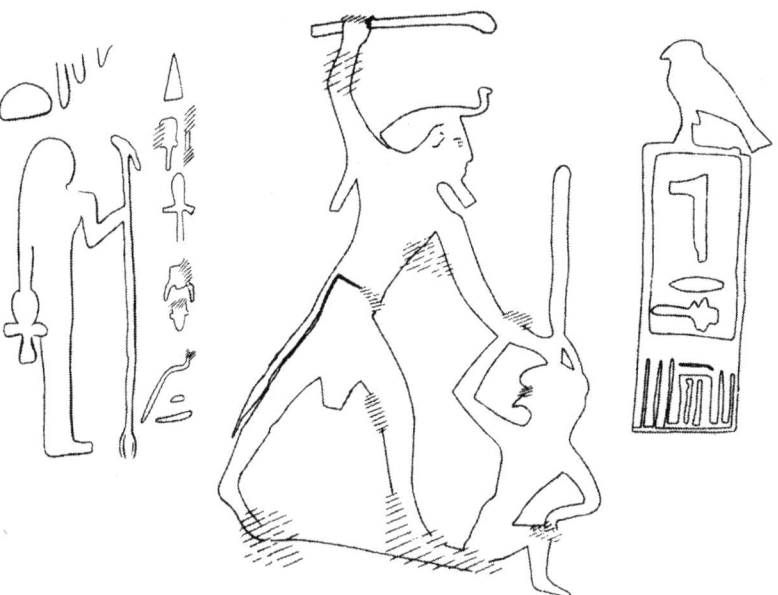

Figure 6.7 Netjerikhet (Djoser) smites an enemy, watched by a goddess. Rock inscription, Wadi Maghara, Sinai. Dimensions: length 240 cm.

of the king. In addition to the captive's hair, the king holds the long staff known from many other smiting scenes in his front hand. No details of dress are clear on the prisoner, but he might sport a kilt and a beard. Behind the dynamic scene of violence stands a goddess in a long dress, clutching an *ankh* and a scepter. She is at a smaller scale than the king. Between the two is a line of inscription noting that the king has been granted dominion, stability, life, and joy for eternity. No frame contains this image, though there is a sloping groundline beneath the king and his victim. On the same rock face and belonging to the same overall composition are images and titles of two officials and what appear, though worn, to be some words about an expedition.

The next smiting images in the landscape of Wadi Maghara date to the Third Dynasty king Sekhemkhet. There are two sets of scenes about 35 m from one another. They are the only known images of this king, whose step pyramid complex at Saqqara was never finished. The two sets are largely the same in composition, except for the rightmost figure. The first is unfinished and is more sketchily drawn than the second, which is of high quality.[21] It has been suggested that the first image was a preliminary draft, found unsatisfactory and so remade elsewhere;[22] if so, it must have been copied from a drawing rather than directly, since the unfinished inscription is not visible from the more complete scene. Both images have five figures: three instances of the king, one of a prisoner, and one of an official. If the scene is to be understood narratively, it is not clear what order or relation there is between the images of the king.

The sketchier of the two Sekhemkhet reliefs has its five figures shown at three different levels (Figure 6.8).[23] On the left, the king in smiting pose and his

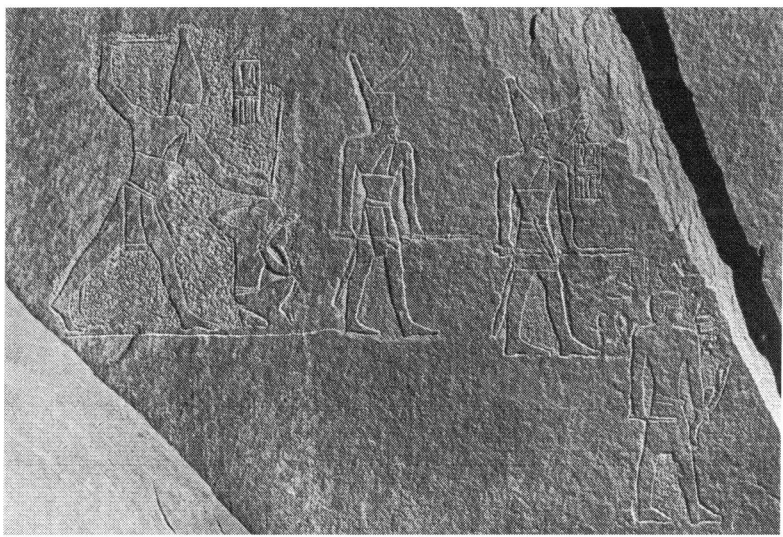

Figure 6.8 One of two sets of images of King Sekhemkhet at Wadi Maghara, Sinai. On the left, the king in the White Crown smites a captive who clutches a feather.

captive can be seen on a groundline. The king to the immediate right of this scene is at a similar level, while the other two figures are at progressively lower levels, perhaps because of a crack in the rock.[24] The smiting scene is the most finished part of the relief, with the background pecked out behind these two figures. The king is in the classic pose, striding to the right, his back heel raised as he leans into the blow. He wears a kilt with an unusual hanging portion and a tab at the belt, and a tail is just visible falling behind his back leg. His torso has the same half-wrapped, one-strapped garment that Sanakht will wear (Figure 6.11). He wears a rather long, narrow beard and the White Crown. His mace, held by the very end of the handle, has a comically small head. His front arm grasps his captive by the hair, a lock of which comes out of his head, and also holds the long staff. His *serekh* is in front of his face, also facing to the right.

The captive kneels, one knee on the ground and one raised in front of him. He turns so that his torso faces his captor and raises one hand toward his head. He wears a belted garment and a wig and holds what appears to be a feather; this is the only aspect of his iconography that might serve to identify him, but it is not static enough in developed visual stereotypes for us to be confident of what it means. He is not labeled.

To the right of the smiting scene and facing away from it come the other figures of this tableau. The king is shown separately walking in the Red and White Crowns. His *serekh* is present before him when he wears the White but not the Red Crown. The Horus falcon on this second *serekh* itself wears a Red Crown. In both of these walking depictions, the king is dressed with the tail, the single shoulder strap, and the kilt, though the front parts of different kilts differ. The White Crown-wearing, rightmost iteration of Sekhemkhet may have a dagger held in his belt. In each case he carries a long staff, held horizontally. At a lower level, the rightmost figure in the tableau is a kilted official in a short wig. He holds a short staff and a weapon and is given a variety of titles, including expedition commander and seal-bearer of the king.

The issue of visibility is particularly acute with this image, which is so difficult to find that it was lost for more than 100 years after its first discovery by scholars, and was thus left out of Gardiner and Peet's seminal survey of Sinai rock inscriptions.[25] In fact, the relatively regular new discovery of Egyptian rock inscriptions as a whole demonstrates how difficult to see they often are, and this in turn must make us question who was intended to see them and under what circumstances. There seems to be a discrepancy in the corpus of landscape images between those that were very obvious, even intervisible, and those that were almost hidden.

The more complete of the Sekhemkhet reliefs, slightly lower down and rather more visible than the first, is in most respects similar (Figures 6.9 and 6.10).[26] Here the same five figures occur, in largely the same relative relationship, with the official at the far right and not watching the action. All of the figures are shown at the same level, made possible here because there is no major fracture in the rock. The kings and official are shown at the same scale, with the captive at a slightly smaller scale. The smiting scene is at the left.

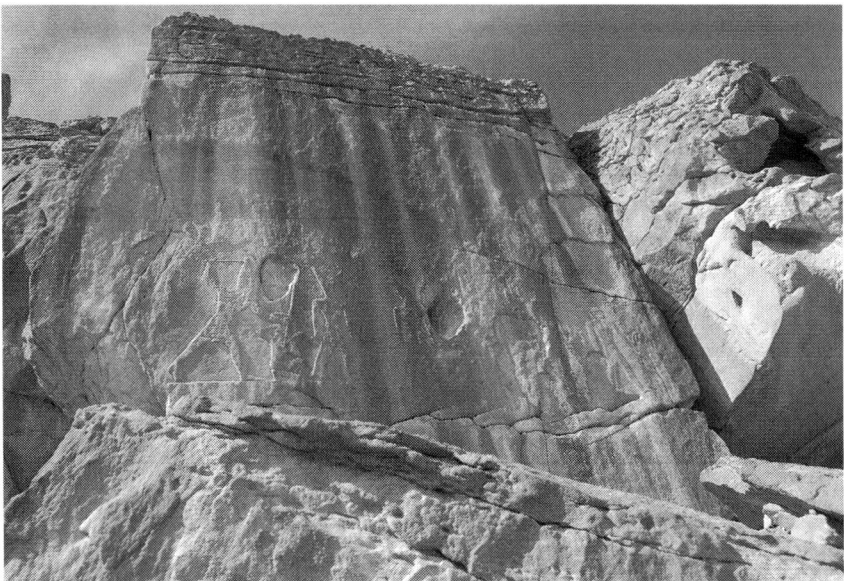

Figure 6.9 The more finished of the two Sekhemkhet reliefs at Wadi Maghara. It again
shows the king three times, once smiting, and an official.

As was true in the other Sekhemkhet relief, the king appears three times. On
the left he smites, again with a comically small mace gripped in an ineffective
place—holding the weapon at the very end of the handle would make the blow
land with the handle, not the macehead—on a victim grasped by the hair. The
king's dress, crown, and *serekh* before his face are also equivalent to those in the
other relief, both in the smiting image and in the two walking figures. The victim,

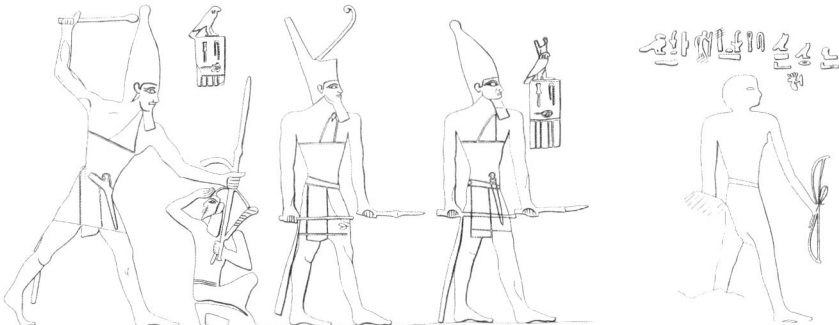

Figure 6.10 A line drawing of the more complete Sekhemkhet relief. Dimensions:
62 × 120 cm (royal figures); 58 × 40 cm (leader of the expedition).

who adopts the same posture as described above and again clutches a feather, has a clear beard here and a wig or hairstyle that leaves his left shoulder uncovered; this emphasizes his otherness rather more than was the case in the first relief.

The official is so far removed from the royal figures that Gardiner and Peet regarded him as almost a separate image, and their line drawing does not accurately show the relationship between him and the king. Here the weapon he holds is clearly a bow. The titles given again include commander of the expedition, and probably king's seal-bearer.[27] It is noteworthy in both of these cases that the inscription accompanies and gives details about the official—not about the king, who is only labeled, or about the action. The importance of the official, who is at the front of the queue and is well labeled, should make us ask whether this is truly a royal monument at all or if it could have been carved at the behest of the official himself, a question that could already be asked with regard to the First Dynasty images.

Also from the early Third Dynasty at Wadi Maghara come two reliefs carved during the reign of a king with the Horus name of Sanakht. Sanakht is ill-attested in the Nile valley and has no known remaining pyramid complex; even his precise position within the Third Dynasty is uncertain.[28] One of these reliefs preserves a partial smiting scene (Figure 6.11),[29] now in the British Museum. The fragment was found loose in a bank of stone chips below the rock face on which was

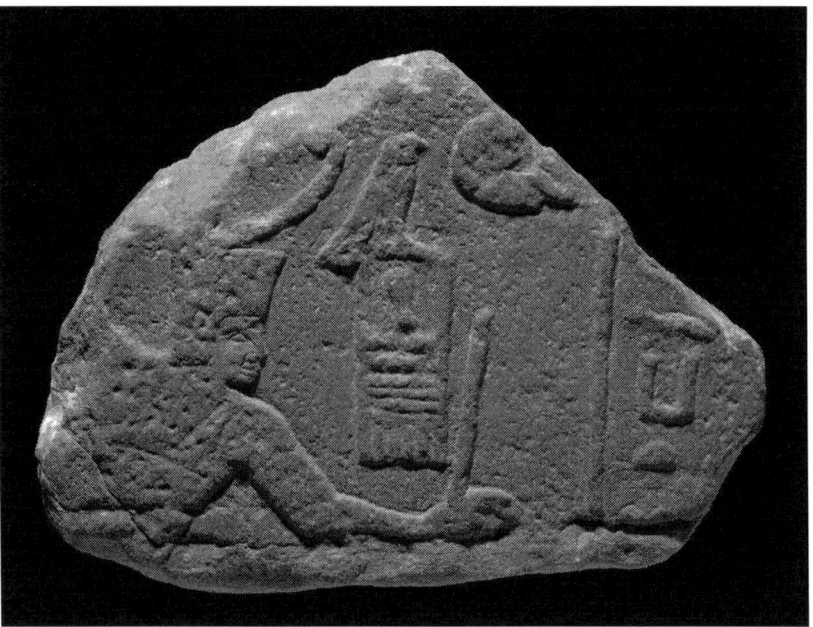

Figure 6.11 King Sanakht smites a captive, now missing, in a raised relief from Wadi Maghara, Sinai. The word *mfkt*, turquoise, can be seen on the right. Dimensions: 33 × 41 cm.

found an image of this king striding with a staff and mace, wearing the White Crown, and following a standard of the god Wepwawet; these may originally have belonged to the same tableau.[30] While the British Museum piece is only a fragment, some of its details, rendered in high relief, are more easily visible than in the earlier rock inscriptions. Here the king is shown in an active smiting pose, torso leaning into the blow. His outstretched front arm has a slightly flexed elbow, and his hand grips the customary long staff. He wears a garment that wraps the lower part of his torso and has a strap crossing his front shoulder. On his head, which has details of ear, eye, mouth, and nose clearly indicated, sits a Red Crown—the first known from a smiting scene. The top of his prisoner's head is barely visible beneath the king's hand; the rest of him is missing. The king's *serekh* is in front of his face, also facing to the right. To the right of the preserved fragment can be seen part of the standard associated with Wepwawet and part of the word *mfkt*, which means turquoise. The use of both crowns in Third Dynasty Sinai images may suggest that the totality of his territorial control, as well as his specifically violent ability to dominate the Sinai, were being insisted upon here. The inclusion of the word for turquoise serves as an overt link between this image and the mining activities of the Egyptian state at this site.

The Fourth Dynasty

The first king of the Fourth Dynasty, Snefru, is pictured smiting on two reliefs at Wadi Maghara. The higher of the two scenes has much in common with the Sekhemkhet reliefs, including multiple images of the king (Figure 6.12).[31]

In this relief, Snefru is shown actively striding, again facing toward the right, with a small mace held high behind his White Crown. He wears a *shendyt* kilt, and the tip of a hanging tail falls just behind his back calf. His much smaller victim is in a more active pose than Sekhemkhet's captives were; one leg is outstretched before him and the other is bent to support him on his knee. He twists to face the king and raises his hand in supplication or against the blow. His beard is clear, but whether or not he is clothed is less certain. The king's *serekh* is shown twice in this scene: there is a small one at some remove behind his head and a larger one facing in the same direction as the king and to the right of the whole scene. A short inscription between the king and his own name is identical to that seen in the Djoser relief, "given dominion, stability, and joy eternally." The smiting scene is on a groundline, below which are two solitary images of the walking king in separate crowns. A plain *serekh* labels each of these. The overall arrangement, the inscription, and the absence of an accompanying official differentiate this relief from the Sekhemkhet examples.

The second of the Snefru smiting reliefs is lower down the hill, closer to the floor of the wadi (Figure 6.13).[32] It incorporates a much greater amount of text, including a more elaborate royal titulary and now the label "subduing the foreign lands." Also notable is one of the most remarkable pieces of headgear ever worn by an Egyptian king. In this case, the smiting scene is the only figural part of the carving. Snefru stands in the classic smiting pose, back heel raised, wearing a

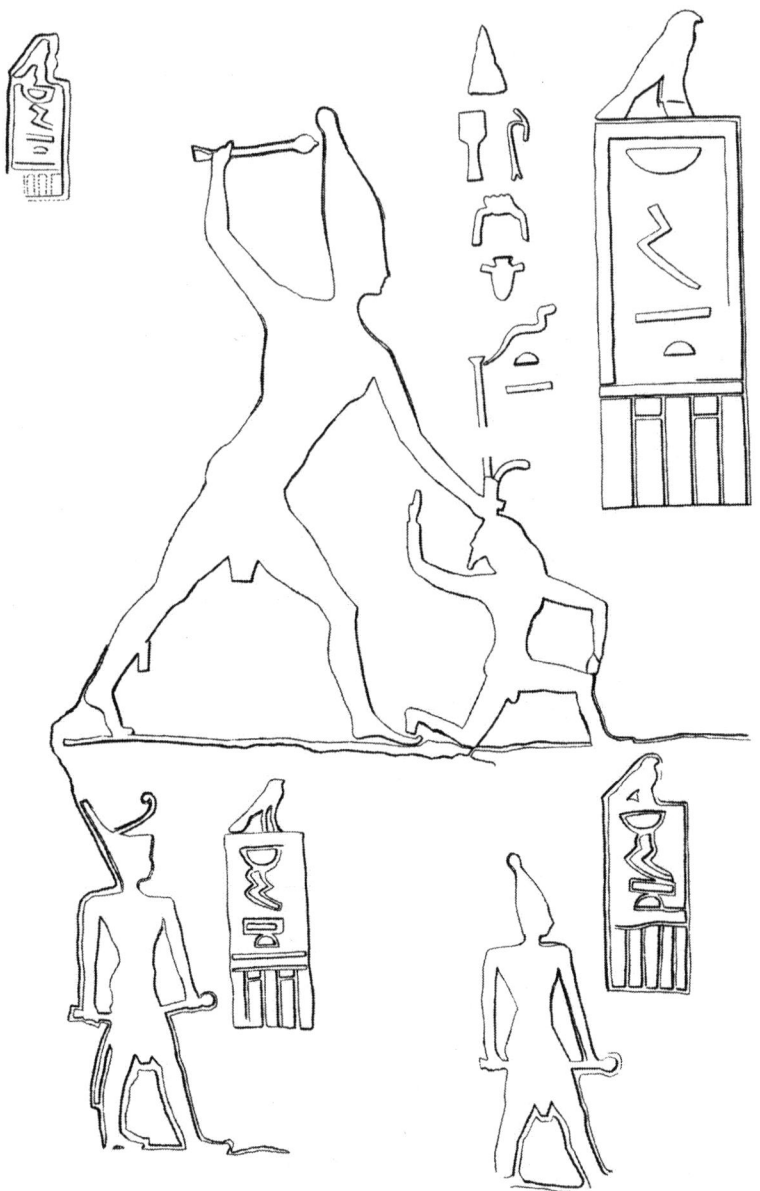

Figure 6.12 Snefru smites an enemy at Wadi Maghara, Sinai. Dimensions: 111 × 73 cm.

shendyt kilt with its elaborate pleating shown. A tail hangs down, visible behind his calf. His mace is again very small. He has a short, curved wig, and wears a narrow collar or necklace. The headdress consists of two pairs of animal horns of different shapes, and two feathers. The king's outstretched arm, with which he grasps his captive's hair and a long staff, wears a bracelet.

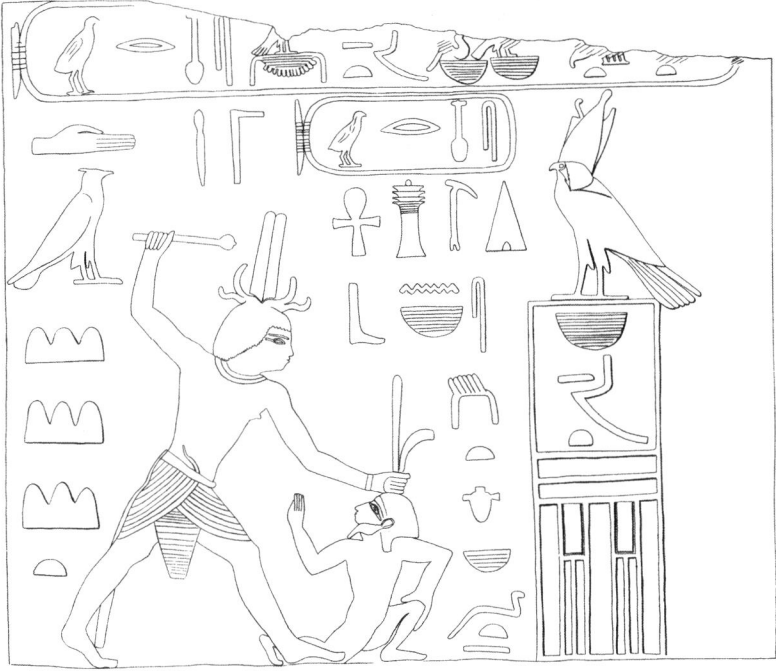

Figure 6.13 Snefru smites again at Wadi Maghara. Dimensions: 112 × 125 cm.

The slightly smaller captive is in a rather awkward and scrunched position, with his right leg extended behind him and overlapped by the striding foot of the king. His other leg, bent knee up, is before him. The apparently naked smitee turns to face the king, raising one hand while his other is on his knee. His hair falls over his shoulder and his beard has side whiskers. The inscription "subduing the foreign lands" is present behind the king.

Khufu's smiting image from the Sinai appears largely classic, though some elements eroded prior to their recording (Figures 6.14 and 6.15).[33] The carving as a whole was a two-part panel, measuring over 3 m long. The king is on the far left, facing right and striding with legs far apart. His mace-holding hand is above his head, with the now expected mace that looks more like a matchstick; his front hand sits atop the head of his victim and clutches the standard long staff and tuft of hair. The king wears a *shendyt* kilt, recognizable by the flap between his legs, and a broad collar. He now wears the double crown. To this point in these images, the smiting king has only been pictured wearing the same headgear between reigns once—the White Crown on both Sekhemkhet and Snefru. The headgear variety in the corpus as a whole is almost funny, particularly in contrast to the near total standardization of elements such as the staff or tuft of hair. Khufu's smitee had largely eroded by the time the epigraphers captured him, but his position is entirely expected. He turns back to face the king, one hand to his head and one bent before him, presumably with his hand resting upon his knee. He wears crossed straps across his chest, but otherwise has no preserved iconographic details.

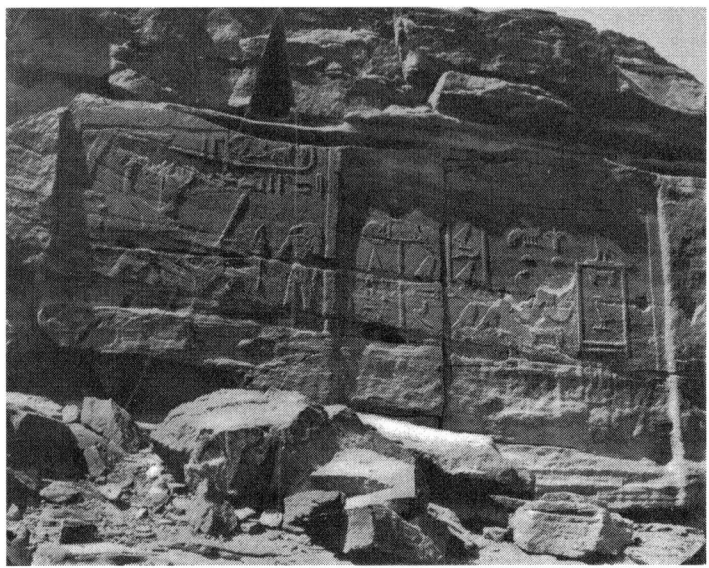

Figure 6.14 Photograph of a now lost double-panel rock inscription dated to the reign of Khufu. On the left, the king wears a Double Crown while smiting a captive with crossed chest straps. The ibis-headed god Thoth watches the scene.

Facing the smiting scene on the right is the ibis-headed god Thoth. He wears a moderately elaborate thigh-length dress with a tail hanging down his back. He holds a *Was*-scepter before him. To the right and above the scene is the king's name and a short inscription, badly decayed, probably to be read "smiting the nomads"; another behind the king reads "the protection of [life] behind [him]!"[34] A falcon, with wings spread at a right angle, protects the king from behind his head. The panel on the right includes a Wepwawet standard facing toward the smiting scene, as well as a longer titulary of the king.

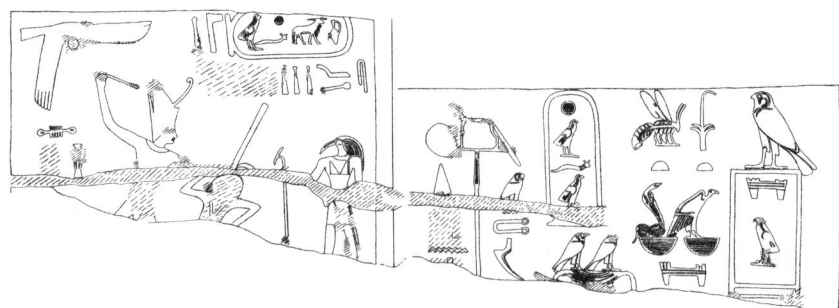

Figure 6.15 Khufu smiting from Wadi Maghara.

The Fifth Dynasty

From the Fifth Dynasty comes a rock relief of Sahure smiting (Figure 6.16).[35] This image solidified a trend, which had begun previously, of making the carving into a bounded rectangular tableau. Here we have not only a contained scene, but also a groundline, *Was*-scepters on either side facing in, and a band of stars supported by the scepters, which together frame what goes on inside. Some of the names of the king are written below the stars. The scene thus framed is split into two by the vertical device of a standard with a jackal, the god Wepwawet, atop it. To the left, the king is shown twice—once in White Crown and once in Red—both times walking with a staff and a mace in his hands. On the right is our smiting scene, with the White-Crowned king brandishing his matchstick mace. His belted kilt is a bit strange looking, with a square central part reminiscent of Sekhemkhet's, but in other ways he is as expected, with a tail hanging down behind his muscled back calf. He holds a long staff in his forward hand, but damage to the rock face at this point makes it impossible to say if there was a tuft of hair in it. Behind the king is the inscription "subduing all the foreign lands," and in front of him it says "smiting the *Mentiu* of all lands." A figure who we can only assume is a member of the *Mentiu* kneels in the expected position before the king. He wears a belt, his hair falls over his shoulder, and he appears to have a small pointed beard. In this case, the scene is quite complete and so it is certain that there is neither god nor official looking on except for the Wepwawet standard.

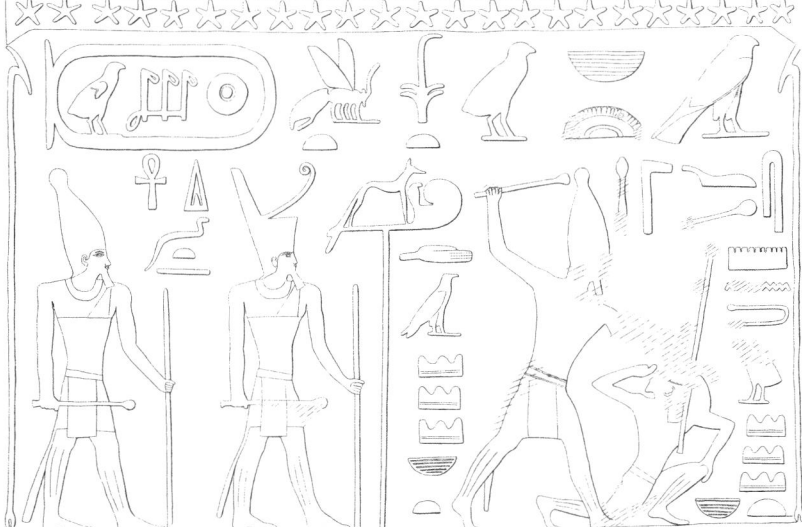

Figure 6.16 Sahure smites the *Mentiu* of all lands. A Wepwawet standard separates the smiting image from two other figures of the king, wearing the White and Red Crowns. Dimensions: 117 × 240 cm.

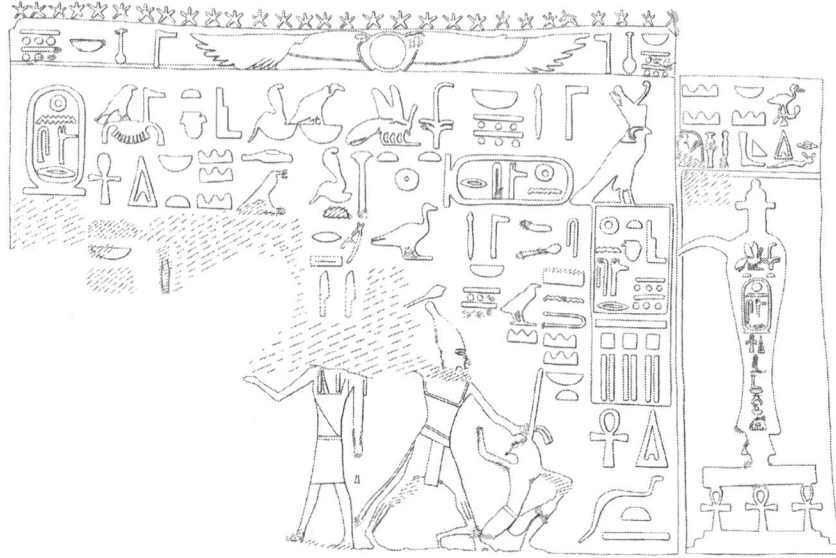

Figure 6.17 Niuserra smites a member of the *Mentiu*, with a god behind his back facing a now-missing additional element of the scene. Dimensions: 164 × 256 cm.

From the reign of Niuserra comes a panel measuring 164 × 256 cm, in a low location near the corner of a branch of the Wadi Maghara (Figure 6.17).[36] This panel continues the trend of providing a frame for the scene, now much more elaborate, with not only a winged sun-disc beneath the stars but also a fancy huge libation jar to the right. The inscription is also more elaborate, without, however, adding much to what we have seen previously. The king, here with a wider range of titles, subdues all foreign lands; the king smites the *Mentiu* of all lands. We can see him doing it just right of center on the groundline. He wears a White Crown and flourishes above his head a mace with a head big enough to convince us it might do some real damage. His kilt is like Sahure's, with its squared central portion, and his tail, if the line drawing captures it well, bounces off his hind leg slightly rather than hanging down inertly.[37] The victim, whose tuft of hair is gripped in the king's hand with the entirely expected long staff, is in the standard position, though the hand with which he wards off the blow is not held as close to his head as usual. He wears a belted kilt, his hair falls over his shoulder, his beard is short and pointed. One becomes a bit bored describing such a homogeneous set of images, until one remembers how rare this uniformity is in the broader corpus of images of violence, and thus how provocative. The left portion of the panel is not well preserved. A god, possibly Thoth on the basis of his headdress and the inclusion of the name of that god in the inscription above the libation vessel, stands with his back to the smiting king and his arm outstretched to the left. Whatever he faced is now gone. The inscription above this hole mentions once

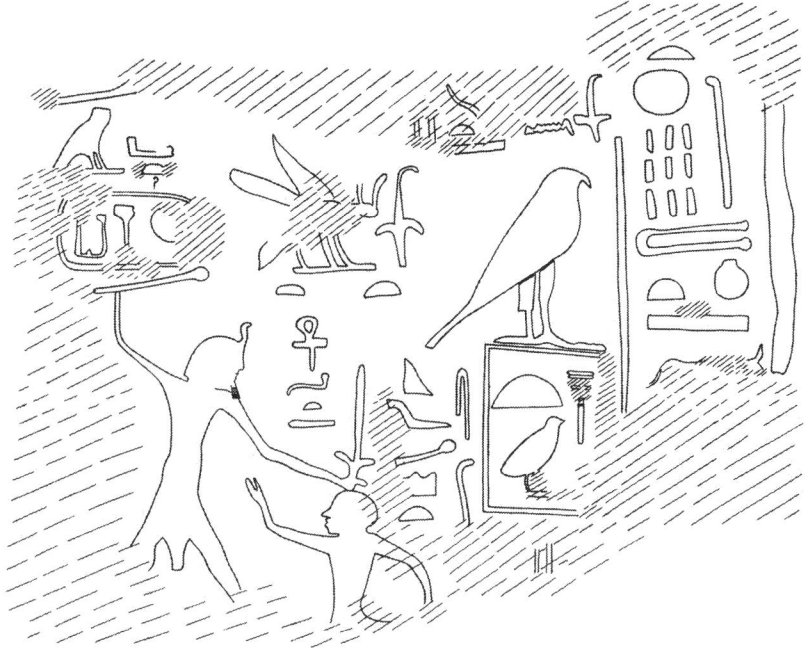

Figure 6.18 Djedkare Izezi smites the leader of a foreign country. Dimensions:
50 × 68 cm.

more subduing all the foreign lands, and so it is at least possible that a second smiting image was once here.

A more poorly preserved smiting panel from Maghara that does in fact present a small number of differences, along with a spate of similarities, dates to the reign of Djedkare Izezi (Figure 6.18).[38] The published line drawing was made on the basis of squeezes; the precise original location is unknown.[39] It is not clear if it was framed in the same way as its predecessors, and its text is somewhat more loosely organized; it is also comparatively small, measuring 50 × 68 cm. The image itself is standard, though in a *shendyt*-clothed king wearing a uraeus on a wig it returns to iconographic details that have not been seen in this context for some time. The victim is too poorly preserved to determine if he has any identifying iconographic features. The accompanying inscription placed between the king's *serekh* and the smiting itself says "smiting the chief of the foreign country." The scene is dated on the right side of the panel, with the year given as that of the ninth cattle count (a standard means of marking years on the basis of a major taxation event in early Egypt). The inscription below this has eroded; the writing of the month and day is not unlikely to have once been present.

The inclusion of a date, and the statement beside the victim that he is the chief of a foreign country rather than representative of a generic "smiting of the foreign lands," seem to render this panel substantially more specific than any we have previously seen in this context. However, it is probable that behind the king once was the more usual inscription "subduing all foreign countries."[40] Furthermore, it is unlikely that the date given refers to the smiting; a reference to an element of the expedition when the image was carved is much more likely (see below, the panel of Pepy I, Figure 6.19). As such, this inscription appears to be a lovely reminder of the concision with which the Egyptians could fold the royal, rhetorical, general, and specific together without conflict.

The Sixth Dynasty

The last of the smiting scenes known from Wadi Maghara dates to the reign of Pepy I in the Sixth Dynasty (Figure 6.19).[41] This is a somewhat more elaborate carving than previous ones, largely because it includes a long inscription beneath the bounded icons above it; as with the previous example, this longer inscription gives a date, here certainly not only by year (the year after the eighteenth cattle count), but also down to the month and day (fourth month of summer, day five). The rest of this inscription lists the names and titles of the participants of the expedition, and it seems clear that the date given refers to some aspect of the

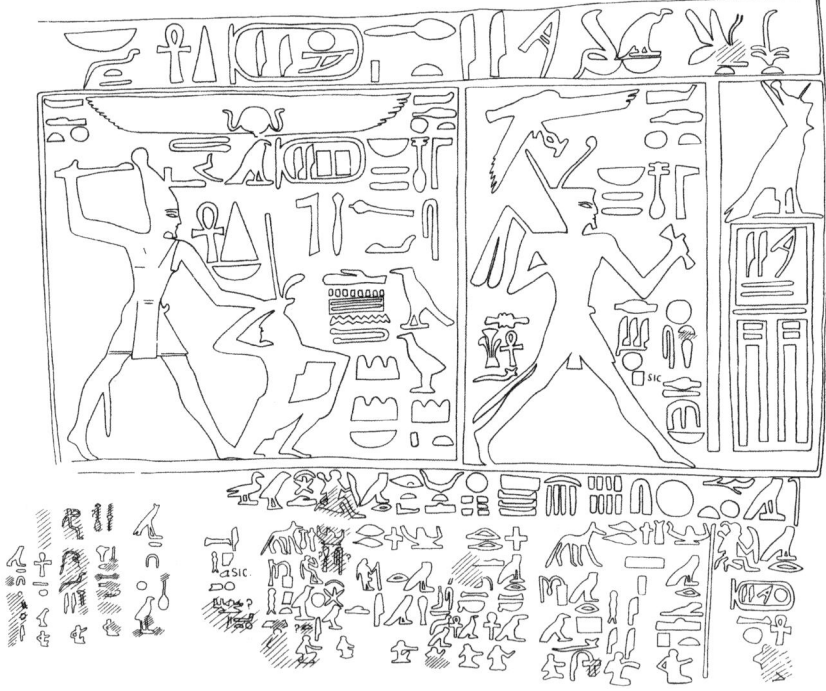

Figure 6.19 Pepy I smites beside a second panel showing the king running. Dimensions: 58 × 71 cm.

expedition itself, possibly even the carving of this monument, rather than to the smiting or jubilee scenes of the king depicted above.

The top part of the panel, with which we are principally concerned, consists of two tableaux separated by a vertical line. Above them both runs an inscription with titles of the king. The right-hand vignette is the king running, labeled as an event of his first jubilee festival; the left is our smiting scene. The king, on the left as always here, strides forward, small-headed mace behind his White-Crowned head. He wears the kilt with the square central portion and his lower torso is wrapped in a tight garment that includes straps going over his shoulders. His tail hangs behind his leg. Tuft of hair, long staff—everything is as we would expect. While the record does not allow us to see many details of the victim, his silhouette tells us that he wore a kilt, hair that went past his shoulder, and a short, pointed beard. The inscription is a variation of what has become familiar: "the great god smites and subdues the *Mentiu* of/and all lands."

The inscription at the base of the Pepy panel is representative of a definitive shift. While Maghara continued to be used, and other areas in the Sinai were also opened for exploitation, the later inscriptions focus more on expedition members and do not include images—usually not at all, and never of smiting.

Reading rock carvings of smiting

The landscape is in many ways the most "other" of the contexts within which images of violence are found. Approaching how these images worked requires us—as is true for all of our contexts but is particularly clear here because of the otherness—to address both the images themselves and how their context itself worked. The first, the issue of the images themselves, requires looking at both the familiarity of the motif employed but also at ways in which it is visually different from the smiting scenes we have seen used in Egypt proper. The second, in this case, turns particularly on issues of audience. Who might see what and understand what when looking at images on rock faces in the Sinai? Why here? Did the accumulation of such images over time contribute to their meaning, as at Naqsh-e Rustam? Why are there no such images in other peripheral places, or in times other than the Early Dynastic and Old Kingdom?

In many ways, the content of the smiting icon in the corpus of landscape images is remarkably uniform and consistent, particularly if we exclude the earliest First Dynasty example. In no case is there more than one victim at a time. Position varies extremely little. The king is always on the left. The posture of the victim changes little, with the only variations being two of the Wadi el-Humur victims who face the king. Otherwise, the victim always has one knee down, one up, always heads away from the king but turns his head and torso back toward his tormentor. The king always holds a tuft of his victim's hair, and at Maghara always holds the long staff. Details of dress on both king and victim seem more variable, and the king certainly can wear either the *shendyt* kilt or the square-centered kilt, with or without chest straps. But some of the differences here may be due to details within the outlines of the carving being variably preserved. When it is possible to see, the victim wears a short and pointed beard. The intense continuity of this central iconic scene can perhaps be best pointed out by noting how the king's tail sometimes lies atop his back leg, and sometimes hangs down. This is the tiniest, tiniest of details; it is hard to see how it could carry meaning. But we notice it here because so much is so similar across the smiting scenes. The lack of variety may relate to a restricted means of transmission of this image—maybe even based largely on seeing earlier examples in this very context—and this could support an argument that those both carving and seeing smiting imagery in the landscape might not have had much access to similar imagery in Egypt proper.

Only one thing is quite variable within the smiting image, and several things are more so within the compositions as a whole and in the accompanying texts. The one big visual variable is the headgear of the king. We have wigs or nemes headdresses with the uraeus; we have the White Crown; we have the Red Crown; there is a Double Crown; there is the impossible confection on Snefru's head. Only the White Crown becomes common. The specific meaning of any crown in this context is unclear, but collectively they give a bit of a sense that while the king may only *do* one thing out here in the Sinai, he is king in many ways or of many things.

Aside from the smiting icon, the visual elements of the Maghara images vary, though within quite narrow limits. The degree to which the violent scene is contained in a box, made into a sort of stela, increases over time. Figures or other elements aside from the two protagonists vary. The two Sekhemkhet examples include an official off to the side, not watching the action; the last two examples, of Djedkare and Pepy, include references in their texts to expedition details, including officials. Does this call into question the degree to which these are royal inscriptions at all? Three examples have divinities present in the scene as observers, twice Thoth and once a goddess. Wepwawet standards are also present in three cases (only one of which also has a god as an observer). Two further examples have winged sun-discs above the smiting scene. The most common other figure is in fact the king himself repeated, though this is often separated by a register or line from the smiting itself. When the king is shown other than smiting, he is striding and holding a mace. In one instance he is also shown running. None of these other figures of the king are present except in combination with smiting.

The inscriptions also vary within quite limited confines. Only three images, those of Sahure, Niuserra, and Pepy, include the word "*Mentiu*," but no other specific names of peoples and none of places are ever used. This name occurs regularly, but not nearly so ubiquitously, among the inscriptions associated with violence from royal pyramid complexes. In the Sinai, Djedkare Izezi grants his victim the title of prince, or chief, but does not make him chief of a specific place. The early inscriptions note the giving of life to the king, a slightly jarring accompaniment to the king taking life away. Snefru adds the subduing of lands, which later became standard. Khufu gets "nomads" in. While the mention of people is thus not very specific and certainly not on the name level seen in the Libyan Family Scene, it is always either vague or in reference to the approximate geographic location of the images and inscriptions themselves. The impression is of a set of images that are context-specific but not event-specific. That specificity increased over time, with the first use of the term *Mentiu* occurring well after the iconic image of smiting a person with the visual ethnic stereotype of an Asiatic had become familiar in this location.

Audience

The landscape as a context immediately suggests that these images were not as restricted as those in built structures within Egypt; they were accessible by foot, carved on a large scale, and lit by the sun in a way that made them eminently visible. While a few were tucked in hard-to-access places, most were not. A largely human audience is conceivable in this case, and much unlike the heavily ritualized and protected contexts for smiting images in Egypt itself, part of that audience might have included non-captive people of the groups victimized in the images; it is not remotely unreasonable to hypothesize that *Mentiu* moved through this landscape and saw these pictures. An Egyptian audience of members of expeditions, as well as a divine audience, are also extremely likely. All three parts of this audience would have had much less regulated access to the imagery than would have been the case in other contexts.

Whether or not there was an indigenous audience for the smiting imagery is surprisingly difficult to answer definitively, relying on circumstantial evidence and inference. The imagery itself certainly makes us want to believe that there was such an audience—that people with short pointed beards and at least latterly called *Mentiu* were supposed to see pictures of themselves being bashed. It is a simple jump from there to assume how they were supposed to react: cowering submission, of course. Direct evidence of this audience is lacking for the Old Kingdom, but the circumstantial evidence is reasonably convincing.[42] Arguments for an indigenous presence at the mines themselves have been advanced on the basis of speculations about tool types; these are not implausible, but the destruction of ancient mines by more recent mining has limited our ability to test them.[43] The presence of fortifications at Egyptian sites in the Sinai, including at Maghara and at the associated harbor on the Gulf of Suez, might also be seen as evidence that there were local people from whom the Egyptians felt need of protection.[44] The presence of Semitic names among the expedition crews listed in Middle Kingdom inscriptions suggests inclusion of local or at least non-Egyptian people on crews at that time, and if so it is possible that this practice was in place earlier.[45] On the whole, it seems to me a reasonable hypothesis, though not a proven point, that *Mentiu* saw these pictures of *Mentiu*. If Egyptian expeditions to the Sinai were seasonal or irregular, and there was no permanent presence at the mining camp, this audience would also have seen these images at times when the presence of the Egyptian state was not otherwise so obvious, and such a reminder might be one reason the images were important.

That Egyptians on expeditions saw these pictures is certain, and that they included people who are unlikely to have seen similar images in their more confined contexts within Egypt seems probable. Though expedition leaders may have been men of rank, the majority of miners would certainly not have been. Furthermore, while Wadi Maghara is far from the Nile, and while we cannot assume that a large swath of the Egyptian population ever passed this way, this remains the only place in which smiting imagery was demonstrably visible to living non-royal humans.[46] This mixed Egyptian audience would thus have had access to images of the king, but also in the case of several of these tableaux, to images of gods. In the Sinai, this imagery was present without the mediation of architecture, meaning that it was approachable in non-ritualized behaviors by Egyptians. The immediacy and accessibility of this imagery in this situation may reflect the apparent less structured, more pervasive presence of the divine in areas outside Egypt proper.[47]

In this regard, it is notable that one Egyptian in particular is very unlikely to have seen these images: there is no reason to think that kings themselves ever came to this place. Whether kings actively led military campaigns in this period is unknown; even if they did, southern Sinai is not particularly likely to have been a place of campaigning. It was a place for mining, an activity that did not require the presence of the king, even though the products most certainly enabled the construction and equipping of royal establishments in Egypt.

Not only did kings likely not see these monuments themselves, but it is also unclear that kings commissioned them. Officials on expeditions may have been at least partly responsible for determining that they were made in the first place, as suggested by the official present in Sekhemkhet's reliefs and the longer inscriptions from the later examples. That there are no images or texts relating to officials from the chronological middle of these scenes might call this suggestion into question, but not necessarily. Representations of the king and gods are contra decorum in private monuments in Egypt proper at the time of the Maghara inscriptions, but the Sinai is not Egypt and has this odd relationship with the divine. As such, there may have been no codified way for officials to represent their relationship to the king at all, and this may explain the variability of direct references to officials even if they commissioned the carving of the monuments. In sum, without being quite sure of the balance or reasons for changes, I am most comfortable seeing the Sinai smiting scenes as a somewhat hybrid type of monument, neither entirely royal nor entirely elite, but very much a vehicle of the state. This reminds us, too, that on the ground it would have been the officials and members of the expeditions who dealt with any *Mentiu*, not the king, and that these images were one aspect of the mediation of this relationship.

In all ways but for the central motif itself, then, we are struck by the otherness of these images in the landscape and required to accept that they had a different decorum, a different audience, and a different function than the same images used in other contexts. Were these intended to make *Mentiu*, who had never seen the Egyptian king at all, cower in fear? Would they even have recognized themselves in the stereotypical guise adapted for them by the Egyptian artists? When the images spoke to an audience of Egyptian miners, did they include such people in the "us" of the image, the part of the world protected by the power of the king? Or did they rather remind those abject miners, conscripted to hard labor, that they, too, were subject to the violent coercion of the Egyptian state? In their inclusion of gods, did these images remind the divine of its pact with the king to protect activities that were in service of his effective running of Egypt? These possibilities are far from mutually exclusive and may even be said to complement one another, even if we include the ambiguity of the us/them perspectives of Egyptian viewers.

Given the issues of decorum and audience in play, the disappearance of smiting scenes in the landscape in the Middle Kingdom may reflect changes in the expression of the relationship between officials and kings, even between people and the divine. However, that these images were only ever found in the Sinai does suggest to me that there was also something specific about this place, not just about the ideology of kingship on the margins, that made it particularly vulnerable. The people identified as the *Mentiu* are named, and presumably were felt either to be or to embody the threat to Egyptian activities here. The ubiquity of smiting as opposed to other depictions of kingship supports the suggestion that the need was not for a general extension of the ideology of kingship to this place, but rather for the countering of a specific type of threat. Images might accomplish this through a combination of apotropaic action and inducement of fear in their audiences. And while the inscriptions often mention all foreign lands, the imagery itself is far more specific and less varied than in any other context where this icon occurs. The enemy is always physically and sometimes textually marked as from this area. The enemy is always singular.

I do think that the smiting images at Maghara acted collectively, their gathered presence over centuries defining and defending a place that was important to but separate from Egypt itself. The very permanence and continued visibility of the early examples must have played a role in convincing their audiences that their message of royal dominion was accurate; while Maghara was not nearly so central a royal project as Naqsh-e Rustam, it likewise communicated a sense of royal legitimacy and continuity through the repetition of royal motifs over time. It should be remembered that Middle Kingdom Maghara was still visibly marked by this imagery, even if new examples were not being created. In the end, it is the otherness of this context that stands out. It is other geographically, and it seems to have been other in terms of the nature of the threat faced there. Incorporating this place within the structures of the ideal Egyptian worldview made use of developed icons of that worldview, but used them differently than in Egypt proper.

Notes

1 Westend61 GmbH/Alamy Stock Photo.
2 The relief was previously entirely covered by soil and was discovered only during excavations in the 1930s. The foot of the rider is not visible currently, perhaps because the base of the relief was slightly lower than current ground level. Georgina Herrmann, *Naqsh-I Rustam 5 and 8: Sasanian Reliefs Attributed to Hormuzd II and Narseh* (Berlin: Dietrich Reimer Verlag, 1977), 6–9. For more information on the reliefs at Naqsh-e Rustam and Sasanian ideology, see: Matthew P. Canepa, "Technologies of Memory in Early Sasanian Iran: Achaemenid Sites and Sasanian Identity," *American Journal of Archaeology* 114 (2010): 563–96.

3 A.D.H. Bivar, *Cavalry Equipment and Tactics on the Euphrates Frontier* (Washington, DC: The Dumbarton Oaks Center for Byzantine Studies, 1972), 281. For more information about Sasanian coins, see: Robert Göbl, *Sasanian Numismatics* (Braunschweig: Klinkhardt & Biermann, 1971).

4 Leonid Andronov/Alamy Stock Photo.

5 Egyptian presence in Nubia in the Old Kingdom is well documented: David O'Connor, *The Old Kingdom town at Buhen*, Ed. Patricia Spencer (London: Egypt Exploration Society, 2014). The interaction with other peoples was different in this area, however, in part because of the apparent depopulation of Lower Nubia for most of this time: David O'Connor, *Ancient Nubia: Egypt's Rival in Africa* (Philadelphia, PA: The University Museum, University of Pennsylvania, 1993), 23–25. For theories of why the A-Group disappeared, see: Bruce Trigger, *Nubia under the Pharaohs* (London: Thames & Hudson, 1976), 44–48.

6 Pierre Tallet and Damien Laisney, "Iry-Hor et Narmer au Sud-Sinaï (Ouadi 'Ameyra): un complément à la chronologie des expéditions minières égyptiennes," *Le Bulletin de l'institut français d'archéologie orientale* 112 (2012): fig. 11.

7 Tallet and Laisney, "Iry-Hor et Narmer au Sud-Sinaï (Ouadi 'Ameyra): un complément à la chronologie des expéditions minières égyptiennes," 381–398.

8 Tallet and Laisney, "Iry-Hor et Narmer au Sud-Sinaï (Ouadi 'Ameyra): un complément à la chronologie des expéditions minières égyptiennes," 388, state that Ash was already associated with the exploitation of the Sinai in this period. The god is more usually associated with the western desert and oases, and was seen in Chapter 4 in the mortuary complex of Sahure where he was labeled "Lord of *Tjehenu*" (Libyans). He is perhaps more clearly labeled in the Sinai reliefs of Den, below.

9 The inscriptions were first published by Moustafa Resk Ibrahim and Pierre Tallet, "Trois bas-reliefs de l'époque thinite au Ouadi el-Humur: aux origines de l'exploitation du Sud-Sinaï par les Égyptiens," *Revue d'Égyptologie* 59 (2008): 155–180.

10 Ibrahim and Tallet, "Trois bas-reliefs de l'époque thinite au Ouadi el-Humur: aux origines de l'exploitation du Sud-Sinaï par les Égyptiens," fig. 2.

11 Ibrahim and Tallet, "Trois bas-reliefs de l'époque thinite au Ouadi el-Humur: aux origines de l'exploitation du Sud-Sinaï par les Égyptiens," fig. 6.

12 Moustafa Resk Ibrahim and Pierre Tallet, "King Den in South-Sinai: The Earliest Monumental Rock Inscriptions of the Pharaonic Period," *Archéo-Nil* 19 (2009): 182.

13 Ibrahim and Tallet, "King Den in South-Sinai," 182, note 9 for references.

14 Ibrahim and Tallet, "King Den in South-Sinai," 183.

15 Ibrahim and Tallet, "Trois bas-reliefs de l'époque thinite au Ouadi el-Humur: aux origines de l'exploitation du Sud-Sinaï par les Égyptiens," fig. 12.

16 Ibrahim and Tallet, "King Den in South-Sinai," 183.

17 The major collection of these inscriptions was done in 1905 on an expedition led by Flinders Petrie for the Egypt Exploration Fund. The principal publication of these inscriptions was done by Gardiner and Peet, with additional work by Černý: Alan H. Gardiner, T. Eric Peet, and Jaroslav Černý, *The Inscriptions of Sinai. Part I: Introduction and Plates*, 2nd ed. (London: Egypt Exploration Society, 1952) and Jaroslav Černý, Alan H. Gardiner, and T. Eric Peet, *The Inscriptions of Sinai from Manuscripts of Alan H. Gardiner and T. Eric Peet. Part II: Translations and Commentary* (London: Egypt Exploration Society, 1955). Part II not only discusses the inscriptions, but also give notes on provenance and bibliography as well as the evidence available to the authors to prepare the line drawings published in Part I. By the time of publication, many of the inscriptions had eroded or otherwise been destroyed or lost; comparison to records from an earlier expedition by Lepsius show that the loss had started before Petrie's arrival: Richard Lepsius, *Denkmäler aus Ägypten und Äthiopien*, 12 volumes (Berlin: Nicolaische Buchhandlung, 1849–1856). The Sinai is currently, as it has so often been in the past, a place of military conflict in which no scholarship can occur.

18 Gardiner, Peet, and Černý, *The Inscriptions of Sinai. Part I*, pl. 1 (lower left), pl. 15.

19 For a propagandistic consideration of these images and a discussion of how they connected to kingship ideology and foreigners, see: Ingelore Hafemann, "Ägyptens Beziehungen zum Sinai in pharaonischer Zeit," in *Antiker Orient: Landeskunde, Archäologie, Epigraphik; Beiträge anläßlich einer Tagung in Potsdam-Hermannswerder Am 20. Und 21. Januar 1995*, Ed. Christian Tietze (Potsdam: Universität Potsdam, Historisches Institut, 1996), 1–14.

20 Courtesy of the Egypt Exploration Society. Gardiner, Peet, and Černý, *The Inscriptions of Sinai. Part I*, pl. 1 (lower left); Černý, Gardiner, and Peet, *The Inscriptions of Sinai from Manuscripts of Alan H. Gardiner and T. Eric Peet. Part II*, 54.

21 This Sekhemkhet relief was first dated to the First Dynasty king Semerkhet. The re-dating of the relief to the Third Dynasty shows that kings became interested in this particular area of the Sinai then, and has implications for our understanding of the chronology of mining activities in the area: William Stevenson Smith, "The Old Kingdom in Egypt and the Beginning of the First Intermediate Period (Volume I, Chapter XIV)," in *The Cambridge Ancient History: Volumes I & II*, Ed. I.E.S. Edwards, C.J. Gadd, and N.G.L. Hammond (Cambridge: Cambridge University Press, 1962), 9.

22 Raphael Giveon, "A Second Relief of Sekhemkhet in Sinai," *Bulletin of the American Schools of Oriental Research* 216 (1974): 17–20.

23 Giveon, "A Second Relief of Sekhemkhet in Sinai," 18, fig. 1. The complete article can be found on JSTOR.

24 Giveon, "A Second Relief of Sekhemkhet in Sinai," 20.

25 Giveon, "A Second Relief of Sekhemkhet in Sinai," 17.

26 Figure 6.9: Francis Lankester. Figure 6.10: Courtesy of the Egypt Exploration Society. Gardiner, Peet, and Černý, *The Inscriptions of Sinai. Part I*, pls. 1 a–b; Černý, Gardiner, and Peet, *The Inscriptions of Sinai from Manuscripts of Alan H. Gardiner and T. Eric Peet. Part II*, 52–53.

27 Giveon, "A Second Relief of Sekhemkhet in Sinai," 19; Černý, Gardiner, and Peet, *The Inscriptions of Sinai from Manuscripts of Alan H. Gardiner and T. Eric Peet. Part II*, 52–53.

28 Toby Wilkinson, *Early Dynastic Egypt* (London and New York: Routledge, 1999), 101–103.

29 British Museum EA691. Courtesy of the Trustees of the British Museum. A.J. Spencer, *Catalogue of Egyptian Antiquities in the British Museum V: Early Dynastic Objects* (London: Trustees of the British Museum, 1980), 16, pls. 8–9; A.J. Spencer, *Early Egypt: The Rise of Civilisation in the Nile Valley* (London: British Museum Press, 1993), 101, fig. 77. Gardiner, Peet, and Černý, *The Inscriptions of Sinai. Part I*, pl. 1 (bottom right); Černý, Gardiner, and Peet, *The Inscriptions of Sinai from Manuscripts of Alan H. Gardiner and T. Eric Peet. Part II*, 56.

30 Gardiner, Peet, and Černý, *The Inscriptions of Sinai. Part I*, pl. 4 (top left); Černý, Gardiner, and Peet, *The Inscriptions of Sinai from Manuscripts of Alan H. Gardiner and T. Eric Peet. Part II*, 54–56.

31 Courtesy of the Egypt Exploration Society. Gardiner, Peet, and Černý, *The Inscriptions of Sinai. Part I*, pl. 4 (upper right); Černý, Gardiner, and Peet, *The Inscriptions of Sinai from Manuscripts of Alan H. Gardiner and T. Eric Peet. Part II*, 57.

32 Courtesy of the Egypt Exploration Society. Gardiner, Peet, and Černý, *The Inscriptions of Sinai. Part I*, pl. 2 (upper relief); Černý, Gardiner, and Peet, *The Inscriptions of Sinai from Manuscripts of Alan H. Gardiner and T. Eric Peet. Part II*, 56–57. This relief has been removed from its context and is now in the Egyptian Museum, Cairo (CG 57102).

33 Figure 6.14: Courtesy of the Egypt Exploration Society. Černý, Gardiner, and Peet, *The Inscriptions of Sinai from Manuscripts of Alan H. Gardiner and T. Eric Peet. Part II*, pl. 1. Figure 6.15: Courtesy of the Egypt Exploration Society. Gardiner, Peet, and Černý, *The Inscriptions of Sinai. Part I*, pl. 3 (upper relief); Černý, Gardiner, and Peet, *The Inscriptions of Sinai from Manuscripts of Alan H. Gardiner and T. Eric Peet. Part II*, 57–58.

34 Černý, Gardiner, and Peet, *The Inscriptions of Sinai from Manuscripts of Alan H. Gardiner and T. Eric Peet. Part II*, 58.
35 Courtesy of the Egypt Exploration Society. Gardiner, Peet, and Černý, *The Inscriptions of Sinai. Part I*, pl. 5; Černý, Gardiner, and Peet, *The Inscriptions of Sinai from Manuscripts of Alan H. Gardiner and T. Eric Peet. Part II*, 58.
36 Courtesy of the Egypt Exploration Society. Gardiner, Peet, and Černý, *The Inscriptions of Sinai. Part I*, pl. 6; Černý, Gardiner, and Peet, *The Inscriptions of Sinai from Manuscripts of Alan H. Gardiner and T. Eric Peet. Part II*, 59.
37 Recent photographs available online are not so convincing on the point of the tail.
38 Courtesy of the Egypt Exploration Society. Gardiner, Peet, and Černý, *The Inscriptions of Sinai. Part I*, pl. 8 (top); Černý, Gardiner, and Peet, *The Inscriptions of Sinai from Manuscripts of Alan H. Gardiner and T. Eric Peet. Part II*, 61–62.
39 Černý, Gardiner, and Peet, *The Inscriptions of Sinai from Manuscripts of Alan H. Gardiner and T. Eric Peet. Part II*, 61.
40 Gardiner, Peet, and Černý, *The Inscriptions of Sinai. Part I*, 62.
41 Courtesy of the Egypt Exploration Society. Gardiner, Peet, and Černý, *The Inscriptions of Sinai. Part I*, pl. 8 (bottom relief); Černý, Gardiner, and Peet, *The Inscriptions of Sinai from Manuscripts of Alan H. Gardiner and T. Eric Peet. Part II*, 62–63.
42 Evidence for a population in south Sinai with largely Caananite material culture connections is present during the Early Dynastic Period. Karin N. Sowada, *Egypt in the Eastern Mediterranean during the Old Kingdom: An Archaeological Perspective* (Fribourg, Göttingen: Academic Press; Vandenhoeck & Ruprecht, 2009), 46.
43 Sarah Parcak, "Egypt's Old Kingdom 'Empire' (?): A Case Study Focusing on South Sinai," in *Egypt, Israel, and the Ancient Mediterranean World: Studies in Honor of Donald B. Redford*, Ed. Gary N. Knoppers and Antoine Hirsch (Leiden, Boston, MA: Brill, 2004), 52.
44 Parcak, "Egypt's Old Kingdom 'Empire' (?): A Case Study Focusing on South Sinai," 53; Gregory Mumford, "Wadi Maghara," in *The Encyclopedia of the Archaeology of Ancient Egypt*, Ed. Kathryn Bard and Steven Shubert (London: Routledge, 1998), 288–292.
45 Jaroslav Černý, "Semites in Egyptian Mining Expeditions to Sinai," *Archív orientální* 7 (1935): 384–389.
46 The accessibility of smiting imagery more generally has been a matter of some discussion. For a discussion of imagery of violence on portable objects, see Chapter 7.
47 See, for instance, a discussion by Baines and Parkinson of the use of oracles prior to expeditions. One Sinai inscription of the late Old Kingdom may refer to such an oracle: "An Old Kingdom Record of an Oracle? Sinai Inscription 13," in *Essays on Ancient Egypt in Honour of Herman te Velde*, Ed. Jacobus van Dijk (Groningen: Styx, 1997), 22.

7 Out and about

Images of violence on portable objects

Three elaborately carved figures face forward, surrounded by intricate ornaments that make their attributes difficult to pick out. The largest, central figure wears a pointed hat and a banded skirt, a collar and chest straps, and beaded anklets. His left arm is straight by his side, while his right arm is raised and grasping a pierced sword with curving sides. The smaller figures wear helmets, patterned garments, and simpler chest straps. They, too, clutch objects in their right hands, but the nature of these objects is less clear. Their heads tilt to the sides, toward the central figure, though the gazes of all three are directed forward to the viewer. The image is one of pageantry more than violence, but the raised weapon and the obvious

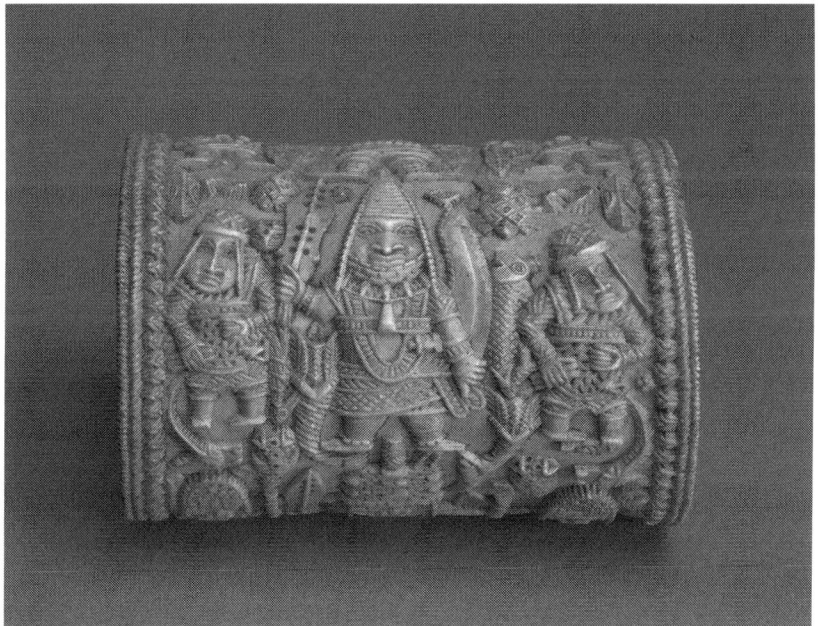

Figure 7.1 An elaborately dressed warrior brandishing a sword is flanked by two smaller figures. Ivory armlet from Benin, eighteenth century.

hierarchy suggest a connection to military themes even to an uninitiated audience. To those in the know, who recognize the particulars of dress and weaponry, are familiar with the relationship between military and ceremony in Benin, and can tell that the two smaller figures are European though they are given some attributes of Benin warriors, the complexity of violent associations would be much greater. If one turns this armlet around, this scene is repeated once, separated by two groupings of three people that show the Edo king flanked by warriors. The legs of the king can be seen above our warrior, and his headdress below.

This eighteenth-century elite artifact (Figure 7.1)[1] is one of a pair, and the pair belongs to a larger but still restricted corpus of carved ivory objects that displayed prominent military themes. The armlet itself is clearly not a military object but instead one that marks status; it has been suggested that the central figure shown above is a military commander who commissioned these objects on which he is shown as of equal status to the king.[2] The size of its carvings suggests that the image, while on an object that was portable and intended for display, might not have been seen and read by a large number of people; the outfits, weapons, and symbols on it, however, would have been broadly familiar.

While the ivory armlet shows warriors rather than an act of war, it also references a larger body of art—including architectural bronzes—that utilizes images of fighting among a broader iconography about an ideology of kingship. The question of how violent an image of violence might be was already raised with the Waterloo coin, which we saw was of restricted circulation precisely because the relation of its image to violence was problematic. On the Benin ivory, the presence of such a nonviolent reference to violence—particularly one that includes markers of ethnicity and hierarchy and that was accessible only to the most elite of elites—is particularly apt for raising questions about portable Egyptian objects. Violent imagery is known from a small handful of such items, while additional objects have images that are related to violent themes expressed in imagery elsewhere. As with the Benin ivory, we might ask who owned these images, who saw them, and what their relation is to the larger corpus of violent pictures.

In Egypt, these objects are of a limited number and variety. Despite their scarcity, they are important because they offer at least the possibility that such imagery was much more accessible to a general audience within Egypt than is otherwise clear. Furthermore, the earliest violent imagery known to us comes from portable objects, and it is possible that they might have served a role in transmitting this iconography across periods when it does not seem to have been employed on buildings. Despite the extremely small sample size and the likelihood that much is missing, I think that the contexts of such portable objects, their size, and some aspects of their content suggest that particularly royal Egyptian icons of violence were not much more accessible to general audiences on objects than they were on architecture. What role they played in transmission is unfortunately unanswerable, but I would again suggest that it is unlikely to have been critical. I suspect instead that images of violence on portable objects, at least after the Early Dynastic Period, were essentially secondary: they made references to the larger body of violent imagery and could stand as shorthand for an ideology of dominance, but were probably never the location in which such imagery was primarily intended to function.

As is true for the other contexts examined in this book, the function of the whole, be it building or jewel or label, must be considered in order to ask how violence aided in the accomplishment of the purpose of that which it adorned. Unlike previous chapters, the context "portable objects" is not bounded by a coherent definition—different objects did different things, and we might expect that violence played different roles on different types of objects. Objects known to me with explicit images of violence after Narmer's reign are restricted to three ivory tags of the First Dynasty and two pieces of jewelry from the Twelfth Dynasty. The tags represent the end of a tradition and sit more comfortably with earlier material. It seems probable that jewelry with such imagery was once more common, as suggested by the smiting scene on an armlet in a relief from the pyramid complex of Niuserra (Figure 4.13) and by the fact that jewelry, of all artifact categories, is probably the least likely to survive. All known such images show triumph; battle scenes are unknown from portable objects prior to the New Kingdom. Images of captivity are likewise known from only a small number of object categories with apparently quite restricted usage. Here we will consider an ivory carved in relief from the First Dynasty; execration figurines of the Old and Middle Kingdoms; and mud stamps from Middle Kingdom fortresses. Because I have separated these objects in terms of the explicitness of their references to violence, this chapter is not arranged chronologically. I will not consider here images of foreigners on portable objects more broadly, because foreigners could play roles other than victim and we cannot be certain in all cases that an ideology of violence is being displayed whenever we have a visual ethnic stereotype.[3]

Images of triumph on portable objects

Early Dynastic tags

Tags with smiting scenes are a transitional type of artifact, in some ways more at home with the late Predynastic Period than with the more developed pharaonic state. We have seen one of them already as a vehicle for violent imagery in the reign of Narmer, when it was one of many types of objects that bore pictures of the king or his name smiting (Figure 3.18). While most of the artifact types known to carry such imagery for Narmer disappeared after his reign, tags continued, and along with the landscape these represent our only extant Early Dynastic evidence for the codification of the smiting scene. That is enough, however: these smiting scenes are clearly fully developed icons in this period. There are only three remaining tags known to me that bear smiting images after the reign of Narmer. All were found at Abydos, in the disturbed fill in and around the royal tombs of the First Dynasty.[4]

The first of the tags dates to the reign of Aha, Narmer's direct successor and the first king of Egypt to build a monumental tomb. This tomb, an entire complex

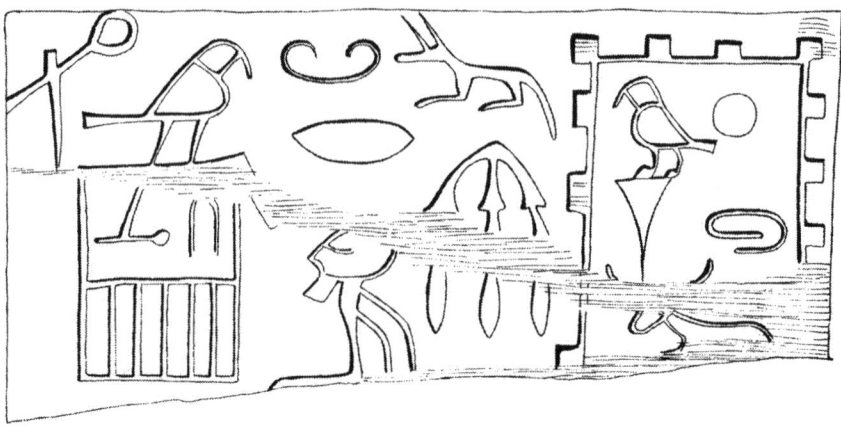

Figure 7.2   An ivory tag from the tomb of Aha at Umm el-Qaab, Abydos. The *serekh* of
the king smites a captive.

at the already ancient site of Umm el-Qaab at Abydos, and in fact located almost
directly on top of the much smaller tomb usually attributed to Narmer, included
separate chambers for a number of probably sacrificed royal retainers and lions.[5]
Artifacts found in association with the tomb were so heavily disturbed that it is
rarely possible to be certain which chamber they came from, and if they were
from the royal burial or one of the subsidiary burials. One of the numerous ivory
tags known from the reign of Aha has a smiting image (Figure 7.2).[6]

This is a close parallel to that on the previously discussed tag of Narmer
(Figure 3.18). Here, Aha's name is enclosed in a *serekh* on the left of the tag.
The *serekh* is provided with one and possibly two schematic arms. The rear arm
is raised in a smiting pose and grasps a mace. A hint of a second arm may reach
toward the kneeling, bearded captive who faces the royal name. The inscription
above the captive includes a bow, usually understood as indication that he is
from the south.[7] While the medium dictated that the representation be small and
schematic, the visual differentiation between these two opponents is total: one is
so much shown as a representation of his office that he is only a name and title,
while the other is given a human body. This is even more extreme than was the
case with Narmer's smiting name, as here the king's name is enclosed in that
most royal of symbols, a *serekh*. This prisoner is being killed by Egyptian kingship in its current incarnation of Aha.

A final example of a smiting *serekh* is known from the reign of Djet, two
generations after Aha. This example, excavated recently and in fragments, is
somewhat more difficult to read visually but includes an accompanying inscription that makes the nature of the scene clear.[8] The smiting scene occurs in the
largest and highest of the three registers. In this case the *serekh* itself is quite
clear, but the victim or victims are difficult to disentangle. There appear to be

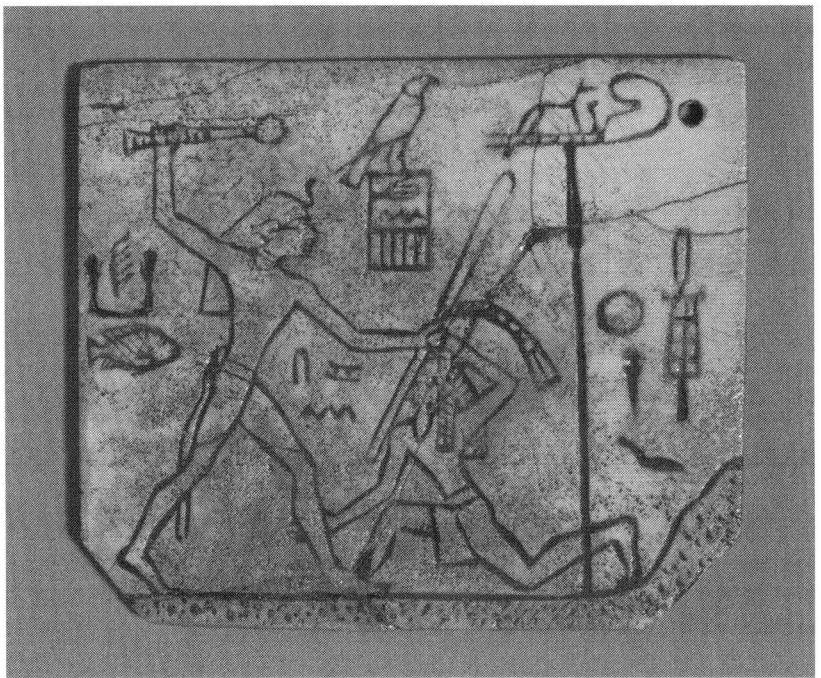

Figure 7.3 Ivory tag showing king Den smiting, from Abydos. Dimensions: 5.3 × 4.5 cm.

more legs than one person could have, unless the central portion represents a kilt. What does seem clear is that the hand that comes from the *serekh* to grasp the victim(s) holds a long stick of the sort that is more clearly rendered in the label of Den, below. A bow in the upper right corner, near the piercing of the label, suggests we should once more understand the victim as belonging to the border region between Egypt and Nubia. If the victims are indeed two wrestlers as the excavators of the object suggest, the scene is unprecedented.[9] Interestingly, deliberate damage to the tag has erased the raised arm that presumably swung the mace of destruction.

An ivory label from the reign of Den (Figure 7.3),[10] in the middle of the First Dynasty, preserves the best-known smiting scene from the Early Dynastic Period aside from the Narmer Palette. The tag was probably originally tied to a pair of sandals, as indicated by the picture on its reverse. The importance of sandals and even their relation to smiting can already be seen on the Narmer Palette, where the king's sandal bearer is the only figure to accompany Narmer as he smites; he also follows again behind him in procession on the other side. Den's own connection with smiting and sandals was also observed in one of his rock inscriptions at Wadi el-Humur (Figure 6.5). On the Den label, the king is shown as human, his *serekh* identifying him before his face. The king strides, feet widely apart, right hand raised and grasping a mace. The mace is shown in detail, with its segmented handle. The king wears a kilt, a tail that falls behind his rear leg, a headdress or wig that falls behind his shoulders, and a uraeus on his brow—a very early example of the latter. Den's left, forward hand grabs both the hair of the captive before him and the implement so common in smiting scenes. The captive, who is not bound, is in a more active stance than we have seen previously: down on one knee with his other leg stretched toward the king. One hand is held to his head, while the other reaches forward and is overlapped by the king's front leg. The captive wears a kilt of a squarer sort than the king's and has a long plaited wig and a pointed beard. Behind him, facing to the right, is a standard of Wepwawet. At the right edge of the tag an inscription reads "first time of smiting the east." An inscription between the two figures cannot be read with confidence. A groundline beneath the scene turns into a small hill on the right, and the whole of the ground is dotted in a way that may represent sand. It seems probable that this is intended to represent a place outside of Egypt.

The depictions and inscriptions on this object include the expected play between specific and general elements. The two figures are distinguished principally by their hair and by the king's uraeus and tail. It is unclear if the hair and beard of the captive are yet explicit references to ethnicity or geographic origin, though similar features will become elements of the visual ethnic stereotypes of easterners in the future. Unless the inscription between the men is the name of the captive, he is only a representative—not an individual—in this image. What the inscription on the right adds is a more definite general reference to place, and a specific reference to time. The latter is in fact a reference to time in a repeated way—"first time" implies other times. Such smiting could have been ritual and regular and so one might expect, even at the first instance, that it would be repeated; or the label might have been made after multiple smitings of the east had happened and therefore refer to an historical event. Either scenario, and the two are not mutually exclusive, suggests an element of ritual in the commissioning of the depiction. Despite its small size, Den's label is a dense object that includes an icon of royal power, the king referred to as both an individual and an office, divine associations provided by his *serekh* and the standard, and his perpetration of violence to a representative of otherness.

These tags with their smiting scenes are royal, but not monumental, in size or presumably in use; they labeled other objects rather than served as primary objects in their own right. In this rather secondary labeling regard they remind me of the not-much-later scene of dead people on the base of the Khasekhem statues from Hierakonpolis (Figures 5.3 and 5.4). Not only does violence play a secondary role on these tags—probably as a way of naming a vintage year—but it is also quite rare. Though many tags are known from Early Dynastic contexts, only those discussed above have smiting scenes; other types of violent action are referred to occasionally on labels, but only in text. For instance, three or four additional tags of Den may include references to the destruction of enemy fortresses; these include an image of an opened fort, but it is essentially a hieroglyph rather than a separate picture.[11] Of interest is that smiting is only an image on Den's labels, not the subject of the lengthier inscriptions, whereas these apparent references to military action are only found in text. This tends to underscore the iconic nature of the smiting scene and the ritual nature of smiting itself.

Middle Kingdom jewelry

The triumph motif, including smiting, is also known from two of the many spectacular pieces of jewelry found with the burials of royal women of the Twelfth Dynasty. These burials were within the kings' tomb complexes broadly defined. Their themes closely mirror what is found in royal relief decoration, but it is reasonable to assume that these pieces were made to be worn in life and were thus not exclusive to the mortuary sphere.

These two pieces of jewelry, both with images of violent royal triumph, were discovered with the burial of Mereret (B), probably a daughter of Senwosret III, in her tomb in the lower galleries of his pyramid at Dahshur.

A gold pectoral with colored inlays shows a trampling scene (Figure 7.4, top).[12] Set within an architectural framework and topped by a vulture, this piece shows the king Senwosret III as a trampling griffin. Color is used to great effect in differentiating the protagonists of this image. The king wears a parti-colored headdress of incredible elaborateness, with two sets of horns, a uraeus, and two enormous plumes (see also figure 6.13). His back, too, displays all the colors of the piece among its feathers. His leonine limbs, though, are pure light blue. Their awkwardly straight lines are the purest pools of color on the piece. On each side—the piece is mirrored—he tramples the same two enemies. In front of him is a red figure with long blue hair and a blue penis sheath and bracelet. Let's call him a Libyan. He kneels, his body facing away from the king but his head turned back and his arm upraised to plead for mercy. The king's forepaws pin him, one atop his head and one holding his knee to the ground. Beneath the king and trodden by him is a dark blue captive. He lies on his back, both arms and one leg thrown in the air, his belly pinned by one of the king's paws. His light blue kilt has a red belt, and his chin has a clearly square short beard. There is little text on this piece and, in keeping with trampling scenes from reliefs in the pyramid complexes themselves, an emphasis on the visual variety of the victims.

A second pectoral, which hung at the end of a jeweled necklace, is fashioned in a similar manner; it shows king Amenemhat III (probably Mereret's brother) in a classic smiting pose (Figure 7.4, bottom).[13] Set within a somewhat heavier architectural framework, the scene is presided over by a vulture with outstretched wings. In her talons she holds the symbols for life and dominion out to the aggressive king. Beneath her and in the center, the king is identified as the good god, lord of the two lands and foreign countries. On either side he is shown facing in, smiting an enemy. The king is dressed elaborately, with a bag wig with a uraeus, a kilt with a striped apron down its front, and a half-shirt with a shoulder strap. A blue collar around his neck is balanced by a counterweight visible behind his back. In his raised hand he holds a mace augmented with a blade.

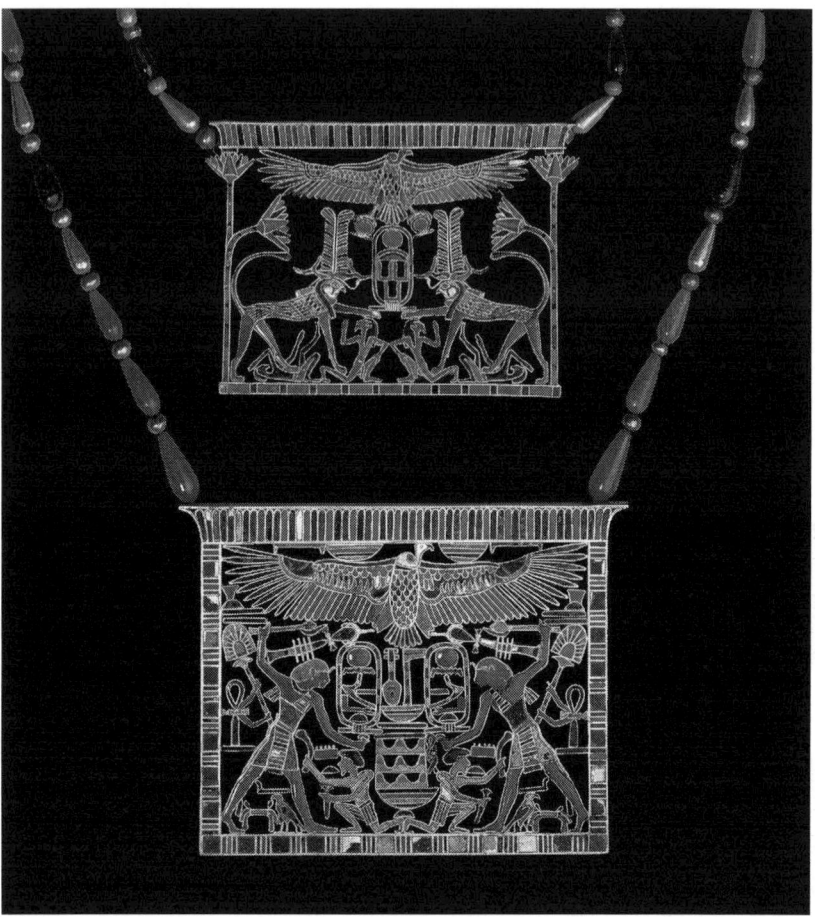

Figure 7.4   *Top*: pectoral showing Senwosret III as a griffin trampling multiple types
of enemies. *Bottom*: pectoral with the name of Amenemhat III showing
almost exact mirror images of the king smiting an Asiatic captive. Both
were discovered with the burial of Mereret, a royal woman of the reign of
Senwosret III, who was buried within his pyramid complex. Twelfth Dynasty.

The victim preparing to meet this nasty weapon kneels and faces the king. He
has lighter skin, is unbound, wears a striped kilt, has mushroom-shaped blue hair,
and reaches forward with two implements. In front of him he grasps a dagger; it is
unprecedented to see an armed and unbound captive next to the king in this way,
but the scene as a whole certainly does not permit us to think he has a chance of
harming the king, meaning that the dagger should probably be read as an element
of identifying iconography rather than a weapon at the ready. He also holds a

curved object and raises it toward the king. His elongated chin probably indicates a small, rounded or pointed beard. On both sides he is labeled *Menet*; this is a variation on the same group name we saw regularly in the Sinai rock carvings, and also in the inscription accompanying Sahure's bound captives.

For our study, the importance of these two masterpieces lies in their suggestion that the contexts we know for such imagery are more limited now than was the case anciently, and that there was a continuation of the trampling motif during a period when it is not otherwise attested. They are also significant in the way they use ethnic stereotypes and in their symmetry, which shows the adaptability of this motif specifically to the context of adornment. While these pieces might well have been worn during Mereret's life, that life was likely to have been very restricted—Middle Kingdom royal women in particular do not seem to have gotten out much—and so these might have been seen only by a narrow court circle. But seen they might have been, with their unmistakable images of the triumph of the king over different peoples.

We must be missing the vast majority of ancient Egyptian jewelry. If walls were sometimes repurposed, as we saw above, this was even more true for meltable things such as precious metals. That motifs of violence appear in jewelry (which also employs a number of non-violent motifs) suggests that these depictions were much more common than we can be aware of. There is still, however, no reason to question the restriction of the motifs of triumph to royal spheres or the protagonist of smiting to the king himself, even when the image adorned another. Ethnic stereotyping here is also similar to what we have seen on walls. The medium—very small and nitpicky to work with—dictated an abbreviated use of those stereotypes, with an atypical set of colors, too. But distinct attributes are recognizable, such as the penis sheath and fancy kilt, and the presence of labeled enemies on one of the pectorals shows that specificity could have a place even in the abbreviated space of jewelry. One wonders a bit, and certainly anachronistically, if anyone bending to read the inscription would have been slapped.

Images of captivity on portable objects

Captivity as a motif on portable objects is more common than direct violence, but still appears relatively little in the extant material from before the New Kingdom. The two contexts in which it appears regularly—execration rituals and mud stamp sealings from the Nubian fortresses (see below)—are themselves very specific and explicitly linked to foreigners. While one is ritual and the other more on the administrative side, both might be said to be practical applications of imagery that reflect an ideology of domination rather than the more abstract and theoretical uses of ideological imagery that we have grown familiar with thus far. Of note is that while the uses of such imagery in such cases are thus quite direct, the images themselves are some of the least explicit and detailed representations of foreigners known from any context. This is less true of the first object to be considered, an ivory from an Early Dynastic royal tomb complex, but that object is more linked to earlier tradition than to later pharaonic practice and is difficult to bring into conversation with other images of captivity from portable objects.

A captive relief on ivory

A number of images of captives are known from carved ivory found in the area of the royal tombs of Umm el-Qaab, Abydos; in most cases their date is not certain and they may date to the Protodynastic Period rather than the First Dynasty itself.[14] One that was found in the tomb of Qa'a, late in the Dynasty, appears to show that the motif on ivory persisted well into the Early Dynastic Period (Figure 7.5).[15] This long, narrow, and thin object was interpreted by its excavator

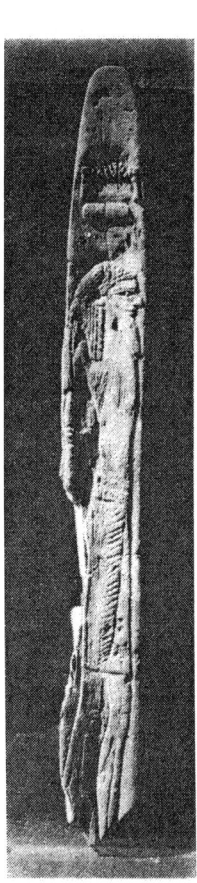
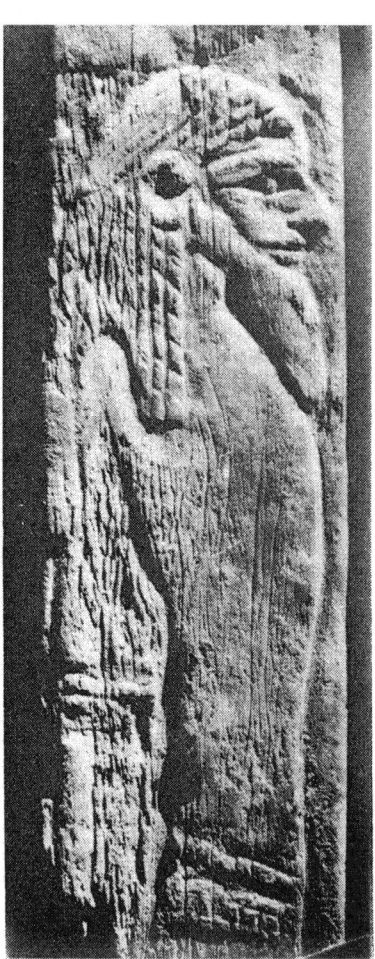

Figure 7.5 Ivory rod, possibly for gaming, with a relief carving of a bound prisoner. From the tomb of Qa'a at Abydos, First Dynasty.

as a gaming rod.[16] The back is carved in imitation of a reed while the front shows a standing man, arms bound at the elbow behind his back. His kilt has an elaborate decorated belt and hanging strip. He is bare-chested. His long and rounded beard creep up his cheeks to meet his elaborate hairstyle, which may show plaited locks falling over his shoulders. The hair atop his head is also segmented in parts that are arranged almost horizontally; it is unclear if a fillet is part of this. What appears to be an inscription above the captive's head is not legible in photographs and was not discussed in the publication of its excavation.

The closeness of this image to a particular ethnic stereotype is not easy to establish.[17] The beard, hair, and elaboration of kilt all distinguish him, but from what? This is not a time when depictions of Egyptians are common, which makes it much more difficult to reliably discuss depictions of others. The beard and hair are close enough to those on the nearly contemporary smitee on Den's tag, which is labeled, that I am happiest seeing him as a representative of the east, if indeed he is intended to represent a specific place and not simply captivity in general. If the interpretation of this object as a game piece is correct we can envision the object thrown, perhaps with others of its kind. While we cannot be sure if this came from the royal burial itself or from one of the subsidiary sacrificial graves in the royal complex, it certainly belonged to a member of the royal court.

Execration figurines

Egyptian execration rituals, in which a text was read and an action performed to damn an enemy and prevent him from causing harm in the future, are known from a variety of places and periods starting in the Old Kingdom. The long form of the text itself was relatively standardized and was particularly concerned with preventing rebellion; large-scale repeated execration rituals were clearly state affairs.[18] The entities identified could be groups or individuals, foreign or Egyptian; they could also be left vague, and multiple entities could be included in a single object. Inscriptions often include specific dates. The damning action best represented archaeologically consisted of burying objects that had been, through inscription and/or speech, imbued with the properties of that which was to be damned; sometimes these were broken before burial but often not. Buried items from execration rituals include ceramic vessels, plaques, figurines, and in the most notable case, a decapitated human being.[19] Deposits of execration materials have been found at a wide variety of sites, including cemeteries and the Middle Kingdom fortresses in occupied Nubia. While it seems likely that there are differences in specific function between deposits, particularly by location, that they were generally intended as protective is clear.[20]

While execration was not primarily a matter concerned with imagery, in many cases the use of figurines provided a visual component. Though the figurines are generally extremely schematic, some of them clearly represent bound prisoners and this might be a general expectation of the more abbreviated forms as well.[21] The number of execration figures excavated is large and continues to grow;[22] here I will illustrate only one example of a particularly clear bound captive execration figurine.

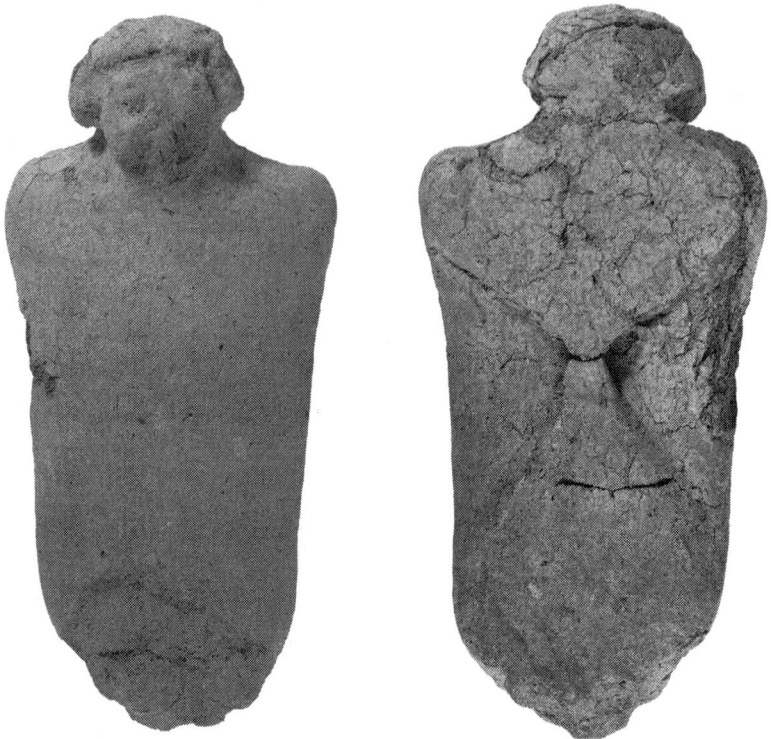

Figure 7.6 Unfired clay execration figurine with schematically rendered arms tied behind the back at the elbow, Twelfth Dynasty.

A figurine currently in Brussels provides an example of the more fully formed textual execration figurines (Figure 7.6).[23] Although its precise provenance is uncertain, it comes from Saqqara and dates, on the basis of its inscription, to the late Twelfth Dynasty.[24] The body of the figurine is a slightly tapered cylinder, with relatively squared shoulders. The head is somewhat broken, making it difficult to see if the features were modeled, but what certainly remains is a slightly poofy, perhaps mushroom-shaped hairstyle, and an elongated chin that may represent or at least refer to a beard. These features would not be out of place on the depiction of an Asiatic, but are also not sufficiently finely rendered to be positively identified as such.[25] The arms, however, are very clear. Invisible from the front, which is not modelled, they can be seen on the back as two rounded triangles, pointing in toward the center. They give the figure the aspect of an envelope. A line between them per-haps indicates a rope but none is needed to tell us that these are arms bound behind the back at the elbow: the classic pose of captivity in Egypt. The figure is reduced to the essentials and covered by text, which stands in stark contrast to the image by its inclusion of specifically named people and places, both Nubian and Asiatic.[26]

In some ways the use of the execration ritual as a whole, particularly if used by kings, might be said to parallel the use of images of violence that we have already seen. It was an effective indirect (excepting the sacrificed victim) means of upholding ideology; it emphasized elements of both generality and specificity that enabled it to link particular actions and people to the overall mission of upholding the theory of kingship; it was repeated; and it had a place in the mortuary sphere. Like imagery, while execration must have been considered to some degree effective in itself, it also presumably had and needed a relationship to the actual practice of violence.[27] In this case the execration ritual suggests the projection of an ideology of violence into future events, rather than the incorporation of past events into primarily ideological tableaux that is assumed to represent the relationship of relief scenes to occurrences.

While we are concerned here primarily with the form of the execration figures, some aspects of the texts found on some of them require mention in this context and can be queried particularly in terms of this element of time. We have seen elsewhere that bound captives in reliefs can be called *seqer-ankh*—something like "living stricken one," combining the word for smiting with the word for life (Figure 4.15). On execration figures, the *ankh* is left off.[28] In case we were wondering how deliberate or meaningful this might be, it has often been noted that Egyptians in execration texts are referred to as *mwt*—dead. The relationship between image and time thus seems quite complicated: a bound captive in relief, which is usually assumed to represent a past event, is referred to by a term that indicates he is alive, at least at the time represented. A bound captive in figurine misses this reference, though it is presumed to represent a hoped-for future action rather than a past one. Though reliefs and execration figures might thus be said to have different relations to time, both can be seen as folding specific events, whether past or future, into an understanding of ritual royal time as cyclical and repeated.

A further point of note about the texts is that they unambiguously list both Nubians (as well as other foreigners) and Egyptians as enemies. This is in contrast to relief scenes of violence, where we have seen that both Nubians and Egyptians are possibly present but not nearly as clearly marked or as consistently depicted as enemies as Libyans and Asiatics. In execration rituals of the periods under consideration here, it is primarily the texts, not the images, which bear direct reference to specific peoples.[29] This is surely a meaningful absence in the figurines, given that the visual vocabulary of ethnic stereotyping was so well developed in other contexts at this time. It reminds us that the execration ritual was not primarily a matter of imagery, and that words, images, and practices had overlapping but not identical functions in Egypt.

Mud sealings

The final category of objects to be considered here as an important bearer of imagery of captivity is itself an odd and ill-understood type, with very limited distribution. Stamp seals on mud lumps, moderately smoothed and between 5–10 cm in diameter, are known from a number of the Twelfth Dynasty fortresses in Nubia. The precise function of these objects is unknown; they were certainly not used as seals on vessels, documents, or doors, and may have served rather as tokens of some sort.[30] They are unknown from elsewhere and so quite probably had a function limited to the fortress context. The stamps that impressed these mud objects have not been recovered.

Wegner identified three different categories of image type in the sealings, one of which is a scene of captivity that is repeated in different iterations. The scene as a whole is unlike any other known image of captivity, but is clearly Egyptian in its iconography.[31] The captives alone might have had a close parallel on a contemporary and local artifact: the base of the year 8 Semna Stela of Senwosret III has been reconstructed to show kneeling figures with arms behind their backs who look much like the figures on the stamp sealings.[32]

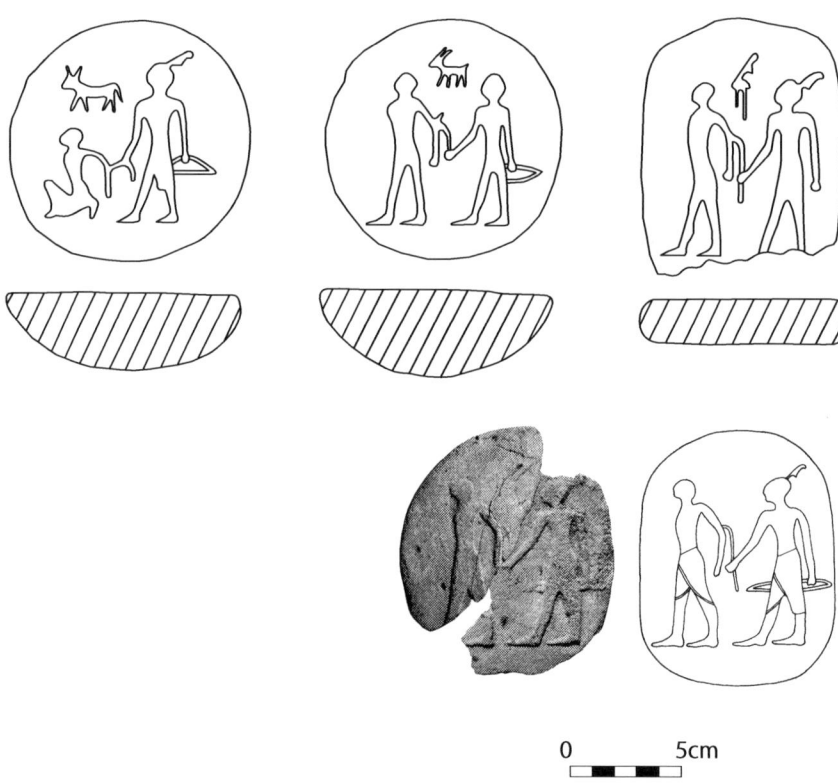

Figure 7.7 Three mud stamp sealings with images of captivity from the fortress of Kubban (top) and one from the fortress of Buhen (bottom). Twelfth Dynasty. In each a man holds a captive who faces away from him, with elbows bound behind him.

Three stamp sealings from the site of Kubban and one from Buhen serve to illustrate some of the varieties of captive depictions in this object group (Figure 7.7).[33] In each there are two human figures, both facing to the left. The figure on the right always stands, striding, and holds a length of what should presumably be read as a rope, which binds the figure before him. The standing figure in three cases has a bow in his back hand, while in the third case he holds nothing but his prisoner. In three cases he has a feather in his hair, and in two he clearly wears a kilt. No other details of clothing or hair can be distinguished or, for that matter, could have been indicated precisely in such a medium. The victim on these objects variously stands, chest thrust out, or kneels. His arms, bound at the elbow, are shown as one. In one case his kilt is clear. The iconography of the captive is never sufficiently distinguished to suggest that he is meant to clearly and visually represent a particular person or group. In three of these cases there is an additional small sign above the scene, twice an animal and once the sign for "west."

The military nature of the captor on the stamp sealings is clear on the basis of his weapon and show of dominance. Short inscriptions are rarely included, and on one known example the captor is shown kneeling as well;[34] the variety in the corpus is very limited. In no instance is the captor actively menacing the captive—this is not a smiting scene in any way, shape, or form, though it is also unambiguously one of captivity. Comparison between these images and other captives we have seen from Dynastic Egypt highlights their differences. In most cases, except when a captive is imminently to be smote by a king, in which case he is usually unbound, there is no direct connection between a captor and a captive. In sculpture and in relief we have seen images of captives without a specific dominator; when we have seen their leashes held in depictions from after the Protodynastic Period, we have seen them held by gods. On these seals, presumably a much more mundane type of object, the captives are directly held by other human beings, shown at the same scale.

Who the actors are in these images is of course an issue of concern. The feather and bow mark the captor as a military person in line with depictions of Egyptian soldiers in other contexts (for instance, Figures 4.37 and 8.7) and perhaps even identify which type of troop he belonged to.[35] The assumption that the person being dominated is a Nubian is based entirely on context; that it was not necessary to make this visually obvious perhaps suggests how little the specific iconography attached to this image mattered. Both the differences between types of stamps and, more minutely, between captive stamps, presumably served to identify groups. But aside from such identification, these images—small, on a material that was easily crumbled or melted, and lacking in much distinguishing detail—cannot have been intended to convey a message of domination very far or very strongly. Perhaps they did not have to in such a situation, where domination was quite literally built onto the landscape in the form of the fortresses and was presumably part of the every day interaction between peoples. But given that there was a fully developed iconography of royal domination, and that these captive stamps exist in circumstances where state domination was a fundamental aim, the failure of such objects to utilize the icons we are familiar with suggests limitations on the dissemination of that imagery. The limitation was itself contextual and historically explicit. In the Sinai in the Old Kingdom, monumental images of smiting kings were as permanent as you could ask. Here, in Nubia in the Middle Kingdom, our scenes of domination are tiny, portable, and non-royal.

Movement and meaning

The very fact of their portability means that objects serve a different role than architecture or the landscape in transmitting messages that are encoded in imagery. On the one hand, they offer the possibility that those images will travel more broadly and thus be seen by a larger and more diverse audience than is the case for something like the interior wall of a royal mortuary complex. On the other hand, also by their very nature, they do not allow for such a static and controlled relationship between the function of the image itself and the function of its context. Nor, in general, are they very large—a not inconsiderable factor when thinking of how they might engage an audience. We have a limited number of objects remaining from ancient Egypt that bear violent imagery, and all of those with explicit violence come from object types and contexts that were likely to have been highly restricted.

The First Dynasty images of smiting from tags are on a type of object that was not only limited but also transitional; they are characteristic of that period in which the Egyptian state first came into being and are known only from royal and high elite tombs. The use of writing, of labeling at all, was very restricted; the meanings carried by writing were not just linguistic but also social and hierarchical.[36] Because of this, the portability of the object does not argue for a particularly widespread audience for it, though presumably it would have been seen at least by those in the administration who were responsible for the gathering and labeling of goods for the royal tomb. This was a small but perhaps not tiny group; a study of labels from a single early First Dynasty mastaba at Saqqara, the tomb of one of the members of the royal administration, identified nine probable hands as having carved the tags found there.[37] The administration seems to have grown during the reign of Den, from whom our last smiting tag is known.[38] But even if tags of this nature would have been familiar to the growing scribal class of the Early Dynastic Period, the images on them seem largely secondary, designed to label rather than to serve independently. "The First Time of Smiting the East" is a vintage, not foremost a statement about smiting. Nonetheless, the image of smiting on Den's tag is so entirely canonical, so like both Narmer's Palette and Djoser in the Sinai, that there must have been a regular means of transmitting this icon during this period as well as a more general understanding of violence as part of royal ideology.

A labeling function can also be argued for the mud stamp sealings; they show captors because they were used in some way that required distinguishing between groups of people who were, in fact, on opposite ends of domination. There is an ideological element to that, but the function of the image seems oblique, not concentrated on defining or upholding that ideology but reflecting the fact that it was part of life in the time and place where the sealings were used. In fact, on none of the preserved objects discussed here does the visual impact of the motif of violence or captivity employed seem to have been the primary purpose. We can understand that even such passive reference would have played a role in perpetuating the social relations at the fortresses, but this is still a different function than a monumental smiting scene might have played. Portable imagery of violence is most direct and prominent on jewelry, but even there the viewer might well have been struck most with the message of wealth and craftsmanship communicated by the pieces, with the particular motif less critical to its meaning. Trampling on a necklace may reflect the fact that violent domination was a part of kingship, but there is no reason to think it was necessary to display smiting on the bosom of the royal daughter in the way it was necessary to display smiting in the royal tomb, or in the Sinai.

The effectively secondary, labeling nature observed here may be one reason why violent images on portable objects are not common—they were not necessary in the way they were in other contexts—and we can be quite confident that we are missing much evidence. But their scarcity also probably reflects decorum regarding the image of the king. Pictures of the king at all are extremely rare in the periods included in this book, and almost entirely restricted to royal spheres. We will not see any in private tombs in the next chapter, and in the last chapter it was noted how anomalous their presence in perhaps official rather than strictly royal inscriptions in the Sinai was. Pictures of triumph always include the king and it is precisely those motifs, rather than battle scenes, which were easily adapted to portable objects. Thus we see smiting on tags, on jewelry. Images of captivity are really not the same thing, in part because they can be more thoroughly divorced from royal ideology, as we see with the stamp sealings.

The separation of objects into two groups on the basis of explicit violence as opposed to captivity can also be seen to have further patterns. Those with explicit violence not only show the king, but they were also found in royal tombs. The same cannot be said about the execration figures or the stamp sealings. Those objects with explicit violence are relatively detailed regarding the visual details of the enemies, as well as the king; there is, however, a noted lack of specificity on the figurines and sealings. The limits of the argument are suggested by the paucity of evidence and by the gaming rod, which was found at a royal tomb and has an unaccompanied and possibly ethnically identified captive. But the boundary on the other extreme is not known to have been crossed: objects with images of the king being violent are not known from non-royal contexts, nor should we expect them there. Those objects from royal contexts that do show the king being violent show scenes that are entirely consistent with the icons also present on walls.

The messages of royal ideology that are quite bluntly made by triumph scenes in the royal tombs, in temples, and in the landscape thus do not seem to have been widely dispersed via imagery on portable objects. Though such pictures do not seem to have littered the country, we should not think for a second that a knowledge of violence and royal control was not a perfectly familiar part of everyday life in ancient Egypt. It only suggests once again that the imagery itself was used in scripted and controlled ways for particular purposes, and that those purposes were largely speaking to an internal audience. The Sinai was a potential exception to that audience, but portable objects do not convince me that they were a similar exception.

That imagery of violence was transmitted in ways we no longer have access to is certain. The smiting icon is too consistent to have been reinvented multiple times from a more generalized understanding of royal domination. It was transmitted across the generations between Narmer and Den, and through the desert (in terms of our available evidence) of the Second Dynasty into the reign of Djoser in the Third. We do not know how that was done, and it is possible that portable objects played a role. Despite the certainty of missing evidence, it seems probable to me from what objects do remain that icons of royal violence were almost as restricted on portable objects as they were on architecture. A less iconic and more generalized imagery of captivity and domination seems to have been somewhat more broadly available, but even this was relatively rare. It is with such observations in mind that we turn to private tombs, in which violence is a repeated but never common motif, and in which that violence never includes the king or the icons available to kings.

Notes

1 British Museum Af1922, 0313.5. Courtesy of the Trustees of the British Museum.
2 Barbara W. Blackmun, "Pair of Armcuffs," in *Benin Kings and Rituals: Court Arts from Nigeria*, Ed. Barbara Plankensteiner (Gent and Vienna: Snoeck and Kunsthistorisches Museum mit MVK und ÖTM, 2007), 352.
3 This is a matter of contention. See, for instance, Parcak, who has taken the presence of heads of foreigners on clappers from the Early Dynastic Period as proof of the widespread dissemination of images of domination. Sarah Parcak, "Egypt's Old Kingdom 'Empire' (?): A Case Study Focusing on South Sinai," in *Egypt, Israel, and the Ancient Mediterranean World: Studies in Honor of Donald B. Redford*, Ed. Gary N. Knoppers and Antoine Hirsch (Leiden, Boston, MA: Brill, 2004), 46, note 13; she notes a pair of clappers in the form of foreigners, Francesco Tiradritti, *Egyptian Treasures from the Egyptian Museum in Cairo* (New York: Harry N. Abrams, 1999), 29, but I am not so willing to assume that every image of a foreigner is related to domination.
4 Not addressed here are labels that may have images of human sacrifice on them. These are left out because I am so uncertain of their reading. Morris' suggestion that they depict the sacrifice of the people buried in First Dynasty subsidiary graves is unlikely, given that none of the bodies found in that context were said to have cut marks on the ribs. Ellen F. Morris, "Sacrifice for the State: First Dynasty Royal Funerals and the Rites at Macramallah's Rectangle," in *Performing Death: Social Analyses of Funerary Traditions in the Ancient Near East and Mediterranean*, Ed. Nicola Laneri (Chicago, IL: Oriental Institute of the University of Chicago, 2007), 20–21, 31. While it does look rather as though an implement is being plunged into the chest of a bound captive on the three labels Morris cites, the lack of more detailed parallels for this imagery makes me uncomfortable asserting that it can be read this way.

5 Günter Dreyer, "Umm el-Qaab: Nachuntersuchungen im frühzeitlichen Königsfriedhof. 3./4. Vorbericht," *Mitteilungen des Deutschen Archäologischen Instituts, Abteilung Kairo* 46 (1990): 53–90.
6 Courtesy of the Egypt Exploration Society. W.M. Flinders Petrie, *The Royal Tombs of the Earliest Dynasties: Part II* (London: The Egypt Exploration Fund, 1901), pl. 11.1; picture: pl. 3.2. For a more recent reference of the objects of the tomb, see Jochem Kahl et al., "Die Funde aus dem 'Menesgrab' in Naqada: ein Zwischenbericht," *Mitteilungen des Deutschen Archäologischen Instituts, Abteilung Kairo* 57 (2001): 171–185.
7 Toby Wilkinson, *Early Dynastic Egypt* (London and New York: Routledge, 1999), 191. The problems with bows as markers of either geographic origin or ethnicity have been encountered previously in this book, see Chapter 4 note 35.
8 Günter Dreyer et al., "Umm el-Qaab Nachuntersuchungen im frühzeitlichen Königsfriedhof: 13./14./15. Vorbericht," *Mitteilungen des Deutschen Archäologischen Instituts, Abteilung Kairo* 59 (2003): 93, pl. 18.f.
9 Two wrestlers are shown inside one of the cities in the Libyan Palette (see Figure 3.2). The figures on the palette are the only possible parallels known for two wrestling figures as victims of another's violence, and the parallel is not exact. Günter Dreyer et al., "Umm el-Qaab: Nachuntersuchungen im frühzeitlichen Königsfriedhof: 9./10. Vorbericht," *Mitteilungen des Deutschen Archäologischen Instituts, Abteilung Kairo* 54 (1998): 162–163.
10 British Museum EA55586. Courtesy of the Trustees of the British Museum. Émile Amélineau, *Les nouvelles fouilles d'Abydos: compte rendu in extenso des fouilles, description des monuments et objets découverts, Vol. 1* (Paris: Ernest Leroux, 1899), pl. 33; Jeffrey Spencer, *Catalogue of Egyptian Antiquities in the British Museum V: Early Dynastic Objects* (London: Trustees of the British Museum, 1980), 65, pls. 49, 53 (cat. 460); Peter Kaplony, *Die Inschriften der ägyptischen Frühzeit* (Wiesbaden: Harrassowitz, 1963), 423.
11 Wilkinson, *Early Dynastic Egypt*, 157. Readings of the associated inscriptions are not entirely certain, but two may include a Semitic word for well, and others a word possibly translated "stronghold." Raymond Weill, *Recherches sur la Ire dynastie et les temps prépharaoniques* (Cairo: Institut français d'archéologie orientale, 1961), 18–21.
12 Cairo Museum JE30875. Photographed by Jürgen Liepe.
13 Cairo Museum CG52003. Photographed by Jürgen Liepe.
14 W.M. Flinders, *The Royal Tombs of the Earliest Dynasties: Part II* (London: The Egypt Exploration Fund, 1901), pl. 4.
15 Courtesy of the Egypt Exploration Society. W.M. Flinders, *The Royal Tombs of the First Dynasty. Part I* (London: The Egypt Exploration Fund, 1900–1901), pl. 12.
16 Flinders, *The Royal Tombs of the First Dynasty. Part I*, 23–24.
17 Petrie, who tended toward near-total self-confidence, was unquestioning in his reading of this figure as a Libyan. Petrie, *The Royal Tombs of the First Dynasty. Part I*, 23.
18 Kerry Muhlestein, "Execration Ritual," in *UCLA Encyclopedia of Egyptology*, Ed. Willeke Wendrich and Jacco Dieleman (Los Angeles, CA: UCLA, 2008), http://digital2.library.ucla.edu/viewItem.do?ark=21198/zz000s3mqr; Joachim Friedrich Quack, "Some Old Kingdom Execration Figurines from the Teti Cemetery," *The Bulletin of the Australian Centre for Egyptology* 13 (2002): 149–160.
19 More attention has been paid to the textual aspects of execration than the material. For a corrective, see Linda Borrmann, "Form Follows Function: der Zeichencharakter der altägyptischen Ächtungsfiguren," in *Bild: Ästhetik—Medium—Kommunikation. Beiträge des dritten Münchner Arbeitskreises Junge Ägyptologie (MAJA 3), 7. bis 9.12.2012*, Ed. Gregor Neunert, Alexandra Verbovsek, and Kathrin Gabler (Wiesbaden: Harrassowitz, 2014), 103–117.
20 A recent MA thesis addresses the difference between such deposits in the sacred space of a cemetery within Egypt and at the fortresses in occupied Nubia. I am grateful

to Brooke Norton for sharing her thesis with me. Brooke Norton, "Destruction of an Image: An Archaeological Examination of Ancient Egyptian Execration Figures" (Master's thesis, New York University, 2013).

21 It has also been suggested that some represent decapitated people. A.M. Abu Bakr and Jürgen Osing, "Ächtungstexte aus dem Alten Reich," *Mitteilungen des Deutschen Archäologischen Instituts, Abteilung Kairo* 29 (1973): 98; Robert Ritner, *The Mechanics of Ancient Egyptian Magical Practice* (Chicago, IL: The Oriental Institute of the University of Chicago, 1993), 137–139.

22 See, for instance, Teodozja I. Rzeuska, "Execration Again? Remarks on an Old Kingdom Ritual," *Polish Archaeology in the Mediterranean* 22, research 2010 (2013): 627–634. Georges Posener, *Cinq figurines d'envoûtement* (Cairo: Institut français d'archéologie oriental du Caire, 1987) gives an inventory of the figurines known at that time.

23 Brussels E7440. Georges Posener, *Princes et pays d'Asie et de Nubie: textes hiératiques sur des figurines d'envoûtement du Moyen Empire* (Brussels: Fondation Égyptologique Reine Élisabeth, 1940), pls. 1–2.

24 Georges Posener, *Princes et pays d'Asie et de Nubie*, 14, 31.

25 Some figurines may have had additional iconography now missing, as suggested by holes in the heads of some of them that may have held feathers or tufts of hair or some such. Posener, *Princes et pays d'Asie et de Nubie*, 19.

26 Posener, *Princes et pays d'Asie et de Nubie*, 47–96.

27 Quack, "Some Old Kingdom Execration Figurines from the Teti Cemetery," 156.

28 Andrés Diego Espinel, "A Newly Identified Old Kingdom Execration Text," in *Decorum and Experience: Essays in Ancient Culture for John Baines*, Ed. Elizabeth Frood and Angela McDonald (Oxford: Griffith Institute, 2013), 26–33 and notes.

29 Bochi has suggested that the figurines always represent types "derived from [the] canonical prototype[s]" (79) as seen in the statues of bound prisoners from Old Kingdom pyramid complexes. However, it is not clear to me that those statues so unambiguously represent foreigners—certainly they do not do so with the more narrow and relatively consistent set of features we see in relief (see Chapter 4). Even if Bochi is correct for some periods, the examples she cites of execration figurines with observable physical attributes of defined foreign groups are later than this study covers. I think the ambiguity clearly embodied in the schematic nature of the representations must be as important as any specific reference could be. Bochi notes that the abstract quality of many figurines "obliterates the individual's human essence" (81); I think this is true of the visual representation of group identity, too. Patricia A. Bochi, "Death by Drama: The Ritual of Damnatio Memoriae in Ancient Egypt," *Göttinger Miszellen* 171 (1999): 73–86.

30 Josef Wegner, "Regional Control in Middle Kingdom Lower Nubia: The Function and History of the Site of Areika," *Journal of the American Research Center in Egypt* 32 (1995): 144–149, establishes their date, makes tentative suggestions as to their general function, and discusses their iconography.

31 Torgny Säve-Söderbergh, *Ägypten und Nubien: ein Beitrag zur Geschichte altägyptischer Aussenpolitik* (Lund: Ohlsson, 1941), 132.

32 Berlin Stela 14753. A line drawing of it can be found in Georg Meurer, *Nubier in Ägypten bis zum Beginn des Neuen Reiches: zur Bedeutung der Stele Berlin 14753* (Berlin: Achet, 1996), pl. 1.

33 Line drawing by author; Josef Wegner's image.

34 David Randall-MacIver and Leonard C. Woolley, *Buhen. Volume II (Plates)* (Philadelphia, PA: University Museum, 1911), pl. 42.

35 Wegner, "Regional Control in Middle Kingdom Lower Nubia: The Function and History of the Site of Areika," 147.

36 John Baines, "On Functions of Writing in Ancient Egyptian Pictorial Representation," in *Iconography without Texts*, Ed. Paul Taylor (London: Warburg Institute, 2008),

95–126; John Baines, "The Earliest Egyptian Writing: Development, Context, Purpose," in *The First Writing: Script Invention as History and Process*, Ed. Stephen D. Houston (Cambridge: Cambridge University Press, 2004), 150–189.

37 Ilona Regulski, "Scribes in Early Dynastic Egypt," in *Zeichen aus dem Sand: Streiflichter aus Ägyptens Geschichte zu Ehren von Günter Dreyer*, Ed. Eva-Maria Engel, Vera Müller, and Ulrich Hartung (Wiesbaden: Harrassowitz, 2008), 581–611.

38 Miroslav Bárta, "Kings, Viziers, and Courtiers: Executive Power in the Third Millennium BC," in *Ancient Egyptian Administration*, Ed. Juan Carlos Moreno García (Leiden: Brill, 2013), 159–160.

8 Who is who?

Private monumental images of war

Sweat and fear and determination are everywhere—on horses, on men. Spears thrust; glistening horses in disarray; a man falling; a leader sweeping his hand before him in passionate gesture—this scene graced the floor of the entryway to a wealthy house in Pompeii, the first image to greet visiting, illustrious guests. They walked over this episode of violence in their jeweled sandals on their way to dinner. They owned it, beneath the soles of their feet. Created in about 100 BC, the so-called Alexander Mosaic (Figure 8.1)[1] is one of the best-known images of the great conqueror as well as a particularly fine example of the mosaicist's art. Its subject is presumed to be the Battle of Issus, fought between Alexander the Great of Macedon and Darius III of Persia.[2]

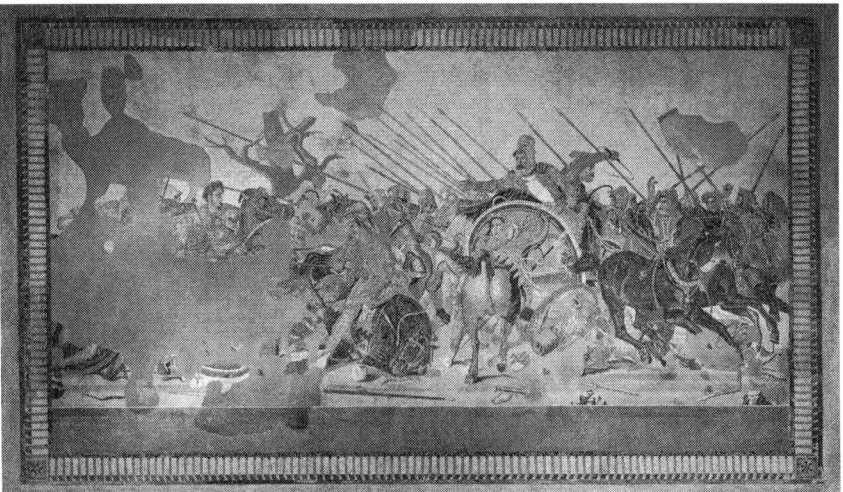

Figure 8.1 The Alexander Mosaic. House of the Faun, Pompeii, *c.*100 BC. A warrior presumed to be Alexander the Great, wearing a Medusa breastplate and thrusting his spear, is partly visible in a fortunate island of preservation amongst the damage on the left. A Persian identified as Darius, his head higher than any other participant's, reaches forth his hand toward Alexander.

The image itself contains both violence and pathos. The setting is deliberately vague: a dull grey sky; no indications of landscape but a single dead tree, which marks the space where the forces collide; and a few small rocks in the foreground. The men in the scene are a difficult to disentangle mass, differentiated primarily by clothing; two figures stand out. The most visible is the figure slightly right of center, whose head is far higher than that of any other participant in the battle. Wearing a white shirt beneath a darker coat, a cloak on his shoulders, and a golden torque at his collarbones, his head and chin swathed in hay-colored wrapping, this bearded figure turns his wide eyes to the left and stretches out his right hand before him. In his left hand he holds a bow, but this is not raised in use. He rides in a chariot, and behind him is a whip-wielding driver in similar dress who grips the reins of two plunging black horses. Two of the men to his right raise their hands in faint echos of the leader in his chariot, with whom they are also associated on the basis of headdress style. The wheel of the chariot, a great circle just right of center, draws the eye. Its shape is echoed in the shield of a falling man in a headdress, as well as in the rump of a horse that partly blocks the chariot. A headdressed man standing at this horse's head attempts to control him.

Few of the figures on the left are preserved, but one is there in steely perfection. In complete profile, his face is an impassive mask. We see his armored body, a Gorgon's head on his chest, in full frontal view as his right arm drives a spear through an opponent. The still-living victim throws one hand above his head and uses the other to grasp the haft of the spear that has run him entirely through. His black steed is already down, blood issuing from its mouth, the curve of its dead neck picking up the other curves in the center of the composition. The steely leader's chestnut-colored horse rears, its hooves ready to trample the fallen. Only a few pieces of the men following this leader can be seen. In contrast to his waving locks, they wear plumed metal helmets.

Aside from its emotional impact, this image raises questions about ambiguity, historical allusion, and the relationship between pictured events and those who commissioned them, which are relevant to a discussion of imagery of war in private contexts in Egypt. As stated above, this mosaic is generally understood by scholars to represent the Battle of Issus. That understanding is key to the way we read the image but relies on information that is not present in the mosaic itself. Even if we accept—on the basis of iconography mixed with expectation—that these are Alexander and Darius, those two fought more than one battle. The choice to depict this battle or campaign at all brings up questions about the connection between the house owner and this event, separated by two centuries. The campaign as a whole was an important stage in the expansion of Alexander's empire to the east and was celebrated in Roman histories by many authors, including in the first century BC. The fact that the image signals rather than dictates to its audience suggests that the audience was being complimented on its cultural literacy—"I don't have to tell you what this is; you know already, and know why it is relevant to us, here, today."[3] The same might be said of more recent depictions of Alexander's battles, both individual and conflations; we still assume that this is part of our western heritage and that it counts as common knowledge for an educated audience.[4]

How can the Alexander Mosaic help us pose questions about private violent images in Egypt? The contexts are certainly quite different—all of our non-royal images of war from Egypt come from the walls of elite decorated tombs, and none include the king. But many provocative questions are nonetheless relevant to both. The most immediate is the degree to which they are historical at all: did they really represent particular battles, in which case a first question might reasonably be "which battles?," or are they conflations, or even fictions? Is the need to see a specific historical episode in these images that of the ancient patrons or of modern scholars? Do ambiguities in the imagery, of persons, places, and of who is winning, carry meaning? What is the relationship between the patron of the art, its audience, and its depiction? Are any of these, in private contexts, related to the state?

Images of violence in Egyptian tombs of people other than the king—those commonly referred to as private people, though many of them were actively engaged in the royal administration and/or were members of the royal family— are relatively rare. While they have little direct bearing on royal ideology, they do speak to the Egyptian elite worldview and to the role of picturing violence for such an audience. In particular, they are useful for their differences from much royal material, which serves to highlight the particularly ideological nature of kingly depictions of violence. Most immediately in this regard, all of these images show combat rather than triumph; attacks on fortified places are the norm. The corpus is also notable for the range of people depicted—from yellow-skinned Asiatics with fancy clothes to black-skinned Nubian archers. Stereotypes are not used to mark bounded categories involved in ethnic conflict. Nubians fight along-side Egyptians; Egyptians fight against Egyptians; Asiatics are shown peacefully in the same tombs where they are also shown being attacked.

Though military action is a motif in tombs in both autobiographical inscriptions and visual depictions, the ways in which it appears in these different source types is notably divergent. This provides a path to examining how images of violence served a role separate from accounts of violence. I will argue below that the non-participation of the tomb owner as well as the lack of historical specificity and the unresolved nature of some of the combat scenes suggest that these should not be read as images of war at all, at least not in the sense of Qadesh. Rather, I think they function as a subset of the more eternal "daily life scenes" that enabled a tomb owner to have access to his accustomed surroundings in perpetuity. In this they may have a similarity to scenes of combat in royal contexts. Unlike scenes of royal triumph, royal combat scenes were rare; there is no evidence that they involved the king himself prior to the New Kingdom; and there is inherently less insistence on outcome than on process when compared to triumph scenes. That a tension between specificity and generality allows images that appear to show events to serve eternal goals is, of course, a point of similarity between these and royal images already seen in various contexts.

All of the private tombs that have preserved images of violence are elite tombs; Egypt's poor did not have elaborate tombs, and scenes of violence are known only from tomb walls, not from the coffins that were available to something akin to a middle class. Elite decorated tombs in Egypt served important roles in demonstrating and defining social identity in the land of the living, as well as providing for an afterlife that perpetuated that social identity into the hereafter.[5] Unlike royal tombs, private tombs were accessible to the public. In fact, one of their functions was to serve as the place where the living could interact with the dead, where sons could bring beer to their dead fathers and ask for their help with whatever ailed them. Decoration on tomb walls is understood simultaneously as literal—providing insurance for a physical afterlife that required repeated offerings, particularly of food, and the maintenance of social relations—and as symbolic.[6] The warfare scenes exist within this context. While they are not common, they are also not revolutionary and do not overthrow the decorum or sense typical of Egyptian tombs; as such, they must be addressed as meaningful choices within a system that was not entirely static despite having conservative tendencies, more pronounced in some periods than others.[7]

The dating of private tombs—particularly in the provinces, from which most of these examples come—can be uncertain. I know of two tombs from the late Old Kingdom that retain images of war; one that has been variously dated to the Old Kingdom or First Intermediate Period; three from the First Intermediate Period; and a further five that can be confidently placed in the early to mid Middle Kingdom. The images are carved or painted on the walls in the more public part of the tomb—the chapel in which offerings to the dead could be made after his burial. They are therefore semi-public monuments with an expected elite audience that included both the dead tomb owner himself (they are all men in this corpus) and his living family. In this chapter I will examine only those scenes of active violence that occur on the walls of the tomb chapels, leaving aside images of soldiers on the march, which are known from a small additional number of tombs both on walls and in wooden models.[8] I have included two cases that are perhaps borderline, in which soldiers actively wield weapons but their enemies are not shown.

The Old Kingdom

The two tombs with scenes of violence that can be confidently placed in the Fifth Dynasty, as well as the one that may date to the Old Kingdom, are unfortunately notable neither for their preservation nor their publication. They are found at widely separated sites, and indeed the presence of elite tombs far from the capital and often displaying notably regional styles is characteristic of the late Old Kingdom and early Middle Kingdom.[9] As the dating of these tombs is not entirely secure, I will describe and discuss them in geographical order from north to south.

The Tomb of Khaemhesy at Saqqara

The published scene of violence from the tomb of Khaemhesy at Saqqara, probably dated to the Fifth Dynasty, shows an attack on what appears to be a settlement

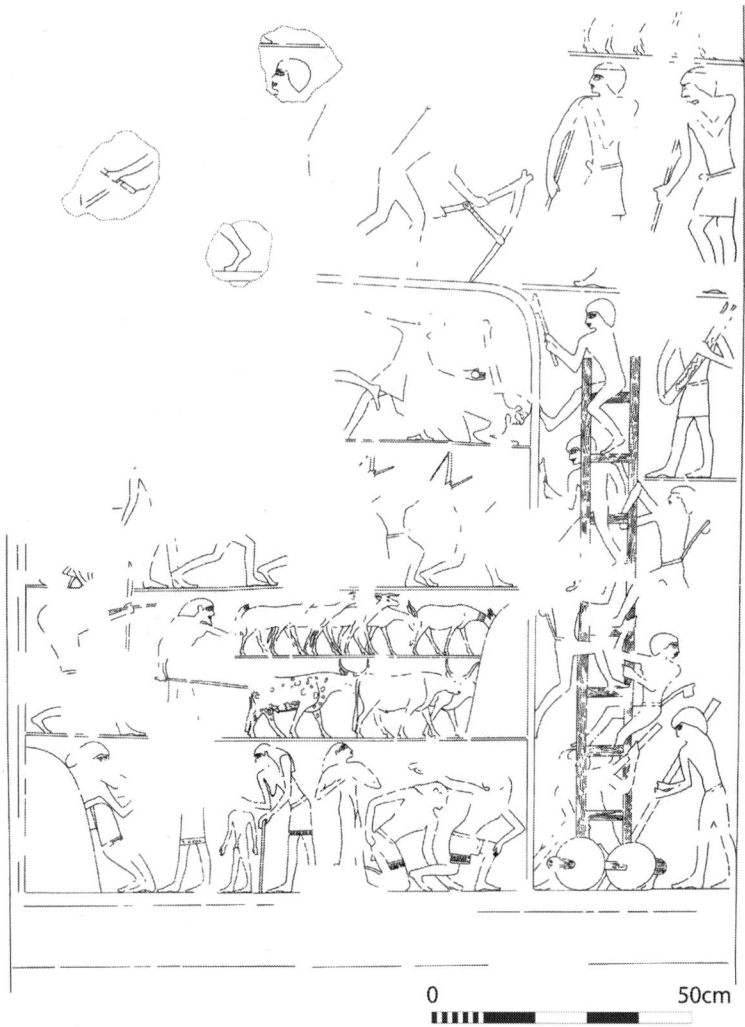

Figure 8.2 Line drawing of an attack on a settlement from the tomb of Khaemhesy at
        Saqqara. The hoe used to compromise the wall recalls the Libyan Palette.

(Figure 8.2).[10] The settlement is marked as separate from that outside it by a line—
not much thicker and no more elaborate than the lines separating registers—that
defines its top and right side, with a curved corner.[11] Inside the presumed settlement are four registers. The bottom, described from right to left, shows two
figures kneeling or crouched, heads bowed, wearing what appear to be short kilts
with bottom fringes. The rightmost figure raises his rear arm, with his forearm
resting on his knee. The figure behind him rests one hand on the ground, with the
other clutching his rear end. Both appear to be in pain or otherwise compromised

but are still alive and unbound. Behind them a standing figure, possibly female, faces to the right and looks skyward, her hands clutched to her breast. Next, facing now to the left, are a woman wearing a short, fringed kilt, with a drooping breast exposed, and a naked child. The woman leans on a stave. To their left is the ill-preserved lower part of a walking person of indeterminate sex and, in the lower left corner, a man leaning against a rounded feature of indeterminate character.

The second register from the bottom has on the far right another rounded feature of indeterminate nature. Beyond this the scene is subdivided into two registers, with the bottom showing three bovines and the top five caprids. These are herded by a bearded figure with a long stick, somewhat bent, who stands to their left and takes up nearly the full height of the register proper. Behind him, not very well preserved but in an unmistakable posture, is an archer in the act of firing an arrow to the right.

The third and fourth registers are more poorly preserved but appear to be filled with active fighters. In the third register are the legs of at least five people, each in a different stance. One clearly shoots a bow; others might be hurling projectiles. All of the legs that can be distinguished indicate figures facing to the right. In the top register, only parts of three figures on the right can be seen. A bearded man is in the act of falling, one hand on the ground and one arm thrown up behind his back. To his left stands the only combatant facing to the left; he stretches one arm before him and leans back, his back hand holding a ball that he is clearly about to launch as a weapon. Crossing his front thigh is the foot of an individual, otherwise now missing, who seems to have been in a position of some distress.

A narrow strip on the right continues the action outside the boundary that defines the settlement. Here a ladder with wheels at its base is shown vertically adjacent to, but not touching the settlement. At the bottom a kilted man with a large lever seems to maneuver the ladder into place. Other men, six in all, clamber up the ladder with axes. Those at the bottom have their semicircular axes tucked into the waistbands of their kilts. The top two men straddle rungs of the ladder and attack the settlement wall with their axes; the top figure even braces himself against the wall with his foot. Behind this man, on a register line of his own and thus not really visually integrated into the scene, is a kilted man walking toward the action with a long quiver or spearcase in his hands.

While fragmentary, the register above the settlement shows a scene that at first might look agricultural, but on closer examination reveals itself to be intimately related to the violence below. On the right are two kilted men with fillets around their wigs who appear to be variations on classic supervisors, standing at ease and leaning against long staffs. Their postures differ slightly from one another; the variation of stance and the lack of visual patterning are quite noticeable in the composition as a whole. While two of the figures to the left of these supervisors wield hoes, they are not using them to plow fields but to plow the wall—presumably mudbrick—that encloses the settlement. This is a theme that echoes a much older composition, having been clearly seen on the Libyan Palette of the late Predynastic Period (Figure 3.2). The register above this is too ill preserved to offer any help.

What is the nature of the place, its people, and the contest being fought in this scene from Khaemhesy's tomb? The supposed defensive wall of the settlement under attack is not marked by any visible types of fortification; it is only the presence of the ladder that makes its nature as a defended space really clear, and the presence of women and animals suggests it is at least as much a town as a fortress. There are relatively few identifying marks on the people inside the settlement, though beards and perhaps fringes on some kilts could argue for a population from the northeast.[12] While some of the figures certainly seem to be in distress, there are no clear attackers inside the settlement, no one inside is bound or dead, and defenders appear to be actively contesting the onslaught. Only the settlement is under attack; no hand-to-hand fighting is shown outside. This is thus a situation in progress, perhaps even early in progress, and not the aftermath of a battle. There is no evidence that the tomb owner himself had any place in this composition.

The Tomb of Inti at Deshasha

The narrative is a bit more advanced in the tomb of Inti at Deshasha, also perhaps to be dated to the Fifth Dynasty.[13] In this scene, the place being attacked is on the lower right (Figure 8.3).[14] Here an oval-shaped enclosure with semicircular protrusions on its exterior contains figures on five registers. The bottom register has four figures; one man is lying face down on the left, rear arm raised. In the center are two stooped figures, one with a long kilt. Behind them a striding figure with

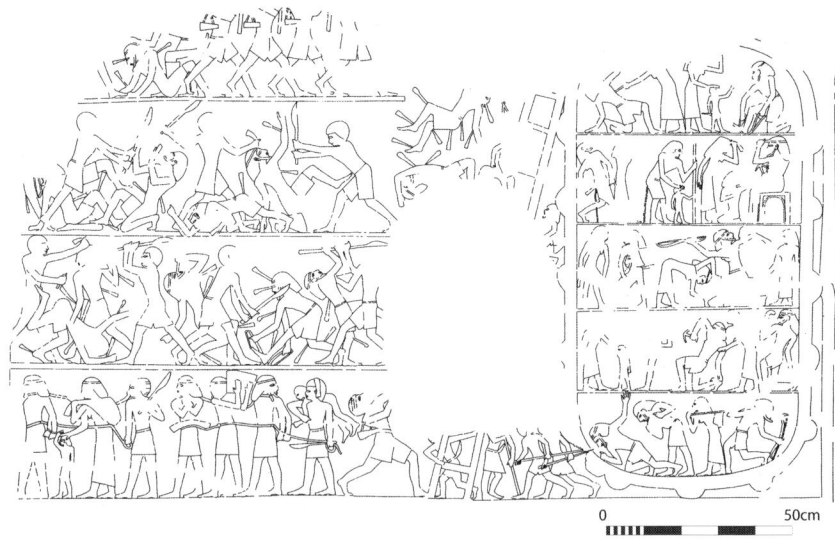

0   50cm

Figure 8.3 Line drawing of an attack on a fortified place from the tomb of Inti at Deshasha, late Old Kingdom. Dotted lines are reconstructions. This is one of the most violent scenes known from ancient Egypt.

chest thrust forward clutches a long implement in his rear hand, but what he does with it is unclear due to poor preservation.

The register above them is unclear except for two figures actively engaged in the center; both face to the left. The fore-figure kneels, his arm to his chest. There is a dagger in this hand; possibly he pulls it out of his own chest. The figure behind him wears a long kilt and perhaps a long hairstyle, and appears to embrace the kneeling person in front. The middle register has dramatic scenes of close personal combat. Figures on the sides watch. The central figure is bent double in clear distress; to the right a combatant grasps a bow in his back hand, apparently wielding it like a club. To the left of the central figure two people are engaged, one standing and one on the ground. It is again unclear if this shows the standing figure stabbing or comforting the seated person.

The fourth register from the bottom shows two distinct scenes. On the left, two figures stand facing one another and perhaps in violent combat; he on the left is leaning back and has a string of round pieces descending from his rear end that make it look as though he is defecating. On the far right a man wearing a fillet and beard sits on a stool, with one hand raised to his head and the other holding a dagger; his posture, seat, and the attitudes of those who approach him might suggest that he is a leader in the town. Four figures—one certainly a child, one a man supporting himself on a long staff, and one or probably two women—approach the seated man. They are in various attitudes of distress or supplication, one with a hand to her head, one on the ground reaching forward. The man with the staff again appears to be defecating.[15] The top register once again preserves a variety of actions. On the right a kneeling figure appears to snap a tool or weapon with his foot. Toward him walk a woman and child, arms raised. On the left a kilted combatant falls backwards while another of our ambiguous women either stabs or supports him, this time from the front rather than the back.

Outside the fortified place are again a variety of scenes split into registers. A major hole in the middle causes some confusion, but the overall picture and many of its details are clear. At the bottom right are figures actively engaged in attacking the fortified place itself. Two men with their backs to the wall hold long sticks that poke into an apparent breach. They appear to be engaged in destroying part of the wall itself.[16]

As we asked of Khaemhesy's tomb, we want to know here what the nature of the attacked place is, who its defenders are, and what is happening in the contest being fought. We must ask, too, how the scene compares to that of Khaemhesy. While superficially similar, this scene and Khaemhesy's have significant differences. The most notable similarities are the use of a ladder to attack a fortified place that includes women and children, with beards and clothing suggesting that the population is Asiatic. However, the town wall in Inti's tomb is more clearly fortified and more obviously represents an attempt to show a town in plan-view than was the case in Khaemhesy, where the "wall" line did little more than divide the composition into meaningful parts. The enclosed space does include women, but not animals in this case. Even more notable, while there is still active fighting in this scene, the campaign seems considerably more advanced and the outcome less in question: there are attackers within the fortified walls, a substantial number of captives are being led away in ropes, and some of the inhabitants of the town seem to have lost control of their bowels. Similarly to Khaemhesy's image, Inti's also does not appear to include the tomb owner or any other person of identifiable rank within the combat scene, with the possible exception of a seated and non-participant leader inside the town.

Inti's tomb is the only one to preserve an inscription that can with some confidence be connected to the battle scene. While poorly preserved, this includes a variety of martial words, crenelated ovals one of which encircles a captive, and at least one place name that has been thought to refer to a city in the Levant.[17]

The Tomb of Setka at Qubbet el Hawa, Aswan

The tomb of Setka was found long after the first wave of discoveries at Aswan and has never been thoroughly studied.[18] Setka held a variety of titles, some tied to Aswan and some to more regional and national levels. He was governor, inspector of the priests of the pyramid of Pepy II, overseer of the phyles of Upper Egypt, and overseer of foreign lands. The elite tombs at Aswan are rock cut; some but not all have courtyards in front. The regional style includes relief-carved or painted panels on only a minority of the flat walls and pillar surfaces, and Setka's tomb, which was also used by his son Meri, keeps with this tradition. One of these panels preserves a register of firing bowmen. The dating of this tomb relies on analyses of both Setka's titles and the image in question here, and so the painting will be described prior to a discussion of date.

Pieces of seven soldiers are preserved in the combat depiction on this wall (Figure 8.4). The six on the left face to the right. In the rear stands a man who holds a black and white skin-covered shield, the top of which is just preserved above a destroyed area. Before him two men stand, legs apart, bows raised, taut, and fitted with arrows. The leading figure of these two has a bent back leg, particularly evocative of an active stance. In front of them another man kneels on one knee in the act of fitting an arrow to his yet undrawn bow. Before him is yet another standing man, in this case not firing but instead fired upon. His right arm clutches a quiver of arrows and his bow, held above his head rather than at the ready. His left hand reaches toward his stomach, apparently grasping the haft of a weapon that has pierced him. Comparing this impassive and upright figure with the dying Persian in the Alexander Mosaic provides a good reminder of the almost total lack of emotion conveyed in these Egyptian combat scenes as a whole. While the enemy of our troop is not well preserved, there is just enough of the curve of a top part of a bow firing toward them, visible directly below the leg of a red-spotted cow in the register above, to be certain that they were opposed by other archers in this register. The tomb owner is not part of the preserved section of this scene but is instead present at a much larger scale, standing behind the archers.

Any attempt to analyze the firing men with regard to historical meaning rests on the details of their visual depiction, as there are no indications of place in the

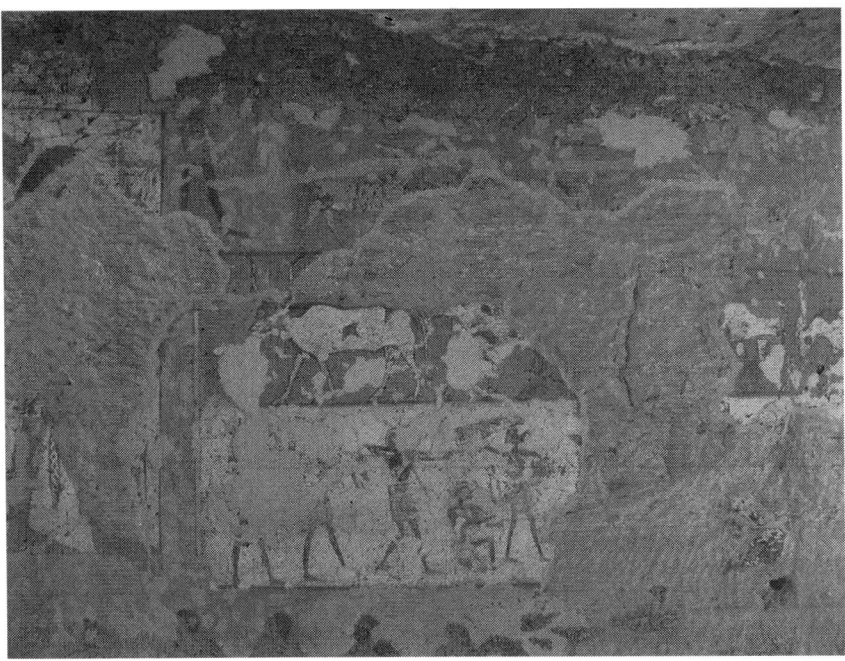

Figure 8.4 Tomb of Setka, Aswan. Bowmen with dark skin and red kilts fire their weapons at an unseen enemy, who may have been depicted in the now missing area to the right. A similar person at a larger scale herds or hunts animals in the top register. The tomb owner is shown at a larger scale to the far left.

image, nor is there any accompanying text. They are all shown with very dark skin, chin-length bobbed hair, fillets tied around their foreheads, feathers stuck in the back of the fillets, white straps running across their chests, and short patterned red kilts with greenish aprons. This is not clearly related to earlier visual ethnic stereotypes but is a version of the stereotypical depiction of Nubians from the Middle Kingdom on. The depiction of soldiers firing in Setka's tomb is specific only in terms of the ethnicity of its participants; there is no preserved trace that suggests it was a reference to a specific place or battle.

That Nubians are shown at all, let alone as warriors, is one factor that has been brought to bear on dating this tomb. This visual stereotype is not present in any securely dated art from the Old Kingdom. What few depictions of Nubians we have from the Old Kingdom, identifiable by texts that call them Nubian, utilize something very close to the standard conventions for showing Egyptian men.[19] The earliest securely dated instances of a Nubian visual stereotype belong to the First Intermediate Period at Gebelein, where a community of Nubian mercenaries who appear to have in many ways adopted Egyptian customs commissioned funerary stelae for themselves that showed them with many of the same elements seen in Setka's tomb. On these grounds, Fischer dated the tomb of Setka to the First Intermediate Period.[20] Jenkins has challenged this dating, principally on the grounds that one of Setka's titles is "inspector of priests of the pyramid of Pepy II"; while royal pyramid cults could last much longer than the kings they served, this does suggest at least the possibility of a very late Old Kingdom date.[21] In the end, I am not confident we can offer a secure date for this tomb. The inclusion of dark-skinned bowmen may be a dating criterion, but also may reflect the geographic location of Aswan, the position of the tomb owner as overseer of foreign lands, and the distinctive local tomb traditions that were developed in this borderland.[22]

The First Intermediate Period

In three tombs of the First Intermediate Period, images of violence have been interpreted as direct illustrations of civil war as mentioned in the autobiographical texts found in the same tombs. Given the fragmentary nature of the images and in all cases the lack of captioning texts, this is somewhat difficult to maintain. While it is intuitively pleasing, it can be questioned on the basis of the much better preserved Middle Kingdom examples from Beni Hasan, in which clear images of civil war are not possible to connect to particular battles (see below).

The Tomb of Iti-ibi at Asyut

The tomb of Iti-ibi at Asyut was recently found to contain an image that has been interpreted as showing part of a battle; there is no question that it is violent (Figure 8.5).[23] In this badly preserved scene on the northern wall of this elite tomb are two preserved figures. On the left, a man with a kilt tied at the back stands, slightly bent over, with both arms swinging long sticks with curved ends. His hair is shoulder-length and his face is not preserved. The stick in his right hand lands squarely on the face of a man at his feet, who kneels but also leans back upon one arm while defending his face with the other. He has no visible weapon. His kilt and hair are the same as those of his attacker. While punishment is not absent from private tomb scenes, the use of multiple weapons seems to suggest rather more in this case. This scene has been interpreted as showing an Egyptian fighting an Egyptian, which seems reasonable, and as the illustration of a particular battle fought between the tomb owner and Thebes.[24] This is harder to maintain; while the scene is fragmentary, there is nothing preserved in it that suggests such specificity.

The Tomb of Ankhtifi at Moalla

One of the best-known tombs of a violent warlord of the First Intermediate Period retains probable traces of images of war; these are unfortunately very badly preserved. Ankhtifi of Moalla has a tomb autobiography that is notable for how little

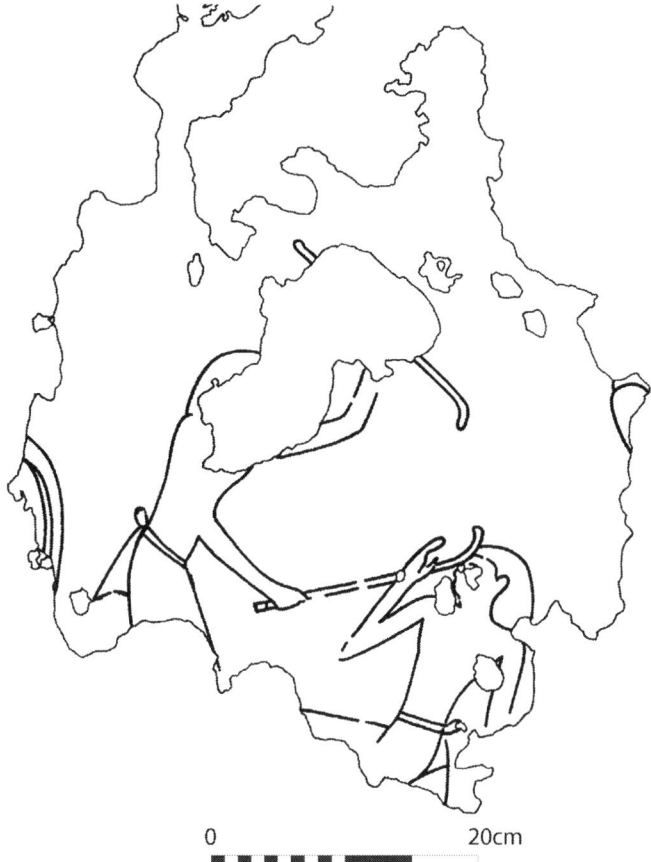

0 ▬▬▬▬▬▬ 20cm

Figure 8.5 Scene of an Egyptian soldier smashing the head of another from the north
wall of the tomb of Iti-ibi at Asyut, First Intermediate Period.

concerned he is with showing his relationship to the king, and for its cursory but
colorful descriptions of civil war.[25] The imagery from this tomb includes three
fragments of figures who appear relatively unambiguously to be in the midst of
combat (Figure 8.6).[26]

One, with dark skin and a white kilt, has an arrow sticking out of his chest.
Another, with red skin, is on the ground, legs in disarray, with what may be arrow
shafts around him. The third, again red skinned and now clearly wearing a white
kilt, straddles a stick, perhaps a long weapon, held by another man. Because
Ankhtifi is so well known for his autobiography, it has been easy to connect these
scenes with the known battles, but once more the preserved images are insufficient to make this certain.

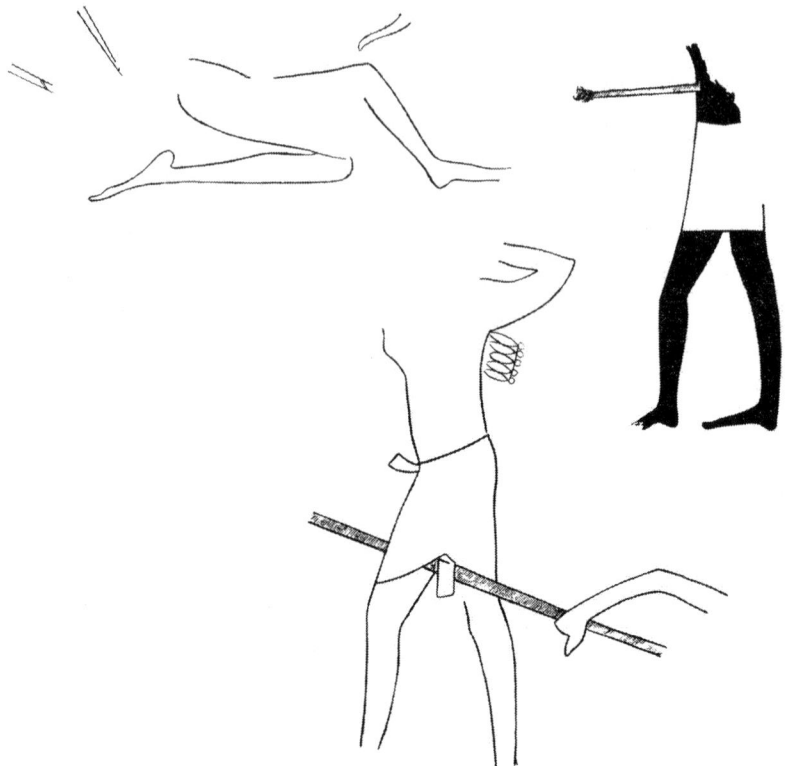

Figure 8.6 Fragmentary figures engaged in combat from the west wall of the tomb of
Ankhtifi at Moalla.

The Tomb of Iti-ibi-iqr at Asyut

The north wall of the tomb of Iti-ibi-iqr at Asyut has a scene that, while badly
damaged, is much more complete than any other with military actions from the
First Intermediate Period.[27] The top of the wall is taken up by a long inscription
that concentrates on the titles of the deceased, including "Overseer of Troops
of the entire 13th Nome."[28] The tomb owner can be seen on the left, taking up
the entire height of the wall and leaning against his staff; his much smaller wife
reaches his knee. The top two registers show men leading animals toward Iti-ibi-
iqr. The bottom two registers include soldiers. While most are marching calmly,
weapons at ease, at least one from the bottom register is shown leaping, and the
eighth man in the upper register is firing his bow.[29] No enemy is shown, and as
the wall is complete it is clear none ever were. This renders the scene less a battle
and more a celebration of battle skills, or of the position of the tomb owner as the
overseer of battle troops.

The Middle Kingdom

Middle Kingdom tombs with images of violence are known from the sites of Thebes and Beni Hasan. Thebes in the early Middle Kingdom was enjoying its first period of prominence and was not yet the major center that it would become in the New Kingdom; we have seen it previously as the site of the mortuary complex of king Nebhepetra Mentuhotep, considered the reunifier of Egypt at the end of the First Intermediate Period and thus the inaugurator of the Middle Kingdom. There are contemporary private tombs in the hills not far from that mortuary temple, one of which includes a scene of war that is closely related to the battle scene(s) from his royal monument (for example, Figures 4.34 and 4.44). Beni Hasan lies farther to the north, in Middle Egypt, and is also the location of private elite tombs that bridge the gap between the First Intermediate Period and the Middle Kingdom. It has four closely related tombs with elaborate combat scenes.

The Tomb of Intef at Thebes

Intef was a general of the Eleventh Dynasty under Nebhepetra Mentuhotep. His titles included overseer of troops. There are two scenes relevant to this study in his tomb, both painted on the sides of square pillars.[30] The tomb itself is a *saff* tomb, with a courtyard in front that ends in a rock-cut portico with square pillars. The pillars and the wall behind them include large areas of decoration in both painting and relief, utilizing styles that have been understood as variously local and canonical.[31] The two scenes showing violence are painted on the rear, wall-facing sides of the first two square pillars on the north; they are rendered in the local style. The first shows a battle against a fortified place and is thus related to those we have already seen in the Old Kingdom. The second scene teeters on the edge of meeting the criteria for this study. In it, three boats full of soldiers are rowed across the water, some of the soldiers menacing unseen enemies with their weapons.

The second pillar from the end wall preserves a scene that is divided into five registers, of which the bottom three are slightly taller than the top two (Figure 8.7).[32] What can be read as the two most important elements of the scene break the register system, occupying a double height: at the top right this is a fortification, and in the bottom left a striding figure of an Egyptian man, presumably the tomb owner. The most notable difference among the many people shown is skin color, which can be found in red-brown, dark brown, orange-brown, and yellow. People of these colors, their additional identifying iconography, and their actions will be described from top to bottom as there appears to be a narrative structure to the composition as a whole.

The fortress in the upper right is shown as a plain mass in side-view, in contrast to the plan-view known from the Old Kingdom examples above. It has straight walls and scalloped crennelation at the top. Nine men with orange-brown skin can be seen above the top of the fort, all facing left. Four standing men are in different poses: one clutches his hands to his chest, another fires a bow, two raise their arms

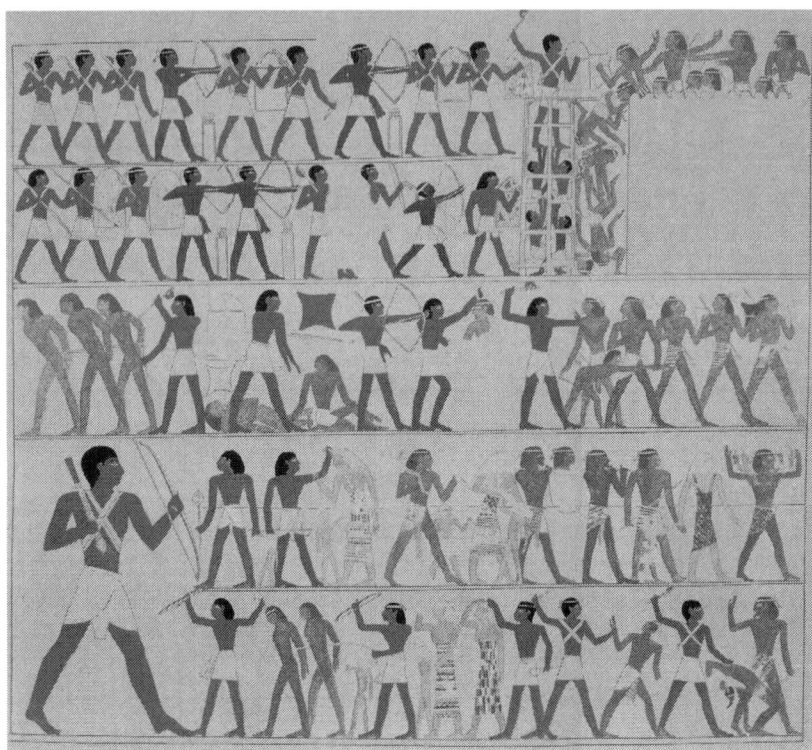

Figure 8.7 Watercolor facsimile of the scene of battle from one of the square pillars in the Theban tomb of Intef, Overseer of Troops. Eleventh Dynasty.

in MLB-worthy poses to hurl small white balls. The standing man in front is at the very edge of the fortification and holds a shield as well as his projectile. There is an arrow stuck in his forearm. All of the standing men wear kilts with fancy patterns, different from one another. Interspersed between the standing men are five men lower down, perhaps crouching to load weapons, whose heads are their only visible parts. All the defenders, whether standing or not, have white fillets tied around their dark, shoulder-length hair. The rightmost man appears to have a small pointed beard, but at least some and perhaps all of the others may be clean-shaven.

The left two-thirds of the top two registers are taken up by men in formation, all facing to the right in opposition to the fortress. They all stand with legs apart and all wear white kilts, but there are a variety of ways in which they are not repeated and therefore do not fall into a simple pattern. A description is both monotonous and broken by little changes in detail, little signals that someone was paying attention and that not all is the same or easy to categorize. In the top register, the first two men have red-brown skin, hold large shields, and carry fenestrated axes at their shoulders. They have straps across their chests and plain short hair.

Behind them is a dark-brown man who is in the act of firing an arrow, with a quiver of more arrows standing on the ground by his forefoot. He wears a fillet tied around his short hair and a red sash hangs down the front of his short kilt. Next are two more red-brown men with hair and dress similar to the first two, but the first has different weapons: a dagger and a curved stick and no shield. Next, another dark-brown archer who is fitting rather than firing his bow. Bringing up the rear are three red-brown-skinned men with chest straps, a variety of the weapons seen by the other red-brown men in the register, and fillets in their hair.

The second register is similar to but not the same as the top. The first two men are notably short, a full head-height shorter than those behind them, but also definitely portrayed as men and not children. The first has red-brown skin, a shield, and an axe held at waist height. Behind him a dark-brown short person shoots at an upward angle. He has a feather at the back of his hair fillet, and the sash at the front of his kilt is white. He has no quiver. Next in line are two red-brown men: the first with a fillet, a white sash, and a bow that is not held at the ready; the second with an axe and probably a shield, now missing. Next are two dark-brown, fillet- and sash-wearing archers with bows drawn, quivers standing on the ground. Behind them are two red-brown, fillet-wearing, shield-bearing men, one with an axe, the other with a long straight stick. The stick holder has longer hair than any other man in these two registers. The last man in the row is the only one with chest straps. He is red-brown and filletless.

There are no indications of landscape in this scene and no accompanying text, omissions we have become familiar with in the corpus of private images and that preclude identifying this battle or town with any specific event or place. Once more, however, the details of dress and skin color allow us to be reasonably certain, at least on a general level, of who is meant to be represented. This image depicts Egyptians and Nubians attacking a fortified place defended by Asiatics; the bottom registers show captured Asiatics being led toward the tomb owner. While this basic interpretation of the scene is easy to arrive at, the wealth of details and differences among the "ethnic" groups is also striking and keeps them from being quite so entirely stereotypes. This is true even among the red-brown-skinned men, those we read as Egyptians. Some have plain hair but some wear hair fillets, as do all the men of other colors. One even has a red sash and a feather in his hair and shoots a bow—these are features more closely tied to the dark-skinned men and usually seen as signs of Nubian identity. This image is a superb illustration of the fact that the relationships between attributes considered to be ethnic markers are not static even on one wall in Egyptian art, and that our assumptions about notions of the bounded nature of groups and their stereotypical representation are too simple.

Despite the complexity of visual ethnic stereotypes in Intef's attack scene, divisions are perhaps not the most important part of the image: all men act together. They are clearly one body of soldiers moving in military action against the fortress on the right. Their differences even highlight that they work together; for instance, most bowmen are positioned directly behind shield bearers, and no bowman is more than one other person away from a shield. This is presumably a reasonably realistic rendering of the fact that when one shoots an arrow, one cannot simultaneously shield oneself.

Between the ordered registers of the attacking force and the bulk of the fortress is the actual place of confrontation, the least ordered part of the composition. A scaling ladder, the same height as the fort's walls, has been wheeled to within arm's length of the fortification. Atop the ladder stands a red-brown man with a shield, axe held high to swoop down upon his enemy, who is the shield-wielding orange-brown man standing at the left corner of the fort. Below the axe-swinger atop the ladder are four red-brown men, smaller in scale, climbing the rungs. Two of them have axes stuck into their waistbands, freeing their hands for climbing. Between the ladder and the fortress are tumbling orange-brown men. One lies on the ground already, knees up and head at an impossible angle. Three others, one with a checkerboard pattern kilt, fall in disarray.

The defeat of the orange-brown defenders is thus in process in the scene of the attack on the fortress, and the remaining three registers show its further development and aftermath. These registers all have a combination of additional fighting, now only between red-brown and orange-brown men, and of captivity. In the middle register are orange-brown men: some naked, some in striped kilts, some in plain. Several have small pointed beards. On the right several march away from the center, three still holding their shields and pointed spears; they are beleaguered by an axe-swinging red-brown man who attacks a weaponless fifth orange-brown man. There is also a smaller, naked orange-brown man bent double and held by the hand by a comrade; three arrows stick out of his back and leg. The axe wielder in this tableau wears a tripartite *shendyt* kilt; this is almost certainly a marker of elite status, though his attributes otherwise keep with the range of norms for the red-brown men here. Elsewhere in this register we see a fallen orange-brown man sprawled on the ground, and three more led off to captivity with bound wrists, driven by an axe holder. The colors get confusing! An image is better than a description for this complex scene, and we can appreciate that we are being shown rather than told.

The bottom two registers introduce a new category of person: yellow-skinned, long-dress-wearing women. Five of them are present here, all but one associated with small yellow or orange-brown children, one even extending her breast to a nursing boy. The women's dresses are elaborately patterned and each is different. One, whose hair is grasped by a red-brown man with an axe held at his waist, appears to have tattoos on her forearms. They all have long, light-colored hair. Some of the orange-brown men in these registers are also associated with children; in one instance a single man is carrying four tiny children upon his shoulders. There is also still some fighting in these registers—two or three men are being beaten on the lower right —but, for the most part, the subduing is in the past.

The clear focus of these bottom two registers is the striding red-brown man on the left who takes up the height of both registers and is thus twice as large as any other person in the composition. He holds a bow loosely in one hand and clutches a small bundle of arrows in the other. He has short hair, crossed straps, and a *shendyt* kilt. While he is not labeled, his size marks him as exceptional, and most probably he represents Intef himself. He does not engage in any of the fighting, but the figures nearest him on these two registers, also wearing *shendyts*, are in the act of presenting prisoners to him, including men, women, and juveniles.

This painting is exceptional as a record of violence when compared to all others we have seen so far. It does appear to show ethnic groups with clear but not entirely static bounds, with some mixing between the allied red-brown Egyptians and the dark-brown Nubian archers integrated into the attacking troops. The enemy is more homogeneous, though the variety of patterns on their clothing lends visual interest as well as indicates a lack of total sameness. Victory is portrayed in this image. The nature of the battle—an attack on a fortified place—and its outcome—the defeat of the orange-brown men and their yellow women and children—are presented in an unambiguous manner. The composition quite carefully does not suggest total annihilation of these people, however. Finally, this scene is unique for showing the tomb owner in direct relation to the image of combat. There is something more obviously personal about this battle than we have seen or will see again in private imagery.

Despite these differences, the Intef fortress attack is in other ways quite comparable to previously seen private imagery. There is a focus on a fortress, which is not named or given any type of landscape or architectural details that might help identify it. The combination of massed troops acting not in step but still in concert is likewise familiar, and the tomb owner is not fighting. There is no way to identify this as a specific battle from the image itself, and generality can still be said to dominate over specificity.

The second martial image from the tomb of Intef is located on the back, western side of the adjacent pillar, the one farthest to the north (Figure 8.8).[33] The condition of this painting is not as good as the previous one, but it is still sufficient to make out many details. This scene has three registers, each with a band of water at the bottom (indicated by a repeated pattern of zigzagging lines) and a boat rowed by oarsmen above. In each boat there are archers with arrows raised to their bows. The enemy at whom these arrows are to be fired is very definitively not shown in this case. The boats are all headed toward the left and occupy the entire back face of the pillar on which they are shown. If one walks around the pillar, the adjacent side is also decorated, but this has a peaceful scene of craftsmanship and certainly cannot be the target of the menacing weapons of the soldiers on boats.[34]

The boats themselves are roughly similar in shape in all three registers, with slightly curved prows and sterns, shallow drafts, and large rudders. The boat in the middle register has a small cabin with a slightly concave roof next to the rudder. On this boat, the oarsmen stand and use oars with leaf-shaped blades; in the top and bottom registers, the oarsmen sit and use oars whose blades are shown as narrower, possibly because they are in the process of sweeping the water. The oarsmen are differentiated from one another by hairstyle and by jewelry. In the top row, the three left oarsmen have unusual updos, hair tufted above fillets. The other two visible oarsmen in this boat have shoulder-length hair, also with fillets. All five appear to wear narrow necklaces. In the middle boat the oarsmen are

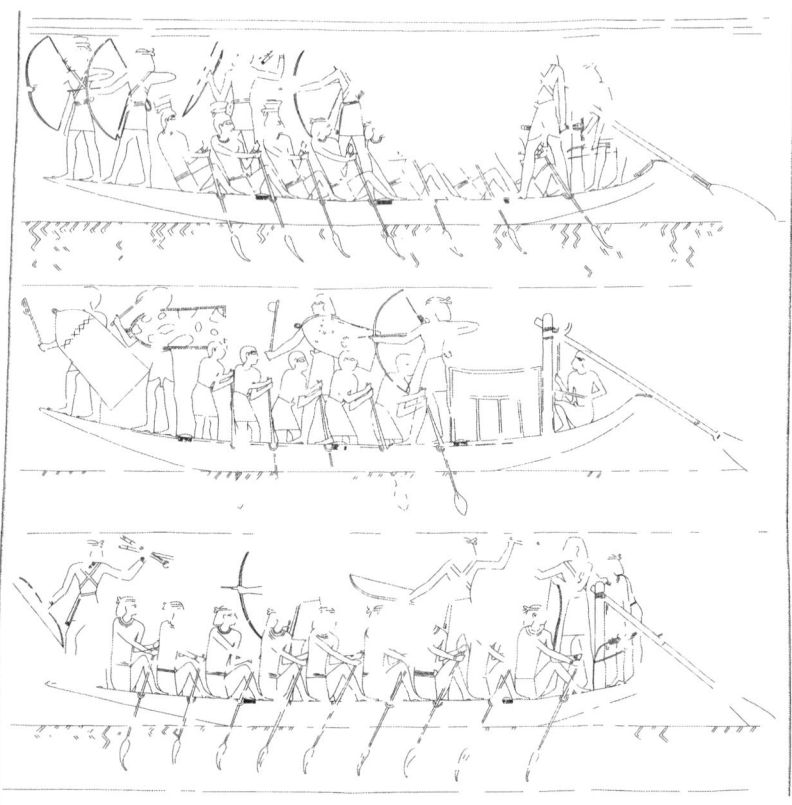

Figure 8.8 Three registers of boats with menacing soldiers aboard, from the tomb of Intef
      at Thebes, Eleventh Dynasty.

quite plain. They have short hair and knee-length kilts, and no ornaments at all.[35]
In the bottom boat all have shoulder-length hair with fillets, and most if not all
wear moderately broad collars. It is not clear whether any of these distinctions
are meant to encode ethnic differences, but they do point once more to the non-
uniformity of depiction. It is even possible that this is a type of visual playing,
rather than an attempt to indicate a specific meaning or group attribution. All three
registers are notable for the overlapping of bodies, with standing people shown
partly obscured by sitting ones.

Active military personnel are present in all three boats. The top boat includes
six preserved standing men, all of whom hold bows and arrows—some fitted to
fire and some not. Most, if not all, of them seem to wear chest straps and sashes,
the latter colored either dark red or black. At least one has the funny hairdo and
at least one the shoulder-length hair. The standing figure just in front of the rudder pole clutches arrows and wears a *shendyt* kilt. He is the only *shendyt*-wearing

figure on the boat, and the only one among the otherwise dark-skinned cohort on this boat to have lighter skin.[36] He also holds a short implement that may be a staff, and though he is the same size as the other figures it is possible that he should be considered a focal point or a commander of the group.[37] Behind him is a standing, slightly stooped figure who appears to be controlling the rudder.

The second boat includes four standing men. The two in the prow of the boat both hold large shields and axes. The shields are particularly well depicted, with the front one showing the stitching where the handle on the back was attached, and the second with its pattern of preserved cowhide; the man who holds it wears a kilt with a front panel that may be a *shendyt*. The axes are of the rounded and fenestrated variety. These men both hold their weapons at the ready but in different positions. Another shield-and-axe-bearing man stands amidships. His axe is the other common type, with an unfenestrated blade, not as wide but a bit longer. Behind him, a full pace back, stands this boat's only archer. There are no differences in skin color in the men of this row; they are uniformly dark red.[38]

The bottom boat is quite similar to the top one. Spaced out in the boat are four bow-holders. The second from the prow has an arrow fitted to his weapon, but the others are not ready to shoot. The first and third hold their bows loose and wave fistfulls of arrows in the air. The one at the back leans on his bow. The first three of these men wear sashes in front of their kilts, and the three whose torsos are preserved have chest straps.

Interpreting this scene is difficult in part because there are no other examples of boats involved in a military action in the corpus considered in this book. Boats with soldiers are well attested from royal tomb complexes, but the soldiers there are not in action poses. Further complicating our understanding, all of the weapon-wielding men on this pillar menace a foe who is not visible, was never visible, but toward whom the oarsmen nevertheless vigorously propel the ships. Are we looking at an attack? Why is the victim not shown? It seems unlikely that we are looking only at military transport or a drill—the men are actively ready to inflict harm with both long-range and melee weapons. Another possibility, suggested by the differences between the boats, is that the cabin on the middle boat was being used to transport something of particular value and that this boat was flanked by the other two, commanders aboard, waiting to intercept anyone who might try to attack the valued element. Arrows to shoot at approaching attackers and axes for close fighting if anyone boarded the transport might make sense in this light. But as usual, we should be wary of too explicit a connection to events.

The Tombs at Beni Hasan

Nowhere is the generalness of references to violence more at issue than in the best-preserved, best-known, and largest images of war from private tombs in Egypt: those in four tombs at the site of Beni Hasan in the center of Egypt. This necropolis of a provincial capital that never rose to national prominence has a large number of impressive rock-cut tombs dating to the First Intermediate Period and early Middle Kingdom; they were owned by local administrators who were tied to the pharaonic government. The cluster of four tombs with images of violence makes this theme markedly more prevalent at this one site than anywhere else in Egypt at any time. While the theme must thus be understood as a local preference in this case, these images are also clearly related to the others discussed in this chapter.

The images of violence in the Middle Kingdom tombs at Beni Hasan are in a way more difficult to deal with than any example previously addressed in this study. This stems predominantly from their size and complexity; it is often not possible to give a single comprehensive image of the combat scenes shown in this context, and in some cases there are multiple such scenes in a single tomb. My approach here will be to give a general description of a whole scene, as much as possible, before diving into details that will be illustrated separately. In the interest of space, I will not deal with every detail, but instead will focus on those that provide for the most fruitful discussion, particularly those that to me raise questions of generalities and specificities with regard to time, place, and people. After such descriptions of each tomb, they will be treated as a group for analysis. The condition of the tombs, which were painted but not relief carved, makes illustrating them difficult, and I will use a combination of line drawings and photographs.[39] The former are more useful for seeing overall scene composition; photographs capture detail better, but some of this cannot be seen without color.

Dating provincial tombs is difficult; they are given here in their presumed chronological order. They all belong to the late Eleventh or early Twelfth Dynasties, in the early part of the Middle Kingdom, probably within the several generations after the tomb of Intef at Thebes. The basic structure of the tombs consists of a rectangular chamber, often with columns of living rock left standing; the paintings are on the walls of the chambers.[40]

Beni Hasan Tomb 15, Tomb of Baqt III

One of the largest tombs at Beni Hasan, that of Baqt III, contains a massive war scene that takes up the entirety of the lower part of the east wall of the main chamber (Figure 8.9).[41] The wall as a whole, from top to bottom, is decorated first with a stylized frieze; next with a short register of text giving a standardized offering formula and the name and titles of Baqt; then with six registers showing nothing but endless variations of wrestling men, each pair including one man with darker skin, perhaps simply as a way of making the two visually distinct in their closely intertwined positions; three registers dedicated to war; and finally a plain dado, not shown below. The blank space on the right was never painted rather than having been destroyed.[42]

The visual focus of the wall, if it can be said to have one given its size and the generally chaotic nature of all of the small figures, is a fortified place that is two registers high toward the lower left. This is a poorly preserved section of the painting. This blocky white structure has a single rectangular door, outlined in red; a slightly protruding top with crenelations; and a sloping glacis at its base.

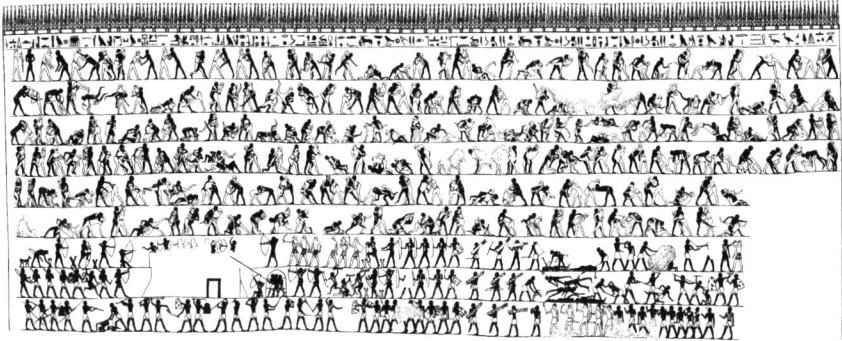

Figure 8.9 Beni Hasan Tomb 15, belonging to Baqt III, east wall of the main chamber. The top registers contain wrestling imagery; the bottom three show an attack on a fortified place. The line drawing elides the complexities of skin color.

The torsos of nine men are visible above the battlement, in various attitudes of shooting, throwing, or beseeching. They face outward in both directions.

From the left, the fortress is menaced by two registers of men. Some shoot arrows, with crossed stacks of arrows waiting for them to reload. There are shield-men, though here most bowmen are not protected by shields, and men with long weapons, some curved. The bowmen all wear dark kilts with tucked up sashes; those with long weapons wear white *shendyt* kilts. In this attacking troop we would seem to have a fairly straightforward visual distinction between "Egyptian" long weapon and shield holders and "Nubian" bowmen, working in concert.

Right of the fortress the attack has a different nature. Again, two registers of men face the fortress with a variety of weapons. In front this time, on the lower of the two registers, is a sort of siege engine, which appears to be a light structure to protect its three occupants. They together hold a long pole, which pokes up across the two registers, hitting the men atop the fort.[43] In front of these pokers an archer crouches and shoots up at an extreme angle. The attacking force on this side includes a wider variety of people. Many of the archers here wear crossed white straps on their chests, in addition to their sashes, and in the case of some particularly acrobatic leapers also feathers in their hair. A group of six men in the upper register is distinguished in a variety of ways, from yellow skin to patterned kilts to different weapons—some of them hold short bows, some axes, one a throw stick, one a small shield. The patterned kilts and yellow skin probably mark these as Asiatics, though they lack the hair and beards that Asiatics have been seen with elsewhere.

In addition to the attack on the fort, this scene includes personal combats and more general melee. At the far right in the upper of the war registers, a dark-skinned man with white chest straps and a sash hits the face of a yellow-skinned, fancy-kilt-wearing man who clutches his attacker's forearm. Beside them two men hit each other with sticks. Immediately below them small groups, all accoutered as Egyptians, attack one another—one particularly graphic vignette shows a man filleted on a spear in the act of falling. The bottom row consists almost entirely of *shendyt*-wearing Egyptians with various weapons. Only in one place is the rule broken, where five light-skinned men are among the troop; they carry weapons and march with the others and are clearly engaged as part of the Egyptian force. All march on the right side of the register, but combat has also erupted on the left, below the attack on the fortress. Here multiple groups of men, all Egyptian, bash at each other with long sticks or axes. A result of all of this violence can be seen in the second register, about two thirds of the way to the right. Here a pile of naked dead bodies, some with arrows sticking out of them, lies. The paint is badly worn, but four of the men seem to have the red-brown skin characteristic of Egyptians while the last is darker.[44]

Diving into the details of the composition provides almost endless interest and amusement, but never a hint of individuality. On the upper war register toward the right, two prone men lie with others standing above them. On the right, a straight line connects the hands of the standing figure to the head of the prone man. Is he dragging him by a rope, or hitting him with a stick? To the left, the prone figure lies face up and raises an arm, but looks quite dead. He has an arrow sticking out of him and the bow-holding man standing above him touches his chest, as though checking for a heartbeat. The interest of these two dead figures, aside from their total inertness, lies in their hair or fillets, which hang over the register line and offer a tiny disruption to the organizing principle of the scene. Aside from such small visual games, there is nothing individualized about any of these people. They represent groups, as indicated primarily by skin color. There is no dominant character anywhere on the wall.

The only text on the east wall of Baqt III's tomb is the offering formula at the very top. The absence of captioning inscriptions is not only notable in itself, but is also in marked contrast to other parts of the same tomb. The north wall, for instance, has a range of daily life scenes, including various kinds of manufacturing, fishing, hunting, etc. Short captions litter the wall, simple statements or labels. These give the scenes additional human interest but do not really locate their activities at a specific time or place. Still, their absence from the war scenes further generalizes those and removes them one step further from particularity.

Beni Hasan Tomb 17, Tomb of Khety

The east wall of Khety's tomb (Figure 8.10)[45] is extremely similar to that of Baqt III, usually identified as Khety's father due to the proximity of their tombs and the fact that they share considerable architectural and decorative similarities,[46] though differences are also present. Khety's east wall is topped by a *kheker* frieze; below that run an offering formula; five registers of wrestlers; and three rows of war, with the same essential elements in largely the same arrangement as Baqt's. The only major difference is on the right of the wall, where there is a double-register-high offering formula that sits above a register of offering-related activities. This is the area that was unfinished in Baqt's tomb, and quite possibly

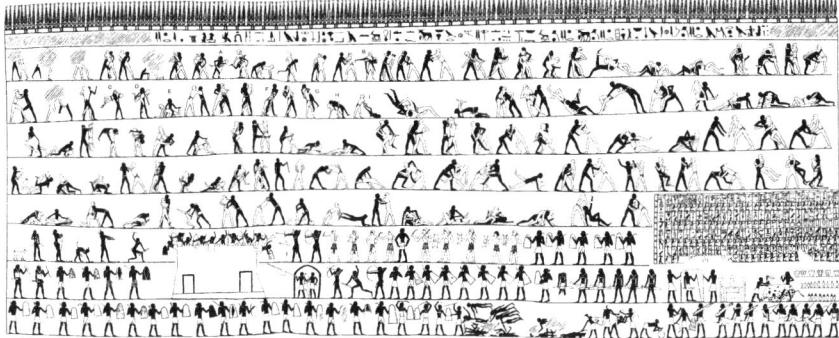

Figure 8.10 Beni Hasan Tomb 17, belonging to Khety, east wall of the main chamber. The scene is closely analogous to that of Baqt III.

a similar inscription and image were intended there. Within the offering-related activities is a statue inside a basic shrine, shown at the same scale as the living human figures around it. This may represent a statue of the tomb owner, who does not otherwise appear to be present on the wall.

The fortress itself is for the most part similar to Baqt's, with the addition of a second doorway the most notable difference (Figure 8.11).[47] Atop it are ten men, again varied in weapon and posture but all engaged in defending the fortress from those below. These men all look similar to one another, with dark brown skin and white straps crossed on their chests. It is not clear if they are to be understood as Egyptians or Nubians, but as these groups are always shown allied elsewhere in

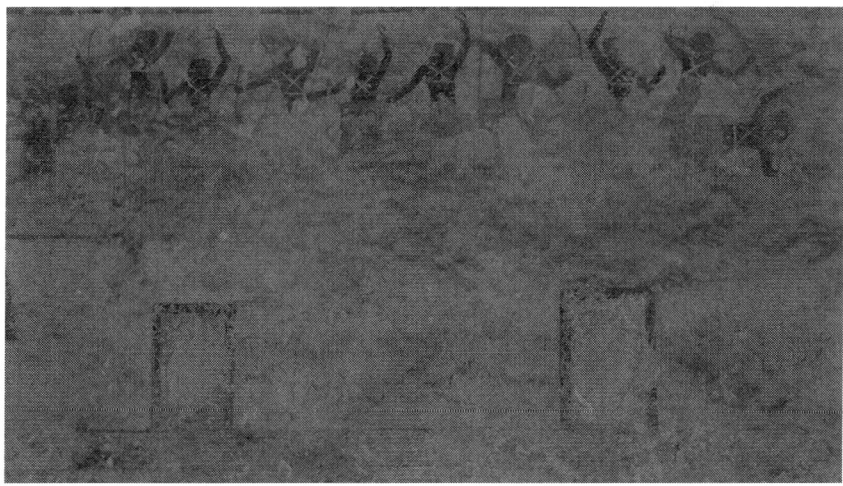

Figure 8.11 The fortress and its defenders on the east wall of the tomb of Khety at Beni Hasan.

this Beni Hasan tomb the distinction might mean little; there are similar looking men among those attacking this fortress.

As was the case in Baqt's tomb, here the fortification is being menaced by archers on the left and by a light siege engine on the right. Once more, the smaller group on the left includes "Nubians" (now in two distinct kinds of outfit) and "Egyptians," while that on the right includes a complement of light-skinned fancy dressers in addition to its somewhat variously clad Egyptians and Nubians. The light-skinned men in this tomb sometimes hold oddly shaped shields with triangular notches out of their tops and bottoms. Scenes of individual combat as well as troops on the march appear to the right and in the bottom register, with minor changes in placement, such as the pile of dead being moved to the bottom register. The number and variety of violent encounters is lower here than in Baqt's tomb, though there are more arrows suspended in mid-flight and the pile of dead bodies is more impressive. To the right of the pile of dead are two vignettes that seem to show physical punishment, perhaps as a matter of discipline.[48]

Beni Hasan Tomb 14, Tomb of Khnumhotep I

The tomb of Khnumhotep I has suffered from water damage and no complete publication of its decorative program has ever been made.[49] As with the other tombs at Beni Hasan with images of violence, its scene of war is on the east side. Newberry published an excerpt from that scene and a color facsimile of two of its "foreigners," but no drawing of the wall as a whole. As such, comparing the composition to those of other tombs is not possible, though published descriptions and photographs give some help. I have not visited the tomb, not even the site, myself.

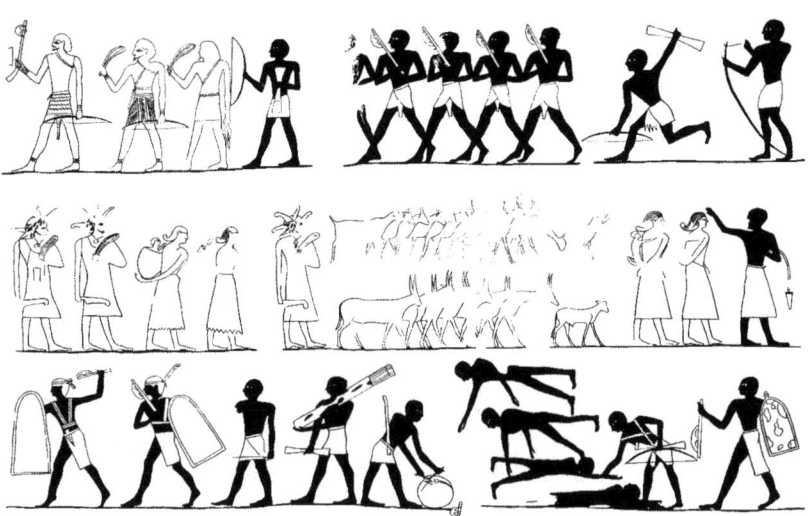

Figure 8.12 Scenes from the east wall of the tomb of Khnumhotep I at Beni Hasan.

Many aspects of the east wall (Figure 8.12)[50] of Khnumhotep I's tomb have parallels in the previously discussed tombs. The top registers again show wrestlers.[51] The martial aspects are also largely familiar, including the attack on a fortified place.[52] Those familiar aspects published in Newberry's drawing include the stringing of a bow; men running while holding bows and arrows; *shendyt*-clad axe bearers on the march; a pile of dead bodies, near which a man ties a bundle; and light-skinned fancy dressers holding weapons.

Also shown on this wall, however, are groups of people and animals that have no direct parallels on the east walls of other tombs. These are men with knee-length dresses and large numbers of feathers stuck in their elaborate hair; they carry even more feathers. The women have long, fringed kilts, and babies held in baskets on their backs. The hair of the women ends in unusual large curls. In one case two such women, led by a presumed Egyptian, walk in front of a herd of animals while a man brings up the rear. The visual stereotype in this case perhaps points west, to Libyans, but the iconography is notably different than the very codified Libyans we see in royal smiting scenes. The theme of pacific foreigners under Egyptian control is a theme elsewhere at Beni Hasan, most famously in the case of Asiatics in the tomb of Khnumhotep II.[53]

Beni Hasan Tomb 2, Tomb of Amenemhat

The tomb of Amenemhat has both notable similarities to and differences from the other three tombs with scenes of war from Beni Hasan. The most obvious difference is the nature of the east wall itself, which rather than a continuous flat surface is here broken in its middle by a recessed niche to hold a rock-cut statue of the deceased, flanked by two smaller figures of his wife and mother. This has the effect of dividing the composition of the east wall into two equal halves, as well as, perhaps, giving the tomb owner's image a presence in the scenes of that wall. The effect of the latter is certainly limited not only by the depth of the recess but also by the bands of text that frame the door to it and the presence of his family; at most we might say that he looks on the scenes rather than takes part in them. The tomb is well dated, with its autobiographical inscription stating that its construction took place in year 43 of the early Twelfth Dynasty King Senwosret I.[54]

The east wall as a whole contains a largely familiar set of themes, with some additions. Beneath a *kheker* frieze is a band of formulaic inscription. Next come three registers of wrestlers, the top of which stretches across the whole wall while the bottom two are broken by the statue niche. The following registers, though split by the statue niche, are balanced across the two sides. On the north we have the assault of a fortress (Figure 8.13),[55] described below. Beneath this is a scene with three water-borne vessels. Two ships with raised sails, one of them also with oars, tow a smaller boat. In the front vessel there are some men holding shields, but this is not a military scene: the boat has a canopy protecting the coffin of the deceased as it is taken on pilgrimage to Abydos. This is made clear by the inscriptions accompanying the scene. While the pilgrimage to Abydos has not been an element of the other walls with martial imagery at Beni Hasan, it is not a rarity in

Middle Kingdom tombs in general or at Beni Hasan more specifically; in other tombs here it is typically present on the west wall.[56]

The southern section of the wall, below its wrestlers, contains two registers of soldiers, some of whom fight (Figure 8.14).[57] Here the bottom of the wall is taken up with another scene of ships towing a boat, this time on a pilgrimage to Busiris.[58]

The image of attacking a fortress on the north side of the east wall is familiar. The fortress here is a steel-grey, with its single yellow door outlined in red; as always, the height of the fortress takes up two registers. It has a sloping glacis at the base and a top more complicated than previous examples, with an alternation between steel-grey and white sections, both with scalloped crenelations. Its width is a bit abbreviated—the statue niche limits available space—and only six men

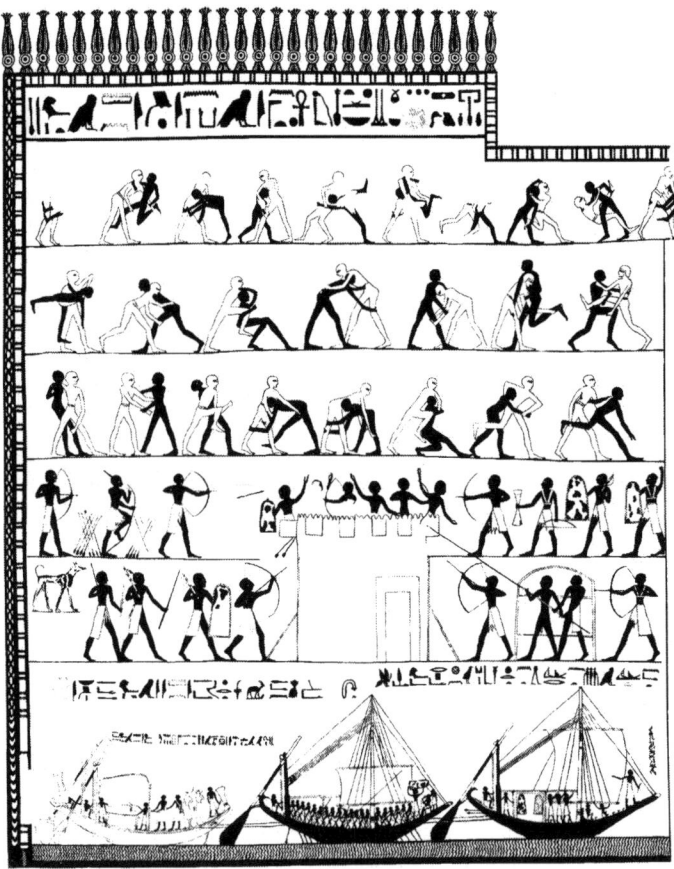

Figure 8.13 The north side of the east wall of the tomb of Amenemhat at Beni Hasan. In addition to the familiar themes of wrestling and the attack on a fortress, this panel includes a labeled image of two ships towing a funerary boat with a coffin to Abydos, one of the cult sites of the god Osiris.

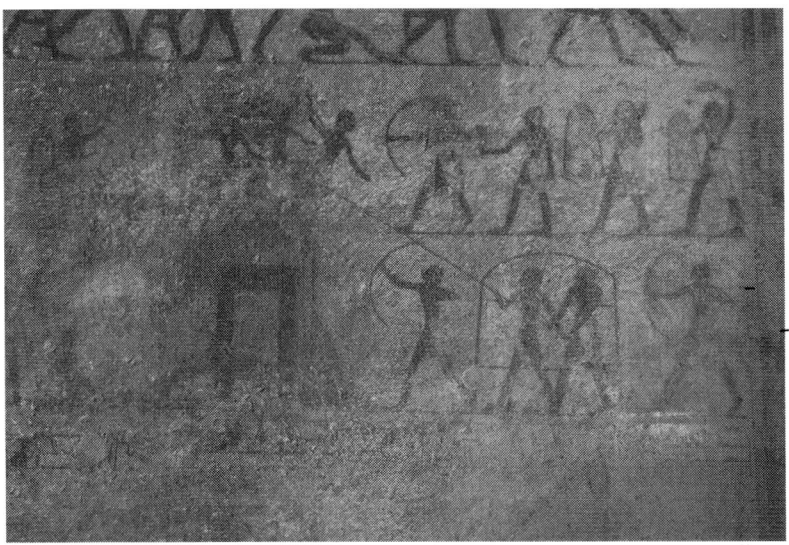

Figure 8.14 Archers and pole-men attack a fortified place on the east wall of the tomb of Amenemhat, Beni Hasan.

defend the fort. They have red brown skin; their clothing is not visible. One holds a bow, one a shield, three have arms raised to throw things. From the left they are attacked by men on foot. All of these wear split kilts that cover only their back legs. In the top register three archers are in different stages of firing or readying bows. The man in the middle, who bends his leg to string his weapon, wears a feather in his hair. Stacks of arrows once more indicate that this is a position held rather than a troop firing while on the march. In the second register there are four men. The first shoots a bow; there are already two arrows lodged in the undersides of the projecting battlements. The archer is followed by a shield- and axe-bearer and two men with long weapons. The dog, also present in the tombs of Baqt and Khety on the left side of the fortress attack, is here on its own groundline behind the men of the second register.

The right of the fortress is, as expected, menaced by foot soldiers bearing a variety of weapons, including a light siege engine in the lower half. Here this protects only two men, who use the expected pike to poke at either the battlements or the men on them. Archers before and after the protective light structure have arrows fitted to their bows. They wear split kilts, now with red sashes (while the Newberry drawing shows the sashes as uncolored, their color is clear in some photographs). The rear archer has white straps across his chest. Skin color can be difficult to determine here, but it seems that the archer at the front, at least, is somewhat darker. The top register has two bowmen and two shield-bearers. The archers are in front, one with a drawn bow and the other holding his bow at rest, with arrows in his hand. The former certainly wears a red sash and the latter, who has white chest straps, may as well. The front shield bearer carries a fenestrated axe and wears a sash; his partner to the rear has no weapon, just a raised hand, a sash, and chest straps.

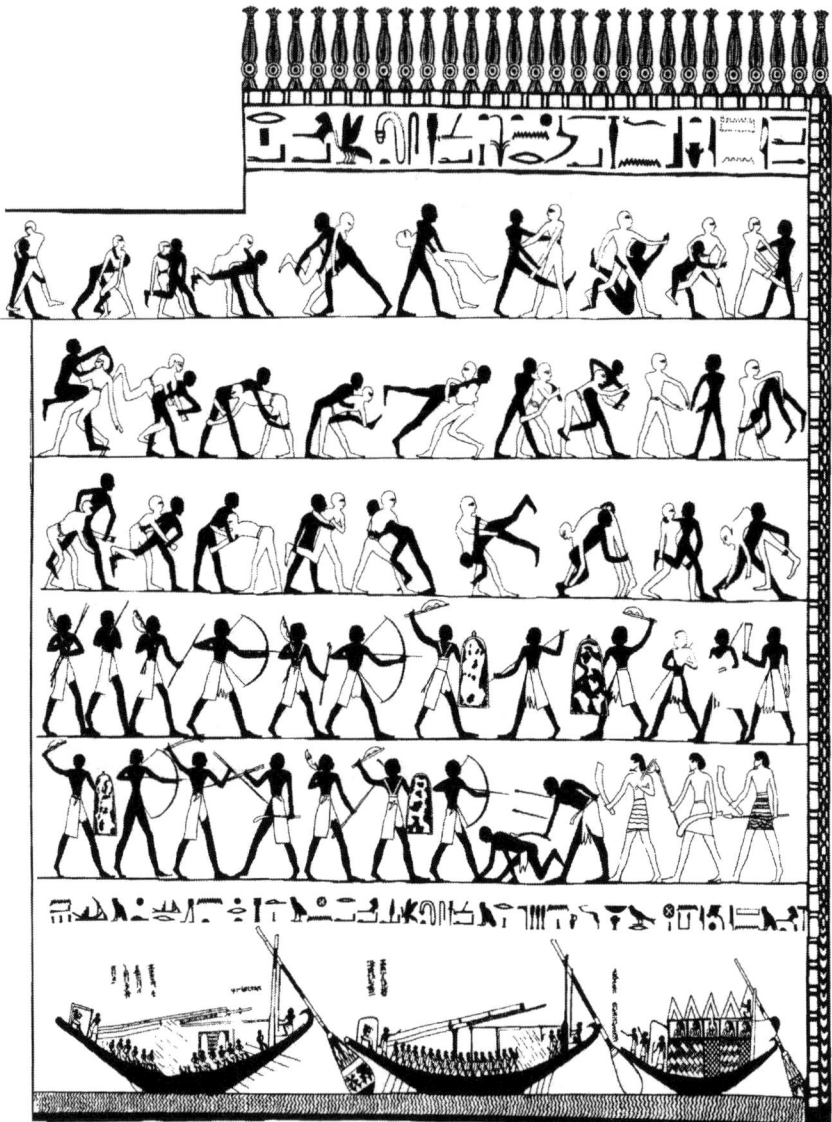

Figure 8.15 The south part of the east wall of the tomb of Amenemhat at Beni Hasan. Three registers of wrestlers top two rows of fighting men, including the now-familiar complement of light-skinned fancy dressers. At the bottom are two ships towing a boat en route to Busiris; the lack of specificity in the war scene compared to that of the journey, with its inscriptions, is clear.

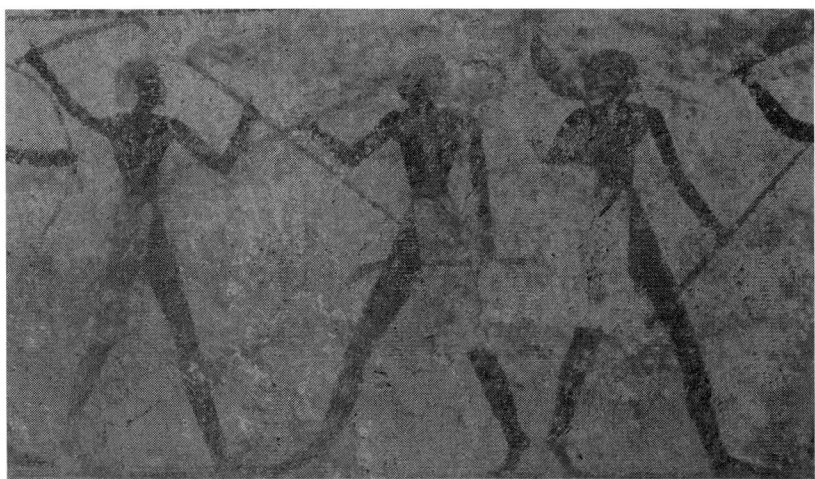

Figure 8.16 Detail of combat from the tomb of Amenemhat at Beni Hasan.

On the south side of the east wall, the expected scene of war in the open is presented in somewhat abbreviated form over two registers (Figure 8.15).[59] There is no pile of dead bodies, and combat itself is limited to three places. In the top register, five men march in from the right and are opposed by seven coming from the left. Aside from the presence of archers on the left but not the right, it seems that considerable care has been taken to make sure that the two sides look similar to one another. All of the men have red-brown skin. Of the middle three characters in the most direct clash, two—one on each side— wear split white kilts with black sashes, hold cow-hide shields, and brandish fenestrated axes (Figure 8.16).[60] The only things that distinguish them from one another are the chest straps on the right-hand man. The spearman between them, who faces left, wears a red sash. But then so does the archer on the left, facing right, who stands behind the shield-holding axeman. The very right of the register has three men in darker kilts.

In the lower register there are confrontations in two places. Toward the left, two men with spears and clubs or axes fight; they each have stuck a spear in the other. They are dressed identically in split white kilts with no sashes, and have the same red-brown skin color. Behind the figure on the left are an archer and a shield- and axe-wielder, also with weapons raised to the fray. The right half of the register shows a confrontation between three red-brown men, the middle perhaps a bit darker, with no sashes and a variety of weapons, and five figures on the right. The first two of these are red-brown to dark-brown, with dark kilts. Both are stuck with arrows and in the process of falling to the ground. Behind them are three men with lighter skin closer to yellow, thick clubs, and fancy kilts. Possibly one could read this as falling Nubian and Asiatic auxiliaries; but the falling is far from complete and the same register has presumed Egyptians spearing one another, so it seems overly simple to assign much weight of ethnic identity to particular sides of the combat shown.

In addition to its scenes of war, the tomb of Amenemhat has an autobiographical inscription that mentions his participation in three military expeditions, two within Egypt and one to the south. As the relationship between autobiographical inscriptions and imagery in tombs is not straightforward, the comparison between the text and pictures from Amenemhat is best addressed in a general discussion of martial tomb autobiographies.

Inscriptions and images in private tombs

Images of war in Egyptian private tombs have almost universally been assumed to depict particular historical battles. I do not think this can be sustained. While the focus of this book is on imagery rather than texts, if there *were* such a relationship between the two it would be critical to understanding the images; it is therefore worth some time to examine the assumption. The argument against it depends not only on the lack of specificity in the battle scenes, as shown above, but also on the lack of a close relationship between images of war and contemporary tomb inscriptions.

Autobiographical inscriptions that mention military activity are not particularly common in the period under consideration and those that explicitly mention violence are even rarer, but they are moderately well attested from the same class of tombs as the images in question. The images of violence do not appear to illustrate or supplement these biographical texts. First, there are very few tombs that have both, so they were clearly not mutually dependent. Second, the nature of the depictions of battle in these two media overlap little, showing that texts and images of war served fundamentally different purposes and that we cannot assume a connection between the two. A few quotes will first demonstrate the nature of texts about military campaigns and how they differ from the images shown above, and then an examination of one of only two tombs that clearly has both image and text referring to military activity will put the nail in the coffin.

Two of the best-known inscriptions that mention campaigns come from the late Old Kingdom; there are notable differences between them. In his tomb at Abydos, the Sixth Dynasty official Weni says, in a brief taste of a longer passage:

> His majesty sent me at the head of this army, there being counts, royal seal-bearers, sole companions of the palace, chieftains and mayors of the towns of Upper and Lower Egypt, companions, scout-leaders, chief priests of Upper and Lower Egypt [...]
>
> > This army returned in safety,
> > It had ravaged the Sand-dwellers' land [...]
> > This army returned in safety,
> > It had sacked its strongholds.
> > This army returned in safety,

It had cut down its figs, its vines [...]
This army returned in safety,
It had slain its troops by many ten-thousands.
This army returned in safety,
[It had carried] off many [troops] as captives.

His majesty praised me for it beyond anything. His majesty sent me to lead this army five times, to attack the land of the Sand-dwellers as often as they rebelled, with these troops.[61]

This passage asserts Weni's own position at the head of the army, stressing its importance by showing how elite those under him were. Weni's relationship with the king is also stressed; this is a passage about hierarchy as much as about violence. Details about the actual fighting are not present, and the use of a poetic and repetitive structure that generalizes the action is arguably the closest parallel between this and the rather programmatic scenes of attacking fortresses seen in the imagery. Some of the details can be compared: "Sand-dwellers" is a reference to people from the east, an ethnic and geographic moniker. We have seen captives in the aftermath of battles, and strongholds, if not quite their sacking, also appear in the images. But the totality of the annihilation, including the places and produce of the enemy, is not reflected in the images. Interestingly, the total security of the Egyptian army—a trope common in textual references to military action—is both unlikely to be literally true and quite different from what we see in the imagery, where even some of the attackers are shown stuck with arrows or otherwise harmed. This particular difference demonstrates both that we should no more regard texts as "true" relations of events than we do images, and that the two focused on different things.

In his rock-cut tomb at Qubbet el-Hawa, Harkhuf speaks of his missions to the south (bracketed additions are mine for clarity):

[Long string of titles] who casts the dread of Horus into the foreign lands, who does what his lord [the king] praises; the royal Seal-bearer, Sole Companion, Lector-priest, Chief of scouts, honored by Sokar [a god], Harkhuf, says:

The majesty of Merenre, my lord, sent me together with my father, the sole companion and lector-priest, Iri, to Yam [a place in Nubia] to open the way to that country. I did it in seven months; I brought from it all kinds of beautiful and rare gifts, and was praised for it very greatly.

His majesty sent me a second time alone. I went up on the Yebu road and came down [...] in the space of eight months. I came down bringing gifts from that country in great quantity, the likes of which had never before been brought back to this land. I came down through the region of the house of the chief of Setju and Irtjet, I explored those foreign lands.[62]

In this case the absence of mention of violence, even of troops, is almost glaring. Harkhuf went exploring for months on end in foreign lands, he opened ways to far off lands, and came back with loads of unprecedented gifts (including a dancing pygmy that delighted the king and for which this inscription is best known). That these were military expeditions undertaken with troops is certain: when discussing his third expedition, he speaks of "the army that had been sent with me" as well as the "strong and numerous . . . troop from Yam" that attached itself to him. But the military quality of the action is curiously elided. Not even the prowess of Harkhuf is celebrated in these passages. The overwhelming focus of the autobiography as a whole is on the relation of Harkhuf to the king, on Harkhuf's ability to bring good things to Egypt for his lord. The alluded to military actions were in service of this, and so they are not reported in a way that makes it possible to reconstruct their particulars, though they are treated as distinct and differing episodes in the life of the worthy Harkhuf.

Even during the First Intermediate Period, when the stress on the king in autobiographies was often less or absent and a celebration of military virtues became more common, verbal depictions of the military served chiefly to showcase the importance of the tomb owner, sometimes also highlighting the value of his troops. The autobiography of Ankhtifi, a local magnate of Moalla who was an active warlord in the battles of that period, includes boasting of both his achievements and that of his companions; events are treated summarily, as in the previous inscriptions.[63] The somewhat maddening, from our perspective, refusal to give the details that would allow us to reconstruct an historical episode is an element the inscriptions have in common with the images described above, but it is close to the only one. The episodes mentioned here are not, and could not have been, illustrated because of the narrow range of types of images used to decorate tombs. We can almost see the strutting figure of Ankhtifi, the cowering Thebans, Weni's despoliation of fig trees and vines, or Harkhuf at the head of his men traversing distant deserts through the shimmering heat. But we could not illustrate any of this from the Egyptian canon, and most elements common to the images do not appear in the texts. No one speaks of piles of dead bodies, no one brags of scaling the ladders, no one explains to us the curious shelters from which men poke at the walls of fortified towns. What the texts do—use military campaigns to glorify the deceased—is fundamentally different from what images of war do. The tomb owner is absent from the latter.

Confirmation that images of war in tombs do not illustrate autobiographies comes from the Beni Hasan tombs of Khnumhotep I and Amenemhat, the only known cases with extensively preserved imagery and texts of war.[64] The autobiography of Amenemhat is the better comparison, since his martial imagery is better preserved and published. While it has been claimed that the combat scenes in Amenemhat's tomb illustrate his military life,[65] it is difficult to assert that the scenes and autobiography cover any of the same territory. This inscription was carved on the jambs of the doorway leading from the tomb's portico into its main chamber.[66] The most relevant passage reads:

I followed my lord when he sailed south to overthrow his enemies among the foreign peoples. As a Count's son, Royal Sealbearer, and Chief Troop Commander of the Oryx nome did I sail, as a man replaces his aged father through the favor of the king's house and his being beloved in the palace.

> I by-passed Kush in sailing south,
> I reached the ends of earth;
> I brought back gifts of all kinds,
> And praise of me reached the sky.

Then his majesty proceeded in safety, having overthrown his enemies in wretched Kush. I returned in his following in alertness and no loss occurred in my troops.[67]

Elsewhere Amenemhat speaks of sailing with military expeditions accompanying treasure, once to the king and once specifying the city of Coptos, in Upper Egypt, as his destination. He gives the numbers of his troops, 400 and 600, and says that he returned without losing any—a theme, as we have seen.

Amenemhat's military concerns as expressed in his autobiography are primarily centered around his relation to the king and the movement of valuable goods, themes we saw in the inscriptions above, too. No actual fighting is mentioned at all—in fact, he always notes that he came back without loss. The reference to the king overthrowing enemies is a bit confused, given that he proceeded in peace and his accompanying general lost no men. All of the expeditions mentioned in the text include sailing, none include fighting, all include treasure, none include any mention of the composition of the army, all result in everyone who matters coming home alive. In the images, we have fighting on land, against a fortified place (unmentioned in the text), no representation of booty, armies that are notably and deliberately depicted as diverse, and actions that seem likely to have led to death on both sides; that there is no pile of dead bodies in this tomb is probably just a concession to space, given the comparison to other Beni Hasan tombs. Both images and inscriptions use a mix of specificity and generality to achieve their purposes, neither one of which is a straightforward report on events. They are specific about different things. For the texts, it is clear that one function is to show the excellence and uniqueness of the actions of the tomb owner, and particularly, at most times, his relationship to the king. This is not what the imagery does, and it seems improbable that this is only because depicting the king was not possible in private tombs in these periods.

Interpreting private images of war

If images of war in private tombs do not illustrate autobiographies, what do they do? Because the Beni Hasan tombs are the most complete and coherent set of images of this sort still extant, it is useful to begin with them and then ask to what degree our observations of them apply to the rest of the corpus described.

Several immediate points jump out in gathering and describing the images of war in Beni Hasan tombs. First, the tomb owner is not pictured in any of them. Nor is any other individual given visual prominence. Second, it is not clear who is who on a group level either, in the sense that while ethnic identifiers of skin and dress are given, the combinations of peoples on any "side" are complex. Third, it is in no instance clear which "side" is winning, partly because the sides themselves are impossible to distinguish visually and partly because the action is never represented as complete.[68] Finally, the scenes are not labeled, not even with brief captions, and this is in marked contrast to other scenes in the same tombs, sometimes even on the same walls.

Taken together these points make it impossible for us to identify representations of particular battles, and impossible to say that the scenes are used to display the personal glory of the tomb owner, as indeed it was impossible to say that battle scenes in royal tombs glorified the king. They are vague both regarding events and participants. The question is, would they have been originally? We saw with the Alexander Mosaic that we can be certain who was winning not because it was encoded in the image, but because we know that Alexander beat the Persians. Would the descendents of the tomb owners at Beni Hasan who have these scenes have known so well what they represented, been raised with tales of the wars on grandpapa's knees, that no visual clues were needed? I doubt it. For me, the very consistent adherence to visual ambiguity in the Beni Hasan corpus, along with the more general disconnect between military images and texts in private tombs, is convincing. The Beni Hasan wars were not primarily intended to depict specific events, but apparently have no trouble referring to a more general state of civil war.

Apart from depicting particular events, which we cannot be certain the Beni Hasan scenes do, what might be the reason for showing Egyptians fighting Egyptians? Kanawati and Woods suggest that the prominent display of the "local" army on the wall opposite the entrance to the tomb in these four cases might be a show of independence from the royal administration.[69] We should be cautious with this interpretation for two reasons. First, there is nothing that marks the unlabeled and clearly diverse armies on these walls as local; it is not unreasonable to think so, only not demonstrable. Second, and more critical, no scene can show "independence" from the pharaonic government because no scene shows its opposite: the depiction of the king is counter to decorum in private tombs prior to the New Kingdom. Showing the relation of the tomb owner to the king was the role of texts, not images. Thus even if the imagery here could be said to clearly show local concerns, this would not count as a claim of independence. That there is a regional preference for such imagery does show that regional identity existed and that tombs were not ordered from a kingly catalog, homogeneous across the land. But that is not news and says nothing about the relationship of these administrators to pharaonic structures of governance, including war making.

In the end, the images of war at Beni Hasan seem best interpreted as a variety of daily life scenes. Daily life scenes in Egyptian tombs show *types* of activities rather than specific instances of activity. They show the background to the life of the tomb owner, the activities of his estates, the preparation of his food and his furniture. He never participates, except in the extremely restricted and probably symbolic activities of fishing and fowling in the marshes. Such an understanding lessens the discomfort that arises from the similarity of the scenes, which has suggested that each generation copied the previous one's images of war at Beni Hasan. Why not copy a daily life scene? If you are not claiming to have had a personal presence at a particular event, it hardly matters if it is copied. It does not even matter much if the event shown was contemporary.

Despite this disconnect between tomb owner and battle scene, we still must recognize that these particular images were chosen for a reason, and that the tomb owner must have had some relationship to war *in general*, presumably even civil war, even if these images were not reports of his participation in a specific battle. Remember our Pompeiian aristocrat who commissioned a mosaic of a long-past battle. This leads to the next section of our discussion, in which we can first ask if all of the images considered here, not just the Beni Hasan ones, can be considered daily life scenes. And, if they are, what does this say about the daily life and values of at least those members of the Egyptian elite who chose to decorate their tombs in this way?

Are all private images of war daily life scenes? The argument is not as strong outside of Beni Hasan because the degree of ambiguity present there is not so clear elsewhere. In both Old Kingdom examples we do seem to have ethnic wars or geographically specific wars of a sort, with Egyptians fighting against towns of people represented as Asiatics. In Inti we have something approaching a victory, with prisoners led off, though fighting continues. The same is true in the Middle Kingdom example of Intef, where we not only have a war between visually distinguished antagonists, but we also have the only example of a tomb owner himself even remotely related to the scene. But while these include more specificity, they also all retain a level of generality. Where are the labels? Where are the specific episodes, or elements of geography, that would distinguish particular fortress sackings from one another? The point is strengthened when we recall soldiers and sailors attacking non-pictured enemies. How can that illustrate something like one of the autobiographies?

To me, the maintenance of a level of ambiguity and generality in all of these scenes as well as the failure to correspond well to autobiographical texts makes it more probable that all of these scenes should be taken as some form of daily life scene, imagery in which timelessness mattered more than specific events—similarly to how much of the violent imagery functioned in royal tombs, as we have seen. This does not mean that Intef did not fight a town full of Asiatics and carry off its women. He may have, and that may have informed his choice to include this scene in his tomb. But the scene is utilized in his tomb in a way that allows it to stand as a perpetual war, providing the backdrop to the rhythm of his life and perhaps a symbolic statement about his own role in the violent domination of pharaonic Egypt. And perhaps we should not be surprised: this is, in fact, primarily what images do in tombs. To have pictures of war in tombs serve as reports of events would have required a notable change in the fundamental function of tomb imagery.

And what is the daily life thus depicted by these scenes? The most basic point, of course, is that it was violent. Violence in this way is shown to be normal. In early Middle Kingdom Beni Hasan, even civil war was apparently a more or less unremarkable background in the lives of the elite for generations.

Life as shown is also full of diverse peoples, physically distinguishable from one another, but the relationships between peoples and places is not straight-forward. Both Old Kingdom tomb scenes utilized visual stereotypes of groups of people; both of those instances seem to show attacks against peoples associated with the east. It is easy and probably correct to read these as attacks against Asiatic fortified places. In the tomb of Intef we saw that Egyptians and Nubians fought together on the same side, but also that they clearly fought against an ethnically homogeneous foe. Not so at Beni Hasan. There is ethnicity, and there is war, but we do not have an ethnic war in any of the Beni Hasan tombs. Everyone gives it, and everyone gets it, and the defenders of the forts look like subsets of the people attacking the forts. The relative absence of Libyans among the private imagery is also of note given their prominence, and the consistency of their visual representation, in triumph scenes in contemporary royal mortuary complexes. Taken collectively, the ethnic stereotypes in private violent scenes do fairly consistently show Asiatic peoples as victims and Nubians as more or less integrated into Egyptian society. But there are no hard and fast rules and Asiatics also appear in more pacific guises, and it would be a mistake to read a simple understanding of ethnicity or otherness into these images.

A final connection that may support the identification of war scenes with daily life scenes is the frequent relationship of the category as a whole with production. Daily life scenes show things being made, or grown, or otherwise acquired. The war scenes sometimes show the acquisition of human captives and it is quite possible that this was understood even when it was not shown; that one of the points of war was booty, which was part of a larger category of sustaining material goods for the afterlife of the deceased. Battle was never popular in imagery, but its inclusion need not and should not change our understanding of how tombs worked. Unlike the case with royal scenes of triumph, this is not a fundamentally different category of image and it does not allow us to draw dramatically new conclusions about the worldview of those who employed it.

Perhaps most surprising about imagery of violence in private tombs is that it stopped being used after the early Middle Kingdom: Amenemhat of Beni Hasan, in the reign of Senwosret I, is the last known person to commission such a picture. Military prowess would continue to be an important part of elite identity, as shown by autobiographies, and would in fact greatly increase in importance during the Eighteenth Dynasty of the New Kingdom. At that time scenes of daily life in tombs also continued to be utilized and even expanded. But there are no more pictures of war. This is unlikely to be just a matter of taste; while they were never common, such scenes were also well enough established as to not be odd. I would suggest, rather, that in the New Kingdom battle scenes did become places of glorifying individuals, as we have seen with Qadesh, but that this use elevated them above the sphere of daily life and made them unsuitable for private tombs.

Notes

1 Museo Archeologico Nazionale di Napoli 10020. Adam Eastland Art + Architecture/ Alamy Stock Photo.

2 The attribution rests in part on a much-cited statement by Pliny the Elder that there was a well-known Hellenistic painting of a battle between Alexander and Darius: John Bostock and H.T. Riley, *The Natural History: Pliny the Elder* (London: Taylor & Francis, 1855), Book XXXV, Chapter XXXVI, Section 110. There is a commonly accepted theory that wall paintings and mosaics from the Roman Period were often copied from or inspired by earlier Greek paintings. Though this assumption has become less satisfying over time, since it diverts attention from Roman accomplishments, several of its characteristics suggest that the Alexander Mosaic was indeed a copy of a Greek work; see: Ada Cohen, *The Alexander Mosaic: Stories of Victory and Defeat* (Cambridge: Cambridge University Press, 1997), 51–82.

3 For a detailed discussion of the possible different meanings of the Mosaic to its Pompeiian audience, see: Cohen, *The Alexander Mosaic: Stories of Victory and Defeat*, 187–199.

4 This includes such diverse treatments as Oliver Stone's movie *Alexander* (2004), which conflates several battles, to an oil painting of Issus by Rossi d'Providence that hangs in the graduate lounge of the Classics Department of Brown University.

5 For discussions of the meaning of tombs in ancient Egypt and how they functioned with regards to both the life and afterlife, see: Steven Snape, *Ancient Egyptian Tombs: The Culture of Life and Death* (Chichester and Malden, MA: Wiley-Blackwell, 2011). For an in-depth look at the decoration program of specifically Old Kingdom tombs, see: Yvonne Harpur, *Decoration in Egyptian Tombs of the Old Kingdom: Studies in Orientation and Scene Content* (London and New York: Routledge & Kegan Paul, 1987).

6 The balance between literal and symbolic significance is still a matter of debate. See: René van Walsem, "The Interpretation of Iconographic Programmes in Old Kingdom Elite Tombs of the Memphite Area. Methodological and Theoretical (Re)considerations," in *Proceedings of the Seventh International Congress of Egyptologists, Cambridge, 3–9 September 1995*, Ed. C.J. Eyre (Leuven: Peeters, 1998), 1205–1213.

7 For an agency-centered discussion of choice in Old Kingdom tomb plan and decoration, see: Deborah Vischak, "Agency in Old Kingdom Elite Tomb Programs: Traditions, Locations, and Variable Meanings," in *Dekorierte Grabanlagen im Alten Reich: Methodik und Interpretation*, Ed. Martin Fitzenreiter and Michael Herb (London: Golden House Publications, 2006), 255–276. One important factor she discusses is regional variation.

8 Some examples of non-combat images of soldiers include a handful of tombs at Asyut from the First Intermediate Period and early Middle Kingdom. That of Khety II (tomb 4) shows rows of marching soldiers and has a biographical inscription that mentions the war between Thebes and Herakleopolis: Mahmoud El-Khadragy, "The Decoration of the Rock-Cut Chapel of Khety II at Asyut," *Studien zur Altägyptischen Kultur* 37 (2008): 219–241. Numerous examples of naval expeditions include soldiers/sailors. Models of armies or military equipment are known from the early Middle Kingdom; the best known are the troops of Egyptian spearmen and Nubian bowmen from the tomb of Mesehti, also at Assiyut (both are now at the Cairo Museum, numbers JE30968 and JE30969).

9 An important discussion of regionalism and the conscious construction of communal identity using, in part, the style of art can be found in Deborah Vischak, *Community*

and Identity in Ancient Egypt: The Old Kingdom Cemetery at Qubbet el-Hawa (Cairo: Supreme Council of Antiquities, 2007).

10 Courtesy of the Australian Centre for Egyptology. Ann McFarlane, *Mastabas at Saqqara. Kaiemheset, Kaipunesut, Kaiemsenu, Sehetepu and Others* (Oxford: Aris and Phillips, 2003), pl. 48. See also Anna-Latifa Mourad, "Siege Scenes of the Old Kingdom," *The Bulletin of the Australian Centre for Egyptology* 22 (2011): 135–158.

11 This has been interpreted as showing a fortified place from a side-view: Brett H. Heagren, "The Art of War in Pharaonic Egypt: An Analysis of the Tactical, Logistic, and Operational Capabilities of the Egyptian Army (Dynasties XVII–XX)" (Master's Thesis, University of Auckland, 2010), 103. It is not so clear to me that this is an attempt to represent this wall from any particular aspect at all; the line serves clearly only to distinguish inside from outside. William Stevenson Smith, *Interconnections in the Ancient Near East: A Study of the Relationships Between the Arts of Egypt, the Aegean, and Western Asia* (New Haven, CT and London: Yale University Press, 1965), 149. A detailed discussion of the scene is provided in Regine Schulz, "Der Sturm auf die Festung: Gedanken zu einigen Aspekten des Kampfbildes im Alten Ägypten vor dem Neuen Reich," in *Krieg und Sieg: Narrative Wanddarstellungen von Altägypten bis ins Mittelalter; Internationales Kolloquium, 29–30. Juli 1997 im Schloß Haindorf, Langenlois*, Ed. Manfred Bietak and Mario Schwarz (Vienna: Verlag der Österreichischen Akademie der Wissenschaften, 2002), 25–28. Both Smith and Schulz identify the inhabitants as Asiatics.

12 Mourad, "Siege Scenes of the Old Kingdom," 136 addresses the ethnicity of the occupants of the town, with notes.

13 This has been variously dated to the Fifth and Sixth Dynasties, sometimes relying on the war scene itself as a dating tool. Since this type of scene is so rare, and the only other certain example from the Old Kingdom is itself not unambiguous of date, this is not a secure means of assessing date. Mourad, "Siege Scenes of the Old Kingdom," 139–140.

14 Courtesy of the Australian Centre for Egyptology. Naguib Kanawati and Ann McFarlane, *Deshasha: The Tombs of Inti, Shedu and Others* (Sydney: The Australian Centre for Egyptology, 1993), pl. 27.

15 This interpretation, though uncomfortable as it is unparalleled in Egyptian art, has also been suggested by Mourad, "Siege Scenes of the Old Kingdom," 143 and Kanawati and McFarlane, *Deshasha: The Tombs of Inti, Shedu and Others*, 25.

16 An alternate explanation, argued for by both Herbert Senk, "Zur Darstellung der Sturmleiter in der Belagerungsszene des Kaemhesit," *Annales du Service des antiquités de l'Égypte* 54, no. 2 (1957): 210; and Schulz, "Der Sturm auf die Festung," 27, is that these figures are in some way securing the mobile ladder shown immediately to their left.

17 See Mourad, "Siege Scenes of the Old Kingdom," 143–144 and notes there; Kanawati and McFarlane, *Deshasha: The Tombs of Inti, Shedu and Others*, 25, pl. 26.

18 The most complete discussion is that of Michael R. Jenkins, "Notes on the Tomb of Setka at Qubbet el-Hawa," *The Bulletin of the Australian Centre for Egyptology* 11 (2000): 67–81, pls. 13–19. I am grateful to Deborah Vischak for providing me a photograph she took of this wall.

19 Henry George Fischer, "The Nubian Mercenaries of Gebelein During the First Intermediate Period," *Kush* 9 (1961): 62–63. Examples from Giza can be found in: Hermann Junker, *Giza II: Grabungen auf dem Friedhof des Alten Reiches bei den Pyramiden von Giza: Band II: die Maṣṭabas der beginnenden V. Dynastie auf dem Westfriedhof* (Wien and Leipzig: Hölder-Pichler-Tempsky, 1934), fig. 28 (right side); Hermann Junker, *Giza III: Grabungen auf dem Friedhof des Alten Reiches bei den Pyramiden von Giza: Band III: die Mastabas der vorgeschrittenen V. Dynastie auf dem Westfriedhof* (Wien and Leipzig: Hölder-Pichler-Tempsky, 1938), fig. 27 (right side).

See Chapter 4, note 5. None of these wears the chevron armlet, and of course the depiction is entirely different from what we see at Setka.

20 Fischer, "The Nubian Mercenaries of Gebelein During the First Intermediate Period," 62.

21 Jenkins, "Notes on the Tomb of Setka at Qubbet el-Hawa," 69 develops this argument and gives citations for others who have dated the tomb to the First Intermediate Period.

22 Vischak, "Agency in Old Kingdom Elite Tomb Programs," 273–276.

23 Copyright: The Asyut Project; drawing: Ilona Regulski. Jochem Kahl et al., "The Asyut Project: Fourth Season of Fieldwork (2006)," *Studien zur Altägyptischen Kultur* 36 (2007): 91, fig. 2.

24 Kahl et al., "The Asyut Project: Fourth Season of Fieldwork (2006)," 82.

25 The text was originally published by Jacques Vandier, *Mo'alla: la tombe d'Ankhtifi et la tombe de Sébekhotep* (Cairo: Institut français d'archéologie orientale, 1950). A full translation of the autobiography into German was undertaken by Wolfgang Schenkel, *Memphis, Herakleopolis, Theben: die epigraphischen Zeugnisse der 7.–11. Dynastie Ägyptens* (Wiesbaden: Harrassowitz, 1965), 45–57. The first part of the autobiography has also been translated to English: Miriam Lichtheim, *Ancient Egyptian Literature. A Book of Readings, Volume I: The Old and Middle Kingdoms* (Berkeley, CA and London: University of California Press, 2006), 85–86.

26 Jacques Vandier, *Mo'alla: la tombe d'Ankhtifi et la tombe de Sébekhotep* (Cairo: Institut français d'archéologie orientale, 1950), 127–128, figs. 61–63.

27 The image is not shown here because the final publication of the tomb is currently in process of being finalized. A preliminary drawing was published in Mahmoud El-Khadragy, "Some Significant Features in the Decoration of the Chapel of Iti-Ibi-Iqer at Asyut," *Studien zur Altägyptischen Kultur* 36 (2007): 123, fig. 3.

28 El-Khadragy, "Some Significant Features in the Decoration of the Chapel of Iti-Ibi-Iqer at Asyut," 109.

29 El-Khadragy, "Some Significant Features in the Decoration of the Chapel of Iti-Ibi-Iqer at Asyut," 110.

30 The name of this general is variously transliterated Antef; the most proper transliteration is Jnj-jtj.f. The tomb has been published in the series Grabung im Asasif; the wall paintings are dealt with in volume 5 of this series: Brigitte Jaroš-Deckert, *Grabung im Asasif. 1963–1970. Band 5: das Grab des Jnj-Jtj.f. Die Wandmalereien der 11. Dynastie* (Mainz: Zabern, 1984).

31 A plan with the location of decorated elements is given by Jaroš-Deckert, *Das Grab des Jnj-Jtj*, pl. 12.

32 Painting by W. Ruhm. © German Archaeological Institute Cairo. Jaroš-Deckert, *Das Grab des Jnj-Jtj*, folding plate 1.

33 © German Archaeological Institute Cairo. Jaroš-Deckert, *Das Grab des Jnj-Jtj*, 27–30, pl. 14, 7a, folding plate 2.

34 Jaroš-Deckert, *Das Grab des Jnj-Jtj*, pl. 13.

35 Jaroš-Deckert interpreted the differences of the middle register to a different artistic hand: *Das Grab des Jnj-Jtj*, 27.

36 The images are published only as black and white line drawings, but the descriptions include mention of skin-color. Jaroš-Deckert, *Das Grab des Jnj-Jtj*, 28; the coding system she derived based on Munsell colors is not always applied, including to the men in this ship, making it somewhat difficult to compare skin color from different parts of this pillar. There is also the possibility that the skin color has decayed. Settgast noted that all the men in the top boat had a coat of red and all but the standing figure had speckles of darker color, which suggested they had had a second coat of paint, darker, applied: Jürgen Settgast, "Zu ungewöhnlichen Darstellungen von Bogenschützen," *Mitteilungen des Deutschen Archäologischen Instituts, Abteilung Kairo* 25 (1969): 136.

37 Settgast implies but does not state that this might be Intef himself, shown at an earlier stage of his career than on the pillar where he (presumably) receives prisoners

at the attack on the fortification. It raises the issue of how a tomb owner could have been actively included in such a scene at all. Jürgen Settgast, "Zu ungewöhnlichen Darstellungen von Bogenschützen," 136–138.

38 Jaroš-Deckert, *Das Grab des Jnj-Jtj*, 29.
39 Percy E. Newberry, *Beni Hasan: Part I* (London: The Egypt Exploration Fund, 1893); Percy E. Newberry, *Beni Hasan: Part II* (London: The Egypt Exploration Fund, 1894). Naguib Kanawati and Alexandra Woods, *Beni Hassan: Art and Daily Life in an Egyptian Province* (Cairo: Supreme Council of Antiquities, 2010): this publication was not intended to be comprehensive. It covers four tombs at the site, three of which include images of war. Tomb 14, belonging to Khnumhotep I and that also has images of war, is in much poorer condition and was not treated in their study.
40 A detailed discussion of the architectural variations in these tombs, grouping them into types, is given by Abdel-Ghaffar Shedid, *Die Felsgräber von Beni Hassan in Mittelägypten* (Mainz: Zabern, 1994), 16–22.
41 Courtesy of the Egypt Exploration Society. Newberry, *Beni Hasan: Part II*, pl. 5.
42 Newberry, *Beni Hasan: Part II*, 48.
43 This has been called a battering ram by various scholars. Yigael Yadin seems to have been the first in "Hyksos Fortifications and the Battering-Ram," *Bulletin of the American Schools of Oriental Research* 137 (1955): 31; and others have done so since, including Alan R. Schulman in "Siege Warfare in Pharaonic Egypt," *Natural History Magazine* 73, no. 3 (1964): 15. This is not a battering ram, and the action of attacking a fortress is not necessarily a siege. For a complete discussion of the pole and its likely use, see: Nicholas Wernick, "Once More unto the Breach: A Re-Evaluation of Beni Hasan's 'Battering Ram' and 'Glacis,'" *Zeitschrift für Ägyptische Sprache und Altertumskunde* 143, no. 1 (2016): 106–128. He takes the scenes to be useful commentary on battle tactics without assuming them to be particularly helpful historically.
44 Visible in Kanawati and Woods, *Beni Hassan: Art and Daily Life in an Egyptian Province*, fig. 72.
45 Courtesy of the Egypt Exploration Society. Newberry, *Beni Hasan: Part II*, pl. 15.
46 Kanawati and Woods, *Beni Hassan: Art and Daily Life in an Egyptian Province*, 49. Newberry, *Beni Hasan: Part II*, 3 thought they were so similar that Khety's must have been a copy of Baqt's.
47 Courtesy of the Australian Centre for Egyptology.
48 Punishment, often including beating, is a theme in other types of scenes at Beni Hasan as well.
49 See Shedid, *Die Felsgräber von Beni Hassan in Mittelägypten*, 6, fig. 7 for an image of the rainwater damage in this tomb.
50 Courtesy of the Egypt Exploration Society. Newberry, *Beni Hasan: Part I*, pl. 47.
51 Shedid, *Die Felsgräber von Beni Hassan in Mittelägypten*, 32.
52 Shedid, *Die Felsgräber von Beni Hassan in Mittelägypten*, 32, 71.
53 Susan Cohen, "Interpretative Uses and Abuses of the Beni Hasan Tomb Painting," *Journal of Near Eastern Studies* 74, no. 1 (2015): 19–38.
54 Newberry, *Beni Hasan: Part I*, 24–27, pl. 8.
55 Courtesy of the Egypt Exploration Society. Newberry, *Beni Hasan: Part I*, pl. 14.
56 Shedid, *Die Felsgräber von Beni Hassan in Mittelägypten*, 68.
57 Courtesy of the Australian Centre for Egyptology.
58 Angela Tooley, "Middle Kingdom Burial Customs: A Study of Wooden Models and Related Material. Volume I" (PhD thesis, University of Liverpool, 1989), 142–166.
59 Courtesy of the Egypt Exploration Society. Newberry, *Beni Hasan: Part I*, pl. 16.
60 Courtesy of the Australian Centre for Egyptology.
61 Lichtheim, *Ancient Egyptian Literature*, 20.
62 Lichtheim, *Ancient Egyptian Literature*, 25.
63 Vandier, *Mo'alla: la tombe d'Ankhtifi et la tombe de Sébekhotep*, 185–215.

64 There were probably more from the First Intermediate Period, as suggested for instance by the tomb of Ankhtifi, with its martial autobiography and fragments of men shot with arrows.

65 Kanawati and Woods, *Beni Hassan: Art and Daily Life in an Egyptian Province*, 9, state this explicitly, but the assumption is implicit in the majority of discussions of the war scenes from Beni Hasan.

66 Newberry, *Beni Hasan: Part I*, 28.

67 Miriam Lichtheim, *Ancient Egyptian Autobiographies Chiefly of the Middle Kingdom: A Study and an Anthology* (Fribourg: Universitätsverlag Freiburg Schweiz Vandenhoeck & Ruprecht Göttingen, 1988), 138.

68 As Wernick, "Once More unto the Breach," 108, notes, even if we assume these scenes to illustrate successful episodes from the lives of the people whose tombs they decorate, we have no idea if the tomb owner attacked a town or defended a town.

69 Kanawati and Woods, *Beni Hassan: Art and Daily Life in an Egyptian Province*, 9.

9   Violence, power, ideology

On the left an *ankh*—the hieroglyph for life—labeled "Egypt Then." On the right, the *ankh* inverted, turned upside down and with a cord wrapped around its stem, becomes a noose: "Egypt Now." I encountered this cartoon on a blog that I have read regularly since Egypt erupted in 2011—*Egyptian Chronicles*. There, this graphic juxtaposition of the peace of ancient Egypt with the violence of modern Egypt illustrated a story on 23 May 2015 about the handing down of 105 death sentences.[1] One of these was to Muhammad Morsi, the recently deposed elected president of Egypt from the Muslim Brotherhood. That sentence has yet to be carried out, and issuing it might be seen as a sort of ideological display parallel to some of our imagery: the point was not the stated event itself nearly so much as to show that the current military leader of Egypt has the power to make such an event happen, and that the former president has no power to resist it.

The immediacy of the *ankh* icon, the simplicity of the picture, and the context within which I discovered the cartoon make this an extremely powerful visual statement about politics in modern Egypt, even though it relies on a simple and, as we have seen, erroneously ideal image of a non-violent past. Ancient Egypt was not all life. In fact, the ancient Egyptian ideal of their own society was to some degree defined by violence, not its absence, and this image itself would not have worked in ancient Egypt, for the concept of violence as a category that could be opposed to non-violence did not exist. However, I would not call this a misuse of the past. Rather, I would say that the cartoon as a whole is about the present and that to be effective it requires an immediately understandable reference to the past, though that reference itself need not be accurate, only immediately understood. The idea conveyed—that ongoing turmoil in Egypt in the wake of the January 25th Revolution is not only deadly but also heartbreakingly unEgyptian—is one I accept viscerally. I do not want to quibble about lack of peace in the past because I do not want to undercut the cry about lack of peace in the present. I think the image makes the point far more effectively than any more accurate or more complex image or set of words could do. To me, there is no better illustration that historical accuracy in imagery is a separate issue from the impact, importance, and perhaps we might even say "truths" from the perspective of a particular worldview, that a picture can convey. This theme of accuracy, and why it is a red herring unless our aim is to try to write history, is one of several that have recurred in this work and to that I turn in conclusion.

In part because the contexts within which violence as a part of the ancient Egyptian worldview was conveyed by images are themselves so different, no neat conclusions can be drawn about the totality of the material covered in this book. As such, I will not attempt to summarize the arguments presented above as to how imagery of violence worked in each individual context in which it was found; however, there are a few interpretive issues that cross contexts with which I would like to end. The "truths" conveyed by violent imagery in ancient Egypt in terms of royal ideology are quite simple, but worth highlighting. As noted above on the basis of the cartoon, we cannot end without returning to the issue of accuracy and why we should not stop asking about the relationship between events and images, even if we ought not use pictures to write history. I will reiterate my interpretation that ancient Egyptian triumph scenes were intentionally restricted to royal spheres, where they spoke to an audience that was part of the worldview on display. Finally, in noting how distant our own historical and emotional contexts are from those in which these images were made, I say that there is much we will never know, much we can never feel, when confronted with them.

The primary truth communicated by the images considered here, particularly in triumph scenes, was not complicated and has never been in doubt: that of a ritually violent king. No one else had the right or the ability to be shown smiting and trampling; the king had the obligation to be shown doing so. In this, he was not a charismatic individual nearly so much as the incarnation of an institution. Even if officials could appropriate the image in the Sinai, they did so within a state context, and the smiter shown was always the king. Kingship did not legitimize violence; violence needed no legitimacy, it was part of life. Rather, a monopoly on scripted types of violence legitimized the king. He was rightful king in part because he controlled the means of control. This was only one part of royal ideology and it is notable that other aspects of kingship that we might expect to be rendered with reference to violence, most notably the king's role as unifier of the Two Lands, are only very rarely communicated with this iconography.

The need to reflect and uphold royal truths, and more broadly the fact that all such images were used in contexts where they had to support the function of a space, meant that there was never a straightforward relationship between images and historical events. This is the case for every image in this book, ancient or modern, Old World or New. Discarding history in relation to these images would be no better than thinking them accurate reports, and we have seen over the course of this book two particular ways in which events must be allowed into the conversation. The first is the ways in which the images themselves claim to refer to events. This is separate from the accuracy of such references. Again and again we have seen historicism, the incorporation of specific elements that give an image a semblance of accuracy: numbers, names, and an iconography of foreigners that, while certainly characterized by stereotypes, was not as codified and static as it has often been assumed. We cannot trust those details as details, but we can trust that they were included meaningfully; that *seeming* like a report, at least in part, was needed in some contexts. The second point about history is a related but largely negative one. Because we cannot trust those details, and since we have relatively little additional information about war and violence from these periods, we have no way of knowing how audiences would have connected these pictures to events. That there was such a connection to real events seems clear; for instance, the only two kings who have given us images that couple smiting and the unification of Upper and Lower Egypt are Narmer, who might have waged wars of unification, and Nebhepetre Montuhotep, who almost certainly did. The significance of our inability to integrate imagery into history well will be returned to in the final paragraphs below.

The relationship of these images to events—real or ritual, accurately or inaccurately referenced in the image—differs based on type. It is hard to see how a trampling scene can be an accurate reflection of any event and there is no reason to think that was its purpose; it is at most a quite oblique allegorical rendering of an event in which a king hurt people, but perhaps should better be considered as lacking any referent in historical occurrences at all. Smiting scenes, on the other hand, could have represented real events, and the Libyan Family Scene is certainly one of our clearest indications that images were intended to carry specific references and resemble history. Even so, it really is impossible to read these possibly real events as the aftermath of individual battles, both because of the repetition of names and the inclusion of people of different stereotypes depicted simultaneously as enemies. If they reflect a reality, then that reality is deliberately cast as ritual killing, not martial killing.

Battle scenes seem to have played a fundamentally different role than triumph scenes in the periods studied here, and at least carried the potential to refer more accurately to a different type of event. Both kings and elite private individuals could show battle in their tombs. These scenes show a tension between the specific and general that, I have argued, allowed them to both reference events and tie those events into cycles of time and ritual; in this way they are parallel to triumph scenes. But neither in their imagery nor in their deployment are they otherwise very similar. Battle as a category, I think, even civil war, was not fraught or loaded with exceptional significance. It does not seem to have been asked to carry the ideologically heavy load of triumph scenes even in the royal tomb, and triumph is not, as far as the evidence allows us to see, presented as the conclusion to fighting.

The distribution of battle scenes as compared to that of triumph scenes suggests that they were neither as restricted nor as necessary as the more ideologically charged categories. Private people could put battle in their tombs, and did so, even in times when kingship was strong. This was no challenge to the king, even though such scenes were not used, as autobiographies were, to glorify the relationship between the deceased and his monarch. Some of our contexts either did not need or could not have battle scenes. There is no evidence they were ever carved in the landscape. With somewhat more caution, given issues of preservation, we note that they are not known from divine temples or on portable objects. The differences in the use and apparent meaning of battle and triumph scenes demonstrates how much the category "imagery of violence" is my own, and not intrinsic to the Egyptian material. However, considering them beside one another has helped clarify how each of them work.

If battle scenes—by virtue of being in elite tombs—were public, how much access to the much more loaded triumph scenes would most Egyptians have had, and was their restriction part of the way they functioned across the board, or only in particular contexts? I have argued cautiously above that there were restrictions on audience and visibility that were fundamental to the divine temple, to the jewelry that adorned a princess, and to the royal tomb, and have argued against seeing these images as primarily designed for a public audience. In fact, the most certainly circulated and accessible images discussed here are those—execration figures and mud stamp sealings—that are the least closely connected to the royal canon, those that are notable for the schematic and abbreviated way they reference captivity and ethnicity. While it seems to me not unlikely that iconic triumph scenes were seen by elite Egyptians—such as those serving as priests— or for that matter the artisans who crafted the images, such an audience does not seem the primary target of the pictures in any case: audience and addressee are not necessarily the same thing. What people thought of such statements of royal violence was probably largely secondary, and even those people most likely to come into contact with the images were very much part of the group that benefited by having the theory and practice of Egyptian kingship coincide.

The Sinai offers us the spectre of much more visible scenes carrying this ideological burden, and even hints that non-royal people could commission them. This might suggest that the idea of restriction within Egypt is not sound, but I think it is better interpreted as a sign of how different this context itself was. It had a built-in means of replication: the first Sinai smiting images come from the First Dynasty, during a period when changes with the media for their display were still occurring. From that point on, the image could have been copied from visible iterations, and indeed it is a much more static image in this location than in others, and its use ends earlier. The Sinai does not convince me that there was regular and dynamic interaction between Egyptians and smiting images outside of this location itself. It serves as a fitting reminder of how critical context was to all elements of the display of violent images: who commissioned them; what they looked like; what they showed; who saw them; to whom their message was directed; and even, I suggest, how they made their audience feel.

In our world, images of violence can cause intense emotional reactions, and we recognize that this is one reason why they are powerful. A visual allusion to Waterloo can lead to outrage, a political cartoon to anger and sadness, a beheading video to disgust and fear. The images both point to feelings we already had and intensify those feelings, bringing them to the fore at the moment we engage with the picture. They are disseminated and restricted with intent, as arguments made for or against particular power structures, and their effect on how we understand violence in our world lasts much longer than our viewing of the pictures. The ISIS beheading in particular illustrates these points. It is a deliberate icon that gains its power to revolt us through what it depicts, through its repetition, through our inability to avoid it, through our knowledge that what it shows really happens; it represents a much larger practice of violence in which the imposition of a worldview on others leads to death.

Our observation of Egyptian pictures is divorced from their original time and can include neither the kind of visceral emotional reactions nor the background knowledge that once made them effective. We lack the corroborative evidence to give us much understanding of the historical context in which we find pictures, and this book has argued that we cannot use the pictures themselves to build a reliable understanding of that context. This book has also argued that the variety of places where images of violence were shown, and the restrictions placed on them, means they were deliberately employed to convince different audiences of different things, contextually eliciting different emotions to different ends. That is the case at any given period, and across periods. Even if they can no longer disgust, excite, or comfort us, we can still marvel at the complexity of use of these rather simple pictures of harm.

Note

1 "It Is a Sign of Changing Times Indeed," *Egyptian Chronicles*, May 23, 2015, http://egyptianchronicles.blogspot.com/2015/05/it-is-sign-of-changing-times-indeed.html.

Bibliography

Abu Bakr, A.M., and Jürgen Osing. "Ächtungstexte aus dem Alten Reich." *Mitteilungen des Deutschen Archäologischen Instituts, Abteilung Kairo* 29 (1973): 97–133.

Adams, Barbara. *Ancient Hierakonpolis*. Warminster: Aris & Phillips, 1974.

Adams, Barbara. *Predynastic Egypt*. London: Shire Publications, 1988.

Adams, Barbara. "A Fragment from the Cairo Statue of Khasekhemwy." *Journal of Egyptian Archaeology* 76 (1990): 161–163.

AhramOnline. "Saudi Arabia May Stop Beheading Due to Swordsmen Shortages." March 10, 2013, http://english.ahram.org.eg/News/66531.aspx.

Alexander, Edward P. *Military Memoirs of a Confederate: A Critical Narrative*. New York: C. Scribner's Sons, 1907.

Allen, James P. *The Ancient Egyptian Pyramid Texts*, Writings from the Ancient World 23. Atlanta, GA and Leiden: Brill, 2005.

Amélineau, Émile. *Les nouvelles fouilles d'Abydos: compte rendu in extenso des fouilles, description des monuments et objets découverts, Vol. 1*. Paris: Ernest Leroux, 1899.

Anđelković, Branislav. "The Molding Power of Ideology: Political Transformations of Predynastic Egypt." *Issues in Ethnology and Anthropology, n.s.* 9, no. 3 (2014): 713–722.

Anselin, Alain. "Le scorpion et la rosette: essai de lecture des deux sémogrammes naga-déens." *Apuntes de Egiptología* 1 (2005): 15–33.

Appelbaum, Yoni. "The Great Illusion of Gettysburg." *The Atlantic*, February 5, 2012. www.theatlantic.com/national/archive/2012/02/the—great—illusion—of—gettysburg/238870/.

Arkell, Anthony. "Varia Sudanica." *The Journal of Egyptian Archaeology* 36 (1950): 24–40.

Arnold, Dieter from the notes of Herbert Winlock. *The Temple of Mentuhotep at Deir el Bahari*. New York: Metropolitan Museum of Art Egyptian Expedition, 1979.

Arnold, Dorothea, Christiane Ziegler, and Krzysztof Grzymski, Ed. *Egyptian Art in the Age of the Pyramids*. New York: Metropolitan Museum of Art, 1999.

Assmann, Jan. *The Mind of Egypt: History and Meaning in the Time of the Pharaohs*. Translated by Andrew Jenkins. Cambridge, MA: Harvard University Press, 2003.

Assmann, Jan. *Ma'at: Gerechtigkeit und Unsterblichkeit im Alten Ägypten*. 2nd ed. Munich: Beck, 2006.

Awady, Tarek El. *Abusir XVI: Sahure—The Pyramid Causeway: History and Decoration Program in the Old Kingdom*. Prague: Czech Institute of Egyptology, 2009.

Baines, John. "Temples as Symbols, Guarantors, and Participants in Egyptian Civilization." In *The Temple in Ancient Egypt: New Discoveries and Recent Research*, edited by Stephen Quirke, 216–241. London: British Museum Press, 1997.

Baines, John. "The Earliest Egyptian Writing: Development, Context, Purpose." In *The First Writing: Script Invention as History and Process*, edited by Stephen D. Houston, 150–189. Cambridge: Cambridge University Press, 2004.

Baines, John. "On Functions of Writing in Ancient Egyptian Pictorial Representation." In *Iconography without Texts*, edited by Paul Taylor, 95–126. London: Warburg Institute, 2008.

Baines, John, and Richard Parkinson. "An Old Kingdom Record of an Oracle? Sinai Inscription 13." In *Essays on Ancient Egypt in Honour of Herman te Velde*, edited by Jacobus van Dijk, 9–27. Groningen: Styx, 1997.

Bárta, Miroslav. "Borderland Dynamics in the Era of the Pyramid Builders in Egypt." In *Understanding Life in the Borderlands: Boundaries in Depth and Motion*, edited by William Zartman, 21–39. Athens, GA and London: The University of Georgia Press, 2010.

Bárta, Miroslav. "Kings, Viziers, and Courtiers: Executive Power in the Third Millennium BC." In *Ancient Egyptian Administration*, edited by Juan Carlos Moreno García, 153–175. Leiden: Brill, 2013.

Baumgartel, Elise. *The Cultures of Prehistoric Egypt II*. London: Oxford University Press, 1960.

Baumgartel, Elise. "About Some Ivory Statuettes from the 'Main Deposit' at Hierakonpolis." *Journal of the American Research Center in Egypt* 7 (1968): 7–14.

Bénédite, Georges. "Le couteau de Gebel el-'Arak: étude sur un nouvel objet préhistorique acquis par le Musée du Louvre." *Monuments et mémoires de la Fondation Eugène Piot* 22 (1916): 1–34.

Bestock, Laurel. "Brown University Abydos Project: Preliminary Report on the First Two Seasons." *Journal of the American Research Center in Egypt* 48 (2012): 35–79.

Bickel, Susanne. "Peace in the Ancient World: Concepts and Theories." In *Peace in the Ancient World: Concepts and Theories*, edited by Kurt A. Raaflaub, 43–66. Chichester and Malden, MA: John Wiley & Sons, 2016.

Bivar, A.D.H. *Cavalry Equipment and Tactics on the Euphrates Frontier*. Washington, DC: The Dumbarton Oaks Center for Byzantine Studies, 1972.

Blackmun, Barbara W. "Pair of Armcuffs." In *Benin Kings and Rituals: Court Arts from Nigeria*, edited by Barbara Plankensteiner, 352. Gent and Vienna: Snoeck and Kunsthistorisches Museum mit MVK und ÖTM, 2007.

Bochi, Patricia A. "Death by Drama: The Ritual of Damnatio Memoriae in Ancient Egypt." *Göttinger Miszellen* 171 (1999): 73–86.

Boehmer, Rainer. "Gebel-el-Arak und Gebel-el-Tarif-Griff: keine Fälschungen." *Mitteilungen des Deutschen Archäologischen Instituts, Abteilung Kairo* 47 (1991): 51–60.

Borchardt, Ludwig. *Das Grabdenkmal des Königs Ne-user-Re'*. Leipzig: J.C. Hinrichs'sche Buchhandlung, 1907.

Borchardt, Ludwig. *Das Grabdenkmal des Königs S'aḥu-Re (Band 2): die Wandbilder: Abbildungsblätter*. Leipzig: J.C. Hinrichs'sche Buchhandlung, 1913.

Borchardt, Ludwig. *Das Grabdenkmal des Königs S'aḥu-Re (Band 2): die Wandbilder: Text*. Leipzig: J.C. Hinrichs'sche Buchhandlung, 1913.

Borrmann, Linda. "Form Follows Function: der Zeichencharakter der altägyptischen Ächtungsfiguren." In *Bild: Ästhetik—Medium—Kommunikation. Beiträge des dritten Münchner Arbeitskreises Junge Ägyptologie (MAJA 3), 7. bis 9.12.2012*, edited by Gregor Neunert, Alexandra Verbovsek, and Kathrin Gabler, 103–117. Wiesbaden: Harrassowitz, 2014.

Bostock, John, and H.T. Riley. *The Natural History: Pliny the Elder*. London: Taylor & Francis, 1855.

Breasted, James Henry. *The Battle of Kadesh: A Study in the Earliest Known Military Strategy*. Chicago, IL: The University of Chicago Press, 1903.

Breyer, Francis. "Die Schriftzeugnisse des prädynastischen Königsgrabes U-j in Umm el-Qaab: Versuch einer Neuinterpretation." *Journal of Egyptian Archaeology* 88 (2002): 53–65.

Bussmann, Richard. *Die Provinztempel Ägyptens von der 0. bis zur 11. Dynastie*. Leiden: Brill, 2010.

Bussmann, Richard. "Local Traditions in Early Egyptian Temples." In *Egypt at Its Origins 3: Proceedings of the Third International Conference "Origin of the State: Predynastic and Early Dynastic Egypt," London, 27th July–1st August 2008*, edited by Renée Friedman and Peter Fiske, 747–762. Leuven: Peeters, 2011.

Canepa, Matthew P. "Technologies of Memory in Early Sasanian Iran: Achaemenid Sites and Sasanian Identity." *American Journal of Archaeology* 114 (2010): 563–96.

Case, Humphrey, and Joan Crowfoot Payne. "Tomb 100: The Decorated Tomb at Hierakonpolis." *Journal of Egyptian Archaeology* 48 (1962): 5–18.

Černý, Jaroslav. "Semites in Egyptian Mining Expeditions to Sinai." *Archív orientální* 7 (1935): 384–389.

Černý, Jaroslav, Alan H. Gardiner, and T. Eric Peet. *The Inscriptions of Sinai from Manuscripts of Alan H. Gardiner and T. Eric Peet. Part II: Translations and Commentary*. London: Egypt Exploration Society, 1955.

Chaloupka, George, and Northern Territory Museum of Arts and Sciences. *From Palaeoart to Casual Paintings: The Chronological Sequence of Arnhem Land Plateau Rock Art*. Darwin: Northern Territory Museum of Arts and Sciences, 1984.

Ciałowicz, Krzysztof. *Les têtes de massues des périodes prédynastique et archaïque dans la Vallée du Nil*. Warsaw: Nakładem Uniwersytetu Jagiellońskiego, 1987.

Ciałowicz, Krzysztof. *Les palettes egyptiennes aux motifs zoomorphes et sans décoration: études de l'art prédynastique*. Kraków: Uniwersytet Jagielloński, 1991.

Ciałowicz, Krzysztof. "Le manche de couteau de Gebel el-Arak: le problème de l'interprétation de l'art prédynastique." In *Essays in Honour of Prof. Dr. Jadwiga Lipińska*, edited by Joanna Aksamit, Monika Dolińska, Aleksandra Majewska, Andrzej Niwiński, Sławomir Rzepka, and Zbigniew Szafrański, 339–352. Warsaw: National Museum in Warsaw, 1997.

Ciałowicz, Krzysztof. "Le plus ancien témoignage de la tradition du heb-sed?" *Folia orientalia* 33 (1997): 39–48.

Ciałowicz, Krzysztof. *La naissance d'un royaume. l'Egypte des la période prédynastique a la fin de la 1ère dynastie*. Kraków: Jagiellonian University, 2001.

Ciałowicz, Krzysztof. "Early Egyptian Objects of Art." In *Tell el-Farkha I: Excavations 1998–2011*, edited by Marek Chłodnicki, Krzysztof Ciałowicz, and Agnieszka Mączyńska, 201–244. Kraków: Institute of Archaeology, Jagiellonian University, 2012.

Cohen, Ada. *The Alexander Mosaic: Stories of Victory and Defeat*. Cambridge: Cambridge University Press, 1997.

Cohen, Susan. "Interpretative Uses and Abuses of the Beni Hasan Tomb Painting." *Journal of Near Eastern Studies* 74, no. 1 (2015): 19–38.

Ćwiek, Andrzej. "Relief Decoration in the Royal Funerary Complexes of the Old Kingdom: Studies in the Development, Scene Content and Iconography." PhD dissertation, Warsaw University, 2003.

Daressy, Georges. "Chapelle de Mentouhotep III à Dendérah." *Annales du Service des antiquités de l'Égypte* 17 (1917): 226–236.

Darnell, John C. "The Rock Inscriptions of Tjehemau at Abisko." *Zeitschrift für Ägyptische Sprache und Altertumskunde* 130 (2003): 31–48.

Darnell, John C. "The Wadi of the Horus Qa-a: A Tableau of Royal Ritual Power in the Theban Western Desert." In *Egypt at Its Origins 3: Proceedings of the Third International Conference "Origin of the State. Predynastic and Early Dynastic Egypt," London, 27th July–1st August 2008*, edited by Renée Friedman and Peter Fiske, 1151–1194. Leuven: Uitgeverij Peeters en Departement Oosterse Studies, 2011.

Davis, Whitney. *Masking the Blow: The Scene of Representation in Late Prehistoric Egyptian Art*. Berkeley, CA: University of California Press, 1992.

de Morgan, Jacques. *Recherches sur les origines de l'Égypte: ethnographie préhistorique et tombeau royal de Négadah*. Paris: Ernest Leroux, 1897.

de Rachewiltz, Boris. "Scavi sulla via sacra di Unis." *Archivio Internazionale di Etnografia e Preistoria* 2 (1959): 35–42.

Dee, Michael W., David Wengrow, Andrew J. Shortland, Alice Stevenson, Fiona Brock, and Christopher Bronk Ramsey. "Radiocarbon Dating and the Naqada Relative Chronology." *Journal of Archaeological Science* 46 (2014): 319–323.

Dreyer, Günter. *Elephantine VIII: der Tempel der Satet: die Funde der Frühzeit und des Alten Reiches*. Mainz: Philipp von Zabern, 1986.

Dreyer, Günter. "Umm el-Qaab: Nachuntersuchungen im frühzeitlichen Königsfriedhof. 3./4. Vorbericht." *Mitteilungen des Deutschen Archäologischen Instituts, Abteilung Kairo* 46 (1990): 53–90.

Dreyer, Günter, Robert Hartmann, Ulrich Hartung, Thomas Hikade, Heidi Köpp, C. Lacher, Vera Müller, A. Nerlich, and Albert Zink. "Umm el-Qaab: Nachuntersuchungen im frühzeitlichen Königsfriedhof: 13./14./15. Vorbericht." *Mitteilungen des Deutschen Archäologischen Instituts, Abteilung Kairo* 59 (2003): 67–138.

Dreyer, Günter. *Umm el-Qaab I: das prädynastische Königsgrab U-j und seine frühen Schriftzeugnisse*. Mainz: Philipp von Zabern, 1998.

Dreyer, Günter, Ulrich Hartung, Thomas Hikade, E. Christiana Köhler, Vera Müller, and Frauke Pumpenmeier. "Umm el-Qaab: Nachuntersuchungen im frühzeitlichen Königsfriedhof: 9./10. Vorbericht." *Mitteilungen des Deutschen Archäologischen Instituts, Abteilung Kairo* 54 (1998): 77–167.

El-Khadragy, Mahmoud. "Some Significant Features in the Decoration of the Chapel of Iti-Ibi-Iqer at Asyut." *Studien zur Altägyptischen Kultur* 36 (2007): 105–135.

El-Khadragy, Mahmoud. "The Decoration of the Rock-Cut Chapel of Khety II at Asyut." *Studien zur Altägyptischen Kultur* 37 (2008): 219–241.

Erman, Adolf, and Hermann Grapow. *Wörterbuch der ägyptischen Sprache, Band 3*. Leipzig: J.C. Hinrichs'sche Buchhandlung, 1929.

Espinel, Andrés Diego. "Blocks from the Unas Causeway Recorded in Černý's Notebooks at the Griffith Institute, Oxford." In *Old Kingdom, New Perspectives*, edited by Nigel Strudwick and Helen Strudwick, 50–64. Oxford and Oakville, ON: Oxbow Books, 2011.

Espinel, Andrés Diego. "A Newly Identified Old Kingdom Execration Text." In *Decorum and Experience: Essays in Ancient Culture for John Baines*, edited by Elizabeth Frood and Angela McDonald, 26–33. Oxford: Griffith Institute, 2013.

Etienne, Marc. "À propos des représentations d'enceintes crénelées sur les palettes de l'époque de Nagada III." *Archéo-Nil* 9 (1999): 149–163.

Finegold, Andrew. "Battle Murals: Violence, Representation, and Time in Epiclassic Mesoamerica." Paper presented at the conference The Art of War at Brown University, Providence, Rhode Island, November 7, 2015.

Finkenstaedt, Elizabeth. "The Location of Styles in Painting: White Cross-Lined Ware at Naqada." *Journal of the American Research Center in Egypt* 18 (1981): 7–10.

Fischer, Henry George. "Eleventh Dynasty Relief Fragments from Deir el Bahri." *Yale Art Gallery Bulletin* 24, no. 2 (1958): 28–38.

Fischer, Henry George. "The Nubian Mercenaries of Gebelein During the First Intermediate Period." *Kush* 9 (1961): 44–80.

Fischer, Henry George. "Varia Aegyptiaca." *Journal of the American Research Center in Egypt* 2 (1963): 15–51.

Friedman, Renée. "Excavating Egypt's Early Kings: Recent Discoveries in the Elite Cemetery at Hierakonpolis." In *Egypt at Its Origins 2: Proceedings of the International Conference "Origin of the State: Predynastic and Early Dynastic Egypt," Toulouse (France), 5th–8th September 2005*, edited by Béatrix Midant-Reynes, Yann Tristant, Stan Hendrickx, and Joanne Rowland, 1157–1194. Leuven: Peeters Publishers, 2008.

Friedman, Renée. "The Early Royal Cemetery at Hierakonpolis: An Overview." In *Recent Discoveries and Latest Researches in Egyptology: Proceedings of the First Neapolitan Congress of Egyptology. Naples, June 18th–20th 2008*, edited by Francesco Raffaele, Massimiliano Nuzzolo, and Ilaria Incordino, 67–85. Wiesbaden: Harrassowitz Verlag, 2010.

Gaballa, G.A. *Narrative in Egyptian Art*. Mainz am Rhein: Philipp von Zabern, 1976.

Galassi, Giuseppe. "L'arte del più antico Egitto nel Museo di Torino: preistoria e proto-storia mediterranea." *Rivista dell'Istituto Nazionale d'Archeologia e Storia dell'Arte*, Nuova Serie 4 (1955): 5–94.

Gardiner, Alan H., T. Eric Peet, and Jaroslav Černý. *The Inscriptions of Sinai. Part I: Introduction and Plates*. 2nd ed. London: Egypt Exploration Society, 1952.

Gautier, Patrick. "Analyse de l'espace figuratif par dipôles: la tombe décorée No. 100 de Hiérakonpolis." *Archéo-Nil* 3 (1993): 35–47.

Gautier, Patrick, and Béatrix Midant-Reynes. "La tête de massue du roi Scorpion." *Archéo-Nil* 5 (1995): 87–127.

Giannese, Alberto. "Conflict-Related Representations in the 4th Millennium Egypt. A Study on Ideology of Violence." Master's thesis, University College London, 2012.

Gilbert, Gregory. *Weapons, Warriors and Warfare in Early Egypt*. Oxford: Archaeopress, 2004.

Giveon, Raphael. "A Second Relief of Sekhemkhet in Sinai." *Bulletin of the American Schools of Oriental Research* 216 (1974): 17–20.

Göbl, Robert. *Sasanian Numismatics*. Braunschweig: Klinkhardt & Biermann, 1971.

Godron, Gérard. "À propos d'une inscription de l'Horus Khâsékhem." *Chronique d'Égypte* 43, no. 85 (1968): 34–35.

Goedicke, Hans. *Re-Used Blocks from the Pyramid of Amenemhet I at Lisht*. New York: Metropolitan Museum of Art Egyptian Expedition, 1972.

Goelet, Ogden. "Kemet and Other Egyptian Terms for Their Land." In *Ki Baruch Hu: Ancient Near Eastern, Biblical, and Judaic Studies in Honor of Baruch A. Levine1*, edited by Robery Chazan, 23–42. Winona Lake, IN: Eisenbrauns, 1999.

Graff, Gwenola. *Les peintures sur vases de Nagada I—Nagada II: nouvelle approche sémiologique de l'iconographie prédynastique*. Leuven: Leuven University Press, 2009.

Grajetzki, Wolfram. *The Middle Kingdom of Ancient Egypt.* London: Duckworth, 2006.

Habachi, Labib. "King Nebhepetre Menthuhotp: His Monuments, Place in History, Deification and Unusual Representation in the Form of Gods." *Mitteilungen des Deutschen Archäologischen Instituts, Abteilung Kairo* 19 (1963): 16–52.

Hafemann, Ingelore. "Ägyptens Beziehungen zum Sinai in pharaonischer Zeit." In *Antiker Orient: Landeskunde, Archäologie, Epigraphik; Beiträge anläßlich einer Tagung in Potsdam-Hermannswerder am 20. und 21. Januar 1995,* edited by Christian Tietze, 1–14. Potsdam: Universität Potsdam, Historisches Institut, 1996.

Hagen, Fredrik. "Local Identities." In *The Egyptian World,* edited by Toby Wilkinson, 242–251. London and New York: Routledge, 2007.

Harpur, Yvonne. *Decoration in Egyptian Tombs of the Old Kingdom: Studies in Orientation and Scene Content.* London and New York: Routledge & Kegan Paul, 1987.

Harris, James. "A New Fragment of the Battlefield Palette." *Journal of Egyptian Archaeology* 46 (1960): 104–105.

Hartung, Ulrich. "Hippopotamus Hunters and Bureaucrats: Elite Burials at Cemetery U." In *Recent Discoveries and Latest Researches in Egyptology: Proceedings of the First Neapolitan Congress of Egyptology. Naples, June 18th–20th 2008,* edited by Francesco Raffaele, Massimiliano Nuzzolo, and Ilaria Incordino, 107–120. Wiesbaden: Harrassowitz Verlag, 2010.

Hawass, Zahi, and Miroslav Verner. "Newly Discovered Blocks from the Causeway of Sahure." *Mitteilungen des Deutschen Archäologischen Instituts, Abteilung Kairo* 52 (1996): 177–186.

Hayes, William C. *The Scepter of Egypt: A Background for the Study of the Egyptian Antiquities in The Metropolitan Museum of Art. Vol. 1, From the Earliest Times to the End of the Middle Kingdom.* New York: Metropolitan Museum of Art, 1978.

Heagren, Brett H. "The Art of War in Pharaonic Egypt: An Analysis of the Tactical, Logistic, and Operational Capabilities of the Egyptian Army (Dynasties XVII–XX)." Master's Thesis, University of Auckland, 2010.

Heagy, Thomas C. "Who Was Menes?" *Archéo-Nil* 24 (2014): 59–92.

Helck, Wolfgang. "Maat." In *Lexikon der Ägyptologie, Band III,* edited by Wolfgang Helck and Eberhard Otto, columns 1110–1119. Wiesbaden: Harrassowitz, 1981.

Helck, Wolfgang, and Eberhard Otto. "Buto." In *Lexikon der Ägyptologie, Band I,* edited by Wolfgang Helck and Eberhard Otto, 887–889. Wiesbaden: Harrassowitz, 1975.

Helck, Wolfgang, and Eberhard Otto. "Djebaut." In *Lexikon der Ägyptologie, Band I,* edited by Wolfgang Helck and Eberhard Otto, 1098–1099. Wiesbaden: Harrassowitz, 1975.

Hendrickx, Stan. "The Relative Chronology of the Naqada Culture: Problems and Possibilities." In *Aspects of Early Egypt,* edited by Jeffrey Spencer, 36–69. London: British Museum Press, 1996.

Hendrickx, Stan. "Peaux d'animaux comme symboles prédynastiques. À propos de quelques représentations sur les vases White Cross-lined." *Chronique d'Égypte* 73 (1998): 203–230.

Hendrickx, Stan. "Arguments for an Upper Egyptian Origin of the Palace-Facade and the Serekh during Late Predynastic-Early Dynastic Times." *Göttinger Miszellen* 184 (2001): 85–110.

Hendrickx, Stan. "Iconography of the Predynastic and Early Dynastic Periods." In *Before the Pyramids,* edited by Emily Teeter, 75–82. Chicago, IL: The Oriental Institute of the University of Chicago, 2011.

Hendrickx, Stan, and Merel Eyckerman. "Continuity and Change in the Visual Representations of Predynastic Egypt." In *Recent Discoveries and Latest Researches in Egyptology: Proceedings of the First Neapolitan Congress of Egyptology. Naples, June 18th–20th 2008*, edited by Francesco Raffaele, Massimiliano Nuzzolo, and Ilaria Incordino, 121–144. Wiesbaden: Harrassowitz Verlag, 2010.

Hendrickx, Stan, and Merel Eyckerman. "Visual Representation and State Development in Egypt." *Archéo-Nil* 22 (2012): 23–71.

Hendrickx, Stan, Nabil Swelim, Francesco Raffaele, Merel Eyckerman, and Renée Friedman. "A Lost Late Predynastic–Early Dynastic Royal Scene from Gharb Aswan." *Archéo-Nil* 19 (2009): 169–178.

Herrmann, Georgina. *Naqsh-I Rustam 5 and 8: Sasanian Reliefs Attributed to Hormuzd II and Narseh*. Berlin: Dietrich Reimer Verlag, 1977.

Heuzey, Léon. "Un prototype des taureaux de Mycènes et d'Amyclées (Pl. I)." *Bulletin de correspondance hellénique* 16, no. 1 (1892): 307–319.

Hornung, Erik. "Maat—Gerechtigkeit für alle? Zur altägyptischen Ethik." In *Wegkreuzungen/ Crossroads/La croisée des chemins*, edited by Rudolf Ritsema, 385–427. Frankfurt am Main: Eranos Foundation Ascona, 1988.

Howley, Kathryn. "A Re-Examination of Early 'Sed Festival' Representations." Paper presented at the annual meeting for the American Research Center in Egypt, Providence, Rhode Island, April 27, 2012.

Huang, Reyko. "The Islamic State as an Ordinary Insurgency." *Washington Post*, May 14, 2015. www.washingtonpost.com/blogs/monkey-cage/wp/2015/05/14/how-the-islamic-state-compares-with-other-armed-non-state-groups/?wpisrc=nl_cage&wpmm=1.

Huyge, Dirk. "The Painted Tomb, Rock Art and the Recycling of Predynastic Egyptian Imagery." *Archéo-Nil* 24 (2014): 93–102.

Ibrahim, Moustafa Resk, and Pierre Tallet. "Trois bas-reliefs de l'époque thinite au Ouadi el-Humur: aux origines de l'exploitation du Sud-Sinaï par les Égyptiens." *Revue d'Égyptologie* 59 (2008): 155–180.

Ibrahim, Moustafa Resk, and Pierre Tallet. "King Den in South-Sinai: The Earliest Monumental Rock Inscriptions of the Pharaonic Period." *Archéo-Nil* 19 (2009): 179–184.

"It Is a Sign of Changing Times Indeed." *Egyptian Chronicles*, May 23, 2015. http://egyptian chronicles.blogspot.com/2015/05/it-is-sign-of-changing-times-indeed.html.

Iversen, Erik. *Canon and Proportions in Egyptian Art*. 2nd ed. Warminster: Aris & Phillips, 1975.

Jánosi, Peter. *The Pyramid Complex of Amenemhat I at Lisht: The Reliefs*. New York, New Haven, CT: Metropolitan Museum of Art, Yale University Press, 2016.

Jaroš-Deckert, Brigitte. *Grabung im Asasif. 1963–1970. Band 5: das Grab des Jnj-Jtj.f. Die Wandmalereien der 11. Dynastie*. Mainz: Zabern, 1984.

Jenkins, Michael R. "Notes on the Tomb of Setka at Qubbet el-Hawa." *The Bulletin of the Australian Centre for Egyptology* 11 (2000): 67–81.

Jéquier, Gustave. "Les talismans *ankh* et *shen*." *Bulletin de l'Institut français d'archéologie orientale* 11 (1914): 121–143.

Jéquier, Gustave. *Fouilles à Saqqarah: le monument funéraire de Pepi II. Tome II: le temple*. Cairo: Institut français d'archéologie oriental du Caire, 1938.

Jéquier, Gustave. *Douze ans de fouilles dans la nécropole memphite 1924–1936*. Neuchatel: Secrétariat de l'Université, 1940.

Jéquier, Gustave. *Fouilles à Saqqarah: le monument funéraire de Pepi II. Tome III: les approches du temple*. Cairo: Institut français d'archéologie oriental du Caire, 1940.

Jiménez-Serrano, Alejandro. *Royal Festivals in the Late Predynastic Period and the First Dynasty.* Oxford: Archaeopress, 2002.

Jucha, Mariusz A. "New Protodynastic Serekhs from the Nile Delta: The Case of Finds from Tell El-Farkha." *Polish Archaeology in the Mediterranean (Research 2009)* 21 (2012): 625–641.

Junker, Hermann. *Giza II: Grabungen auf dem Friedhof des Alten Reiches bei den Pyramiden von Giza: Band II: die Maṣṭabas der Beginnenden V. Dynastie auf dem Westfriedhof.* Wien and Leipzig: Hölder-Pichler-Tempsky, 1934.

Junker, Hermann. *Giza III: Grabungen auf dem Friedhof des Alten Reiches bei den Pyramiden von Giza: Band III: die Mastabas der vorgeschrittenen V. Dynastie auf dem Westfriedhof.* Wien and Leipzig: Hölder-Pichler-Tempsky, 1938.

Junker, Hermann. "Die Feinde auf dem Sockel der Chasechem-Statuen und die Darstellung von geopferten Tieren." In *Ägyptologische Studien,* edited by O. Firchow, 162–175. Berlin: Akademie-Verlag, 1955.

Kahl, Jochem, Tine Bagh, Eva-Maria Engel, and Susanne Petschel. "Die Funde aus dem 'Menesgrab' in Naqada: ein Zwischenbericht." *Mitteilungen des Deutschen Archäologischen Instituts, Abteilung Kairo* 57 (2001): 171–185.

Kahl, Jochem, Mahmoud El-Khadragy, Ursula Verhoeven, and Monika Zöller. "The Asyut Project: Fourth Season of Fieldwork (2006)." *Studien zur Altägyptischen Kultur* 36 (2007): 81–103.

Kaiser, Werner. "Zur inneren Chronologie der Naqadakultur." *Archaeologia Geographica* 6 (1957): 69–77.

Kanawati, Naguib, and Ann McFarlane. *Deshasha: The Tombs of Inti, Shedu and Others.* Sydney: The Australian Centre for Egyptology, 1993.

Kanawati, Naguib, and Alexandra Woods. *Beni Hassan: Art and Daily Life in an Egyptian Province.* Cairo: Supreme Council of Antiquities, 2010.

Kaplony, Peter. *Die Inschriften der ägyptischen Frühzeit.* Wiesbaden: Harrassowitz, 1963.

Kemp, Barry. "Photographs of the Decorated Tomb at Hierakonpolis." *Journal of Egyptian Archaeology* 59 (1973): 36–43.

Kemp, Barry. *Ancient Egypt: Anatomy of a Civilization.* 2nd Revised ed. London: Routledge, 2006.

Köhler, E. Christiana. "History or Ideology? New Reflections on the Narmer Palette and the Nature of Foreign Relations in Pre- and Early Dynastic Egypt." In *Egypt and the Levant: Interrelations from the 4th through the Early 3rd Millennium BCE,* edited by Edwin C.M. van den Brink and Thomas E. Levy, 499–513. London and New York: Leicester University Press, 2002.

Köhler, E. Christiana. "Theories of State Formation." In *Egyptian Archaeology,* edited by Willeke Wendrich, 36–54. Chichester, West Sussex: Wiley-Blackwell, 2010.

Kousoulis, Panagiotis. "Egyptian vs. Otherness and the Issue of Acculturation in the Egyptian Demonic Discourse of the Late Bronze Age." In *Athanasia: The Earthly, the Celestial and the Underworld in the Mediterranean from the Late Bronze and the Early Iron Age,* edited by Nicholas Chr. Stampolidis, Athanasia Kanta, and Angeliki Giannikouri, 129–139. Herakleion: University of Crete, 2012.

Labrousse, Audran, and Jean-Philippe Lauer. *Les complexes funéraires d'Ouserkaf et de Néferthétepès. Volume 1.* Cairo: Institut français d'archéologie oriental du Caire, 2000.

Labrousse, Audran, and Jean-Philippe Lauer. *Les complexes funéraires d'Ouserkaf et de Néferthétepès. Volume 2.* Cairo: Institut français d'archéologie oriental du Caire, 2000.

Labrousse, Audran, Jean-Philippe Lauer, and Jean Leclant. *Mission archéologique de Saqqarah II: le temple haut du complexe funéraire du roi Ounas*. Cairo: Institut français d'archéologie orientale du Caire, 1977.

Labrousse, Audran, and Ahmed Moussa. *Le temple d'accueil du complexe funéraire du roi Ounas*. Cairo: Institut français d'archéologie orientale du Caire, 1996.

Labrousse, Audran, and Ahmed Moussa. *La chaussée du complexe funéraire du roi Ounas*. Cairo: Institut français d'archéologie orientale du Caire, 2002.

Leclant, Jean. "La 'famille libyenne' au temple haut de Pépi Ier." In *Livre du centenaire 1880–1980*, edited by Jean Vercoutter, 49–54. Cairo: Institut français d'archéologie orientale du Caire, 1980.

Lepsius, Richard. *Denkmäler aus Ägypten und Äthiopien*, 12 volumes. Berlin: Nicolaische Buchhandlung, 1849–1856.

Lichtheim, Miriam. *Ancient Egyptian Autobiographies Chiefly of the Middle Kingdom: A Study and an Anthology*. Fribourg: Universitätsverlag Freiburg Schweiz Vandenhoeck & Ruprecht Göttinge, 1988.

Lichtheim, Miriam. *Ancient Egyptian Literature. A Book of Readings, Volume I: The Old and Middle Kingdoms*. Berkeley, CA and London: University of California Press, 2006.

Luiselli, Maria Michela. "The Ancient Egyptian Scene of 'Pharaoh Smiting His Enemies': An Attempt to Visualize Cultural Memory?" In *Cultural Memory and Identity in Ancient Societies*, edited by Martin Bommas, 10–24. London and New York: Continuum International, 2011.

Macadam, M.F. Laming. *The Temples of Kawa II: History and Archaeology of the Site*. Oxford: Oxford University Press, 1955.

McDermott, Bridget. *Warfare in Ancient Egypt*. Stroud: Sutton, 2004.

McFarlane, Ann. *Mastabas at Saqqara. Kaiemheset, Kaipunesut, Kaiemsenu, Sehetepu and Others*. Oxford: Aris and Phillips, 2003.

McVicker, Donald. "Images of Violence in Mesoamerican Mural Art." In *Latin American Indigenous Warfare and Ritual Violence*, edited by Richard J. Chacon and Rubén G. Mendoza, 73–90. Tucson, AZ: The University of Arizona Press, 2007.

Marochetti, Elisa Fiore. *The Reliefs of the Chapel of Nebhepetre Mentuhotep at Gebelein*. Leiden, Boston, MA: Brill, 2010.

Mawdsley, Lisa. "Two Labels of Aha: Evidence of a Pre-Mortuary Administrative Function for First Dynasty Potmarks?" *Cahiers Caribéens d'Egyptologie* 15 (2011): 51–68.

Mekhennet, Souad, and Adam Goldman. "'Jihadi John': Islamic State Killer Is Identified as Londoner Mohammed Emwazi." *Washington Post*, February 25, 2015. www.washingtonpost.com/world/national-security/jihadi-john-the-islamic-state-killer-behind-the-mask-is-a-young-londoner/2015/02/25/d6dbab16-bc43-11e4-bdfa-b8e8f594e6ee_story.html.

Meurer, Georg. *Nubier in Ägypten bis zum Beginn des Neuen Reiches: zur Bedeutung der Stele Berlin 14753*. Berlin: Achet, 1996.

Midant-Reynes, Béatrix. *The Prehistory of Egypt: From the First Egyptians to the First Pharaohs*. Oxford and Malden, MA: Wiley-Blackwell, 2000.

Millet, Nicholas. "The Narmer Macehead and Related Objects." *Journal of the American Research Center in Egypt* 27 (1990): 53–59.

Millet, Nicholas. "The Narmer Macehead and Related Objects: [Correction]." *Journal of the American Research Center in Egypt* 28 (1991): 223–225.

Moreno García, Juan Carlos. "War in Old Kingdom Egypt (2686–2125 BCE)." In *Studies on War in the Ancient Near East: Collected Essays on Military History*, edited by Jordi Vidal, 5–41. Münster: Ugarit-Verlag, 2010.

Morenz, Ludwig D. *Die Zeit der Regionen im Spiegel der Gebelein-Region: kulturge-schichtliche Re-Konstruktionen*. Leiden: Brill, 2010.

Morris, Ellen F. "Sacrifice for the State: First Dynasty Royal Funerals and the Rites at Macramallah's Rectangle." In *Performing Death: Social Analyses of Funerary Traditions in the Ancient Near East and Mediterranean*, edited by Nicola Laneri, 15–37. Chicago, IL: Oriental Institute of the University of Chicago, 2007.

Mourad, Anna-Latifa. "Siege Scenes of the Old Kingdom." *The Bulletin of the Australian Centre for Egyptology* 22 (2011): 135–158.

Muhlestein, Kerry. "Execration Ritual." In *UCLA Encyclopedia of Egyptology*, edited by Willeke Wendrich and Jacco Dieleman, http://digital2.library.ucla.edu/viewItem. do?ark=21198/zz000s3mqr. Los Angeles, CA: UCLA, 2008.

Muhlestein, Kerry. *Violence in the Service of Order: The Religious Framework for Sanctioned Killing in Ancient Egypt*. Oxford: Archaeopress, 2011.

Müller, Hans Wolfgang, and Ernst Kofler-Truniger. *Ägyptische Kunstwerke: Kleinfunde und Glas in der Sammlung E. und Kofler-Truniger, Luzern*. Münchner Ägyptologische Studien 5. Berlin: Verlag Bruno Hessling, 1964.

Mumford, Gregory. "Wadi Maghara." In *The Encyclopedia of the Archaeology of Ancient Egypt*, edited by Kathryn Bard and Steven Shubert, 875–878. London: Routledge, 1998.

Murnane, William J. "The Gebel Sheikh Suleiman Monument: Epigraphic Remarks." In "The Metropolitan Museum Knife Handle and Aspects of Pharaonic Imagery before Narmer," edited by Bruce Williams and Thomas J. Logan. *Journal of Near Eastern Studies* 46 (1987): 282–285.

Naville, Edouard. *The XIth Dynasty Temple at Deir el-Bahari. Part I*. London: The Egypt Exploration Fund, 1907.

Needler, Winifred. *Predynastic and Archaic Egypt in the Brooklyn Museum*. Brooklyn, NY: The Brooklyn Museum, 1984.

Newberry, Percy E. *Beni Hasan: Part I*. London: The Egypt Exploration Fund, 1893.

Newberry, Percy E. *Beni Hasan: Part II*. London: The Egypt Exploration Fund, 1894.

Norton, Brooke. "Destruction of an Image: An Archaeological Examination of Ancient Egyptian Execration Figures." Master's thesis, New York University, 2013.

Nuzzolo, Massimiliano. "The 'Reserve Heads': Some Remarks on their Function and Meaning." In *Old Kingdom, New Perspectives: Egyptian Art and Archaeology 2750–2150 BC*, edited by Nigel Strudwick and Helen Strudwick, 200–215. Oxford: Oxbow Books, 2011.

O'Connor, David. "The Status of Early Egyptian Temples: An Alternative Theory." In *The Followers of Horus: Studies Dedicated to Michael Allen Hoffman*, edited by Renée Friedman and Barbara Adams, 83–98. Oxford: Oxbow Books, 1992.

O'Connor, David. *Ancient Nubia: Egypt's Rival in Africa*. Philadelphia, PA: The University Museum, University of Pennsylvania, 1993.

O'Connor, David. "The Dendereh Chapel of Nebhepetre Mentuhotep: A New Perspective." In *Studies on Ancient Egypt in Honour of H.S. Smith*, edited by Anthony Leahy and John Tait, 215–220. London: Egypt Exploration Society, 1999.

O'Connor, David. "Context, Function and Program: Understanding Ceremonial Slate Palettes." *Journal of the American Research Center in Egypt* 39 (2002): 5–25.

O'Connor, David. "The Narmer Palette: A New Interpretation." In *Before the Pyramids*, edited by Emily Teeter, 145–152. Chicago, IL: The Oriental Institute of the University of Chicago, 2011.

O'Connor, David. *The Old Kingdom Town at Buhen*, edited by Patricia Spencer. London: Egypt Exploration Society, 2014.

O'Connor, David. "An Expanding Worldview: Conquest, Colonization, and Coexistence." In *Ancient Egypt Transformed: The Middle Kingdom*, edited by Adela Oppenheim, Dorothea Arnold, Dieter Arnold, and Kei Yamamoto, 160–179. New Haven, CT and London: Yale University Press, 2015.

Oppenheim, Adela. "Appendix: Relief Decoration of the King's Temples and Queens' Chapels." In *The Pyramid Complex of Senwosret III at Dahshur: Architectural Studies*, edited by Dieter Arnold, 133–147. New York: The Metropolitan Museum of Art, 2002.

Oppenheim, Adela. "Decorative Programs and Architecture in the Pyramid Complexes of the Third and Fourth Dynasties." In *Structure and Significance: Thoughts on Ancient Egyptian Architecture*, edited by Peter János, 455–476. Vienna Austrian Academy of Sciences Press, 2005.

Oppenheim, Adela. "Aspects of the Pyramid Temple of Senwosret III at Dahshur: The Pharaoh and Deities." PhD dissertation, New York University, 2008.

Parcak, Sarah. "Egypt's Old Kingdom 'Empire' (?): A Case Study Focusing on South Sinai." In *Egypt, Israel, and the Ancient Mediterranean World: Studies in Honor of Donald B. Redford*, edited by Gary N. Knoppers and Antoine Hirsch, 41–60. Leiden, Boston, MA: Brill, 2004.

Partridge, Robert. *Fighting Pharaohs: Weapons and Warfare in Ancient Egypt*. Manchester: Peartree Publishing, 2002.

Patch, Diana Craig. *Dawn of Egyptian Art*. New York: Metropolitan Museum of Art, 2011.

Patch, Diana Craig. "Early Dynastic Art." In *Dawn of Egyptian Art*, 137–179. New York: Metropolitan Museum of Art, 2011.

Patch, Diana Craig. "From Land to Landscape." In *Dawn of Egyptian Art*, 21–81. New York: Metropolitan Museum of Art, 2011.

Payne, Joan Crowfoot. *Catalogue of the Predynastic Collection in the Ashmolean Museum*. Oxford: Clarendon Press, 1993.

Peck, William. "The Ordering of the Figure." In *A Companion to Ancient Egyptian Art*, edited by Melinda Hartwig, 360–374. Chichester, West Sussex: John Wiley & Sons, 2015.

Pérez Largacha, Antonio. "The Libyan Palette: A New Interpretation." *Varia Aegyptiaca* 5, no. 3 (1989): 217–226.

Petrie, W.M. Flinders. "Excavations at Hierakonpolis: The Earliest Monuments of Egyptian History." In *Egypt Exploration Fund Archaeological Report 1897–1898*, edited by Francis L. Griffith, 6–10. London: The Egypt Exploration Fund, 1898.

Petrie, W.M. Flinders. *The Royal Tombs of the First Dynasty. Part I*. London: The Egypt Exploration Fund, 1900–1901.

Petrie, W.M. Flinders. *The Royal Tombs of the Earliest Dynasties: Part II*. London: The Egypt Exploration Fund, 1901.

Petrie, W.M. Flinders. *The Making of Egypt*. London: Sheldon Press, 1939.

Pickett, George E. *Soldier of the South: General Pickett's War Letters to His Wife*. Edited by Arthur C. Inman. Boston, MA and New York: Houghton Mifflin Company, 1928.

Pittman, Holly. "Constructing Context: The Gebel el-Arak Knife. Greater Mesopotamian and Egyptian Interaction in the Late Fourth Millennium B.C.E." In *The Study of the Ancient Near East in the Twenty-First Century: The William Foxwell Albright Centennial Conference*, edited by Jerrold Cooper and Glenn Schwartz, 9–32. Winona Lake, IN: Eisenbrauns, 1996.

Posener, Georges. *Princes et pays d'Asie et de Nubie: textes hiératiques sur des figurines d'envoûtement du Moyen Empire*. Brussels: Fondation Égyptologique Reine Élisabeth, 1940.

Posener, Georges. *Cinq figurines d'envoûtement*. Cairo: Institut français d'archéologie oriental du Caire, 1987.

Posener-Kriéger, Paule, and Jean Louis de Cenival. *The Abu Sir Papyri, Hieratic Papyri in the British Museum. Fifth Series.* London: Trustees of the British Museum, 1968.

Prakash, Tara. "Shoulders, Knees, and Toes: The Bodies of the Prisoner Statues from Pepi I's Pyramid Complex." Paper presented at the annual meeting for the American Research Center in Egypt, Atlanta, Georgia, 2016.

Quack, Joachim Friedrich. "Some Old Kingdom Execration Figurines from the Teti Cemetery." *The Bulletin of the Australian Centre for Egyptology* 13 (2002): 149–160.

Quibell, James. "Slate Palette from Hierakonpolis." *Zeitschrift für Ägyptische Sprache und Altertumskunde* 36 (1898): 81–84.

Quibell, James. *Hierakonpolis: Part I*. London: Bernard Quaritch, 1900.

Quibell, James, and Frederick W. Green. *Hierakonpolis: Part II*. London: Bernard Quaritch, 1902.

Randall-MacIver, David, and Leonard C. Woolley. *Buhen: Volume II (Plates)*. Philadelphia, PA: University Museum, 1911.

Ratcliff, Rebecca. "Isis Tricked Victims into Appearing Calm with Beheading Rehearsals." *Guardian*, March 10, 2015. www.theguardian.com/world/2015/mar/10/isis-tricked-victims-into-appearing-calm-with-beheading-rehearsals.

Regulski, Ilona. "Scribes in Early Dynastic Egypt." In *Zeichen aus dem Sand: Streiflichter aus Ägyptens Geschichte zu Ehren von Günter Dreyer*, edited by Eva-Maria Engel, Vera Müller, and Ulrich Hartung, 581–611. Wiesbaden: Harrassowitz, 2008.

Reisner, George. *The Development of the Egyptian Tomb down to the Accession of Cheops*. Cambridge, MA and London: Harvard University Press and Oxford University Press, 1936.

Riemer, Heiko. "Prehistoric Rock Art Research in the Western Desert of Egypt." *Archéo-Nil* 19 (2009): 31–46.

Ritner, Robert. *The Mechanics of Ancient Egyptian Magical Practice*. Chicago, IL: The Oriental Institute of the University of Chicago, 1993.

Ritner, Robert. "Libyan vs. Nubian as the Ideal Egyptian." In *Egypt and Beyond: Essays Presented to Leonard H. Lesko upon His Retirement from the Wilbour Chair of Egyptology at Brown University June 2005*, edited by Stephen E. Thompson and Peter Der Manuelian, 305–314. Providence, RI: Brown University, Department of Egyptology and Ancient Western Studies, 2008.

Robins, Gay. *Proportion and Style in Ancient Egyptian Art*. Austin, TX: University of Texas Press, 1994.

Rzeuska, Teodozja I. "Execration Again? Remarks on an Old Kingdom Ritual." *Polish Archaeology in the Mediterranean* 22, research 2010 (2013): 627–634.

Säve-Söderbergh, Torgny. *Ägypten und Nubien: ein Beitrag zur Geschichte altägyptischer Aussenpolitik*. Lund: Ohlsson, 1941.

Scamuzzi, Ernesto. *Museo Egizio di Torino*. Turin: Edizioni d'arte Fratelli Pozzo, 1964.

Schäfer, Heinrich. "Das Niederschlagen der Feinde: zur Gesichte eines Ägyptischen Sinnbildes." *Wiener Zeitschrift für die Kunde des Morgenlandes* 54 (1957): 168–176.

Scharff, Alexander. "Some Prehistoric Vases in the British Museum and Remarks on Egyptian Prehistory." *The Journal of Egyptian Archaeology* 14, no. 3/4 (1928): 261–76.

Schenkel, Wolfgang. *Memphis, Herakleopolis, Theben: die epigraphischen Zeugnisse der 7.–11. Dynastie Ägyptens*. Wiesbaden: Harrassowitz, 1965.

Schneider, Thomas. "Das Schriftzeichen 'Rosette' und die Göttin Seschat." *Studien zur Altägyptischen Kultur* 24 (1997): 241–267.

Schneider, Thomas. *Ausländer in Ägypten Während des Mittleren Reiches und der Hyksoszeit. Teil 1: die ausländischen Könige*. Wiesbaden: Harrassowitz, 1998.

Schulman, Alan R. "Siege Warfare in Pharaonic Egypt." *Natural History Magazine* 73, no. 3 (1964): 12–21.

Schulman, Alan R. "The Battle Scenes of the Middle Kingdom." *Journal of the Society for the Study of Egyptian Antiquities* 12, no. 4 (1982): 165–183.

Schulz, Regine. "Der Sturm auf die Festung: Gedanken zu einigen Aspekten des Kampfbildes im Alten Ägypten vor dem Neuen Reich." In *Krieg und Sieg: Narrative Wanddarstellungen von Altägypten bis ins Mittelalter; Internationales Kolloquium, 29–30. Juli 1997 im Schloß Haindorf, Langenlois*, edited by Manfred Bietak and Mario Schwarz, 19–41. Vienna: Verlag der Österreichischen Akademie der Wissenschaften, 2002.

Senk, Herbert. "Zur Darstellung der Sturmleiter in der Belagerungsszene des Kaemhesit." *Annales du Service des antiquités de l'Égypte* 54, no. 2 (1957): 207–211.

Sethe, Kurt. "Die Inschriften." In *Das Grabdenkmal des Königs S'aḥu-Re (Band 2): die Wandbilder: Text*, edited by Ludwig Borchardt, 72–132. Leipzig: J.C. Hinrichs'sche Buchhandlung, 1913.

Sethe, Kurt. "Zur Erklärung einiger Denkmäler aus der Frühzeit der ägyptischen Kultur." *Zeitschrift für Ägyptische Sprache und Altertumskunde* 52 (1914): 52, 55–60.

Sethe, Kurt. *Die altägyptischen Pyramidentexte, nach den Papierabdrücken und Photographien des Berliner Museums, neu Herausgegeben und Erläutert*. Hildesheim: Georg Olms Verlagsbuchhandlung, 1960.

Settgast, Jürgen. "Zu ungewöhnlichen Darstellungen von Bogenschützen." *Mitteilungen des Deutschen Archäologischen Instituts, Abteilung Kairo* 25 (1969): 136–138.

Shaw, Ian. "Battle in Ancient Egypt: The Triumph of Horus or the Cutting Edge of the Temple Economy?" In *Battle in Antiquity*, edited by Alan B. Lloyd, 239–269. London: Duckworth in association with the Classical Press of Wales, 1996.

Shaw, Ian. "Socio-Economic and Iconographic Contexts for Egyptian Military Technology: The Knowledge Economy and 'Technology Transfer' in Late Bronze Age Warfare." In *The Knowledge Economy and Technological Capabilities: Egypt, the Near East and the Mediterranean 2nd Millennium BC–1st Millennium AD. Proceedings of a Conference Held at the Maison de La Chimie Paris, France 9–10 December 200*, edited by M. Wissa, 77–85. Barcelona: Aula Orientalis, 2010.

Shedid, Abdel-Ghaffar. *Die Felsgräber von Beni Hassan in Mittelägypten*. Mainz: Zabern, 1994.

Sievertsen, Uwe. "Das Messer vom Gebel el-Arak." *Baghdader Mitteilungen* 23 (1992): 1–75.

Silverman, David P., Ed. *Searching for Ancient Egypt: Art, Architecture, and Artifacts from the University of Pennsylvania Museum of Archaeology and Anthropology*. Dallas, TX: Dallas Museum of Art, 1997.

Smith, Harry. "The Making of Egypt: A Review of the Influence of Susa and Sumer on Upper Egypt and Lower Nubia in the 4th Millennium BC." In *The Followers of Horus: Studies Dedicated to Michael Allen Hoffman*, edited by Renée Friedman and Barbara Adams, 235–246. Oxford: Oxbow Books, 1992.

Smith, Harry. "Ma'et and Isfet." *Bulletin of the American Schools of Oriental Research* 5 (1994): 67–88.

Smith, William Stevenson. "The Old Kingdom in Egypt and the Beginning of the First Intermediate Period (Volume I, Chapter XIV)." In *The Cambridge Ancient History. Volumes I & II*, edited by I.E.S. Edwards, C.J. Gadd, and N.G.L. Hammond, 1–72. Cambridge: Cambridge University Press, 1962.

Smith, William Stevenson. *Interconnections in the Ancient Near East: A Study of the Relationships Between the Arts of Egypt, the Aegean, and Western Asia.* New Haven, CT and London: Yale University Press, 1965.

Smith, William Stevenson. *The Art and Architecture of Ancient Egypt: Revised with Additions by William Kelly Simpson.* New Haven, CT and London: Yale University Press, 1981.

Snape, Steven. *Ancient Egyptian Tombs: The Culture of Life and Death.* Chichester and Malden, MA: Wiley-Blackwell, 2011.

Somaglino, Claire, and Pierre Tallet. "Gebel Sheikh Suleiman: A First Dynasty Relief after All." *Archéo-Nil* 25 (2015): 122–134.

Sowada, Karin N. *Egypt in the Eastern Mediterranean during the Old Kingdom: An Archaeological Perspective.* Fribourg, Göttingen: Academic Press; Vandenhoeck & Ruprecht, 2009.

Spalinger, Anthony J. *War in Ancient Egypt: The New Kingdom.* Malden, MA and Oxford: Blackwell, 2005.

Spalinger, Anthony J. *Icons of Power: A Strategy of Reinterpretation.* Prague: Charles University in Prague, Faculty of Arts, 2011.

Spencer, A.J. *Catalogue of Egyptian Antiquities in the British Museum V: Early Dynastic Objects.* London: Trustees of the British Museum, 1980.

Spencer, A.J. *Early Egypt: The Rise of Civilisation in the Nile Valley.* London: British Museum Press, 1993.

Steindorff, Georg. "Die übrigen Fundstücke." In *Das Grabdenkmal des Königs Chephren,* edited by Uvo Hölscher, 105–115. Leipzig: J.C. Hinrichs'sche Buchhandlung, 1912.

Stevenson, Alice. "Material Culture of the Predynastic Period." In *Before the Pyramids,* edited by Emily Teeter, 65–74. Chicago, IL: The Oriental Institute of the University of Chicago, 2011.

Stockfisch, Dagmar. "Bemerkungen zur sog. 'Libyschen Familie.'" In *Wege Öffnen: Festschrift für Rolf Gundlach zum 65. Geburtstag,* edited by Mechthild Schade-Busch, 315–325. Wiesbaden: Harrassowitz, 1996.

Taçon, Paul, and Christopher Chippindale. "Australia's Ancient Warriors: Changing Depictions of Fighting in the Rock Art of Arnhem Land, N.T." *Cambridge Archaeological Journal* 4, no. 2 (1994): 211–48.

Tallet, Pierre, and Damien Laisney. "Iry-Hor et Narmer au Sud-Sinaï (Ouadi 'Ameyra): un complément à la chronologie des expéditions minières égyptiennes." *Le Bulletin de l'Institut français d'archéologie orientale* 112 (2012): 381–398.

The Epigraphic Survey. *Reliefs and Inscriptions at Karnak, Volume 4: The Battle Reliefs of King Sety I.* Chicago, IL: The University of Chicago, 1986.

Tiradritti, Francesco. *Egyptian Treasures from the Egyptian Museum in Cairo.* New York: Harry N. Abrams, 1999.

Tooley, Angela. "Middle Kingdom Burial Customs: A Study of Wooden Models and Related Material. Volume I." PhD thesis, University of Liverpool, 1989.

Torfs, Michaël. "Belgium Withdraws 'Controversial' Waterloo Coin under French Pressure, but Has a Plan B." *FlandersNews.be,* March 12, 2015. http://deredactie.be/cm/vrtnieuws.english/News/1.2267618#.

Török, László. *The Image of the Ordered World in Ancient Nubian Art: The Construction of the Kushite Mind.* Leiden, Boston, MA: Brill, 2002.

Trigger, Bruce. *Nubia under the Pharaohs.* London: Thames & Hudson, 1976.

Trigger, Bruce, Barry Kemp, David O'Connor, and Alan Lloyd. *Ancient Egypt: A Social History.* Cambridge: Cambridge University Press, 1983.

Uphill, Eric. "The Nine Bows." *Jaarbericht van het Vooraziatische—Egyptisch Genootschap Ex Oriente Lux* 19 (1967): 393–420.

Valbelle, Dominique. *Les neuf arcs: L'égyptien et les étrangers de la préhistoire à la conquête d'Alexandre*. Paris: Armand Colin, 1990.

van Haarlem, Willem. *Temple Deposits at Tell Ibrahim Awad*. Amsterdam: Van Haarlem, 2009.

van Walsem, René. "The Interpretation of Iconographic Programmes in Old Kingdom Elite Tombs of the Memphite Area: Methodological and Theoretical (Re)considerations." In *Proceedings of the Seventh International Congress of Egyptologists, Cambridge, 3–9 September 1995*, edited by C.J. Eyre, 1205–1213. Leuven: Peeters, 1998.

Vandersleyen, Claude. "La titulature de Mentouhotep II." In *Essays in Egyptology in Honor of Hans Goedicke*, edited by Betsy Bryan and David Lorton, 317–320. San Antonio, TX: Van Siclen Books, 1994.

Vandier, Jacques. *Mo'alla: la tombe d'Ankhtifi et la tombe de Sébekhotep*. Cairo: Institut français d'archéologie orientale, 1950.

Vischak, Deborah. "Agency in Old Kingdom Elite Tomb Programs: Traditions, Locations, and Variable Meanings." In *Dekorierte Grabanlagen im Alten Reich: Methodik und Interpretation*, edited by Martin Fitzenreiter and Michael Herb, 255–276. London: Golden House, 2006.

Vischak, Deborah. *Community and Identity in Ancient Egypt: The Old Kingdom Cemetery at Qubbet el-Hawa*. Supreme Council of Antiquities, 2007.

Vogel, Carola. "Fallen Heroes? Winlock's 'Slain Soldiers' Reconsidered." *Journal of Egyptian Archaeology* 89 (2003): 239–245.

Wegner, Josef. "Regional Control in Middle Kingdom Lower Nubia: The Function and History of the Site of Areika." *Journal of the American Research Center in Egypt* 32 (1995): 127–160.

Wegner, Josef. "A New Temple: The Mahat of Nebhepetre at Abydos." *Egyptian Archaeology* 46 (2015): 3–7.

Weill, Raymond. *Recherches sur la Ire Dynastie et les temps prépharaoniques*. Cairo: Institut français d'archéologie orientale, 1961.

Wendorf, Fred. "Site 117: A Nubian Final Paleolithic Graveyard near Jebel Sahaba, Sudan." In *The Prehistory of Nubia 2*, edited by Fred Wendorf, 954–995. Dallas, TX: Southern Methodist University Press, 1968.

Wengrow, David. "Rethinking 'Cattle Cults' in Early Egypt: Towards a Prehistoric Perspective on the Narmer Palette." *Cambridge Archaeological Journal* 11, no. 1 (2001): 91–104.

Wengrow, David. "The Evolution of Simplicity: Aesthetic Labour and Social Change in the Neolithic Near East." *World Archaeology* 33, no. 2 (2001): 168–188.

Wengrow, David. *The Archaeology of Early Egypt: Social Transformations in North-East Africa, 10,000 to 2,650 BC*. Cambridge: Cambridge University Press, 2006.

Wernick, Nicholas. "Once More unto the Breach: A Re-Evaluation of Beni Hasan's 'Battering Ram' and 'Glacis.'" *Zeitschrift für Ägyptische Sprache und Altertumskunde* 143, no. 1 (2016): 106–128.

Whitehouse, Helen. "The Hierakonpolis Ivories in Oxford: A Progress Report." In *The Followers of Horus: Studies Dedicated to Michael Allen Hoffman*, edited by Renée Friedman and Barbara Adams, 77–82. Oxford: Oxbow Books, 1992.

Whitehouse, Helen. "A Decorated Knife Handle from the 'Main Deposit' at Hierakonpolis." *Mitteilungen des Deutschen Archäologischen Instituts, Abteilung Kairo* 58 (2002): 425–446.

Wilkinson, Toby. *Early Dynastic Egypt*. London and New York: Routledge, 1999.

Wilkinson, Toby. "What a King Is This: Narmer and the Concept of the Ruler." *The Journal of Egyptian Archaeology* 86 (2000): 23–32.

Willems, Harco. "The Nomarchs of the Hare Nome and Early Middle Kingdom History." *Jaarbericht Ex Oriente Lux. Jaarboek van het Nederlands Instituut Te Leiden* 28 (1985): 80–102.

Willems, Harco. "The Social and Ritual Context of a Mortuary Liturgy of the Middle Kingdom (CT Spells 30–41)." In *Social Aspects of Funerary Culture in the Egyptian Old and Middle Kingdoms*, edited by Harco Willems, 253–372. Leuven: Peeters, 2001.

Williams, Bruce. "The Lost Pharaohs of Nubia." *Archaeology* 33, no. 5 (1980): 12–21.

Williams, Bruce. "A New Collation of the Gebel Sheikh Suleiman Monument." Paper presented at the annual meeting for the American Research Center in Egypt, Atlanta, Georgia, April 16, 2016.

Williams, Bruce, Thomas J. Logan, and William J. Murnane. "The Metropolitan Museum Knife Handle and Aspects of Pharaonic Imagery before Narmer." *Journal of Near Eastern Studies* 46, no. 4 (1987): 245–285.

Williams, Lauren. "The Ethics of Banning a Brutal Beheading Video." *ThinkProgress*, August 21, 2014. http://thinkprogress.org/world/2014/08/21/3473831/ethics-behind-blocking-foley-beheading-video/.

Winkler, Hans Alexander. *Rock-Drawings of Southern Upper Egypt*. London: Egypt Exploration Society, 1938.

Yadin, Yigael. "Hyksos Fortifications and the Battering-Ram." *Bulletin of the American Schools of Oriental Research* 137 (1955): 23–32.

Index

Page numbers in italics indicate illustrations; page numbers followed by 'n' refer to footnotes.

US spelling is used in this index.

1830 revolution, France 86
2011 revolution, Egypt 264

abstraction in violent images 74, 165–7
Abusir: Niuserra pyramid complex 104–7;
  Sahure pyramid complex 87, 93–103
Abydos: figurines 61; ivory rod 210–11,
  217; ivory tags 203–7; pilgrimage to
  247–8; Weni tomb 252–3; White Cross-
  Lined Ware 18–24, 36n13
agricultural scene, Scorpion Macehead
  56, 57
Aha ivory tag 203–4
Alexander Mosaic 222–4
Amenemhat I pyramid complex 139–40
Amenemhat III pectoral 207–8
Amenemhat tomb (at Beni Hasan) 7,
  247–52, 254–5, 258
American Civil War 4–5, 12–13n4
animal skins, depiction of 30, 31
animals: Battlefield Palette 45, 46; bulls
  49, 50, 65, 67; captive 20, 22, 31;
  carrion birds 45, 46; catfish 70, 71;
  falcons 42, 48, 57, 66, 176; Gebel
  el-Arak knife handle 53; herons
  47; Hierakonpolis Tomb 100 31;
  hippopotami 20–1, 22; horses 172–3,
  222–3; hunting 44; Libyan Palette 47,
  48; lions 45, 46, 47, 48, 49, 50, 53,
  55, 105, 106, 204; Narmer Palette 65,
  67; rekhyt 57; Scorpion Macehead 57;
  vultures 207; White Cross-Lined Ware
  20–1, 22, see also feathers; griffins;
  mythical creatures
ankh 109, 213, 264

Ankhtifi tomb 232–3, 234, 254
archers: Amenemhat tomb 249–50, 251;
  Baqt III tomb 243; Intef tomb 236,
  237–9, 240; Khafre pyramid complex
  91–3; Khety tomb 245, 246; Nebhepetra
  Mentuhotep tomb complex 130,
  131, 132, 135, 136, 137, 138; Sahure
  pyramid complex 99–100; Senwosret III
  pyramid complex 142; Setka tomb 230,
  231; Unis pyramid complex 111, 112,
  see also bows
architectural innovation 156
armlet, chevron (as indication of ethnicity)
  90, 125; ivory 201–2
Arnhem Land rock art, Australia 14–15
Ash (divinity) 94, 176, 177
Asiatic identity/stereotype: 11, 89; Asiatic
  Family Scene 96; Baqt III tomb 243;
  beards 90, 91, 96, 98, 99, 105, 106,
  111, 134, 141, 184, 195, 228, 229, 243;
  execration figures 212–3; Gebelein
  chapel reliefs 162–4; Intef tomb 236,
  237; Inti tomb 228–30; Khafre pyramid
  complex 90–1; Khnumhotep II tomb
  246–7; Mentiu 11, 189,190, 193, 194,
  195, 196, 197, 209; Mereret pectoral
  208; Nebhepetra Mentuhotep tomb
  complex 129, 130, 133, 134, 137–8;
  Niuserra pyramid complex 105, 106;
  pacific Asiatics 96, 247; Pepy II
  pyramid complex 123; prisoner statues
  126–7; private tomb imagery 257–8;
  royal tomb imagery 89, 145; Sahure
  pyramid complex 98, 99, 102–3;
  Senwosret I pyramid complex 141;
  Senwosret III pyramid complex 142;
  Unis pyramid complex 111, 112

Aswan: Harkhuf tomb 253–4; Setka tomb 230–2

Asyut: Iti-ibi tomb 232, *233*; Iti-ibi-iqr tomb 234

attacks on fortifications/settlements: Amenemhat tomb 248–50; Baqt III tomb 242–4; Bull Palette 49, *50;* Intef tomb 235–9; Inti tomb 228–30; Khaemhesy tomb 226–8; Khety tomb 244–6; Khnumhotep I tomb 246–7; Libyan Palette 47–9; Narmer Palette 65, 67; Nebhepetra Mentuhotep tomb complex 128–130, 137; Senwosret I pyramid complex 141–2; Unis pyramid complex 114, *see also* battle scenes

audience 3, 5, 10, 41, 77, 266; images as, 10; portable objects 216–8; private tombs 224–5;

restrictions on 267; rock carvings/reliefs 195–7; royal tombs 88, 143–4

Australia, Arnhem Land rock art 14–15

autobiographical inscriptions 252–5

axes, depiction of: Amenemhat tomb *251;* Intef tomb 238, 241; Khaemhesy tomb 226–7; Unis pyramid complex *113*

Baqt III tomb 242–4

battering rams, depiction of 262n43

Battle of: Gettysburg 4–5; Issus 222, 223; Qadesh 7–8; Waterloo 1–3

battle images/scenes 3, 6, 9, 11–12, 75, 255–9, 266–7; absence of 168, 203; Amenemhat tomb 248–52; Amenemhat I pyramid complex 139; Ankhtifi tomb 232–3, *234*; Baqt III tomb 242–4; Battlefield Palette 44–7, 64; and daily life scenes 257–9; differences between actors 75; function of 266–7; Gebel el-Arak knife handle 53–5; Hierakonpolis Tomb 100 29–31; historical accuracy of 145–6, 256–7; Intef tomb 235–41; Inti tomb 228–30; Iti-ibi tomb 232, *233*; Khaemhesy tomb *226*, 227–8; Khafre pyramid complex 91–3; Khety tomb 244–6; Khnumhotep I tomb 246–7; and kingship 146; Libyan Palette 47–9; Nebhepetra Mentuhotep tomb complex 129–39; naval 239–41, 255; private tombs 255–9; Qadesh 7–8; royal tombs 88–9, 146; Sahure pyramid complex *92;* Senwosret I pyramid complex *141*, 142; Senwosret III pyramid complex 142; Setka tomb

230–2; Unis pyramid complex 107–8, 111–15

Battlefield Palette 44–7, 64, 102

beards: Asiatic stereotype 90, *91*, 96, 98, *99*, *105*, 106, 111, 134, *141*, 184, 195, 228, 229, 243; Battlefield Palette *45*, 46; Bull Palette 49, *50*; captive figurines 60, 61; ivory objects 58, 70–1 *205*, 206, 210–11; Libyan stereotype 94, *95*, *108*, 109, 116, 118, *164*, 165; *Mentiu 189, 190*, 195; Narmer Palette *65*, 66–8; prisoner statues 125–7; Sekhemkhet rock relief *183*, 184; southerner stereotype *97*, *101*, 123

beheading images 41, 66, 73, 76–7, 267–8

Belgium, Battle of Waterloo commemoration 1–3

Beni Hasan, private tombs at 241–52, 255–9

Benin, ivory armlet 201–2

Bickel, Susanne 13n11

binding *see* ropes; captivity images/scenes

birds: carrion birds *45*, 46; falcons 42, 48, 57, 66, 176; herons 47; *rekhyt* 57; vultures 207

boats, depiction of: Amenemhat tomb 247, *248*, *250*; Decorated Ware *25*; Gebel el-Arak knife handle *53*, 54; Gebelein textile *26*, 27; Gebel Sheikh Suleiman 63–4; Hierakonpolis Tomb 100 28–9, 32; Intef tomb 239–41; Wadi Ameyra rock carvings 175, *see also* ships

Bochi, Patricia A. 220n29

bows, depiction of: Aha ivory tag 204; Djet ivory tag 205 Gebel Sheikh Suleiman relief 63, 82n55; Khafre pyramid complex 91–3; Khasekhem relief *158*, 159; Nebhepetra Mentuhotep tomb complex *131*, *132*, *137*; Sahure pyramid complex 99–100; Setka tomb 230, *231*, *see also* archers

bracelet, depiction of *107*

Buhen, Nubia, mud stamp sealings *214*, 215

Bull Palette 49, *50*

bulls 49, *50*, *65*, 67

C-Ware *see* White Cross-Lined Ware

captions: absence of 232, 244, 256; in battle scenes 138; on jewelry 209; in Libyan Family Scene 93, 109

captive figurines, Protodynastic Period 59–62, *see also* execration figurines; prisoner statues

captivity images/scenes: Amenemhat I pyramid complex 139; animals *20, 22*; Battlefield Palette *45*, 46; execration figurines 211–13; captive figurines 59–62; Gebel Sheikh Suleiman relief 63–4; Gebelein textile *26, 27*; Intef tomb *236*, 238; Inti tomb *228*, 230; ivory objects 50–4, 59, 210–11; Khafre pyramid complex 90–1; Khasekhem relief *158*, 159; Khasekhem statue *161*, 159; Narmer Macehead *69*, 70; ; Pepy II pyramid complex 118–9, *120*, 123; prisoner statues 125–7; Sahure pyramid complex 94, *95*, 96–8; Senwosret III pyramid complex 142; Scorpion Macehead *56*, 57; stamp sealings 214–16; Unis pyramid complex 108–10; White Cross-Lined Ware 18–24; Yaxchilan (Maya) Stela 11 155, *see also* domination images/scenes; smiting images/scenes
carrion birds *45*, 46
cartoon, *Egyptian Chronicles* blog 264
causeways: 88–9, 143; Amenemhat I pyramid complex 152n103; Niuserra pyramid complex *105*; Pepy II pyramid complex 119, *121, 122, 123*; Sahure pyramid complex 96–100, 103; Senwosret I pyramid complex 142; Senwosret III pyramid complex 142; Unis pyramid complex 110–15
censorship 41
ceramics: Decorated Ware 24–5, 27, 32, 43; White Cross-Lined Ware 18–24, 30–1, 68
ceremonial relief palettes *see* palettes
chaos versus order 33–5, 76–7, 146, 167
chariots *8*, 145, *222*, 223
Civil War, American 4–5
civil war: 266; Khasekhem 156–8, 169; Nebhepetra Mentuhotep 145, 156, 169; private tombs 232, 256–8
clubs, depiction of 28, *29*, 54
coin, Battle of Waterloo commemoration 1–4
combat images/scenes *see* battle images/scenes
crowns: development of 68; Double Crown 165, *166, 187, 188*; Red Crown *65, 67, 69*, 70, 106, *107, 177, 178, 181*, 182, *183, 184*, 185, *186, 189, 192*; unusual 185, *187*; White Crown *56, 65*, 66, *160, 162*, 163, *164*, 165, *177, 181*, 182, *183, 186, 189, 190, 192*; variation in smiting images/scenes 194

cycloramas 4–5
cylinders, ivory 57, *58*, 70, *71*, 72

D-Ware *see* Decorated Ware
daggers, depiction of: Mereret jewelry 208; Niuserra pyramid complex *104*, 105; Unis pyramid complex *111*, *see also* knives
Dahshur: Mereret jewelry 207–9; Senwosret III pyramid complex 142
daily life scenes 224, 256–9
Darius III of Persia *222*, 223
Darnell, John 82n52
dead figures: Battlefield Palette *45*, 46; Baqt III tomb *243*, 244; Gebel el-Arak knife handle *53*, 54; Gebel Sheikh Suleiman relief *63*, 64; Khasekhem statue 160–1; Khety tomb *245*, 246; Khnumhotep I tomb *246*, 247; Narmer Palette *65*, 66–7; *rekhyt 56*, 57; Senwosret III pyramid complex 142
Deaf Adder Gorge, Arnhem Land 14–15
Decorated Ware (D-Ware) 24–5, 27, 32, 43
Deir el-Bahri, Thebes, Nebhepetra Mentuhotep tomb complex 88, 128–39
Delacroix, Eugene 85
Den (king): ivory tag 205–7, 216; rock reliefs 176–8
Denderah, chapel relief 165–9
Deshasha, Inti tomb 228–30
divine temples *see* temple decoration
Djedkare Izezi: prisoner statues 125; rock relief 191–2, 194
Djer rock relief 82n59, 175–6
Djet ivory tag 204–5
Djoser (Netjerikhet), rock relief 179–81
domination images/scenes: 75–7; of animals *20, 22*, 31–2, 34, *53*, 56–7, *65*, 67; Hierakonpolis Tomb 100 27–8, 33; mud stamp sealings 215–16; and kingship 27, 41, 43, 70, 144, 146; and practice of violence 16, 74; and royal iconography 34; and sculpture 62, 127; White Cross-Lined Ware 16, 18–24; Yaxchilan (Maya) Stela 11 155, *see also* captivity images/scenes; smiting images/scenes; trampling images/scenes
Double Crown 165, *166, 187, 188*
Dreyer, Günter 51–2
Dynamic Figures Period (Australia) 14–15
Dynasty 0 42, *see also* Protodynastic Period

Early Dynastic Period: ivory rod 210–1, 217; ivory tags 203–7, 216; rock reliefs 175–9; temple decoration 157–61; transition to 17, 42–4, 73–4

Egyptian Chronicles blog 264

Egyptian revolution (2011) 264

Egyptians: audience for violent images 77, 195–6, 267; as captives 97–8, 125–7, 211–13; fighting against Egyptians 224, 232, *233*, 243–4, 251, 256; violence against 57, 145–6, 155–6, 161, *162*, 163–4, 168–9, 185–7, 211–13; visual stereotype 11, 97–8, 101–3, 111, 123, 125–7, 130–1, 134–5, 237, 243–4, 245–6

Eleventh Dynasty: temple decoration 156, 162–9; Nebhepetra Mentuhotep tomb complex 127–39; Intef tomb 235–41

elite tombs *see* private tombs

emblems, smiting of 165–7

ethnic identity/stereotypes: ambiguity and 10, 97–8, 102–3, 258; complexity of 10–11, 89–90, 98, 211, 213, 237; excration figurines 213; private tombs 224, 239, 251–2, 258; prisoner statues 125–7; royal tombs 89–90; 97–8, 128, 137–8; *see also* Asiatic identity/stereotype; Libyan identity/ stereotype; Nubian identity/stereotype; Puntite identity/stereotype; skin color; southerner identity/stereotype

eurozone 1–2

evolution of simplicity 73–4

excration figurines 9, 211–13

Facebook 41

falcons 42, 48, 57, 66, 176; *see also* Horus

feathers, depiction of: Amenemhat tomb at Beni Hasan *249*; Amenemhat I pyramid complex 139; Baqt III tomb 243; Gebelein chapel reliefs *162*, 164–5; Intef tomb *236*, 237; Khnumhotep I tomb 246–7; mud stamp sealings 214–5; Nebhepetra Mentuhotep tomb complex 130–2, 135, *136*; Niuserra pyramid complex 104–5; Sahure pyramid complex *101*, 102; Sekhemkhet rock relief 181–4; Senwosret III pyramid complex 142; Setka tomb 231; White Cross-Lined Ware 18–21

festivals, royal jubilee (*heb-sed*) 32–3

Fifth Dynasty: prisoner statues 125; private tombs 225–30; southerner identity/ stereotype 90; pyramid complexes *87*, 93–115; rock reliefs 189–92

fighting scenes *see* battle scenes

figurines *see* captive figurines; excration figurines; votive figurines

fillets (in hair) *65*, 66, 110, *132*, 135–6, 227, 239–40; Asiatic stereotype 98, 111, 129–30, 229, 236–7; Nubian stereotype *231*, *236*, prisoner statues 126–7; southerner stereotype 90, *101*, *105*, 106, 123

First Dynasty: ivory objects 203–7, 210–11; rock reliefs 175–8, *see also* Narmer

First Intermediate Period, private tombs 230–4

foreigners *see* Asiatic identity/stereotype; ethnic identity/stereotypes; Libyan identity/stereotype; Nubian identity/ stereotype; Puntite identity/stereotype; southerner identity/stereotype

fortifications *see* attacks on fortifications/ settlements; towns, depiction of

Fourth Dynasty: pyramid complexes 90–3; rock reliefs 185–8

France: 1830 revolution 86; Battle of Waterloo commemoration 1–2, 3

funerary boats, depiction of *248*

gaming rod 210–11, 217

Gebel el-Arak knife handle *52*, 53–5

Gebel Sahaba, cemetery 35n8

Gebel Sheikh Suleiman relief 62–4, 174

Gebelein: chapel reliefs 162–5, 168, 169; stelae 231–2; textile 26–7

Gettysburg, Battle of 4–5

Giza, Khafre pyramid complex 90–3

Goddess of the West 94

griffins 74, 88; Mereret jewelry 207, *208*; Niuserra pyramid complex *105*, 106; Pepy II pyramid complex 119, *121*, *122*; Sahure pyramid complex 100, *101*, 102–3; Unis pyramid complex *110, 111*

Harkhuf tomb 253–4

headdresses *see* crowns; fillets

heb-sed (royal jubilee festival) 32–3, 193

heraldic devices *see* serekhs

herons 47

Hierakonpolis: Khasekhem statue 159–61; Main Deposit 44, 50–1, 56–9, 69–73,

77; temple at 158–61, 169; Tomb 100 27–33, 38n30, 54–5, 68, 74, 77

hippopotami *20–1*, 22

historical accuracy: 4, 9–10, 265–6; Den ivory tag 205–6; Khasekhem statues 159–61; Khasekhem temple relief 158–9; Libyan Family Scene 144–5; Narmer Palette 68–9; Nebhepetra Mentuhotep divine temple reliefs 167–8; Nebhepetra Mentuhotep tomb complex 138; private tombs 256–7; royal tombs 143–6

Hittites 7, *8*

hoes, depiction of: Khaemhesy tomb *226*, 227; Libyan Palette 47–9; Scorpion Macehead *56*, 57

Hormizd II rock relief 172–4

horses: Alexander Mosaic *222*, 223; Hormizd II rock relief 172–3; Qadesh *8*

Horus 42–3, 66, 73, 102, 157–8, 169, *see also* falcons

human sacrifice 204, 211, 218n4

hunting, depictions of 44, 56

ideology: Islamic State 40–1; Egyptian royal 11–12, 34–5, 40–84, 146–7, 157, 217–18, 265; French 86

Intef tomb 235–41, 257–8

Inti tomb 228–30

Iran, Naqsh-e Rustam rock relief 172–4

isfet (chaos) 34 *see also* chaos vs. order

Islamic State 35, 40–1, 73, 76–7, 267–8

Issus, Battle of 223

Iti-ibi tomb 232, *233*

Iti-ibi-iqr tomb 234

ivory objects: armlet from Benin 201–2; cylinders 57–8, 70–1; knife handles 50–5; macehead 58–9; (gaming) rod 210–11, 217; tags 70–1, *72*, 203–7, 216

jewelry 203, 207–9, 217, 267; depiction of: 106, *107*

Khaemhesy tomb 225–8, 229–30

Khafre pyramid complex 90–3

Khasekhem: architectural innovation 156; civil war: 156, 157; statues 159–61; temple decoration 158–9

Khety tomb 244–6

Khnumhotep I tomb 246–7

Khufu: pyramid complex 90; rock relief 187, *188*

kilts, depiction of: Amenemhat tomb at Beni Hasan 251; Baqt III tomb 243; Intef tomb 236, 238; ivory gaming rod *210*, 211; Khaemhesy tomb *226*, 228; Mereret pectoral *208*, 209; Narmer Palette *65*, 67; Nebhepetra Mentuhotep tomb complex 128–30; Niuserra rock relief 190; Pepy I rock relief *192*, 193; Sahure pyramid complex 98, 101–2; Sahure rock relief 189; Sekhemkhet rock relief *181*, 182; *shendyt* kilts 163, 180, 193, 238, 240–1; Unis pyramid complex 114–5

kingship 11, 16, 265; battle scenes 146; depiction of kings 32, 33, 34, 217, 256; falcon symbol 48; order versus chaos 34; rock-carved images 62; *serekhs* 42; symbols of 48, 75; Yaxchilan Stela 11, 155, *see also* crowns; royal ideology

knife handles 50–5

knives, depiction of 54, *see also* daggers

Kubban, Nubia, mud stamp sealings *214*, 215

labels *see* ivory tags, captions

ladders, depiction of: Intef tomb *236*, 238; Inti tomb *228*, 229; Khaemhesy tomb *226*, 227–8; Nebhepetra Mentuhotep tomb complex *129*

La Liberté guidant le peuple (Delacroix) 85–6, 147

Libyan identity/stereotype 11, 258; Amenemhat I pyramid complex 139; Gebelein chapel reliefs *162*, 163–5; Khnumhotep I tomb *246*, 247; Libyan Family Scenes 89, 93–6, 104–6, 110–1, 116, 117, 144–5, 151n82, 266; Mereret pectoral 207, *208*; Niuserra pyramid complex *105*, 106; Pepy I pyramid complex 116; Pepy II pyramid complex 117–9, 123; private tomb imagery 247, 258; Sahure pyramid complex 94–5, 98, *101*, 102; Senwosret I pyramid complex 142; Senwosret III pyramid complex 142; *Tjehenu* 47–9, 70–1, 75–6 94; Unis pyramid complex *108*, 109–11

Libyan Palette 47–9

lions *45*, 46, *47*, 48, 49, *50, 53*, 55, *105*, 106, 204; *see* animals

Lisht: Amenemhat I pyramid complex 139; Senwosret I pyramid complex 139–42

Logan, Thomas J. 52

Lord of the Hill Countries (Sopdu) 96

ma'at (order) 34 *see also* order vs. chaos
maceheads 33, 43, 55–9, 60, 69–70
maces: Den ivory tag 206; functional/
    ceremonial uses 55–6; Gebel el-Arak
    knife handle 54; Gebelein chapel reliefs
    163; Hierakonpolis Tomb 100 31; and
    kings 76; White Cross-Lined Ware *20,
    22*; *see also* smiting images/scenes
Maya (Yaxchilan) Stela 154–5
Mentiu (Asiatic group) 11, 189, 190, 193,
    194, 195, 196, 197, 209
Mereret jewelry 207–9
Metropolitan Museum knife handle 51–2
Mexico, Yaxchilan Stela 11 154–5
mfkt (turquoise) 185
Middle Kingdom: Eleventh Dynasty
    127–39, 156–7, 162–9, 235–41;
    execration figurines 211–13; jewelry
    207–9; mud stamp sealings 213–16;
    private tombs 231, 235–52, 254–5; rock
    reliefs 175, 197; royal tombs 86, 89,
    127–42, 143; temple decoration 156–7,
    162–9; Twelfth Dynasty 139–42,
    207–9, 211–13, 213–16
military training, depiction of 99–100, 103,
    see also battle images/scenes
mining/miners 174–5, 195–7
Moalla, Ankhtifi tomb 232–3, *234*, 254
Morris, Ellen F. 218n4
Morsi, Muhammad 264
mortuary complexes *see* royal tombs/
    pyramid complexes
mud stamp sealings 209, 213–17, 267
mudstone palettes *see* palettes
Muslim Brotherhood 264
mythical creatures: Narmer Palette *65*,
    67; Mereret jewelry 207, *208*; Pepy II
    pyramid complex *121–2*; royal tombs
    101, 102; *see also* griffins

Naqada I Period: 16, 33–5; White Cross-
    Lined Ware 18–24, 74, 77, *see also*
    Predynastic Period
Naqada II Period: 16, 24, 33–5, 74;
    Decorated Ware 24–5, 32; Gebelein
    textile 26–7; Hierakonpolis Tomb 100
    27–33, *see also* Predynastic Period
Naqada III Period: 42–4; anonymous
    serekhs 62; captive figurines 59–62;
    Gebel Sheikh Suleiman 62–4; ivory
    objects 50–5, 58–9; kingship 35, 76–7;
    maceheads 55–7; relief palettes 44–50,
    see also Protodynastic Period
Naqsh-e Rustam, Iran, rock relief 172–4

Narmer 6, 42–3, 64–5, 72–4, 6, 266; ivory
    objects 70–2, 203; Macehead 69–70;
    Palette 42, 44, 49, 65–9, 77
naval battles, private tombs 239–41, 255
Nebhepetra Mentuhotep: architectural
    innovation 88, 156; temple decoration
    156, 162–9; tomb complex 88, 90,
    127–39, 145–6
Netjerikhet (Djoser) rock carving 179–81
New Kingdom 7–8
Nine Bows 102, 149n35, 161
Niuserra: prisoner statues 125, 127;
    pyramid complex 104–7; rock relief
    190–1, 194
Nubian identity/stereotype: Baqt III tomb
    243; complexity of 11; development
    of 11, 90, 231–2; execration figurines
    213; Gebelein chapel reliefs 163–4;
    hairstyles 90; Intef tomb 237; Khety
    tomb 246; mud stamp sealings 215;
    Nebhepetra Mentuhotep tomb complex
    135, *136*; private tomb imagery 231,
    237, 243, 246; Setka tomb 231, *see also*
    Puntite identity/stereotype, southerner
    identity/stereotype

oarsmen, depiction of *26*, 239–41
officials 68, 179, 194, 196–7, 265
Old Kingdom: execration figurines
    211–3; Fifth Dynasty *87*, 93–115,
    125–7, 189–92, 225–30; Fourth
    Dynasty 90–3, 185–8; prisoner
    statues 124–7; private tombs
    225–32; rock reliefs 179–93; royal
    tombs *87*, 88, 90–127; Sixth Dynasty
    115–24, 125–7, 192–3, 252–3; Third
    Dynasty 180–5
order vs. chaos 33–5, 76–7, 146, 167
Osiris 106

palettes 43–4; Battlefield Palette 44–7, 64;
    Bull Palette 49, *50*; labels 68; Libyan
    Palette 47–9; Narmer Palette 42,
    44, 49, 65–9, 77
papyrus plants: Denderah chapel reliefs
    165, *166*; Khasekhem statue 160–1;
    Metropolitan Museum knife handle 52;
    Narmer ivory tag 71, *72*, 75; Narmer
    Palette *65*, 66
peace 13n11, 264
pectorals 207–8
penis sheaths, depiction of: Battlefield
    Palette 45, 46; Bull Palette *50*; figurines
    61; Gebel el-Arak knife handle 53–4;

Gebelein reliefs *164*, 165; Mereret pectoral 207–8; Niuserra pyramid complex *105*, 106; Pepy II pyramid complex 118–9, 123; Sahure pyramid complex 94, *95*, 101–2; White Cross-Lined Ware 18

Pepy I: prisoner statues 125–7; pyramid complex 89, 115–16; rock relief 192–3, 194

Pepy II: prisoner statues 125–7; pyramid complex 89, 117–24, *126*, *127*

Peribsen 157

pharaonic ideology *see* royal ideology

photography 73

Pickett's Charge (Battle of Gettysburg) 4–5

Pompeii, Alexander Mosaic 222

pottery: Decorated Ware 24–5, 27, 32, 43; White Cross-Lined Ware 18–24, 30–1, 68

Predynastic Period 16–35, 41, *see also* Naqada I Period, Naqada II Period, Protodynastic Period

preservation issues 33–4, 88–9, 145, 156

prisoner statues 125–7, *see also* captive figurines; captivity images/scenes

private tombs 6, 223–59; Amenemhat 7, 247–52, 254–5, 258; Ankhtifi 232–3, *234*, 254; at Abydos 252–3; at Aswan 230–2, 253–4; at Asyut 232, 234, 259n8; at Beni Hasan 241–52; autobiographical inscriptions in 252–5; Baqt III 242–4; and daily life scenes 256–9; dating of 225; at Deshasha 228–30; First Intermediate Period 232–4; Harkhuf 253–4; historical accuracy in 256–7; Intef 235–41, 257–8; interpretation of imagery 255–9; Inti 228–30; Iti-ibi 232, *233*; Iti-ibi-iqr 234; Khaemhesy 225–8, 229; Khety 244–6; Khety II 259n8; Khnumhotep I 246–7, 254; Middle Kingdom 235–52; at Moalla 232–4; Old Kingdom 225–32; royal tombs comparison 225; at Saqqara 225–8; Setka 230–2; at Thebes 235–41; Weni 252–3

Protodynastic Period 17, 35, 41–77, 174; kingship 35, 76–7; *serekhs* 62–3, *see also* Naqada III Period, Predynastic Period

Puntite identity/stereotype 90

pyramids *see* royal tombs/pyramid complexes

Qa'a ivory rod 210–11, 217

Qadesh, Battle of 7–8

Qubbet el-Hawa, Aswan: Harkhuf tomb 253–4; Setka tomb 230–2

Ramses II, Qadesh scenes 7–8

Raneferef, prisoner statues 125–7

Red Crown: Den rock reliefs *177*, 178; Narmer Macehead *69*, 70; Narmer Palette *65*, 67; Niuserra pyramid complex 106, *107*; Pepy I rock relief *192*; Sahure rock relief *189*; Sanakht rock relief *184*, 185; Sekhemkhet rock relief *181*, 182, *183*; Snefru rock relief *186*; undated rock relief 178

rekhyt 57

relief palettes *see* palettes

reserve heads 125

Riemer, Heiko 81n51

rock art, Australia 14–15

rock carvings/reliefs 174–197; audience for 195–7; Den 176–8; Djedkare Izezi 191–2, 194; Djer 175–6; Djoser 180–1; Early Dynastic Period 175–9; Fifth Dynasty 189–92; First Dynasty 175–8; Fourth Dynasty 185–8; Gebel Sheikh Suleiman 62–4; Hormizd II relief 172–4; interpretation of imagery 193–7; Khufu 188; Niuserra 190; and officials 196–7; Old Kingdom 179–93; Pepy I 192–3; Protodynastic Period 62–4; 174; Sahure 189; Sanakht 184–5; Sekhemkhet 181–4, 194; Sixth Dynasty 192–3; Snefru 185–7; Third Dynasty 180–5; undated 178; Wadi Ameyra 175; Wadi el-Humur 176–9; Wadi Maghara 179–97

rod, ivory 210–11, 217

ropes, binding 21–3, 52, 63, 90, 96–8, 109, 110–11, 118, 212, 215, 230, *see also* captivity images/scenes

rosette symbol 57, 68

royal festival 32–3

royal iconography *see* kingship

royal ideology 11–12, 34–5, 40–84, 146–7, 157, 217–18, 265

royal tombs/pyramid complexes 85–153; Amenemhat I 139; audience for 88, 143; battle scenes 9, 88, 145–6; Eleventh Dynasty 127–39; Fifth Dynasty 93–115, 124–7; Fourth Dynasty 90–3; historicism 143–6; ideology 146–7; Khafre 90–3; layout of 86–8; Middle

Kingdom 89, 127–42; Nebhepetra Mentuhotep 127–39; Niuserra 104–7; Old Kingdom *87*, 88, 90–127; Pepy I 115–16; Pepy II 117–24, *126*, *127*; prisoner statues 124–7; private tombs comparison 225; Sahure *87*, 93–103; Senwosret I 139–42; Senwosret III 142; Sixth Dynasty 115–27; smiting scenes 9, 88, 144–6; trampling scenes 9, 88, 144–6; Twelfth Dynasty 139–42; Unis 107–15; Userkaf 93

saff tombs 235
Sahure: pyramid complex *87*, 93–103; rock relief 189
Sanakht rock relief 184–5
"Sand-dwellers" 252–3
sandals, depiction of *65*, 66, *177*, 178–9, 205
Saqqara: execration figurine 212–13; Khaemhesy tomb 225–8; Pepy I pyramid complex 115–16, 125; Pepy II pyramid complex 117–24, *125*, *126*; Unis pyramid complex 107–15; Userkaf pyramid complex 93
scene types 3, 6, 9, 23, 75, 88, 266–7, *see also* battle images/scenes; captivity images/scenes; smiting images/scenes; trampling images/scenes
Scepters *see Was*-scepter
Scorpion Macehead *56*, 57
sculptures *see* statues
sealings, mud stamp 209, 213–17, 267
Second Dynasty: Khasekhem statues 159–61; temple decoration 156, 157–9, 168; rock reliefs 179
Sekhemkhet rock reliefs 181–4, 194
sema-tawy (binding of the Two Lands) 83n70, 161, 165, *166*
Semerkhet 179
Semna Stela 214
Senwosret I pyramid complex 139–42
Senwosret III: jewelry image 207–9; pyramid complex 90, 142–3; Semna Stela 214
seqer-ankh ("living stricken one") 109, 213
serekh (heraldic device): 42; Aha ivory tag 204; anonymous 62; Djer rock relief 175–6; Djet ivory tag 204–5; Gebel Sheikh Suleiman relief 62–3, 64; Khasekhemwy 157; plain 62–3; Sekhemkhet relief 182–3; smiting *serekhs* 63, 175–6, 204–5

Seshat 93, 94, *95*, 110, 118, *119*, 123, 141
Seth 96, 157
Setka tomb 230–2
settlements *see* attacks on fortifications/ settlements
shendyt kilts, depiction of 108, *162*, 163, *164*, 165, 180, 185, *186*, 187, 191, 193, 238–9, 240–1, 243–4, 247, *see also* kilts
shields, depiction of 30, 134, 141, 230, 236–8, 241, 243, 246, 247, 249–51
ships, depiction of 247, *248*, *250*, *see also* boats
siege scenes *see* attacks on fortifications/ settlements
Sinai: context of violent images 11, 267; rock carvings/reliefs 174–97
Sixth Dynasty: private tombs 252–3; prisoner statues 125–7; southerner identity/stereotype stereotype 90; pyramid complexes 115–24; rock reliefs 192
skin color, as ethnic marker: Amenemhat tomb 249, 251; Ankhtifi tomb 233; Asiatic identity/stereotype 90, 103, 138; Baqt III tomb 243–4; Intef tomb 235, *236*, 237, 238, 241; Khafre pyramid complex 90; Khety tomb 246; Libyan identity/stereotype 103; Nebhepetra Mentuhotep tomb complex 134–5, *136*, 137, 138; Niuserra pyramid complex 104–5; Nubian identity/stereotype 90, 127, 231–2, 237; Pepy II pyramid complex 123; Senwosret I pyramid complex 141; Senwosret III pyramid complex 142; Setka tomb *231*; southerner identity/ stereotype 90
Slain Soldiers burial 171n30
smiting images/scenes 6, 8–9, 10, 88, 144–5, 193–7; Aha ivory tag 203–4; arrow in *140*; beheading images parallel 41, 73, 76; Den ivory tag 205–6; Den rock reliefs 176–8; development of 34–5, 57–8, 73, 77, 58; Djedkare Izezi rock relief 191–2, Djer rock relief 175–6; Djet ivory tag 204–5; Djoser rock relief 180–1; of emblems 165–8; Gebel Sheikh Suleiman relief 63; Hierakonpolis Tomb 100 27–31; historical accuracy of 144–5, 266; iconography of 76–7; ideology and 35, 76–7, 265; interpretation of 145,

193–7; jewelry 207–9; Khufu
rock relief 187–8; of *Mentiu* 189, 190,
192–3, 195–7; Metropolitan Museum
knife handle knife handle 52; Narmer
ivory cylinder 70–1; Narmer ivory tag
71–2; Narmer Palette *65*, 66, 68–9;
Nebhepetra Mentuhotep Denderah
chapel 165–8; Nebhepetra Mentuhotep
Gebelein chapel 162–5; Nebhepetra
Mentuhotep tomb complex 137;
Niuserra pyramid complex 104–5,
106–7; Niuserra rock relief 190–1;
Pepy I pyramid complex 115–6; Pepy
I rock relief 192–3; Pepy II pyramid
complex 117–18, 123–4; prisoner
statues comparison 127; Sahure
pyramid complex 94–6, 103; Sahure
rock relief 189; Sanakht rock relief
184–5; Sekhemkhet rock reliefs 181–4;
Senwosret I pyramid complex 140–1;
Senwosret III pyramid complex 142;
smiting names 63–4, 72, 204–5; Snefru
rock reliefs 185–7; transmission of 218;
undated rock relief 178–9; Unis pyramid
complex 108–9; Userkaf pyramid
complex 93; variation in 193–5; White
Cross-Lined Ware 24, *see also* captivity
images/scenes; domination images/
scenes; triumph images/scenes
Snefru rock reliefs 185–7
social stratification 33
Sopdu (Lord of the Hill Countries) 96
southerner identity/stereotype 90; Niuserra
pyramid complex *105*–6; Pepy II
pyramid complex 119, 123; Sahure
pyramid complex *98*, *101*, *see also*
Nubian identity stereotype, Puntite
identity/stereotype
spears, depiction of: Alexander mosaic
223–4; Amenemhat tomb 251; Intef
tomb *236*, 238; Nebhepetra
Mentuhotep tomb complex *136*;
Arnhem Land rock art *14*, 15; Hormizd
II relief 172–3; Senwosret I pyramid
complex *141*, 142; White Cross-Lined
Ware 23
stamp sealings, mud 209, 213–17, 267
state formation *see* Naqada III Period,
Protodynastic Period
statues: of Khasekhem 159–61; of
prisoners 124–7; reserve heads 125
stereotypes *see* Asiatic identity/stereotype;
ethnic identity/stereotypes; Libyan
identity/

stereotype; Nubian identity/stereotype;
southerner identity/stereotype; Puntite
identity/stereotype
Stick Figure Period, Australia 15

Ta-seti (land of the bow) 159
tags, ivory 70–1, *72*, 203–7, 216
target practice, depiction of 99–100
Tell el-Farkha, figurines 60–1
Tell Ibrahim Awad, figurines 61
temple decoration (divine) 156–69;
audience 156, 267; Denderah 165–9;
Early Dynastic Period 157–61;
Gebelein 162–5, 168; Middle Kingdom
162–9; *see also* royal tombs/pyramid
complexes
textile, Gebelein 26–7
Thebes: Intef tomb 235–41; Nebhepetra
Mentuhotep tomb complex 88, 128–39
Third Dynasty, rock reliefs 179–85
Thoth 188, 190
Tjehenu 47–9, 70–1, 75–6 94, *see also*
Libyan identity/stereotype
tombs *see* private tombs; royal tombs/
pyramid complexes
towns, depiction of 47–9, *50*, 63, *65*,
67, *see also* attacks on fortifications/
settlements
Towns Palette (Libyan Palette) 47–9
trampling images/scenes 9, 88, 265;
Bull Palette 49, *50*; historical
accuracy 144–6, 266; Mereret pectoral
207–9; Narmer Palette *65*, 67;
Nebhepetra Mentuhotep tomb complex
137; Niuserra pyramid complex 105–7,
107; Pepy II pyramid complex 119,
121–*2*; Sahure pyramid complex 99,
100–3; Unis pyramid complex 110–1,
see also triumph images/scenes
transmission of imagery 10, 193–7, 202,
216–8, 266–7
triumph images/scenes 3, 9, 10, 145, 146,
265, 267; portable objects 203–9, *see
also* smiting images/scenes; trampling
images/scenes
turquoise 185
Twelfth Dynasty: execration figurines
211–13; jewelry 207–9; pyramid
complexes 88, 139–43;
stamp sealings 213–5

Umm el-Qaab, Abydos: ivory rod 210–11,
217; ivory tag 204; White Cross-Lined
Ware 18, *20*, *21*, 22–4

Unis prisoner statues 125–7; pyramid complex 107–15, 125–7
uraeus: Den ivory label *205*, 206; Djedkare Izezi rock relief 191; Djoser rock relief 180; Gebelein chapel *162*, 163; Mereret pectoral 207, *208*
Userkaf pyramid complex 89, 93

victory, portrayal of 7, 18, 239, 257
votive figurines 43, 59–62
vultures 207

Wadi Ameyra, Sinai, rock reliefs 175–6
Wadi el-Humur, Sinai, rock reliefs 176–9
Wadi Maghara, Sinai, rock reliefs 179–93, 196
war imagery *see* attacks on fortifications/settlements; battle images/scenes; captivity images/scenes
Was-scepters: Khufu rock relief 188; Pepy II 118, *119*, 123; Sahure pyramid complex 96, *97*; Sahure rock relief 189; Unis pyramid complex *108*, 109
Waterloo, Battle of 1–3
Wegner, Josef 214

Wengrow, David 74
Weni tomb 252–3
Wepwawet 109, 165, 176–8, 185, 188, 189, 194, 206
White Cross-Lined Ware 18–24, 30–1, 68
White Crown: Den rock reliefs 176, *177*; Gebelein chapel reliefs *162*, 163, *164*, 165; Khasekhem statues 159–60; Narmer Palette *65*, 66; Niuserra rock relief *190*; Pepy I rock relief *192*; Sahure rock relief *189*; Scorpion Macehead 56–7; Sekhemkhet rock reliefs *181*, 182, *183*; Snefru rock relief 185, *186*; smiting images 194
Wilkinson, Toby 83n65
Williams, Bruce 52, 64, 81n49
women, depiction of 89, 94–5, 117, 130, 134–6, 138, 227, 229, 238–9, 247
wrestlers: Amenemhat tomb 247–8, *250*; Djet ivory tag 205; Khety tomb 244–5; Khnumhotep tomb 247; Sahure pyramid complex 100

Yaxchilan (Mexico) Stela 11, 154–5

Made in the USA
Las Vegas, NV
15 October 2022